MW01598570

TAX PLANNING
FOR YOU AND YOUR FAMILY

Compliments of
2000
Michael Archibald
Wood Gundy PCI
420-6212
Toll Free N.S. 1-800-789-6084

Prepared by

Editors-in-Chief

S. Brian Fisher, CA
Waterloo

Wayne L. Tunney, FCA
Toronto

Editor

Joseph Petrie, BA
Toronto

Contributing KPMG Editors

Joanne Ivanski, LL.B., CA
Montréal

Carol Bethune, MA
Toronto

George W. Denier, FCA
Toronto

L. Dean Gallimore, CA, CBV
Lethbridge

Benita Loughlin, CA
Vancouver

Deborah A. MacPherson, CA, CFP
Hamilton

Marsha Reid, LL.B, LL.M.
Toronto

Michele A. Wood-Tweel, CA, CFP
Halifax

CARSWELL
Thomson Professional Publishing

©1999 Thomson Canada Limited

All rights reserved. No part of this publication may be reproduced, stored in a retrieval system, or transmitted, in any form or by any means, electronic, mechanical, photocopying, recording or otherwise, without the prior written permission of the publisher.

This publication is designed to provide accurate and authoritative information. It is sold with the understanding that the publisher is not engaged in rendering legal, accounting or other professional advice. If legal advice or other expert assistance is required, the services of a competent professional should be sought. The analysis contained herein represents the opinions of the authors and should in no way be construed as being either official or unofficial policy of any governmental body.

Canadian Cataloguing in Publication Data

Tax planning for you and your family

Annual.
1997-
Continues: Personal tax planning guide (Scarborough, Ont.)
ISSN 1207-5957
ISBN 0-459-57678-X (2000)

1. Tax planning – Canada – Popular works – Periodicals. 2. Income tax – Canada – Popular works – Periodicals. I. KPMG (Firm)

KE5759.Y43   343.7105'2'05   C96-900735-3
KF6499.ZA2Y43

Printed in Canada.

CARSWELL
Thomson Professional Publishing

One Corporate Plaza	**Customer Care:**
2075 Kennedy Road	Toronto: 1-416-609-3800
Scarborough, Ontario	Elsewhere in Canada/U.S.: 1-800-387-5164
M1T 3V4	Fax: 1-416-298-5094

This book has been printed on text paper which meets Environmental Canada's and the Canadian Standards Association's "Environmental Choice Program" guidelines for recycled fibre content and environmentally safe manufacturing processes.

Overview

Table of Contents

Introduction

Many Canadians don't give much thought to how they can reduce their taxes until it's time to file their tax returns each spring. By then, many tax saving opportunities may be lost. Filing your tax return is essentially a once-a-year accounting to the government to settle up your taxes owing or refund due for the previous year. It's the tax planning steps that you take throughout each year that will save the most money at tax time and in the years to come.

In this book we set out the most common rules and tax planning techniques that are currently available to individuals, but our emphasis is on tax planning aimed at minimizing your family's overall tax bill. Although many of the tax rules are designed in contemplation of the traditional family model, our advice is equally relevant to modern households of all types — whether you are part of a dual-income couple with children, a single or divorced parent, a common-law couple, a student or a retiree, you'll find that a few hours invested in reading this book can pay off substantially in tax savings and in the organization of your financial affairs.

Tax planning should comprise only one aspect of your family's overall financial plan. Chapter 1 discusses how tax planning can help you to achieve your financial goals. Your answers to the quiz in Chapter 1 will provide you with a quick check-up on your financial health. The rest of this chapter provides an important overview of the financial planning framework in which your tax planning should take place, including tips for securing your family's financial future, buying a home, and saving for your children's education. Chapter 19 offers specific tax and financial planning advice on building your retirement fund and managing your financial resources during your retirement and Chapter 20 discusses important issues to consider in developing your estate plan.

The balance of this book offers plain-language explanations of Canada's personal income tax system, along with a wealth of tax saving ideas. Key tax planning points are listed at the beginning of each chapter and highlighted in the body of the chapter itself — if you wish, you can skip directly to the planning techniques that will benefit you most.

Due to popular demand, this year's edition features new chapters with advice on:

- the ins and outs of Registered Education savings Plans
- the tax treatment of business-related automobile expenses
- the tax implications of moving into, out of, and within Canada.

At the end of most chapters we include references to publications that are available from Revenue Canada. These publications are a good source of more detailed information on the topics discussed.

What exactly is tax planning?

Tax planning is a perfectly legitimate activity. There is nothing shady about it. You are entitled to arrange your affairs, within the limits of the law, so that you pay a minimum amount of tax.

Tax evasion is a different story. Evasion is illegal. You are evading tax if you fail to report income or if you misstate facts so as to claim deductions or credits to which you are not entitled. If you evade tax, you will be subject to interest, penalties, fines and possibly imprisonment as well as being required to pay the tax owing.

Tax avoidance is the somewhat nebulous activity of using the tax system in a way in which it was not intended. The *Income Tax Act* contains a general anti-avoidance rule (GAAR), which can apply to avoidance activities. If you misuse or abuse the provisions of the Act, you may run into GAAR. The line between tax planning and tax avoidance is not always clear.

Note that Revenue Canada does not make the law. The *Income Tax Act* is enacted and amended by Parliament. Revenue Canada's role is to administer and enforce the Act. In this book we will occasionally refer to "Revenue Canada's position" on a particular matter, to indicate that this is an administrative position rather than a matter of law.

As we'll see in Chapter 8, if you disagree with Revenue Canada's interpretation of a particular rule, and you have a good legal basis for doing so, you can object to an assessment or reassessment by filing a Notice of Objection, and, if you wish, appealing the case to the Tax Court of Canada.

This book cannot replace your tax adviser

This book deals only in general terms. The Canadian tax system is horrendously complex, far more than the book makes it appear. The details fill shelves, not a thin book. Even if your affairs are relatively simple, you should consult a qualified tax professional (not just a tax return preparer). You will likely find the savings far outweigh the fees.

The book does not go very far in dealing with the tax treatment of businesses, whether incorporated or unincorporated. Only brief treatment is given to this topic in Chapters 10, 13 and 15. If you carry on your own business, or manage a corporation, you will benefit greatly from personalized tax advice.

The income tax system is constantly changing. If you thought you knew the rules a couple of years ago, you may find they have been modified. We also cannot predict what changes are in store for the future. This book is current to July 1, 1999, and reflects the law and publicly-announced proposals for changes as of that date.

For current tax information and other KPMG tax publications — including KPMG's *Canadian Tax Letter* — visit our World Wide Web site at *www.kpmg.ca.*

KPMG
Chartered Accountants

Tips for achieving your financial goals

- Define your short-, medium- and long-term financial goals (1.1.2)
- Track your net worth and cash flow, and set an annual growth target (1.1.3 and 1.1.4)
- Save systematically by "paying yourself first" (1.1.4)
- Build an investment strategy that suits your unique circumstances and needs (1.1.5)
- Set benchmarks for measuring the performance of your investment portfolio and your investment manager (1.1.5)
- Contribute $2,000 annually to an RESP to save for your child's education and earn a 20% government grant (1.2.1)
- Encourage your children to invest the money they earn (1.2.1)
- Think about using RRSP funds for a down payment on your first home under the Home Buyers' Plan (1.2.2)
- Consider GST and provincial sales tax when buying a home (1.2.2)
- Increase the frequency of your mortgage payments to reduce your mortgage interest (1.2.2)
- Plan to minimize capital gains tax on dispositions of vacation homes (1.2.3)
- Set up an emergency fund or line of credit (1.3.1)
- Make sure you have adequate insurance and a current will (1.3.2 and 1.3.3)
- Consider a power of attorney (1.3.4)
- Shop around when choosing your financial and investment advisers (1.4)

In this chapter we offer a primer on financial planning with emphasis on the impact of taxes on your ability to meet your family's financial goals. We also point out tax planning ideas elsewhere in this book that may help you to achieve these goals. Given the importance of financial planning for your retirement, this area is discussed separately in Chapter 19.

1.1 Developing your financial plan

For many Canadians, at all stages in life, the very idea of financial planning is mystifying. It shouldn't be. Saving for retirement, financing your child's education or buying a house are within the reach of most of us—the purpose of financial planning is to clarify your objectives, set a realistic timetable for achieving them, and marshal your financial resources to support your plan. Of course, the process may require changing your expectations, paring down your current lifestyle or other compromises. But having a sound financial plan will likely ease your financial anxiety by giving you a realistic picture of your family's finances and a clear path for satisfying your goals.

In Canada, taxes are one of the biggest obstacles to the creation, maintenance and preservation of independent wealth. Tax planning to minimize your family's overall tax bill should be an integral part of your family's financial plan. The balance of this book is full of ideas about how to save taxes; the rest of this chapter is an overview of the financial planning framework in which your tax planning should take place.

1.1.1 The 21st century — will you be financially fit?

Are your financial affairs in order today? How well are you prepared for the future? Take the following quiz to find out. Depending on how high you score, you may wish to simply scan the ideas in the rest of this chapter and go straight to Chapter 2. But if you score less than 16 points, you probably stand to benefit from a more thorough reading of the financial planning overview in this chapter before you move on.

		Yes	No
1.	Have you reviewed your lifestyle goals within the last two years?	❏	❏
2.	Have you determined if your financial resources can meet those goals?	❏	❏
3.	Have you reviewed your personal net orth statement in the last 12 months?	❏	❏
4.	Have you established an emergency fund or personal line of credit?	❏	❏
5.	Are you satisfied with the amount of money you are saving per month?	❏	❏
6.	Do you contribute your maximum amount to an RRSP each year?	❏	❏
7.	If you have a spouse, are you taking advantage of a spousal RRSP for income splitting in retirement?	❏	❏
8.	Do you make the maximum RRSP contribution within the first three months of the year?	❏	❏

	Yes	No
9. Have you determined your short- and long-term investment goals?	❏	❏
10. Are you satisfied with the performance of your investments, both inside and outside of your RRSP?	❏	❏
11. If you are employed, are you aware of all the benefits available through your company pension and other benefits plans?	❏	❏
12. Are you contributing to a retirement fund outside of your company pension plan?	❏	❏
13. Have you determined how much income you can expect during retirement?	❏	❏
14. Do you know if your expected retirement income will meet your lifestyle needs?	❏	❏
15. If you have children, have you established an education fund for them?	❏	❏
16. Are you familiar with the new Canada Education Savings Grant introduced in 1998?	❏	❏
17. Do you have a plan in place to reduce or eliminate your personal debt?	❏	❏
18. Is the interest on your loans tax-deductible?	❏	❏
19. Have you done all you can to reduce your tax liability by sheltering, deferring or splitting your income?	❏	❏
20. Do you know your projected income tax liability for the current year?	❏	❏
21. If you have a future tax liability (e.g., on death), are you able to finance it?	❏	❏

	Yes	No
22. Have you reviewed and, if necessary, updated the following documents within the past two years:		
• Will and last testament?	❑	❑
• Power of attorney?	❑	❑
• Disability income insurance policies?	❑	❑
• Excess liability (umbrella) insurance policy?	❑	❑
23. Do you have sufficient insurance coverage?	❑	❑
24. Have you explored tax and estate planning opportunities involving family trusts?	❑	❑
25. Do you feel in control of your financial future?	❑	❑

Now total your points—if you answered "yes" to…

- **17 to 25 questions:** Congratulations, you're in great shape. Keep up the good work by regularly reviewing your progress toward achieving your goals.
- **9 to 16 questions:** You're on your way but there is still room for improvement. Consider talking to a qualified financial counsellor, who can give objective advice to assist you in becoming financially fit.
- **0 to 8 questions:** You need to do some serious work. Start by reading through the rest of this chapter. Once you know the basics, consider meeting with a qualified financial adviser to develop a plan for getting into shape.

> Define your short-, medium- and long-term financial goals.

1.1.2 Define your financial goals

Putting your dreams on paper is the first step toward realizing them. Start by setting down what you want and when you want it. If you have a spouse or domestic partner, compile your list together, compromising where necessary to make sure that you are both committed to the same objectives. You might also include your children and have them develop their own plan as a teaching exercise.

While your list should take into account your family's well-being and future financial security, be sure to include lifestyle-enhancing items like vacation homes, major renovations, luxury cars or swimming pools. If you want to take a sabbatical from work to spend time with your children or eventually start your own business, write it down. As part of this exercise, consider the discussion of building your investment strategy in 1.1.5, common financial goals in 1.2 and important financial safeguards in 1.3.

When you have completed your list, divide it into short-, medium- and long-term goals and rank them in order of priority within each section. Set down a timeframe for meeting each goal. Then do a bit of research and estimate the cost of achieving your goals, making sure to account for inflation. Don't let the numbers overwhelm you—over time the effects of compound growth can provide significant returns on your investments. Nevertheless, you may need to revise your list by allowing more time to achieve a certain goal or by dropping items that are beyond your means.

As time goes by, your list will serve as a guide for directing your savings and investments and as an indicator of your progress. Since your personal and financial circumstances and goals are bound to change, revisit your list once or twice a year and revise it to reflect new priorities.

1.1.3 Track your net worth

Now that you have a better idea of where you want to go, the next step is to take a snapshot of where you are today—your net worth. Calculating your net worth is simply a matter of adding up your total assets (what you own) and total liabilities (what you owe), and then subtracting your liabilities from your assets. The resulting figure is the springboard for most aspects of financial management and planning.

It's also a good idea to separate your assets by ownership—whether your resources are owned by you, your spouse or jointly, can help in determining potential strategies for income splitting (see Chapter 5) and estate planning (see Chapter 20).

A close look at your assets will show you whether most of your assets are personal items, such as your home or your car, or investment assets, such as savings and shares. It should also indicate how liquid your assets are and help you determine if your investments are spread appropriately to balance expected rates of return with the degree of risk you are prepared to take (see 1.1.5).

Similarly, a close look at your liabilities will show you whether your insurance coverage is adequate (see 1.3.2) and how your debts are affecting your bottom line. As we'll see in 7.2.3, interest incurred for personal reasons on credit cards, consumer loans and mortgages is not deductible for tax purposes, while interest on loans taken out to purchase income-generating investments or business income may be deductible. As a result, the interest on your consumer debts may cost you more than you make on your investments. Where possible, you should try to pay down your consumer debts and make sure that all loans you take out are for a tax deductible purpose.

> **Set an annual target for increasing your net worth.**

Updating your net worth calculation once or twice a year is a good way to track your financial health and progress toward achieving your financial goals. If you are able to increase your net worth by 15% each year, your net worth will double every five years. Ways to increase your net worth include:

- improving the rate of return on your investments;
- investing more of your income by spending less on discretionary items and minimizing taxes; and
- reducing your debt by paying off your credit card balances and accelerating your mortgage and other debt payments.

One simple rule of thumb for determining how quickly your assets will grow is to use the "Rule of 72". By taking the number 72 and dividing it by the average growth rate of your assets, you can calculate the number of years it will take to double your assets. For example, if your annual growth rate is 8%, then your assets will double in value every 9 years ($72 \div 8\% = 9$).

1.1.4 Cash management and budgeting—the cornerstone of financial planning

The formula for accruing the necessary funds to achieve your financial goals is no secret. Unless you expect to inherit money or win a lottery, the way to start building wealth is to save and regularly invest a portion of your income. Through the mathematical "miracle" of compounding, your investment assets will grow exponentially. So the more savings you have to invest and the longer they are invested, the greater your net worth will be.

One way to increase your net worth is to gain better control over your savings and expenses with a personal or family budget. List the amounts of money you expect to receive through your pay cheque or other sources and the amounts you pay out monthly for living expenses, such as mortgage payments, groceries and entertainment. This will allow you to realistically assess your cash flow and help you prioritize so you can spend your money where you need and want to.

If you have never before looked at your living expenses in detail, you could first analyse your previous year's spending by preparing a breakdown of all amounts paid out on your bank statements and charged to your credit cards and lines of credit. Try to group your expenses under logical classifications that fit your particular spending patterns, using as few or as many classifications as you need for budgeting purposes. Separate extraordinary, one-time expenses such as major house renovations or home purchases from basic necessities and discretionary expenses. Now review this information and use it for setting a budget for the next year. Based on your particular goals, add any unusual one-time expenditures and other new categories as necessary.

Without making lifestyle changes, there is usually little you can do about your mortgage payments, car payments and other fixed expenses. However, the exercise of preparing—and sticking to—a budget will probably reveal opportunities to easily reduce your discretionary expenses such as travel, entertainment and gifts. There are plenty of excellent software packages available that can help you create and monitor your family budget.

Save systematically by "paying yourself first".

When preparing your budget, do not simply plan to save the amount left over at the end of each month—chances are there won't be as much left as you intended. Instead, get into the practice of saving a fixed amount of at least 10% of your income at the beginning of each month (or some other period) and using the balance for your expenses. Commonly known as the "pay yourself first" plan, this technique helps you to save systematically and to be less prone to making impulsive or needlessly expensive purchases. Although it may take you a few months to get used to having less cash readily available, you will probably be surprised at how quickly you will adjust. Consider having your financial institution automatically transfer your savings amount to a separate account or registered retirement savings plan ("RRSP") (see Chapter 3) on a monthly or other regular basis.

1.1.5   Develop an appropriate investment strategy

Today's economic realities are forcing Canadians to take care of their own financial health. Even with professional advisers, most investors should take an active interest in their investment activities. But the average investor spends most of his or her time picking individual stocks, mutual funds and GICs, a practice that generally adds little to a portfolio's incremental return.

Build an investment strategy that suits your unique
circumstances and needs.

Modern investment wisdom says that it's not what you select but where
you select it from. Known as "asset allocation", this process works as
well for $100,000 as it does for $1 million. Simply put, asset allocation is
the process of deciding how to invest a pool of resources among a broad
array of assets. It is considered the single most important part of
managing a portfolio. According to Ibbotson Associates of Chicago,
Illinois, over 90% of a portfolio's investment return is derived from the
appropriate asset allocation mix. The actual securities selection
contributes only 5% to 10% of the overall return.

Asset allocation has three levels. The first level entails selecting between
asset classes: cash, fixed income and equities.

After that, a second level decision includes determining market
exposure—in many cases, you would be wise to diversify your
investments geographically. Canada represents less that 3% of the world's
capitalization, and substantial investment opportunities exist beyond our
borders. Most Canadians are satisfied with owning some U.S. stocks, but
this usually doesn't allow for enough diversification because the North
American markets strongly influence each other. As we'll see in 3.1.7,
there is a 20% foreign content limit for registered retirement savings
plans, but there are several strategies for increasing your RRSP's
participation in foreign markets above that level.

The third level of asset allocation is deciding the currency exposure,
commonly known as "hedging". This was illustrated earlier this decade
by a 25% rebound in the Japanese stock market as the yen dropped by the
same value against the U.S. dollar. A North American investor would be
no further ahead unless he or she was hedged.

Along with these three levels, asset allocation comes in two forms:
strategic and tactical. Strategic asset allocation is a long-term scheme that
divides a portfolio among several asset classes according to the inherent
risks and rewards of each asset. Tactical allocation consists of short-term
market predictions that could last an hour or a day. This type of allocation
often proves difficult because variables used in selecting the asset mix
continually change and the portfolio must be adjusted to keep up with
market movements. Other disadvantages include higher fees, lack of
liquidity in esoteric markets like precious metals, and the potential to
misread economic signals.

While there is no perfect asset allocation for any one person, there are definitely wrong ones. The following are some tips for getting the right mix.

Determine your objectives and risk tolerance—Before you make any investment decisions, determine your objectives and risk tolerance and then do an asset allocation. Risk tolerance is influenced by your age, your family situation and investor personality. For example, a 55-year-old with two dependent teenage children may have a dramatically different risk tolerance than an empty-nester or single person of the same age.

Risk tolerance should also reflect your ability to replace losses. For a partner in a major law firm earning $500,000 who owns a house and has thousands of dollars in RRSPs, a loss of $50,000 in the market is replaceable. But for someone with only pension and investment income, such a loss would be devastating. Asset allocation has to be a function of your own profile and risk tolerance. If it's right you should be able to sleep well in any market environment.

For a discussion of revising your investment strategy as you approach retirement, see 19.2.2.

Consider your total portfolio—Most investors make a classic mistake at the outset by separating their registered from non-registered investments; whether investments are in an RRSP or not is irrelevant to an asset allocation decision. Your total investment portfolio should be amalgamated so that the right proportion of assets can be determined. Once the asset allocation is done, then you can decide, from a tax perspective, which investments are more effective to hold inside your RRSP.

Plan for a long horizon and stay on course—Once you have determined your asset allocation, plan to let your investments grow for at least five to seven years, long enough to go through a full market cycle. Average investors often make the mistake of buying what's hot because they think it's a great time to be in the market, then panic and sell as soon as the stock goes down. A disciplined approach to long-term asset allocation will probably give you higher returns in the long run.

Pay attention to fees—Be wary of management fees and commissions. A saving in fees of 1% per annum on a $100,000 investment earning a 10% annual return for 10 years could save you well over $20,000. You can't control the market, but you can control the fees and commissions you pay.

Inflation is a risk—Inflation is another factor you can't control. Depending on the rate of inflation, it can be a costly mistake to think of money in nominal terms instead of its real value. If your money isn't growing, you're losing it. Consider a $1,000 investment earning an average rate of return of 10% per year. After 10 years, the investment will be worth $2,594, but inflation will have eroded its real value. Assuming an annual inflation rate of 3%, this erosion will amount to $627 by the end of the tenth year, bringing the investment's real value down at that time to $1,967.

Rebalance annually—One of the most powerful tools you can use in managing your investments is a regular discipline of portfolio rebalancing. This allows you to manage your investments for profit, by selling high and buying low.

For example, you may have decided originally that an investment mix of 40% in stocks and 60% in bonds met your objectives. However, due to a prosperous period in the economy, you find that the stock component of your portfolio grows to 55% while bonds now represent only 45% by value. In this case, the discipline of strategic asset allocation should force you to take profits and rebalance your original mix so that when the economy reverses—as it always does—you will be positioned to take advantage of the change.

> **Set benchmarks for measuring the performance of your investment portfolio and your investment manager.**

Choose the right investment firm and monitor your investments' performance—Select an investment firm that fits your particular circumstances and needs and has consistently shown strong performance over the long-term, compared to its competitors. Establish appropriate benchmarks that relate to your particular asset mix, such as market indices, to judge the performance of your investment portfolio and your investment manager. See 1.4 for general advice on choosing your professional advisers.

Don't try to outsmart the market—Focus your attention on getting the asset allocation right and then, within each asset class, try to keep your costs at a minimum. Make sure you are well diversified. Be consistent in your investment style. Don't think that what happened in the past will happen in the future. In the financial market, history rarely repeats.

1.2   Some common financial goals

1.2.1   Planning for your children's education

Although post-secondary education may not be the route your child chooses, having a college degree or university diploma can greatly expand their range of occupational choices and will probably enhance their future earning power. But with government support for post-secondary institutions falling and tuition fees on the rise, putting a child through college or university is becoming increasingly costly—depending where your child attends school, the cost is currently about $10,000–$12,000 per year in Canada when you factor in tuition, books and living expenses. If your child decides to study outside Canada, the cost will increase exponentially. Most of us would be hard-pressed to finance these costs out of current income, so planning ahead is crucial.

Like any financial planning endeavour, decisions about funding your child's education should be made with an eye toward the effects of taxation. Below are a few common techniques for reducing your family's overall tax burden so that more funds will be available to finance your child's education.

> Contribute $2,000 annually to an RESP to save for your child's education and earn a 20% government grant.

Over the last few years the federal government has made several improvements to the rules for Registered Education Savings Plans ("RESPs"), making them significantly more attractive. The most welcome change is the introduction of a 20% Canada Education Savings Grant. Under this program, the government will provide a grant of 20% on the first $2,000 of annual contributions made in a year to an RESP, giving you an easy extra 20% return on your first $2,000 of contributions each year.

Another improvement involves situations where your child does not go on to post-secondary school. In the past you could not recover more than your original contributions to your RESP and all of the investment income was lost. Now you can recover all of your contributions plus the growth by either transferring the earnings to your RRSP (if you have enough RRSP contribution room), or withdrawing the funds and paying a 20% penalty tax (plus an additional 20% charge if you live in Québec). The RESP rules are discussed at greater length in Chapter 4.

As an alternative to an RESP, you could invest in tax-efficient growth mutual funds in your child's name. Any income from these funds is normally taxed under the preferential rules for capital gains (see Chapter 6) or dividends (see Chapter 7). In addition, any capital gains distributed by the fund or on the sale of the fund will be taxable in your child's hands at your child's lower tax rate (or not taxed at all if his or her income is low enough). Until your child turns 18, the dividends and interest will be taxed in your hands due to the attribution rules discussed in 5.2.3; however, this will usually amount to a small proportion of the fund's overall return. Choosing a non-registered mutual fund provides some investment control and flexibility—there are no restrictions on the use of the funds and there is no limit on the amount that can be deposited annually.

If you receive Child Tax Benefit payments (see 2.3.1), consider depositing them to an account in your child's name. As with RESP funds, these deposits may add up to a significant investment over time and, since the anti-income splitting rules discussed in Chapter 5 don't apply, any investment income earned on the funds will be taxed in your child's hands. You may wish to withdraw the balance from the account annually and purchase higher-yielding investments on your child's behalf.

If you have a child who works part-time (e.g., summer employment, paper route, etc.) with an income below the basic and supplementary personal amounts of $7,294 that can be earned tax-free (see 2.2), you might consider filing a tax return for him or her to report the earned income for RRSP purposes and allow the build up of an unused contribution limit, which may be of use in a later year when he or she becomes taxable (see 3.1.3). This can be especially useful when your child is in the teenage years and can expect to earn much more income in the future, since the unused deduction room can be carried forward indefinitely. If your child has cash available, he or she can contribute now to start enjoying tax-free investment growth but delay claiming the related tax deduction until a later year when your child has enough income to be taxable.

Also, instead of giving your child money which is easily spent, consider having him or her start an RRSP. The amount you can contribute may seem minimal—only 18% of the child's earned income from a summer or part-time job, plus the $2,000 lifetime overcontribution if the child turned 18 in the prior year (see 3.3.4). But the funds in the RRSP will enjoy tax-free compounding, which will accumulate significantly over time. For example, assuming an 8% rate of return, $1,000 a year invested in an RRSP at the end of each year beginning at age 16 will grow to $7,336 by the beginning of the year in which the child turns 22; at age 30, the RRSP will grow to $24,215, and if the annual contribution is made until the child retires at 65, the RRSP will be $530,000.

> **Encourage your children to invest the money they earn.**

To top up your child's earnings and help finance his or her education (or other pursuits), consider lending your child, interest-free, an amount equal to what he or she earns over the year and would otherwise spend. Your child can use the loaned funds to pay for expenses such as tuition fees and invest his or her own income to earn investment income. That way, the anti-income splitting rules discussed in Chapter 5 will not attribute the investment income back to you and it will be taxed at your child's lower tax rate (or not taxed at all if his or her income is low enough). Later on, perhaps after graduating, your child can pay you back out of the invested funds, or keep the funds as "seed money" for their early working years. (This strategy is discussed in more detail in 5.3.11.)

Chapter 5 discusses a number of techniques for splitting income with children. These strategies can significantly lower your family's overall tax burden, and the savings are bound to come in handy whether or not your child ultimately pursues a post-secondary education.

1.2.2 Buying a home

If you are renting living accommodations, instead of buying, you're missing out on a potential investment opportunity. A home can be a reliable hedge against inflation, a great retirement savings vehicle and a tax shelter—as we'll see in 6.5.2. If you own a home and sell it for a gain, the gain is usually tax-free as long as it has been your principal residence.

So if you can afford to buy a home, don't rent. If you are renting while you are saving for a home, consider moving to less expensive rental accommodations and saving more toward your down payment. The sooner you start putting your money toward a mortgage instead of your landlord's pocket, the better off you will be. Below are a few tax planning and other issues for prospective home buyers to consider.

Most first-time home buyers quickly find out that the price of a new home and the interest cost in financing a mortgage are just the beginning. New home owners also need to cover substantial ongoing costs that were previously included in their rent, such as repairs, utilities, insurance and property taxes. There will also be a number of one-time costs associated with the purchase, including legal fees, moving expenses, and land transfer taxes in certain provinces. Depending on the home you buy, you should also be prepared to bear the costs of decorating a new home, or redecorating or substantially remodelling an existing house.

> **Think about using RRSP funds for a down payment on your first home under the Home Buyers' Plan.**

If you qualify, the Home Buyers' Plan can be a possible source of cash for financing your down payment. If you are saving to buy your first home, think about using your RRSP as your savings vehicle; under the Home Buyers' Plan discussed at 3.3.6, if you qualify, you can generally withdraw up to $20,000 as a loan from your RRSP to buy or build a home, without counting the withdrawal as income for tax purposes. You must then repay the loan, without interest, over the next 16 years.

If you do plan to withdraw RRSP funds under the Home Buyers' Plan, consider making your RRSP contribution for the year at least 90 days before you make the withdrawal to preserve your ability to deduct the contribution amount. If you are depending on your RRSP for retirement income, you will want to forecast the decline in income that will result from the loss of the tax-free compounding when you withdraw a large chunk of RRSP funds now and pay it back over the next 16 years. See 3.3.6 for a more detailed discussion of the Home Buyers' Plan.

> **Consider GST and provincial sales tax when buying a new home.**

Since no sales tax applies to used houses, a resale home may be cheaper than a new home. Sales of new homes in Nova Scotia, New Brunswick and Newfoundland attract Harmonized Sales Tax ("HST"—see 10.2.5) at a 15% rate (the combined 7% federal and 8% provincial rates). In Québec, new home sales attract the 7% Goods and Services Tax ("GST") and Québec Sales Tax ("QST") at 7.5% of the sale price including GST. New home sales in the rest of Canada attract GST at the regular 7% rate. However, if you buy a new home as your principal place of residence (or the principal residence of someone related to you), you may be entitled to a partial sales tax rebate.

Buyers of qualifying new homes priced under $450,000 can claim a partial rebate of the GST payable on the purchase (including the 7% portion of the HST in the above Atlantic provinces). The rebate is available either from Revenue Canada or directly from the vendor—in the latter case, you will pay the vendor less than the full 7% GST. For homes priced under $347,222 (before GST), the rebate is 2.52% of the purchase price and from that point to $350,000 it is capped at $8,750. For homes from $350,000 to $450,000, calculate the rebate as follows: subtract $350,000 from the purchase price, multiply by 0.0875, and subtract the result from $8,750. Once the price hits $450,000, there is no rebate and you pay the full 7% tax. Similar rebates of QST and the 8% provincial portion of the HST in Nova Scotia and Newfoundland are also available for qualifying new homes, although the rebate rates and calculations are quite different.

> **Increase the frequency of your mortgage payments to reduce your mortgage interest.**

Once you have a mortgage, consider making extra payments to reduce your interest costs. Based on a 25-year amortization period, your mortgage will be paid off at the same time whether you pay monthly or weekly and making extra payments can greatly reduce the amount of interest you'll pay over the life of your mortgage.

Accelerating your mortgage payment schedule doesn't necessarily mean that you will be shelling out any more than you do now. Here's the trick: figure out how much you can or want to pay each month and multiply that amount by 12. This is your annual payment. Then divide this number by 52 to determine the amount to pay weekly. Over the course of a year, your total mortgage payments will be identical, but more frequent payments will reduce your principal more quickly and reduce your overall interest cost.

Another way to save on mortgage interest is to maintain your original payment level when your mortgage comes up for renewal, even if interest rates have fallen. Also, each time you renew, consider increasing your payment by whatever you can commit—even an extra $5 or $10 will save you money in the long run.

1.2.3 Vacation properties

Buying a cottage, ski chalet or condo in Florida can provide years of enjoyment for your family. For a variety of reasons, a recreation property can also be a sound investment. You will probably save on your family's vacation costs. You may even find it easy to make up some of the property's costs by renting it out when your family is not using it. Any improvements you make may significantly enhance the property's resale value. Market demand for desirable vacation properties (especially waterfront properties) within a reasonable drive from Canadian urban centres will probably remain steady, and, if historical trends continue, your vacation home could appreciate significantly during the time you own it.

> **Plan to minimize capital gains tax on dispositions of vacation homes.**

Whether you plan to keep the property in the family or sell it for future gain, bear in mind that the capital gains tax (see 6.2) may apply on the difference between the property's cost when you bought it and its fair market value when you sell it or at the time of your death (or your spouse's death). The longer you own your cottage, the bigger the gain is likely to be.

To avoid leaving your survivors with a tax bill which they may have to fund by selling the property, consider purchasing enough life insurance to fund the taxes that will arise on your death. You may be able to shelter some of the gain on the property's sale or on your death (or your spouse's) through the principal residence exemption (see 6.5.2). You may be able to protect future gains from tax by transferring the property to one of your children or to a family trust (see 5.3.7). Consider also our more general discussion of estate planning in Chapter 20.

If your vacation property is situated in the U.S. and you are a Canadian resident, the double hit of U.S. estate tax and Canadian income tax arising on death can carry a potentially high tax burden. The Canada-U.S. tax treaty may ease the potential for double taxation, but, as discussed at 18.4, some rather complex tax planning may be required and you should probably seek professional tax advice.

1.3   Preserving your family's financial security

The achievement of your financial goals can be delayed or derailed by unexpected changes of circumstance. Your family's financial plan should include measures to address risk and protect your family's financial security.

1.3.1   Do you have a line of credit and/or an emergency fund?

> Set up an emergency fund or line of credit.

In today's economic and business environment you can no longer count on having a job for life. Job loss can also affect your company-funded benefits and pension plan. Generally speaking, you should have an emergency fund large enough to handle the loss of a job for six months to one year. Canada Savings Bonds, money market funds and cashable guaranteed investment certificates are good places to park emergency reserves.

Another way to provide an emergency fund is to establish a line of credit with your financial institution. Be careful to only use it when necessary, because the interest you'll incur will be non-deductible and you will have to repay it according to the line of credit's terms.

1.3.2 Do you have enough insurance?

Review your insurance needs with your financial advisers to determine the appropriate amount and form of your insurance coverage in various areas, including property loss, death, disability, sickness, personal liability and liquidity crisis.

> **Make sure you have adequate insurance.**

A review should consider your need for life insurance. In the event of your death, life insurance may be critical for providing replacement income for your dependants and for funding your estate's tax and other liabilities. Life insurance plays many other important roles in estate planning. Some tax planning and other issues involving life insurance are discussed in 20.6.

One of your most valuable assets is your ability to earn income through employment or self-employment. Review your need for disability insurance—if you become disabled, the financial consequences can be devastating. Most disability insurance policies do not provide a level of income over and above what you need for basic ongoing living expenses. In the long-term, this could leave you without enough funds set aside for your retirement since disability income usually stops at age 65.

Make sure you have sufficient insurance to protect you from significant financial loss due to damage or destruction to your home, automobile or other personal assets. Without adequate coverage, the emotional trauma of such losses could be compounded by irreversible damage to your family's finances. Depending on your occupation or circumstances, you should also assess your need for other forms of insurance such as health and professional or director's liability coverage.

1.3.3 Is your will up-to-date?

Have you and your family members reviewed your wills within the past two years, or since there has been a change in your family circumstances? Are your wills effectively tax-structured? Remember that if you die intestate (without a will) your assets will be distributed according to provincial law, possibly differently from what you would have wished. This may be particularly true for those in relationships not covered by provincial law, such as same-sex couples. Be sure to seek advice of a lawyer (or a notary in Québec) to ensure your will is legally valid and accurately reflects your wishes. You should also consult a tax adviser for assistance in reducing your estate's tax liability, including probate fees, income tax, and U.S. estate tax.

For a more detailed discussion of the role of your will in planning for the orderly distribution of your estate and the minimization of taxes on death, see 20.2.

1.3.4 Do you have a power of attorney?

A power of attorney allows you to designate a person who will take control of your financial affairs if you become incapacitated due to illness or injury. If this happens and you do not have a power of attorney, control will yield to a provincial public trustee which may hamstring your family's ability to access your financial resources.

> Consider a power of attorney.

Powers of attorney are usually limited to decisions regarding your finances. In some provinces (including Ontario and Québec), you can empower a different person to make decisions about your health care and medical treatment.

Like your will, your power of attorney should be prepared with professional advice—consider having both drawn up at the same time.

Note that a power of attorney operates only while you are alive. Once you die your will takes over.

1.4 Selecting your professional advisers

Financial planning is broad in scope and you may need advice from professionals with expertise in different areas. For some financial decisions, it will be worth the expense to invest in professional advice, whether from a lawyer, tax adviser, insurance broker, investment counsellor, or a personal financial adviser. And in some financial planning endeavours, such as estate planning, professional legal and tax advice is a must.

> Shop around when choosing your financial advisers.

Given what's at stake—your family's finances—you should take the time to shop around for advisers who are knowledgeable in their fields and with whom you feel comfortable. When interviewing prospective advisers of any profession, be sure to cover the following topics:

- Ask for client references, preferably from three or four people in circumstances similar to your own.

- Inquire into the professional's educational background, qualifications and level of experience, particularly in fields like financial planning which is only regulated in Québec.
- Ask whether the adviser belongs to any professional networks and associations to determine what sorts of resources are available to him or her.
- Make sure that you understand the fee arrangement.
- Be cautious of advisers whose sole objective may be trying to sell you investments, tax shelters, insurance or anything other than independent advice.

The level of your need for advisers will depend primarily on the complexity of your affairs, but to some extent on your own knowledge of financial matters. You will get better value for your fees to advisers if you spend some time up front educating yourself. The personal finance sections of bookstores and libraries are full of excellent, easy-to-read books on retirement and investment planning and the business sections of newspapers are packed with investment, tax, and retirement planning tips. Various organizations also offer frequent, free retirement and investment planning seminars.

If you have a spouse, be sure that he or she is acquainted with your advisers, since your spouse will need to deal with them in the event of your death or disability. It is also a good idea to keep an up-to-date list of your advisers' names and phone numbers in one place, perhaps in the same place as your will.

Tips for claiming tax deductions and credits

2

- The higher-income spouse should claim credits to reduce high-income surtax (2.1.3)
- If you're unmarried and support a family member, don't miss out on the "equivalent-to-married" credit (2.2.1)
- Working parents and students—claim your child care expenses (2.3.2)
- Take advantage of the new tax credit for interest on student loans (2.4)
- Consider withdrawing RRSP funds under the Lifelong Learning Plan to help pay for training or post-secondary education programs (2.4)
- If Revenue Canada challenges your disability claim, consider objecting (2.5.1)
- Disabled persons—weigh the benefits of deducting the costs of an attendant or claiming the costs for purposes of the medical expense credit (2.5.2)
- If you're separating, co-operate to minimize your joint tax bill (2.6)
- Aim to preserve pre-May 1997 child support arrangements where practical (2.6.2)
- Combine two or more years of charitable donations into one year (2.7.1)
- If you're married, combine your charitable donations and claim them on the higher-income spouse's return (2.7.1)
- Consider donating publicly traded securities or other assets to charity (2.7.1)
- Combine your family's medical expenses on one return (2.7.2)
- Choose your own 12-month period for medical expense claims (2.7.2)
- Plan for the timing of your family's medical expense payments (2.7.2)
- Take advantage of Canada's generous tax break for political contributions (2.7.3)
- If you have friends and relatives visiting from outside Canada, have them claim the sales tax rebate for visitors (2.9.4)

In this chapter we highlight some commonly available and sometimes overlooked deductions and credits that can be claimed on your income tax return, depending on your family status and personal circumstances.

2.1 Taxes, credits and deductions

2.1.1 Calculating your tax balance due or refund owing

To understand how deductions and credits work, you need to understand the basic tax calculation. We'll describe it briefly here. (For Québec residents, the provincial tax calculation is completely separate and not as described below. See Chapter 16.)

You start by adding up your various kinds of income: employment, business, interest, grossed-up dividends, taxable capital gains, and so on. This gives you **total income**. From this figure you subtract certain deductions, some of which we'll look at in this chapter, and reach **net income**. The net income figure is used for certain purposes later. Then some additional deductions are allowed, primarily losses carried forward from previous years, giving you **taxable income**.

You then calculate your **federal tax** using the formula shown on Schedule 1 of your tax return. Then you subtract various **non-refundable tax credits** (see 2.1.2), and certain others such as the dividend tax credit (see 7.1.1). This gives you **basic federal tax**.

To the basic federal tax figure you add the **basic** and **high income federal surtax**. Before 1998, the surtax was 3% of basic federal tax, plus an additional surtax of 5% of basic federal tax over $12,500. As of July 1, 1998, the 3% surtax was eliminated for individuals with incomes under $50,000 and reduced for those with income between $50,000 and $65,000. As of July 1, 1999, the 3% surtax is eliminated for everyone. Because of the mid-year implementation date, individuals earning over $50,000 will pay half of the 3% surtax otherwise payable in 1999, to a maximum of 1.5% of federal tax. The 5% high income surtax is unchanged.

Once you've figured in the federal surtax, you add the **provincial or territorial tax**, which is a percentage (anywhere from 40% to 69%, varying by province or territory) of the basic federal tax. Then, depending on the province, you may also have to add a provincial surtax, health care levy and/or flat tax. If you are self-employed, you may also be required to add your Canada Pension Plan ("CPP") contribution on your self-employment income at this point.

Next, you claim as a credit any other non-refundable credits that are federal only, such as the political contributions credit (see 2.7.3), and you end up with two figures: your federal tax for the year and your provincial tax for the year.

Finally, you record all source deductions of tax (withheld by your employer, for example) and instalments paid, both of which are credited to your account. Along with these are the **refundable credits**—including the supplementary medical expense credit (see 2.7.2), the Goods and Services Tax ("GST") credit (see 2.9.3) and the GST rebate (see 2.9.4)—which are given the same treatment so that they can effectively be refunded to you even if you pay no tax for the year. (Some provinces also provide refundable tax credits.) The bottom line is your **balance due** or

refund claimed, and that will be the cheque you send in by April 30 or receive when your return is assessed.

You can see why the non-refundable credits are given that name. They can reduce your tax to zero, but they are not paid to you if you have no tax to pay for the year. In other words, they can trigger a refund, if tax is otherwise payable.

2.1.2 Deductions versus credits—what's the difference?

Before we get into the specific deductions and credits available, you need to understand the different effects of a deduction and a credit. You can refer back to the calculation in 2.1.1 as we go through this.

A **deduction** (or "write-off") reduces your taxable income, on which your federal tax is calculated. The combined effect of the federal and provincial taxes and surtaxes means that, as long as you are still paying some tax, a deduction is worth about 27% where your taxable income is under $29,590; about 41% where it is between $29,590 and $59,180; and about 50% where it is over $59,180.

In other words, a $100 write-off (of, say, deductible moving or child care expenses) is worth about $27 to $50 in tax savings, depending on your tax bracket.

A **credit**, on the other hand, is a direct reduction in tax; $100 of a credit such as the credit for political contributions (2.7.3 below) is worth exactly $100 to you.

There is a twist, however. Most of the credits are calculated as part of getting to basic federal tax, *before provincial tax and federal surtax are calculated*. As a result, these credits are worth about 50% to 75% more than they would otherwise be, because the provincial tax, provincial surtaxes and federal surtax are reduced as well.

Example:

Riley calculates his federal tax for 1999 as being $12,000. For 1999, federal basic surtax is essentially 1.5% of federal tax on income over $65,000 (and reduced for income between $50,000 and $65,000—see 2.1.1). Riley lives in British Columbia where the effective provincial tax for 1999 is 49.5% of the federal tax. Richard's total tax bill is $18,120 ($12,000 federal tax, $180 federal surtax, $5,940 provincial tax).

Riley discovers that he is able to claim an additional credit, which he had not thought of. The credit is $500 against federal tax. Now his federal tax is $11,500, the 1.5% surtax is $173 and his provincial tax is 49.5% of $11,500, or $5,693. His total tax bill is now $17,366.

As you can see, the $500 federal credit is actually worth $754 because of the reduced surtax and provincial tax—even though there is no explicit provincial credit to be claimed. The additional $254 is actually 1.5% + 49.5% (the federal surtax and provincial tax rate) on the $500. (The impact of provincial surtaxes, such as Ontario's Fair Share Health Care

Levy on taxable income over about $51,000, can magnify this effect still more.)

Finally, note the distinction between refundable and non-refundable credits. Because they are treated as having been paid by you, just like source withholdings and instalments, refundable credits are always worth what they say they are. Non-refundable credits, like deductions, become worthless once you reach the point of paying no tax at all for the year.

2.1.3 Transferring credits between spouses

Some of the non-refundable credits outlined below, such as charitable donations (see 2.7.1), can be transferred between spouses if not otherwise usable (see Schedule 2 of the T1 General Return).

> The higher-income spouse should claim credits to reduce high-income surtax.

Where you have a choice as to which spouse will claim certain credits, note that credits are worth slightly more to very high-income individuals. That is because of the additional surtax that applies to individuals with high "basic federal tax". This additional surtax is an extra 5% of basic federal tax in excess of $12,500. Almost all provinces also have surtaxes on high levels of provincial tax, which can boost the effect of credits still further.

If you are paying any of these surtaxes and your spouse is not, it is better for you to claim most of the credits that can be allocated between the two of you.

2.2 Personal, spousal and dependent credits

Every individual gets a basic federal credit, which allows you to receive a basic amount of income on a tax-free basis. In 1999, the basic federal credit is $1,155, which offsets the federal tax on your first $6,794 of income. (On your income tax return, you claim a "basic personal amount" of $6,794, which you later multiply by 17%.)

In 2000, the basic federal credit is scheduled to rise for all individuals to $1,212 (17% of $7,131). For 1999 only, low-income individuals can also claim a supplementary personal amount of up to $250.

2.2.1 Spousal and "equivalent-to-married" credits

If you are married, you can claim a further federal credit of $972 (rising to $1,029 in 2000) if your spouse's income is under $606, or a reduced amount if your spouse has income between $606 and $6,324.

> **If you're unmarried and support a family member, don't miss out on the "equivalent-to-married" credit.**

If you are single, widowed, divorced or separated, and you support another family member (such as a child) in your home, you can claim that person under the "equivalent-to-married" credit. This will allow you the same claim as if that person were your spouse.

For 1999 only, the amounts used to calculate the spousal and equivalent-to-spouse credits for low-income earners are increased by a supplementary amount of up to $250.

Common-law spouses who meet certain criteria (below) are treated identically to legally married couples for all purposes relating to income tax. This means that the spousal credit can be claimed for a dependent common-law spouse. It also means that a taxpayer who has a common-law spouse cannot claim the "equivalent-to-married" credit for a child.

Common-law spouses are treated as spouses if they are two people of the opposite sex who "cohabit in a conjugal relationship", where either they have had a child together, or they have cohabited for at least 12 continuous months. Separation is not considered to terminate this "cohabiting" unless the couple separates for at least 90 days because of a breakdown in their relationship.

2.3   Children

There is no tax credit available for dependent children under 18—this was eliminated in 1993 with the introduction of the Child Tax Benefit. There is a $400 credit for disabled dependants aged 18 and over (see 2.5.1).

2.3.1   Child Tax Benefit and National Child Benefit Supplement

The "Child Tax Benefit" is an annual non-taxable benefit for low and moderate income families of $1,020 per child, an extra $75 for the third and each later child, and an extra $213 for each child under seven if no child care expenses are claimed. It begins to be phased out once family income exceeds $25,921. (These amounts are different for residents of Alberta and Québec.) Depending on the number of children you have and whether you claim child care expenses, you can still receive a portion of the Child Tax Benefit even when your family income is quite high.

The Child Tax Benefit is topped up with the National Child Benefit supplement, the federal government's contribution to the federal, provincial and territorial program to help protect benefits for low-income parents in the workforce. At the time of writing, maximum benefits are $605 for one-child families, $1,010 for two-child families, and $1,010 plus an additional $330 per child for families with three or more children. The supplement is reduced once family income reaches $20,921 and eliminated for families with income over $25,921.

Each province has additional programs and benefits available to aid lower-income families with the cost of raising children under age 18.

2.3.2 Child care expenses

For two-parent families, child care expenses can be deducted, usually by the spouse with the lower income, subject to various limitations. (The assumption is that the lower-income spouse would otherwise stay home with the children.) Single parents can deduct child care expenses from their own income, subject to the same limitations. Common-law couples who meet certain criteria are treated the same as spouses for purposes of calculating child care expenses (as well as for all other tax purposes—see 2.2.1).

> Working parents and students—claim your child care expenses.

Single parents who are full-time students and two-parent families where both parents are full-time students can also deduct their child care expenses. A reduced child care expense deduction is available to part-time students.

You can claim child care expenses for your child or your spouse's child. You can also claim them for a child who was dependent on you or your spouse and whose net income in 1999 is less than $6,956.

Child care expenses include baby-sitting, day nursery services, day camps, boarding schools and camps.

For child care expenses to be claimed, they have to have been made to allow you or your spouse to work, carry on business, attend school "full-time" or "part-time" or carry on grant-funded research. "Full-time" attendance at school for these purposes means that you must be enrolled in a secondary or post-secondary program that is at least three consecutive weeks long and requires you to spend at least 10 hours per week on course work. You are attending school "part-time" if the program lasts at least three consecutive weeks and involves at least 12 hours per month on course work.

Assuming you are a single parent or the lower-income spouse, the deduction for child care expenses is limited to $7,000 times the number of your children who are under seven at the end of the year, plus $4,000 times the number of children seven and over but under 17. It is also limited to two-thirds of your "earned income" (basically salary and business income).

For single parents and two-parent families where both parents are attending school, child care expenses are deductible against all types of income, to a maximum of $150 per child under seven and $100 per child aged seven to 16, for each week that the single parent or both parents are attending school full-time.

For part-time students, the child care expense deduction is limited to $175 per child under seven and $100 per child aged seven to 16, for each month for which the part-time education credit (see 2.4) is claimed. If you have a working spouse, the deduction is also limited to two-thirds of his or her earned income.

The deduction is based on when the services are provided rather than when the amounts are paid, so prepaying in December does not give you the deduction a year earlier.

Payments to a boarding school or camp are limited to $175 per week that the child attends the school or camp, for children under seven, and $100 per week for children over six but under 17.

Example:

Mary and Adam are married and have two children under seven. Mary earns $70,000 and Adam earns $21,000. They pay $12,000 in 1999 to a nanny to take care of their children while they are working.

Adam must be the one to claim the expenses, since he is the lower-income spouse. His deduction is the least of: (a) the amount paid—$12,000; (b) $7,000 per child—$14,000; and (c) two-thirds of his earned income—$14,000. He can therefore claim $12,000 as a deduction against his $21,000 of employment income. This will reduce his tax bill by about $3,240.

If Mary was a single parent, she could claim the same amount as a deduction against her own income of $70,000 and reduce her tax bill by about $6,000.

Where a child, at any age, has a severe and prolonged mental or physical impairment for which the disability credit can be claimed (see 2.5.1), special rules allow a deduction as though the child were under seven. If the child is older than 16, but has a less severe mental or physical infirmity, you are entitled to the same deduction as that allowed for children aged seven to 16.

There are also special circumstances where the lower-income spouse is not expected to care for the children. These are: where the spouse is disabled; in prison or hospital; confined to bed or a wheelchair, for at least two weeks; attending full-time high school or post-secondary school; or where the spouses have separated. In such cases, the higher-income spouse can claim the deduction for up to $175 per child under seven ($100 per child seven and over) for each week that the condition continues.

The tax treatment of child care expenses for Québec purposes is discussed at 16.2.2.

2.4 Students

Tuition fees qualify for a 17% federal credit if you pay them for yourself. Tuition fees paid for your child or other person cannot be claimed by you, subject to the transfer rules discussed below.

To be eligible for a credit, the fees must be paid to a Canadian university, college or other post-secondary educational institution, or to an institution certified by Employment and Immigration Canada. Fees paid to post-secondary institutions in other countries may qualify as well. Any fees you claim must total more than $100 per institution.

Along with admission fees, eligible tuition fees include library and lab charges, examination fees, application fees, mandatory computer service fees, charges for certificates and diplomas, and the cost of books included in the fees for a correspondence course. Also eligible are mandatory ancillary fees for health services, athletics and various other services (but not student association fees, fees covering goods of value that you retain, or ancillary fees at institutions sanctioned by the Ministry of Human Resources Development).

Fees paid to private schools for grade-school or high-school education will not entitle you to a tax credit. However, religious private schools may be able to provide a tax receipt for some of your tuition fees, treating that amount as a charitable donation (see 2.7.1) made toward the school's religious instruction.

As a separate credit from the tuition fees, you are entitled to a further educational status credit of $34 (federal) for each month you are in full-time attendance at a post-secondary educational institution.

For part-time post-secondary students, the education amount is about $10 per month that you attend an eligible program at least three consecutive weeks long and involving at least 12 hours of course work per month. Disabled students qualify for the full $34 per month amount even if they attend the institution only part-time.

If you are not able to use your tuition and education credits (because you have no tax to pay), up to $850 in federal credits for the two combined may normally be transferred to your spouse or to a parent or grandparent. Alternatively, you can carry forward any unused and untransferred tuition and education amounts and claim them against your taxable income in any later year. Note, however, that such amounts carried forward cannot be transferred—only the student can claim them in a later year.

> **Take advantage of the tax credit for interest on student loans.**

Students and former students can claim a 17% non-refundable federal tax credit on their interest on student loans under the *Canada Student Loans Act* or equivalent provincial programs. The credit is available for interest paid in the year or any of the five preceding years (but after 1997). Although the credit is not transferable, it can be carried forward for up to five years.

> **Consider withdrawing RRSP funds under the Lifelong Learning Plan to help pay for training or post-secondary education programs.**

You can tap your registered retirement savings plan (RRSP) to help finance your own or your spouse's education. Under the Lifelong Learning Plan, students in full-time training or post-secondary education and their spouses are allowed to withdraw up to $10,000 per year from their RRSPs over a four-year period, as long as the total amount does not exceed $20,000. Withdrawn amounts must be repaid to an RRSP in equal instalments over 10 years or they will be included in the income of the person who made the withdrawal. The first repayment will be due 60 days after the fifth year following the first withdrawal (or earlier in certain circumstances such as failure to complete courses). (See Chapter 3 for information on RRSPs.)

Full-time students who are single parents, or who are married and both parents attend school, and part-time students may be able to deduct child care expenses paid to attend school; if you are the working spouse of a full-time student, you may be able to deduct them on your own return (see 2.3.2). In certain cases, students may also be able to deduct their moving expenses (see 12.1.2).

If you are a student who lives in Québec, see 16.2.4.

2.5 Disabled persons

2.5.1 Disability credit

If you suffer from a severe and prolonged mental or physical impairment, you get an additional federal credit of $720. Depending on the nature of the impairment, your status must be certified by a medical doctor, an optometrist, an audiologist, an occupational therapist or a psychologist.

To qualify as having a severe and prolonged impairment, your ability to perform a "basic activity of daily living" must be "markedly restricted", and the impairment must have lasted or be expected to last for at least a year. The *Income Tax Act* has specific definitions to determine whether you qualify. The rules can be found on Revenue Canada's disability credit certificate, Form T2201. If you are disabled and reside in Québec, see also 16.2.11.

> **If Revenue Canada challenges your disability claim, consider objecting.**

However, it is often difficult to determine whether one qualifies or not, and the Tax Court of Canada has issued a slew of decisions interpreting these rules. In some cases, the Court has found Revenue Canada's view to be incorrect. Therefore, if you believe you fit within the *Income Tax Act's* definition of disabled, you should consider pursuing your claim if it is denied.

If you have a dependent child who qualifies for the disability credit but does not earn enough income to be able to use all of it, the child's unused credit can be transferred to your return. As well, if you support a dependent child age 18 or over who is disabled, you can claim an additional federal credit of $400. This credit is reduced by 17% of your infirm dependant's income over $4,441 and is thus reduced to zero if the dependant's income is more than $6,794.

You may also be able to claim a portion of your medical expenses for the medical expense credit (see 2.7.2) and for the new refundable medical expense supplement (see 2.7.2).

2.5.2   Attendant for disabled person

If you are disabled, you can deduct some or all of the costs of an attendant needed to allow you to earn income. The deduction is limited to two-thirds of your "earned income" (basically salary and business income). As an alternative, expenses of an attendant can generally be claimed for purposes of the medical expense credit (see 2.7.2), even if you are not earning income.

> **Weigh the benefits of deducting the costs of an attendant or claiming the costs for purposes of the medical expense credit.**

In some cases, it may be more beneficial to claim these costs as medical expenses on your own or your spouse's tax return. To determine which option generates greater tax savings, calculate and compare the net tax results of claiming these costs through the attendant care deduction versus the medical expense credit.

2.5.3 RRSP withdrawals under the Home Buyers' Plan

Under the Home Buyers' Plan (see 3.3.6), you can withdraw up to $20,000 as a loan from your RRSP to buy or build a home and not pay tax on the amount as long as you repay it over the next 16 years. Since the Plan was originally intended to help first-time home buyers, you are generally ineligible if you owned a home in any of the five calendar years up to and including the current calendar year.

For 1999 and later years, the five-year qualifying period under the Home Buyers' Plan no longer applies to disabled persons and their relatives if the new home is more accessible to or better suited to the personal needs and care of a disabled person who will reside there.

See 3.3.6 for a more detailed discussion of the pros and cons of participating in the Home Buyers' Plan.

2.5.4 Caregivers credit

A tax credit of up to $400 is available for caregivers who provide in-home care for elderly or infirm relatives who live with them in the same self-contained home. The credit is reduced if the infirm relative's income is between $11,500 and $13,850 and is not available if the relative's income exceeds $13,850. You cannot claim the caregiver credit if you claim the equivalent-to-spouse or dependant tax credits (see 2.2.1) in respect of the care recipient.

If you support a disabled relative, you can claim the cost of training courses related to the care of the disabled person for purposes of the medical expense credit (see 2.7.2).

2.6 Marital breakdown

> If you're separating, co-operate to minimize your joint tax bill.

While marriage breakdown is often an occasion for bitter disputes, you and your spouse (through your lawyers, if necessary) should co-operate to minimize your joint tax bill and share the resulting savings.

In May 1997, a new system for taxing child support payments took effect for federal and Québec tax purposes. Although these changes were designed to address the widespread perception that the former system was unfair to custodial parents, many divorced or separated couples with child support arrangements may be worse off under the new system than they would have been under the old system.

If you are a party to a child support agreement or court order finalized before May 1997, you can still take advantage of the tax savings available under the old system (see 2.6.2), but you and your spouse or ex-spouse may have to work together to preserve your ability to do so. If your support agreement or order was finalized on or after May 1, 1997, the payments will generally be treated under the new rules discussed in 2.6.1.

2.6.1 Child support paid under post-May 1, 1997 arrangements

Under the pre-May 1, 1997 system, alimony and spousal and child support payments are deductible to the payer and taxable to the recipient if they meet the strict criteria set out in 2.6.2.

Under the new rules, child support paid under orders or agreements made or varied after April 30, 1997 will no longer be taxed as income to the recipient, or deducted from income by the paying parent. The government has also introduced new guidelines for the courts to follow when setting child support awards. Generally, the child support amount will be calculated as a percentage of the support-paying parent's income, and adjusted to account for the impact of federal and provincial taxes, certain special child care expenses and undue hardship.

The purpose of the elimination of the "deduction/inclusion" system for child support payments was to make the system fairer to custodial parents. However, all other things being equal, divorced and separated couples will probably pay more in combined taxes under the new rules, particularly in the usual case where the support-paying spouse is in a higher tax bracket than the recipient spouse.

> Aim to preserve pre-May 1997 child support arrangements where practical.

Because of this result, if you are a party in a separation or divorce agreement entered into before May 1997, you should aim to preserve your ability to use the current inclusion/deduction system where practical. The new system generally will not apply to court orders made before May 1, 1997 unless a new court order or agreement made after that date changes the amount of child support payable under your existing order or agreement, or unless you and your spouse both sign and file a form with Revenue Canada (or Revenu Québec) stating that the new tax rules will apply to payments made after a specified date (which cannot be earlier than April 30, 1997).

Bear in mind that the new rules only deal with child support payments. Alimony and spousal support payments will remain deductible to the payer and taxable to the recipient under the rules discussed in the next section. The same rules apply when a common-law couple separates, if they meet the criteria for common-law spouses outlined in 2.2.1.

2.6.2 Child support paid under pre-May 1, 1997 arrangements and alimony

Alimony and spousal maintenance payments are deductible to the payer and taxable to the recipient if they meet a number of well-defined and strict criteria. Child support paid under arrangements reached before May 1, 1997 are treated the same way. This system is generally of benefit to the separating or divorcing couple, since the person making the payments is often in a higher tax bracket than the recipient.

Note that your ability to claim a deduction does not depend on whether the recipient actually reports the income. Provided you meet all of the requirements, you can go ahead and claim the deduction, and it is up to Revenue Canada (or Revenu Québec) to take action if the recipient does not include the payments for tax purposes.

To be deductible, any payments must be an *allowance* which has been established in advance as a recurring payment. The amounts payable must be predetermined. (Amounts that are required to be adjusted for inflation can still be considered predetermined.)

The further requirements are:

- the allowance must be paid under a written agreement or under a decree, order or judgment of a competent tribunal; and
- it must be payable on a periodic basis for the maintenance of the recipient (your spouse or ex-spouse) and/or the children of the marriage; and
- you must be living apart from your spouse or ex-spouse, at the time the payment is made and throughout the rest of the year. If the payments are alimony (rather than maintenance) and the marriage breakdown occurred before 1993, you must also be separated pursuant to a divorce, judicial separation or a written separation agreement.

Payments to former common-law spouses may be deducted on the same basis, where the recipient is an individual of the opposite sex who cohabited with you "in a conjugal relationship" or you are the natural parent of that person's child. However, if the common-law breakup occurred before 1993, the maintenance payments must be paid under a court order to be deductible.

Note that the "periodic basis" requirement excludes one-time payments and transfers of property in settlement of rights of the marriage.

Payments made directly to third parties, rather than to your spouse or ex-spouse, are allowed in limited circumstances. Such payments can include medical bills, tuition fees and mortgage payments for your spouse or ex-spouse's home. Among other requirements, the court order or written separation agreement must specifically provide for the payments and must specifically provide that the relevant tax rules will apply, to make the payments deductible to you and taxable to your spouse or ex-spouse. For court orders and agreements made after 1992, these rules also apply to most common-law relationships.

In general, you also may deduct payments made before obtaining a court order or signing a written separation agreement, provided the order or agreement is signed by the end of the year following the year in which the payment is made, and that it specifically provides that the amounts paid earlier are to be considered as paid and received pursuant to the agreement.

If you pay alimony or child support to a non-resident of Canada, as of May 1, 1997, you no longer have to withhold any tax on the payment and remit it to Revenue Canada.

If you receive alimony or maintenance payments in circumstances where they are deductible to the payer (i.e., under a pre-May 1, 1997 child support agreement or court order), they are taxable to you. If you receive child support from a resident of the United States, however, it will not be taxed due to the Canada-U.S. tax treaty (see 17.2.3).

If you receive a lump-sum spousal or child support payment over $3,000 relating to prior years, under a 1999 budget proposal, you may ask Revenue Canada to determine whether it is more advantageous to you to recalculate the tax on that income as if you received it in those prior years. This change is intended to relieve the higher tax liability that may result if the entire lump-sum is taxed in the year of receipt, rather than year by year as the right to receive the payments arose. (Once enacted, this change will apply to qualifying lump-sum payments received after 1994. Certain employment-related payments also qualify for this relief— see 3.4.1.)

2.7 Other commonly available credits

2.7.1 Charitable donations

Charitable donations entitle you to a two-tier credit. The first $200 of donations for the year (total to all charities) gives you a 17% federal tax credit, worth about 27% when provincial tax is taken into account. All donations above that level give you a 29% federal tax credit, worth about 50% when provincial tax is factored in (see 16.2.9 if you live in Québec).

For federal purposes, charitable donations above $200 for the year are therefore given the same treatment as if they were deductible, if you are in the top tax bracket (over $59,180 in taxable income). If you are in a lower bracket, the credit for large donations is worth far more than a deduction.

To claim charitable donations, you must have official receipts that show the recipient organization's charitable registration number. Revenue Canada's administrative policy is to allow you to claim receipts made out in either your name or your spouse's.

The maximum amount of donations you can claim in a year is 75% of your net income. To the extent you have receipts for more than this amount, or if you choose not to claim a donation for any other reason, you can save the receipts and claim the credit in any of the following five years.

> **Combine two or more years of charitable donations into one year.**

The annual limit for donations in the year of death and the year before (including bequests and legacies) is 100% of net income for the year. A number of other special rules relating to charitable donations, and creative techniques for use of the credit for donations, are discussed in 20.7, in the chapter on Estate Planning.

> **If you're married, combine your charitable donations and claim them on the higher-income spouse's return.**

If you donate only small amounts over a year, consider combining two or more years of donations into one year to put yourself over the $200 threshold. A $100 donation above the $200 level for the year costs you only about $50 instead of about $73 below that level.

If you and your spouse donate separately, you should combine your receipts and claim them all on one return (Revenue Canada's administrative practice is to permit this), to avoid having to get the low-rate credit on $200 twice. Due to the operation of the federal and provincial high-income surtaxes, the higher-income spouse should claim all the donations.

Once you are over the $200 level, consider making extra contributions in December rather than early in the new year. Your tax saving through the donations credit will come one year earlier.

> ## Consider donating publicly traded securities or other assets.

Instead of donating cash, you should also consider the potential benefits of donating property such as publicly traded securities, artwork or real estate. The tax treatment of donations of property—or "gifts in kind"—is somewhat more complex but may result in greater tax savings for you and may enhance the value of your gift to the charity. Gifts in kind are discussed in 20.7.3.

2.7.2 Medical expenses

Medical expenses over a certain threshold entitle you to a tax credit. The threshold is 3% of your net income, or, if your net income exceeds $53,800, a flat $1,614. All qualifying medical expenses above this amount give rise to a 17% federal credit, worth about 27% when provincial tax is counted (if you live in Québec, see also 16.2.10).

> Example:
>
> Alison's net income is $30,000. She spends $1,500 on qualifying medical expenses in 1999.
>
> Given that 3% of Alison's net income is $900, the remaining $600 qualifies for the medical expense credit. The federal credit is 17% of that, or $102. Alison's provincial tax and federal surtax will be reduced by about $60 as a result. So of her $1,500 in medical expenses, she will get back about $162 in federal and provincial tax.

Low-income workers with higher than average eligible medical expenses and earned income of at least $2,500 can also claim the "medical expense supplement". This refundable tax credit is equal to 25% of the portion of your medical expenses allowable for the medical expense credit, to a maximum of $500. The credit is reduced by 5% of family net income over $16,745. Claiming the supplement will not affect your ability to claim the medical expense credit.

You can claim expenses for yourself, your spouse and any close relative who is dependent on you for support, including your child, grandchild, parent, grandparent, brother, sister, uncle, aunt, niece or nephew; or any of those relatives of your spouse (including a qualifying common-law spouse as outlined in 2.2.1). Except for your or your spouse's child or grandchild, the person must be resident in Canada.

To the extent any close relative dependent on you for support has net income over $6,794, any claim for the medical expense credit will be reduced. If the dependant has net income under $6,794 you can claim the medical expenses without restriction. To the extent the dependant has net income exceeding $6,794, all of the medical expenses you can claim are reduced by 68% of that excess. If a dependant has sufficiently high income, you will not be able to claim that person's expenses at all, since the reduction will exceed the total value of that dependant's medical expenses. (Note that it doesn't matter who paid the expenses; what matters is who the "patient" was.)

The list of qualifying medical expenses is very long, and you should refer to Revenue Canada's Interpretation Bulletin IT-519R2 (see 2.10) if you need specific details. The list includes:

- payments to medical practitioners, dentists and nurses, hospital fees not covered by public health insurance, and diagnostic procedures
- prescription drugs
- travelling expenses and meals and lodging, in some cases
- institutional care (e.g., nursing home)
- part-time attendant for disabled person (up to $10,000, see also 2.5.2)
- guide dogs (both purchase cost and upkeep cost)
- eyeglasses, hearing aids and dentures
- costs of moving to accessible housing, home renovations required for someone with a mobility impairment and driveway alterations made to provide access for persons with severe mobility impairments to a bus, and 20% (to a maximum of $5,000) of the cost of a van adapted for transporting a person using a wheelchair
- cost of training courses related to the care of the disabled relative
- sign language interpreter fee
- a long list of specific devices, ranging from crutches to insulin needles, wheelchair lifts, speech synthesizers, visual fire alarm indicators and TDD devices for the deaf.

As of 1999, you can claim remuneration paid for:

- the care and supervision of persons with severe and prolonged disabilities living in a group home
- therapy for persons with severe and prolonged disabilities
- tutoring for persons with learning disabilities (or other mental impairments).

> **Combine your family's medical expenses on one return.**

Since self-employed individuals are now allowed to deduct premiums to a drug or dental plan (see 10.2.11), these premiums are no longer eligible for the medical expense credit.

Because of the threshold of 3% of net income, you should combine all of the family's medical expenses on one return. It is normally better for the lower-income spouse to make the claim, provided that spouse has enough tax to pay to use up the credit, since the 3% threshold will be smaller. On the other hand, the credit might be slightly more valuable to a high-income spouse because it will reduce the application of high-income federal and provincial surtaxes (see 2.1.3).

> **Choose your own 12-month period for medical expense claims.**

When claiming medical expenses, you can pick any 12-month period ending in the year. If, for example, you made no claim for 1998, and you have large medical expense bills in February 1998, January 1999 and November 1999, you might be better off to use January 1999 as the end of your 12-month period, claim the February 1998 and January 1999 expenses for 1999, and leave the November 1999 expenses to be claimed on your 2000 return.

> **Plan for the timing of your medical expense payments.**

You can also plan for the timing of medical expenses, since they are based on when they are *paid*. If you are using a December end for the 12-month period, and you have pending expenses (perhaps for medical equipment purchases or large dental bills) that are due early in the new year, consider prepaying them so that you can claim them one year earlier.

2.7.3 Political contributions

> **Take advantage of Canada's generous tax break for political contributions.**

If you are interested in the greatest "bang for your buck", consider a contribution to your favourite federal political party or election candidate. Contributions to federal political parties and to candidates in federal election campaigns entitle you to a credit, which is federal only. A donation of $100 will cost you only $25.

In addition, many of the provinces have their own credits for contributions to *provincial* parties and candidates. The Québec credit for political donations is discussed at 16.2.12.

Note that contributions to a candidate in a federal leadership campaign are not eligible for the credit. However, political parties sometimes set up funds that allow you to contribute to the party itself and direct that your contribution be used to support a particular leadership candidate.

To encourage small political donations by many people, the federal credit is most generous at the lowest levels. The credit is 75% for the first $100 of donation; 50% for the next $450; and 33.33% for the next $600. There is no additional credit for donations beyond $1,150.

Example:

Jacquelin contributes $200 to a federal political party in 1999.

Jacquelin's political contribution credit for 1999 will be 75% on the first $100 ($75) plus 50% on the next $100 ($50), for a total of $125. There is no reduction in provincial tax resulting from this credit.

2.7.4 Other credits

There are a number of other credits with a provincial component available when computing "basic federal tax" (thereby reducing provincial taxes and surtaxes, as discussed in 2.1.2). These include the pension income (see 19.3.5) and age credits (see 19.3.4) and the dividend tax credit (see 7.1.2).

Other federal-only credits include the investment tax credit, which is an incentive for those carrying on business to invest in particular regions or sectors of the economy (see 10.2.14); the labour-sponsored funds tax credit (see 7.4.3); and the foreign tax credit (also available in Québec), which offsets the impact of foreign tax paid on one's income from a foreign source, to reduce double taxation.

2.8 Other commonly available deductions

2.8.1 Legal fees

Whether or not you can deduct legal fees you have paid depends on why you paid them.

Legal fees are generally deductible if they are paid for the purpose of earning income from business or property. Legal fees to acquire or preserve a capital asset are normally not deductible, though there are a number of exceptions.

Legal fees associated with an objection or appeal of your income tax assessment (see 8.6) are deductible. This includes the costs of negotiations with Revenue Canada officials prior to filing a formal Notice of Objection. The fees are also deductible if you are appealing a

Québec income tax assessment or an income tax assessment of a foreign government, or an Employment Insurance or Canada/Québec Pension Plan decision.

Legal fees to collect unpaid salary or wages owed to you by your employer or former employer are deductible.

Legal fees can be deducted where they are incurred to obtain a "retiring allowance" (including severance pay) or a pension benefit (see 9.9.5), but only up to a limit of your income from those sources (in the current year or past years).

Finally, legal fees to enforce an existing right to alimony or maintenance that is taxable in your hands (see 2.6 above) are deductible. They are not deductible, however, when incurred to *establish* a right to alimony or maintenance, except for maintenance for which you must sue your spouse or former spouse in a Family Court or under certain provincial legislation. (See also 16.2.8 if you live in Québec.)

2.8.2 Northern residents

If you live in northern Canada, a special deduction is available to help offset the higher costs of living and the hardship and isolation relative to the more populated parts of the country. The deduction is limited to 20% of your net income. A similar deduction is available for Québec tax purposes if you live in northern Québec.

If you live in the "prescribed northern zone", the federal deduction is $15 per day ($5,475 per year). If you live somewhat further south, in the "prescribed intermediate zone", you can only claim half as much. As well, if your employer pays the cost of travel for you and your family (e.g., an annual trip to southern Canada), a deduction is available to offset part or all of the taxable benefit that is thereby included in your income. See 9.9.8.

2.8.3 Other deductions

Some other common deductions are covered in other chapters. See, for example, 3.1.3 (contributions to RRSPs), 6.3.2 (allowable business investment losses), 6.4 (capital gains deduction), 7.2.3 (interest paid), 9.9 (deductions available to employees) and 12.1 (moving expenses). Some of the deductions relating to self-employment (carrying on business) are discussed in Chapter 10.

2.9 Canada/Québec Pension Plan Contributions, Employment Insurance and GST

2.9.1 CPP/QPP contributions and EI premiums

A federal credit of 17% of all Canada (or Québec) Pension Plan ("CPP/QPP") contributions and Employment Insurance ("EI") premiums is available, effectively giving you back about 27% of these amounts when provincial tax and surtax are factored in. If you are employed, these amounts are normally taken off your pay cheque at source by your employer. If you are self-employed, you will normally have to calculate and remit both the employer and employee portions of CPP/QPP (but not Employment Insurance) contributions on your net self-employment income.

2.9.2   EI clawback

If you receive Employment Insurance benefits and your net income exceeds a certain threshold, a portion of your benefits received during the year will be taxed back through a special tax, commonly called a "clawback", paid through your income tax return.

The clawback applies if you received benefits for up to 20 weeks and your net income exceeds $48,750, or if you received benefits for more than 20 weeks and your net income is more than $39,000. You must repay $30 for each $100 of net income over your threshold, up to a maximum of 100% of the benefits received if you have received over 120 weeks of benefits in the past five years. Benefits that are not clawed back are taxed as regular income.

2.9.3   GST credit

The GST credit is aimed at low-income families. It is designed to offset the GST paid by consumers on most goods and services. This credit is normally $199 per adult (but up to $303 in some cases) and $105 per child in the family, reduced by 5 cents for each dollar that the parents' income exceeds $25,921. The credit is generally prepaid in quarterly instalments to qualifying families, based on their previous year's income. If your GST credit is less than $100, you should receive it in one lump-sum payment in July.

Example:

Jeffrey and Margaret are married and have two dependent children. Their combined income is $25,000.

For 1999, their combined GST credit will be $608 ($199 for each parent and $105 for each child). Since their combined income is below $25,921, the credit is not reduced. The $608 effectively offsets the GST paid on $8,686 of taxable goods and services purchased during the year. Thus, although the credit is paid through the income tax system, it operates to alleviate the effects of GST on low-income families.

An extra GST credit supplement of up to $105 is available for singles, including single parents. The supplement is phased in at a rate of 2% of net income over $6,794. As of 1999, the phase-in no longer applies for single parents — they will receive the entire $105 as part of their core GST credit benefit. For all singles, the supplement is reduced by 5 cents for each dollar of income over $25,921.

Many provinces also have sales tax credits for low-income taxpayers. For the Québec credit, which parallels the GST credit, see 16.2.13.

2.9.4 GST rebates

In addition to the GST credit described in 2.9.3, certain employees and members of partnerships can claim a GST rebate on their income tax returns. The rebate is available to employees who claim income tax deductions relating to their employment expenses, and partners who claim deductions on expenses they incur outside the partnership to earn partnership income. (See 9.10, 10.2.4 and 10.3.7 for more details; see also 16.2.13 if you live in Québec.)

Non-residents are eligible for a full refund of the 7% GST and the 15% Harmonized Sales Tax ("HST"—see 10.2.5) paid on most goods they take back with them (but not alcohol and tobacco), as well as hotel accommodation while in Canada. The minimum rebate claim for non-resident visitors is $200 in purchases of goods and accommodation.

Your visitors should keep receipts and apply for a refund once they get home. They can also claim their refunds at duty-free stores at many land border points (all the airport duty-free shops have opted out of the refund program, not being able to handle the volume). Telephone 1-800-66VISIT from within Canada for information on this Visitors' Rebate Program.

The refund does not apply to purchases or services consumed in Canada, such as restaurant meals, gas or haircuts.

Many provinces also provide a refund of provincial sales tax on goods taken out of the province. For Québec and Manitoba, this is handled by Revenue Canada on the same form on which the GST/HST refund is claimed.

2.10 References

The following publications can be obtained (in person or by telephone request) from your nearest Revenue Canada District Taxation Office. Some of Revenue Canada's guides, brochures and forms are also available from Revenue Canada's Internet site at *www.rc.gc.ca.*

> Interpretation Bulletin IT-99R5, "Legal and accounting fees"
>
> Interpretation Bulletin IT-110R3, "Gifts and official donation rec
>
> Interpretation Bulletin IT-118R3, "Alimony and maintenance"
>
> Interpretation Bulletin IT-495R2, "Child care expenses"
>
> Interpretation Bulletin IT-513R, "Personal tax credits"
>
> Interpretation Bulletin IT-515R2, "Education tax credit"
>
> Interpretation Bulletin IT-516R2, "Tuition tax credit"

Interpretation Bulletin IT-519R2, "Medical expense and disability tax credits and attendant care expense deduction"

Interpretation Bulletin IT-523, "Order of provisions applicable in computing an individual's taxable income and tax payable"

Information Circular 75-2R4, "Contributions to a registered political party or to a candidate at a federal election"

Brochure, "Students and Income Tax"

Brochure, "Support Payments"

Brochure, "Tax Refund for Visitors"

Brochure, "Information Concerning People with Disabilities"

Guide, "Your Child Tax Benefit"

Form T778, "Calculation of child care expense deduction for 19___"

Form T929, "Attendant care expenses"

Form T1065, "Child care expenses information sheet"

Form T1156, "Support payments information sheet"

Form T1157, "Election for child support payments"

Form T1158, "Registration of family support payments"

Form T2201, "Disability tax credit information"

Form T2202A, "Tuition and education amounts certificate"

Form T2222, "Northern Residents Deductions"

RRSPs and other tax deferral plans

3

- Contribute as much as you can to an RRSP (3.1.9)

- Contribute early in the year instead of the following February (3.1.9)

- Consider a self-directed RRSP for greater flexibility (3.1.6)

- Think about transferring shares that you already own to your self-directed RRSP (3.1.6)

- Think about holding your own mortgage through your RRSP (3.1.6)

- Think about boosting your self-directed RRSP's foreign content (3.1.7)

- Think twice before borrowing funds to contribute to your RRSP (3.1.9)

- Withdraw funds from your RRSP in low-income years (3.2.1)

- Contribute to your spouse's (or common-law spouse's) RRSP, if your projected income on retirement will be higher (3.3.1)

- Make spousal RRSP contributions in December instead of the following February (3.3.1)

- Transfer retiring allowances or severance pay to your RRSP (3.3.2)

- Top up your RRSP with a non-deductible $2,000 overcontribution (3.3.4)

- Consider shares of a labour-sponsored venture capital corporation for your RRSP (3.3.5)

- Consider Home Buyers' Plan withdrawals to buy or build your first home (but be sure to weigh the loss of RRSP growth) (3.3.6)

- Ask Revenue Canada to recalculate your prior-year tax liability on retroactive lump-sum pension and other payments (3.4.1)

- Consider contributing to your RRSP instead of a money purchase RPP (3.4.1)

- Find out about the vesting of your pension benefits, especially before making a career change (3.4.1)

- Weigh the advantages of establishing an "individual pension plan" (3.4.2)

Deferred income plans, particularly RRSPs and registered pension plans, are the most widely-used tax shelters in Canada. Put simply, almost everyone should have one.

The concept of deferred income plans is quite simple, although the particular rules can get rather complex. In this chapter, we'll take you through the basic rules, so you understand the system in general. We also discuss the options you have and steps you can take for tax planning.

The rules are essentially the same for Québec tax purposes.

3.1   Registered retirement savings plans—RRSPs

3.1.1   What is an RRSP?

You hear a lot about RRSPs every February, when the annual contribution deadline approaches. Although the acronym stands for "registered retirement savings plan", an RRSP does not necessarily have anything to do with retirement. It can be used simply as a tax deferral tool.

The concept behind an RRSP is quite simple. If you agree to put some of your salary or self-employment income away and not have immediate access to it, the tax system will tax that income—along with all the interest and other income it earns—when it is *received* rather than when it is *earned*.

Example:

If you earn $60,000, you pay tax on $60,000.

Suppose you earn $60,000 but you put $2,000 of that into an RRSP. You will be taxed on only $58,000—the amount you have *received*.

If, some years later, the $2,000 you put away has grown (in a tax-free environment) to $3,000, you can take the $3,000 out of your RRSP, and it will be taxed (added to your income) at that point. Again, the original $2,000, now grown to $3,000, is being taxed in the year it is *received* rather than when it was *earned*.

The rules governing RRSPs are more complex than the above example indicates, of course. The amount you can contribute to an RRSP is limited in various ways.

3.1.2   How do you set up an RRSP?

An RRSP can be set up easily at almost any bank or trust company or through a stockbroker, life insurance agent, mutual fund company or mutual fund distributor. Basically, you just fill out a form and contribute money to the plan. Some institutions will give you your official tax receipt immediately; others will mail it to you later, in time for you to file it with your tax return.

3.1.3   How much can you contribute?

Contributions to an RRSP are deductible for any given year if they are contributed *in the year* or *within 60 days after the end of the year*. So if you contribute by February 29, 2000, you can get a deduction for your

1999 tax return (and any resulting refund will come sometime in the spring of 2000 after you have filed your return).

There are three factors that limit the amount you can contribute to an RRSP: a dollar limit, which is $13,500 for 1999; a percentage (18%) of the previous year's "earned income"; and your "pension adjustment". We'll look at each of these in turn.

Dollar limit

The RRSP contribution limit has been frozen at $13,500 until 2003. The limit is scheduled to rise to $14,500 for 2004 and $15,500 for 2005, after which the limit will be indexed.

Percentage of previous year's earned income

The annual deduction (subject to the $13,500 dollar limit and pension adjustment) is limited to 18% of the *previous* year's earned income. That is, 18% of your 1998 earned income will be used to determine your 1999 contribution (made by February 29, 2000).

"Earned income" for most employees is the same as "salary"—the gross amount of salary, before deductions for income tax, EI, CPP, etc., which are withheld at source. "Earned income" includes business income, if you are self-employed or are an active partner in a business. It also includes:

- research grants, net of deductible related expenses
- alties from works or inventions that you wrote or invented
- taxable alimony, maintenance and child support received (see 2.6)
- net rental income from real estate
- disability pension income received under the CPP/QPP.

Earned income is *reduced* by:

- deductible alimony, maintenance and child support you pay
- most deductible employment-related expenses, such as union dues and travelling expenses (but not pension plan contributions)
- rental losses.

Earned income does not include most investment income, such as interest or dividends, or capital gains. Nor does it include pension benefits, retiring allowances, severance pay, death benefits or amounts received from an RRSP, RRIF or deferred profit-sharing plan.

If your 1998 earned income was more than $75,000, your 1999 contribution will be limited to $13,500 (minus the pension adjustment as discussed below). Otherwise, you will be limited by the 18% factor.

Pension adjustment

Once you have calculated your maximum contribution limit as 18% of your previous year's earned income, subject to the dollar limits discussed above, you must subtract your pension adjustment, if any. This figure represents the deemed value of your pension earned for the previous year. In other words, the more that has been put aside (by you and your employer combined) towards your retirement pension, the less the *Income Tax Act* allows you to contribute to an RRSP.

If you are *not* a member of an employer's pension plan or deferred profit-sharing plan, your pension adjustment is zero, and you can contribute the full 18% of your previous year's earned income (subject to the annual $13,500 dollar limit).

Otherwise, your pension adjustment for 1999 should appear on your 1998 T4 slip, as well as on your Notice of Assessment received in the spring of 1999 following the filing of your 1998 return.

For "money-purchase" pension plans (see 3.4.1), the pension adjustment is the total contributions made towards your pension by you and your employer combined. The same applies to deferred profit-sharing plans (see 3.5), except that the contributions are made only by your employer. For "defined benefit" pension plans (the type of pension plan most employees belong to), the pension adjustment is based on a calculation that takes into account the benefit you may receive on retirement based on the past year's employment.

In some situations, the calculation of your RRSP limit may also be reduced by a past service pension adjustment ("PSPA"). In general terms, a PSPA can arise when your pension benefits under a defined benefit pension plan are improved on a retroactive basis.

Example:

Melanie is a chemical engineer who belongs to her employer's pension plan. Her 1998 earned income was $60,000. Her pension adjustment for 1999, as reported to her on her 1998 T4 slip and her 1998 assessment received from Revenue Canada in mid-1999, is $3,200.

Before accounting for her pension adjustment, Melanie's contribution limit for 1999 is 18% of her 1998 earned income, to a maximum of $13,500. For 1998, 18% of her earned income is $10,800. From this amount she must deduct her pension adjustment of $3,200. Melanie may therefore contribute up to $7,600 to an RRSP by February 29, 2000 for a deduction on her 1999 tax return.

If you terminate your employment before retirement, you may be entitled to a pension adjustment reversal ("PAR"). The PAR is designed to give you back some of the RRSP contribution room lost due to pension adjustments ("PAs") while you were a member of a company pension plan.

If you were a member of a defined contribution plan or deferred profit-sharing plan, your PAR will be the total of all PAs reported by your employer since 1990 that have not yet "vested" (see 3.4.1). If you were a member of a defined benefit plan and you have not reported any PSPAs, your PAR will be equal to your total PAs since 1990 less the post-1989 portion of any lump sums paid to you or transferred to an RRSP or money-purchase pension plan (if you have reported any PSPAs, your PAR calculation will be more complex but, whatever your plan, your employer's pension plan administrator will figure it out for you). You will not be entitled to a PAR if you maintain any entitlement to periodic pension payments from the plan.

PARs for 1997 terminations increase 1998 RRSP room. PARs for post-1997 terminations increase RRSP room for the year of termination. If you have ended or will be ending company pension plan membership in 1999, you may want to encourage your employer to report your PAR earlier so you can make use of the related extra RRSP room as soon as possible. Your employer must report your PAR for 1999 by February 29, 2000. If you wish to make an RRSP contribution based on your 1999 PAR, your RRSP contribution deadline for 1999 is extended until April 30, 2000.

Carry forward of unused deduction room and undeducted contributions

If in any year you contribute less than the maximum to an RRSP, you can "carry forward" the extra deduction room and make that much more contribution in any following year. You can also carry forward unused RRSP room created by a PAR. If you contribute an amount for a year but choose not to deduct the amount for that year, you can claim the deduction in any subsequent year (provided you still have contribution room).

Example:

Melanie, from the example above, has $7,600 of contribution room for 1999. She chooses to contribute only $5,000 to an RRSP for the year.

Melanie has unused RRSP contribution room of $2,600 to carry forward. As a result, she may increase her contribution by that amount in any following year. If Melanie's contribution limit for 2000 is again $7,600, she can contribute up to $10,200 for deduction in 2000.

You should carefully review your assessment from Revenue Canada to make sure the contribution limit reported is correct, before relying on it. A wrong statement from Revenue Canada will not entitle you to deduct a contribution you would otherwise be entitled to.

In some cases you might contribute more than you can actually deduct. We discuss overcontributions in 3.3.4.

3.1.4   What's your contribution worth?

What is your contribution worth in tax savings? It depends on your marginal tax rate. The rates vary among the provinces due to different provincial tax rates (see Appendix II), but they are approximately:

- 27% on income up to $29,590
- 41% on income from $29,591 to $59,180
- 50% on income over $59,180

In the example above, if Melanie's taxable income, after other deductions, would be between $34,590 and $59,180, her contribution of $5,000 to an RRSP will save her about 41% of that amount, or $2,050, in tax for 1999. For someone whose taxable income stays over $59,180 even after making the RRSP contribution, the same $5,000 contribution would be worth about $2,500. Clearly, RRSPs are more tax-effective to those with higher incomes.

You should keep the value of your deduction in mind and try to take maximum advantage of the carry-forward mechanism in claiming your RRSP deductions. In a low-income year, for example, it may be advantageous to make your maximum RRSP *contribution*, but to defer claiming the *deduction* until a later year when your income is taxed at a higher marginal rate.

3.1.5   What happens to the funds in the RRSP?

While your funds are in the RRSP, they are not subject to tax at all. No matter what amounts of interest, dividends, capital gains—or losses—result, there will be no tax effect until you withdraw the funds. (As we shall see in 19.4, you must close out the RRSP by the end of the year in which you turn 69, but even then the tax effects can be partially deferred.)

The effects of having income compound without tax are quite dramatic. Compare the following two situations: A, where you invest $5,000 of your salary in an RRSP for 10 or 20 years at 10%, and B, where you earn the same 10% but it is subject to tax. The example assumes a 50% marginal tax rate.

	1999	2009	2019
A. Invest $5,000 in an RRSP After withdrawal	$5,000	$12,969 $6,484	$33,637 $16,818
B. Do not put $5,000 in an RRSP, so you are immediately taxed on the $5,000 as salary and taxed on the income it earns	$2,500	$4,072	$6,633

In case A, you pay 50% in tax when you withdraw the funds, but they have grown substantially in the meantime. After 20 years, your $5,000 is worth $16,818 *after* tax. In case B, since the annual 10% interest is taxed, you have only 5% to reinvest for compounding purposes. The fact that you can use the $6,633 (after 20 years) directly in case B, without having to pay 50% tax on it as in case A, doesn't come close to making up for the tax-free compounding of interest.

Of course, if you are paying non-deductible interest such as mortgage interest, that interest also effectively compounds on a pre-tax basis, and you might be better off to pay down your mortgage rather than contribute to an RRSP. In such a case, you can generally use all your unused RRSP contribution room by making and deducting a "catch-up" RRSP contribution in a later year, when you have the funds to contribute.

As we mentioned earlier, your RRSP can be invested in a number of different forms. The simplest, and usually lowest-paying, is a deposit account that pays interest monthly or twice a year. Many people invest instead in longer-term Guaranteed Investment Certificates ("GICs") or term deposits. Equity mutual funds are growing increasingly popular as a method of indirectly investing RRSP funds in a number of companies, but they do entail a higher level of risk. See 1.1.5 for tips on choosing investments and advice on developing an appropriate investment strategy.

3.1.6   Self-directed RRSPs

> **Consider a self-directed RRSP for greater flexibility.**

If you're ambitious and willing to take a little more risk with your funds by investing in stocks or bonds of your own choosing, you can set up a self-directed RRSP. This is normally done through a stockbroker or financial services institution, and is typically subject to an annual fee in the $100 to $150 range (plus normal commissions on any stock trades or mutual funds, where applicable). You then decide what to invest in with your RRSP. There are restrictions—the system tries to ensure that your money, while not necessarily "safe", is at least invested in reasonable places. "Qualified investments" for an RRSP include:

- cash
- government, Crown corporation or municipal bonds
- GICs, term deposits and treasury bills ("T-Bills")
- certain government-insured mortgages
- shares or bonds of corporations listed on Canadian stock exchanges
- RRSP-eligible mutual funds

- shares listed on certain foreign stock exchanges, bonds of certain foreign governments and mutual funds investing in foreign markets (however, as discussed in 3.1.7, no more than 20% of an RRSP may be directly invested in foreign assets)
- certain small business shares.

The rules governing the details (e.g., which mortgages and small business shares are qualified investments) are extremely complex, and you should consult a professional advisor if you wish to do more with your self-directed RRSP than simply buy, say, T-Bills and Hydro bonds (which are generally regarded as good safe investments, incidentally). If you have the time to give it the attention it needs, a self-directed RRSP can prove to be much more rewarding in the long run. The control you will gain over investment decisions will diversify your risk and give you the flexibility to pursue a different range of investment opportunities— including some that are generally only possible through self-directed RRSPs, like strip bonds, mortgage-backed securities and other less common RRSP investments. If you only plan to invest in mutual funds and GICs, a self-directed RRSP may not be required; in this case, you may be better off using a regular plan to save on annual administration fees.

The broader range of investment options you may acquire with a self-directed RRSP comes with a higher level of risk. It is generally prudent to spread your investments over a wide range of options and to ensure that at least a portion of your investments have fixed rates of return, such as GICs. Studies show that your asset mix is primarily responsible for your portfolio's rate of return—see 1.1.5 for details on developing an appropriate investment strategy.

Think about transferring shares that you already own to your self-directed RRSP.

Consider contributing shares (or interest-bearing investments) that you already own to your self-directed RRSP in lieu of cash contributions. Shares in small businesses can be contributed in limited circumstances (for example, you must not be a controlling shareholder of the corporation). However, most shares and bonds of Canadian public corporations are fair game. If you have shares that you intend to hold for a long time, you can contribute them to your RRSP and get a tax deduction without any cash outlay.

Note that capital gains and dividends are effectively fully-taxed when withdrawn from an RRSP, since you're taxed on the total amount withdrawn. So if you contribute shares (or buy shares inside your RRSP), any capital gains and dividends will eventually be taxed at a higher rate than if you earned them directly (see 6.2 and 7.1.2). If you leave the funds in the RRSP for long enough, the deferral of tax and tax-free compounding of interest should more than make up for the tax rate differential, however. Consider holding fixed income investments inside your RRSP and equities outside your RRSP.

A transfer of investments to your RRSP can trigger a capital gain (see 6.2), since the transfer will be deemed to take place at fair market value. However, you are prohibited from claiming a capital loss (see 6.3) on the transfer of investments to your RRSP.

> **Think about holding your own mortgage through your RRSP.**

It is even possible for you to arrange for your RRSP to hold your own mortgage—in other words, you put funds into your RRSP, receive a tax deduction, and lend the funds to yourself. This is not easy to do, however; the mortgage must be federally insured, and various other restrictions apply.

Investing in your own mortgage may make you feel good, but does not always make sense financially. Since the investment must be at the market rate, you may be no better off depending on the size of the mortgage, once all fees (legal, appraisal, etc.) are taken into account. As a general rule of thumb, to be a worthwhile investment, the mortgage's principal should be in the $50,000 to $100,000 range with a term of at least five years. Alternatively if you don't have that much cash in your RRSP, some financial institutions offer a program through which the mortgage is "shared" between your RRSP and your institution.

3.1.7   Self-directed RRSP investments in foreign properties

One advantage of a self-directed RRSP is that it allows you more scope to maximize your RRSP's foreign content. Through a self-directed RRSP, you can invest in shares listed on certain foreign stock exchanges, certain foreign government bonds and other foreign properties, within limits.

> ## Think about boosting your self-directed RRSP's foreign content.

Generally, only 20% of the cost amount of all property held by your RRSP can be invested in foreign property. The calculation is performed at the end of each month. Foreign property values over the 20% threshold are subject to a special tax of 1% per month payable by the RRSP. The 20% limit is generally based on the property's cost at the time of purchase, not its current market value. Your RRSP's administrator should monitor your RRSP's foreign content holdings and warn you if it is in danger of going off-side.

With the right investment mix, you can boost your self-directed RRSP's foreign content to a maximum of 40% of the cost amount of property held by it. To assist small businesses in obtaining equity financing, a special rule permits you to increase your RRSP's holdings of qualifying foreign property without penalty by $3 for every $1 that you invest in a certain Canadian small business corporation. That means a 6.67% holding of a qualifying small business property will enable you to increase your foreign property holdings by 20% ($3 \times 6.67\%$), up to the 40% maximum.

However, if you own more than 10% of the shares of a small business, your RRSP's ability to invest in that business may be restricted or denied. Since these restrictions and the rules governing the types of small businesses that qualify are quite complex, you should consult your tax advisor if you are considering increasing your self-directed RRSP's foreign content through small business investments.

Another indirect way of further increasing your self-directed RRSP's foreign property content is to invest in a qualifying mutual fund trust. As long as the trust meets certain conditions, the mutual fund trust in which you invest can also invest up to 20% of the cost amount of its holdings in foreign property.

You can also boost your RRSP's participation in foreign markets by investing in:

- RRSP-eligible bonds issued by Canadian governments and corporations
- RRSP-eligible mutual funds that gain exposure to foreign markets through the use of derivatives such as options and futures
- shares of Canadian subsidiaries of foreign corporations
- shares of Canadian corporations with significant foreign operations

- shares of Canadian corporations that trade on foreign stock exchanges.

Don't let periodic downturns in foreign markets scare you away from increasing your RRSP's foreign holdings. As long as you plan to invest for the long term, maximizing your RRSP's foreign content will increase the diversity of your investment mix and thus reduce your overall investment risk.

3.1.8   RRSP fees

Administration, trustee and investment management and counselling fees related to your RRSP are not deductible. However, you can use funds already deposited in your RRSP without having to pay tax on the amount as you would if you withdrew the money for another purpose. Alternatively, you can pay these fees from funds outside your RRSP and the amount will not count as part of your contribution for the year.

If you have not used all of your available contribution room and you do not foresee doing so in the future, consider contributing the amount of the fees and paying them with funds inside the plan so you will get a regular RRSP deduction for that amount. On the other hand, if you have or will be maximizing your RRSP contributions, you will be better off paying the fees with other funds so you do not erode the amount of RRSP funds available to grow tax-free.

3.1.9   How to make the most of your RRSP

> **Contribute as much as you can to an RRSP.**

If you have cash in the bank earning interest, even if you are young and not yet concerned about retirement, you should contribute as much as possible to an RRSP. The example we saw in 3.1.5 above shows how valuable it is to have your funds earning tax-free income.

> **Contribute early in the year instead of the following February.**

If possible, you should contribute early, rather than waiting till the deadline. Your 1999 contribution, for example, may be made any time until February 29, 2000 if you intend to deduct it on your 1999 tax return. If you contribute at the beginning of 1999, all of the income earned for that extra year will accumulate tax-free. The effect of early contributions over several years will be dramatic. Do ensure, however, that you have enough contribution room before you commit your contribution for the year, and remember that each year's contribution will be limited to 18% of your *previous year's* earned income.

You can store up any unused RRSP contribution room if you can't afford to make a contribution now, and make your contribution and claim the deduction in later years.

> **Think twice before borrowing funds to contribute to your RRSP.**

If you're behind on your RRSP contributions, you might be thinking about taking out an RRSP loan. Generally, this strategy only makes sense if you can repay the borrowed funds within about a year, or if your income for the current year falls into a higher tax bracket than usual. Otherwise, the non-deductible interest that you will pay on the loan may negate the tax benefits of your contribution. Instead, consider making regular catch-up payments later when you have the funds to contribute.

If you have the cash and the contribution room, but do not want to claim a deduction in the current year because you are already in a low tax bracket, make the contribution but delay the deduction. As discussed in 3.1.3, you can claim the deduction in any later year. If you are confident of being in a higher tax bracket within the next year or so, this strategy can maximize the tax-free growth of funds while also maximizing your tax savings.

For cash-flow purposes, you may wish to set up a monthly transfer of a few hundred dollars from your regular bank account to your RRSP account. That will ensure steady contributions to the RRSP over the course of the year.

When considering investments within your RRSP, bear in mind the one major drawback of long-term investments such as five-year GICs. If you decide to withdraw the funds sooner for tax purposes (see 3.3.4), or to use the Home Buyers' Plan (see 3.3.6), you may find that you cannot get access to your investment.

3.2 How do you get money out of an RRSP?

At any time, you may withdraw cash from your RRSP. The amount will be included in your income for that year and taxed as ordinary income, just as if it were salary, even if some of the value of the RRSP represents capital gains (which outside an RRSP are normally only partially taxed and, in some cases, could be entirely exempt).

A percentage to cover tax will be withheld at source by the financial institution and remitted to Revenue Canada (and Revenu Québec if appropriate) on your behalf. For federal purposes, a withdrawal of up to $5,000 is subject to 10% withholding; over $5,000 and up to $15,000, 20%; and over $15,000, 30%. In Québec, a withdrawal of up to $5,000 is subject to a combined federal and Québec withholding of 25%; over $5,000 and up to $15,000, 33%; and over $15,000, 38%. You will then report the income and amount of tax withheld on your annual income tax return and either receive a refund or, if not enough tax was withheld, pay the difference.

The government will allow you to make tax-free RRSP withdrawals (within limits) if you use the funds for certain purposes, such as buying a new home (see 3.3.6) or financing training or post-secondary education for you or your spouse (see 2.4). Generally, you must repay the amount withdrawn under these plans over a certain amount of time or it will become taxable.

You must wind up your RRSP by the end of the year in which you turn 69. At any time before then, you can transfer your RRSP funds tax-free to an annuity, a registered retirement income fund or a life income fund. Your various options for maturing your RRSP are discussed in 19.4.

3.2.1 Early withdrawals—your RRSP as a tax averaging tool

As discussed in 3.1.5, the funds in your RRSP are not taxed until the year in which you withdraw the funds. As a result, RRSPs can be used as a tax averaging tool rather than just a mechanism for retirement saving. If you are still fairly young and not too worried about retirement income, you can withdraw funds from your RRSP whenever there is a tax advantage to doing so.

> **Withdraw funds from your RRSP in low-income years.**

Suppose you plan to take some time off to care for your young children, for example, or to go on an extended vacation or take up some other activity. During such years, where your employment income will be low, you can withdraw funds from your RRSP and perhaps pay tax at the 27% rate instead of 41% or 50%. The advantage of low-rate taxation will have to be balanced against the advantage of tax-free growth available by leaving the funds in the RRSP.

In an anticipated low-income year following a high-income year, you can even consider contributing in February, claiming a deduction (say at

41%) for the previous year, and withdrawing the funds, to be taxed at the low (27%) rate.

You will need to plan around the withholding tax on RRSP withdrawals discussed in 3.2, however. You may be able to arrange withdrawals so that they incur the least possible withholding tax, leaving you with the use of the funds until you file your tax return the following April. Bear in mind, however, that you may have a tax liability to settle up on April 30 to the extent that your tax rate on the income exceeds the withholding tax rate.

3.3 Special RRSP rules

A number of rules deal with special situations with respect to RRSPs. We will refer to them only briefly; you should consult your professional advisor if you are in these situations.

3.3.1 Spousal plans

> Contribute to your spouse's (or common-law spouse's) RRSP if your projected income on retirement will be higher.

The RRSP rules allow you to contribute to an RRSP for your spouse, and claim the deduction yourself. Your total contributions (to your own and your spouse's plans) are still subject to your normal limits (18% of your previous year's earned income or $13,500 for 1999, minus any pension adjustment). The advantage is that your spouse will ultimately be the one who reports the income for tax purposes, when the funds are withdrawn on retirement or otherwise. If your spouse has less income than you either on retirement or at some earlier time (including, for example, due to expected maternity leave), this can result in significantly less tax on the income.

> Make spousal RRSP contributions in December instead of the following February.

To prevent spousal RRSPs from being used for "income splitting" (see Chapter 5), the amount you contribute will be taxed back to you (rather than your spouse) to the extent any amount is withdrawn by your spouse in the year *in which* you contribute or *in the next two calendar years.* See 5.3.9.

Example:

Jon and Nancy are married. Jon contributes $5,000 to Nancy's RRSP in February 2000, and claims the deduction on his 1999 tax return.

If Nancy withdraws the funds at any time up to the end of 2002, $5,000 of the amount withdrawn will be treated as Jon's income, not Nancy's. (If, however, Jon's contribution had been made in December 1999, this would only be the case until the end of 2001.)

This rule does not apply if the spouses are separated or divorced. We explore this rule in more detail at 5.3.9, in the chapter on Income Splitting.

If you are over 69 (the age at which you must mature your RRSP; see 19.4) and have "earned income" in the previous year, this will create new RRSP room for you in the current year. As long as your spouse is 69 or younger, you can still claim a deduction for a spousal RRSP contribution.

In general, there will be little effect on the real ownership of the funds under provincial law if you and your spouse separate or divorce. The rule in most provinces is that such funds will be pooled and shared between the spouses. There are rules in place to allow a tax-free division of RRSP funds in such situations.

3.3.2 Transfers to and from RRSPs

RRSPs can generally be transferred, with no tax consequences, to other RRSPs or to registered retirement income funds ("RRIFs"), by simply filling out a form.

> **Transfer pension commuted value, retiring allowances or severance pay to your RRSP.**

Under pension legislation you may be prevented from immediately withdrawing pension benefits (known as the "commuted value") from your employer's plan on your departure from the company. This legislation is commonly referred to as "locking-in" legislation. Pension benefits subject to these rules may be transferred to a locked-in RRSP. Locked-in RRSPs are essentially subject to the same restrictions on withdrawal of funds as the original pension plan. For example, you cannot usually access the locked-in plan funds until you are within 10 years of the retirement date set out in the plan documents and, even then, you can only use the plan funds to purchase an annuity or a special RRIF that will provide a lifetime income, called a "life income fund" ("LIF") (see 19.4.5). With a LIF, you have more flexibility in deciding how to invest the funds.

Where the pension legislation permits a transfer from a registered pension plan to a locked-in RRSP or LIF, there are generally no tax consequences to such transfers, though the tax rules may restrict the amounts that can be transferred from a "defined-benefit" pension plan.

Special rules allow a "retiring allowance" (which, as defined for tax purposes, includes severance pay and amounts received for wrongful dismissal) to be transferred tax-free to an RRSP, rather than taxed as income when received. The amount that can be transferred is normally limited to $2,000 for each calendar year (or part year) of employment before 1996, plus $1,500 for years of employment before 1989 for which employer pension contributions have not vested.

3.3.3 Death

On death, a taxpayer is normally taxed on the entire amount of any RRSPs or RRIFs, except where the funds are left to the taxpayer's spouse, in which case they are included in the spouse's income (see 20.1.1). To the extent the funds come from an RRSP, they can be transferred to the spouse's own RRSP or RRIF for a deduction that offsets the income inclusion. The spouse can also use these funds to acquire an annuity. If there is no surviving spouse, and the RRSP or RRIF funds are left to a financially-dependent child or grandchild, the RRSP or RRIF funds can either be taxed in the hands of the child or grandchild or used to buy a term annuity to age 18. Previously, if the deceased left RRSP or RIF funds to financially dependent children and the deceased had a surviving spouse, the deceased's estate remained liable for tax on these amounts. Under a 1999 federal budget proposal, the amount will be included in the income of the dependent children, whether or not there is a surviving spouse. The executor of the deceased's estate should obtain professional advice on these matters.

See Chapter 20 for a general discussion of the tax effects of death.

3.3.4 Overcontributions

The RRSP contribution limits were discussed in 3.1.3. What happens if you contribute more than the maximum?

First, bear in mind that your financial institution will not prevent you from overcontributing. Your financial institution is not obliged to tell you how much you can or cannot contribute.

Second, any contributions over the maximum are non-deductible. However, once the funds are in your RRSP, they are taxable when withdrawn (whether on retirement or earlier), just like the funds that were deductible when you contributed them. Therefore, there is double taxation—once when you earn the income (and receive no deduction despite putting the funds into the RRSP), and once when you withdraw the funds from the RRSP.

Third, in certain rare circumstances, overcontributing might be valuable despite the double taxation, because of the huge beneficial effect of tax-free compounding (as illustrated in the table in 3.1.5). Also, you can often deduct an overcontribution in a later year as new contribution room is created.

There is a rule preventing excessive overcontributions. At any one time up to $2,000 can be overcontributed without penalty. Above the $2,000 level, the excess is subject to a penalty tax of 1% per month.

> **Top up your RRSP with a non-deductible $2,000 overcontribution.**

The $2,000 figure is designed to catch those cases where you might have miscalculated your pension adjustment (see 3.1.3) and contributed a little too much. However, as long as you are certain about your pension adjustment, you can use the $2,000 deliberately if you wish. So if you are already contributing your maximum for 1999, consider making an additional contribution of up to $2,000 to further benefit from the compounding of tax-free growth.

Until February 27, 1995, the overcontribution limit was $8,000. If you overcontributed before that date, you must use up the excess over $2,000 by deducting it against your RRSP contribution room in 1996 and later years as new room becomes available.

3.3.5 Labour-sponsored venture capital corporation shares

In most provinces, a combined federal/provincial credit of 30% to 35% (depending on the province) is available for an investment of up to $3,500 per year in shares of a "labour-sponsored venture capital corporation", or LSVCC (see 7.4.3). In Newfoundland, Alberta and the Territories, only the 15% federal credit is available.

You can buy shares in a labour-sponsored venture capital corporation and contribute them to your RRSP. You can also generally have the shares bought directly by your self-directed RRSP (see 3.1.6), provided the RRSP uses "new" or previous contribution funds (but not earnings). Either way, you claim the credit on your personal income tax return.

> **Consider shares of a labour-sponsored venture capital corporation for your RRSP.**

When combined with the deduction for the RRSP contribution, a $3,500 investment in an LSVCC may cost you as little as $700 after tax.

Particularly if you are not otherwise making the maximum possible RRSP contribution, an investment in an LSVCC for your RRSP may be worth considering. Before taking the plunge and investing in an LSVCC, make sure you evaluate the relative merits from an investment perspective, as they are generally a higher risk and probably illiquid investment. (See also 7.4.3.)

3.3.6   The Home Buyers' Plan

Under the Home Buyers' Plan, if you qualify, you are allowed to withdraw up to $20,000 as a loan from your RRSP to buy or build a home, without counting the withdrawal as income. You must then repay the loan, without interest, over the next 16 years.

Who may use the Home Buyers' Plan?

The Plan may only be used by what the government calls a "first-time buyer". You are not a "first-time buyer" if you have owned and lived in a home as a principal place of residence at any time during the five calendar years up to and including the current year. (For the current year, you can use the Plan up to 30 days after you acquire a home.) If your spouse has owned and lived in a home during that period, and you have inhabited that home during the marriage, you also do not qualify. (Remember that "spouse" includes a common-law spouse as outlined in 2.2.1.)

Past participation will not prevent you from participating in the Plan again, as long as you have fully repaid to your RRSP the amounts previously withdrawn and you have not owned a home in the past five calendar years (including the current year).

As noted in 2.5.3, starting in 1999, the five-year qualification test is waived for disabled persons and their relatives for purchases of new homes that are more accessible to or better suited to the personal needs and care of a disabled person who will reside there.

How does the Plan work?

You can borrow (withdraw) up to $20,000 from your RRSP under the Plan. If you and your spouse each have RRSPs, you can thus borrow up to $40,000 between the two of you if you are taking joint ownership in the property. A qualifying home must be acquired before October 1 of the year following the year of the withdrawal. You must also begin or intend, not later than one year after its acquisition, to use the home as a principal place of residence. No tax will apply to the withdrawal.

When you withdraw the funds, you fill out Form T1036 (and TP-935.1-V for Québec purposes), certifying that you have entered into a written agreement to purchase a home, and stating its address. Once you have done this, the financial institution will not withhold tax when it pays the funds to you.

Note that the Home Buyers' Plan does not give you any right to withdraw funds from your RRSP if you didn't already have that right. If your RRSP funds are invested in term deposits or other long-term obligations, you will still need to negotiate with the financial institution to have the funds released as cash. Similarly, if your RRSP funds are in your employer's group RRSP or a "locked-in RRSP", you may not be able to get them out.

Once you borrow the funds, you must normally complete the purchase by September 30 of the *following* year. (A one-year extension may be available if the deal falls through and you buy a replacement property.) If you withdraw less than the $20,000 maximum, you can in many cases withdraw a further amount up to the following January 31 and treat the total as one withdrawal.

The requirement to repay the funds begins in the second year following the withdrawal. You can opt to make any year's repayment up to 60 days after the end of the year.

If you do not make repayments as required, you must include the shortfall in income for tax purposes. In effect, it's treated as a permanent withdrawal from your RRSP and you're taxed on it.

Example:

Olivia has $30,000 in her RRSP. She signs an agreement in September 1999 to purchase a new home. In November 1999 she completes Form T1036 and withdraws $15,000 from her RRSP. The purchase closes in January 2000.

No tax will be withheld from the $15,000 that Olivia withdraws, so she can use the full amount towards the home purchase. Since she withdrew the funds in 1999, Olivia must repay $1,000 (1/15 of the total) to her RRSP during 2001 or by March 1, 2002. If she repays only $600, she will have to include $400 in income for 2001 and pay tax on that amount.

If Olivia repays no more than $1,000 in 2001 (or by March 1, 2002), she will be required to repay 1/14 of the balance, another $1,000, in 2002 (or by March 1, 2003). Suppose she repays $8,000 in 2001, leaving a balance owing of $7,000? For 2002, she will still be required to repay 1/14 of the balance, or $500. The fact she has prepaid more than required will reduce but not eliminate her obligation to continue paying the balance in later years.

Contributions in the year you use the Plan

If you contribute to an RRSP and withdraw the same funds within 90 days under the Home Buyers' Plan, you cannot deduct your contribution. For purposes of this rule, any balance that was already in your RRSP can be considered as withdrawn first. Thus, it is only to the extent the amount of your new contribution is needed for the withdrawal (within the 90-day period) that a deduction will be disallowed.

Some special situations

The Home Buyers' Plan may be used for building a new home on an existing lot that you own. Instead of an agreement to purchase the home, you must have an agreement in place to construct it.

If you withdraw the funds but your home purchase does not close, you can generally cancel your participation in the Plan and return the funds to your RRSP with no adverse tax consequences. Alternatively, if you buy another qualifying home as a replacement, you can remain in the Plan.

If you have contributed to a spousal RRSP, your spouse must normally wait two to three years before withdrawing the funds or they will be taxed back to you (see 3.3.1). However, with the Home Buyers' Plan, your spouse can borrow the funds to purchase a qualifying home, and to the extent they are not repaid over the 16 years, it is your spouse that must include the difference in income, not you. (Note, however, that if your spouse withdraws the funds and does not purchase a qualifying home, so that the full amount withdrawn is taxed in the current year, the attribution rule *will* apply and you, not your spouse, will be taxed on the withdrawal.)

If you become a non-resident of Canada, you must repay the entire outstanding balance to the RRSP within 60 days. Otherwise, the balance will be included in your income for the year that you became non-resident.

If you should die while you have an outstanding balance to repay, that balance will be included in your income for the year of death and tax will be payable by your estate (see 20.1.1). However, if you leave a surviving spouse, your executor and your spouse may make a special election to have your spouse take over the obligation to repay the funds over the remainder of the 15-year period, and the balance will not be included in your income for the year of death.

Should you use the Home Buyers' Plan?

At first glance, the Plan seems attractive, since it gives you ready access to a potentially large chunk of cash. However, there are three costs to consider.

Weigh the loss of RRSP growth before using the Home Buyers' Plan.

First, you lose the tax-free compounding in your RRSP (see the example in 3.1.5). Balanced against this is the fact that you have probably reduced the mortgage interest expense you would otherwise have to pay out of after-tax dollars. Nevertheless, the value of the RRSP may be significantly less, at your retirement, than it otherwise would have been. If you are depending on your RRSP for your retirement income, you will want to forecast the reduction in income that will result from withdrawing a large chunk of the funds now and repaying it to the RRSP over the next 16 years.

Second, you have to be able to sustain the cash flow to repay the RRSP; if you cannot, you will end up being taxed on the funds you have withdrawn. When figuring out the cash you need to handle your mortgage and property tax payments, don't forget the 1/15 minimum repayment to the RRSP in each year beginning with the second year after the withdrawal (due by 60 days after the end of the year). Of course, since you are repaying borrowed funds and not contributing new money to the RRSP, no deduction is available for the amounts you repay.

Third, you might not be able to make a contribution to your RRSP for the current year. This will depend on the balance in your RRSP. If your withdrawal does not exceed the value you had in the RRSP 90 days before the withdrawal, you have no problem. Otherwise, you may have to postpone the current year's contribution, and save it up for a later year. The result would be one less year for those funds to have earned tax-free interest, and higher tax to pay in the current year since you will not have a contribution to deduct.

Nevertheless, if you need the funds to help you purchase your first home, the Home Buyers' Plan may be a significant help.

Planning for the Home Buyers' Plan

If you're thinking about tapping your RRSP to purchase your first home but your RRSP is not yet at $20,000 and you intend to use the Home Buyers' Plan to its fullest, make your contribution early enough so that it can sit in the RRSP for 90 days before you withdraw the funds. Then the amount you contributed can be withdrawn as well without affecting your deduction for the contribution.

If you are planning to buy a new home and you are close to the four-year cutoff that will re-qualify you as a "first-time buyer", consider waiting and making your purchase at a time when you can use the Home Buyers' Plan. For example, if you sold your last home in 1995, you can use the Plan as of January 1, 2000.

If you are about to be married and your future spouse owns a home that you will be living in, consider borrowing funds under the Home Buyers' Plan before your wedding. Once you are married, you will not be able to do so. However, you are not restricted by a previous home owned by your spouse, as long as you do not live in it while married. Therefore, if you plan on buying a new home after your wedding, you should not (romantic considerations aside) move into your spouse's current home until you have made your withdrawal under the Plan.

The same applies if you have been living common-law for less than 12 months (and have not had a child together). Once you reach 12 months of living together, you are considered "married" for income tax purposes (see 2.2.1). If your mate owns your present home, but you are planning on "moving up" to a larger home, you should consider withdrawing funds under the Home Buyers' Plan before you have lived together for 12 months. However, you will have to take ownership (or at least part ownership) of the new home in your own name.

3.4   Registered pension plans—RPPs

3.4.1   Ordinary RPPs

A registered pension plan ("RPP") is set up by an employer for its employees. Virtually all large companies, and many smaller ones, have such plans. These are quite different from the Canada Pension Plan (or, in Québec, the Québec Pension Plan), to which all employed and self-employed taxpayers must contribute.

The employer contributes (and deducts for tax purposes) an annual amount on behalf of each employee. Unlike most other employment benefits, these amounts are not taxed as benefits from employment in the year they are contributed. Instead, employees are taxed on the income from the pension when they *receive* it, which is normally after retirement.

In some cases, employees may be required or permitted to make additional contributions to the plan, which they can deduct for tax purposes in the year contributed.

There are two general kinds of pension plans: money-purchase and defined benefit. Money-purchase plans are analogous to RRSPs, in the sense that the amount of the pension payments is determined by the contributions and the investment income they earn. Many large and public employers provide defined benefit plans. With such plans, you know from the beginning how much your pension will be, usually based on a percentage of your actual salary over a specified number of years. It is up to the employer to contribute enough, and to the pension fund management to invest wisely, to make sure that the plan remains sufficiently well funded to make those payments.

Once an employee retires and starts receiving pension income, the pension income is taxed as regular income as it is received. Up to $1,000 per year may effectively be exempted through the pension income tax credit (see 19.3.5).

> **Ask Revenue Canada to recalculate your prior-year tax liability on retroactive lump-sum pension and other payments.**

If you receive a lump-sum payment relating to prior years, under a 1999 budget proposal, you may ask Revenue Canada to determine whether it is more advantageous to you to recalculate the tax on that income as if you received it in those prior years. This change is intended to relieve the higher tax liability that may result if the entire lump-sum is taxed in the year of receipt, rather than year by year as right to receive the income arose. Eligible payments must total at least $3,000 in the year and include superannuation or pension benefits (other than non-periodic benefits), wrongful dismissal and other employment-related payments arising from a court order or similar judgment, and certain other amounts. (This change was introduced in the 1999 federal budget, but will apply to qualifying lump-sum payments received after 1994.)

If you have terminated your employment but are not yet eligible to receive pension income, you are allowed to transfer lump-sum amounts from the RPP to a "locked-in" RRSP or a "locked-in" RRIF (see 19.4.5). Locked-in funds cannot be withdrawn in a lump sum; they must be used to provide a lifetime income. As discussed in 19.4, you must start receiving pension income from an RPP, an RRSP or an RRIF by the end of the year in which you turn 69.

The amount you can transfer from an RPP to an RRSP or an RRIF is limited to the amount of annual pension given up under the RPP multiplied by a factor based on your age at the date of the transfer. The factor is 9.0 if you are under 50, gradually rising to 12.4 at ages 64 and 65. Any amount over this limit must be paid to you in cash and will be taxed as income in the year received.

> **Consider contributing to your RRSP instead of a money-purchase RRSP.**

If you've been making voluntary contributions to your registered pension plan under a money-purchase provision, consider contributing to an RRSP instead. Though the amount you can contribute will normally be the same and your administration and investment management fees may be higher, the RRSP will give you much greater flexibility in terms of your investment choices.

> **Find out about the vesting of your pension benefits before making a career change.**

If you are a member of a company pension plan, find out how long it takes for your contributions to be "vested". Once they are vested, the pension you have earned becomes yours, and almost all employers will allow you to take the full pension benefits with you if you change jobs. On the other hand, if they are not vested, you get your own contributions back when you leave—but no pension down the road. The vesting of your pension benefits can be a major factor in career change decisions.

3.4.2   Individual pension plans—IPPs

An individual pension plan ("IPP") is exactly what the name implies—a defined benefit registered pension plan designed and structured for one individual member. It is possible for owner-managers to meet the qualifications to have this type of pension plan registered with Revenue Canada.

As a defined benefit pension plan, the benefit payable at retirement is specified and IPP contributions are made accordingly. The amount necessary to provide a defined benefit rises at ages closer to retirement since less time is available to accrue investment income in the plan. As such, IPPs are advantageous where the member is close to retirement— the amounts that can be contributed to an IPP are greater than those allowed to an RRSP.

Generally speaking, the IPP concept will be suitable for you if you are

- a key executive and/or owner-manager of a corporation;
- over 53 years old; and
- earning a base salary of more than about $100,000.

An IPP may also be worth considering if you are already in your employer's group RPP but the benefits from that RPP are not as generous as you would like them to be.

At termination or retirement, any surplus in the IPP can be returned to the member after paying personal tax. The surplus is the excess of IPP assets over the actual cost of the defined benefit pension to be provided under the terms of the plan. Alternatively, the tax sheltering may be allowed to continue if your IPP is able to opt to "self-annuitize" upon your retirement (i.e., rather than purchasing an annuity from a life insurance company, have the IPP pay you, the beneficiary of the plan, a lifetime income). This can have the effect of stretching out the additional tax sheltering represented by any accumulated IPP surplus well into the years beyond retirement and quite possibly until the last of you and your spouse dies. However, some provinces do not allow self-annuitization in a plan with no active members, which will be the case for your IPP after you retire.

> **Weigh the advantages of establishing an "individual pension plan".**

The main advantage of the IPP is that, if you are over 53, you and your employer will be allowed to make higher annual contributions than you would otherwise be entitled to under the RRSP route. In addition to maximizing tax savings, the higher allowable contributions under the IPP concept can be looked on as a form of forced savings. Your employer will be required to top up the funds in the IPP if investment performance is poor and there will be insufficient funds (as determined by an actuary) to pay you the defined benefit pension promised under the plan (which could be a point of concern to your employer). A further advantage is that an IPP is generally creditor-proof, while most RRSPs are not.

Depending on your particular circumstances, an IPP could also provide some scope for making past service pension contributions, which can only be made under defined benefit RPPs. This can further enhance an IPP's tax sheltering value.

There are also significant potential disadvantages of an IPP which you should carefully consider. For example, you will lose the flexibility to split income on retirement, since contributions cannot be made to the IPP for your spouse, as can be done with RRSPs. In contrast to RRSPs, which can be cashed in any time, contributions made to the IPP will be locked in under pension benefits legislation until retirement, at which time they must be used to provide retirement benefits (usually in the form of a life annuity or life income fund). An RRSP, on the other hand, provides a variety of options, on termination or retirement (see 19.4). In addition, start-up and ongoing costs of administration of an IPP will be higher than those of your RRSP. This is due to the complex regulatory environment governing pension plans. For example, an actuarial valuation will be required at start-up and every three years thereafter; and certain forms must be filed annually.

The rules regarding IPPs are quite complex. You should consult your professional tax advisor for more information.

3.5   Deferred profit-sharing plans—DPSPs

Deferred profit-sharing plans ("DPSPs") are less common than registered pension plans. They operate the same way in that contributions are made by the employer and are only taxed in the employee's hands when received, normally on retirement.

Employer contributions to DPSPs are based on current or accrued profits but may have a defined minimum contribution. Such plans may be used, for example, by smaller companies which are not sure of profits and do not wish to commit themselves to large pension contributions, especially if they end up losing money for the year.

Employer contributions to DPSPs are generally limited to the lesser of 18% of your earnings for the year or $6,750 for 1999. Employee contributions to a DPSP are not permitted. Contributions to a DPSP are reported as a pension adjustment on your T4 slip and they therefore reduce the amount you can contribute to an RRSP in the following year (see 3.1.3). Employer contributions vest in an employee after 24 months of plan membership.

DPSPs cannot be set up for employees who are also major shareholders (over 10% of any class of shares) in the employer corporation, or for members of their families. They therefore cannot be used for owner-managers of small businesses.

3.6   References

The following publications can be obtained (in person or by telephone request) from your nearest Revenue Canada District Taxation Office. Some of the brochures and forms are also available from Revenue Canada's Internet site at *www.rc.gc.ca*.

Interpretation Bulletin IT-124R6, "Contributions to   registered retirement savings plans"

Interpretation Bulletin IT-307R3, "Spousal registered retirement savings plans"

Interpretation Bulletin IT-320R2, "Registered retirement savings plan—Qualified investments"

Interpretation Bulletin IT-337R3, "Retiring allowances"

Interpretation Bulletin IT-363R2, "Deferred profit sharing plans—Deductibility of employer contributions and taxation of amounts received by a beneficiary"

Interpretation Bulletin IT-528, "Transfers of funds between registered plans"

Information Circular 72-22R9, "Registered retirement savings plans"

Information Circular 77-1R4, "Deferred profit sharing plans"

Information Circular 78-18R5, "Registered retirement income funds"

Information Circular 79-8R3, "Forms to be used to directly transfer funds to plans"

Information Circular 93-3, "Registered education savings plans"

Guide, "RRSPs and Other Registered Plans for Retirement"

Guide, "Registered Education Savings Plans"

Brochure, "Home Buyers' Plan for 19___ Participants"

Form T1023, "Calculation of earned income for 19___"

Form T1036, "Applying to withdraw an amount under the Home Buyers' Plan in 19___"

Form T1037, "Designating contributions you made to your RRSPs as your repayment under the Home Buyers' Plan for 19___"

Form T2097, "Identification of amounts transferred to an RRSP for 19___"

Form T2205, "Calculation of amounts from a spousal RRSP or RRIF to be included in income for 19___"

Registered Education Savings Plans—RESPs

4

- Consider setting up an RESP for your child's post-secondary education (4.1)
- Think about establishing a self-directed RESP to increase your investment options (4.1.2)
- Contribute $2,000 annually to an RESP and earn a 20% government grant (4.2)
- If your child does not pursue higher education, consider transferring up to $50,000 to your own or your spouse's RRSP (4.3.2)

RESPs are tax-assisted savings vehicles similar to the RRSPs and the other deferred income plans discussed in Chapter 3—but the rules governing contributions to and payments from RESPs are quite different. In the past, restrictions on the use of RESP investment income sometimes outweighed the potential benefits of tax-deferred growth. Changes to the RESP system over the past few years have made these plans more attractive as education investment vehicles.

4.1   What is an RESP?

RESPs can help you build an education fund for your child or grandchild (or a friend or relative's child) by allowing you to earn investment income in a tax-deferred environment. You can set up an individual plan with organizations such as life insurance companies, mutual fund companies and financial institutions or you can enroll in a group plan offered by a non-profit scholarship or education trust foundation. If the child goes to college or university, the RESP provides funds to help cover the child's expenses.

> **Consider setting up an RESP for your child's post-secondary education.**

Unlike RRSPs, contributions to an RESP are *not* deductible to the contributor. However, the income in the plan grows tax-free, so RESPs enjoy the effect of tax-free compounding of interest, which we illustrated in 3.1.5. When the child withdraws the funds, the income portion will be taxable to the child. As a student, your child will probably not have much other income and will be eligible for the tuition and education tax credits (see 2.4), so he or she will pay little or no tax. The investment income payments from the RESP are all taxable as income, even if the investment income was earned as dividends or capital gains, which are normally taxed at a lower rate.

4.1.1 How much can you contribute to an RESP?

The maximum contribution to an RESP in respect of any one beneficiary by all contributors is limited to $4,000 per year. There is an overall lifetime contribution limit of $42,000 per beneficiary. Unlike RRSPs, if you contribute less than $4,000 in a particular year, you cannot catch up by contributing more than $4,000 in a later year. Overcontributions are taxed at a rate of 1% for each month that they remain in the plan. Even if overcontributions are withdrawn from the plan, they still count towards the beneficiary's $42,000 lifetime contribution limit, creating a double penalty for overcontributing.

Income generated in an RESP may be sheltered from tax for a maximum of 25 years. You can make contributions to the plan for up to 21 years. The plan can exist and earn tax-sheltered income for four more years, after which the plan must be wound up. You may want to wait until your child is about age five to set up a plan, so it will still be available if your child wants to pursue post-graduate studies. Keep in mind that waiting to set up an RESP means that the funds will have less time to grow.

If an RESP contributor dies, his or her estate can continue to contribute to the plan. However, a trust cannot contribute to an RESP. If you've already established and funded a formal trust for your child, you will have to find other sources of funding for an RESP.

If you wish, you can withdraw your own contributions to an RESP without any tax consequences since you did not get a tax deduction when you contributed the funds. However, you can't withdraw the income earned by the RESP tax-free. You may also be required to pay some or all of any Canada Education Savings Grants upon a RESP withdrawal for non-education purposes—see 4.2.

4.1.2 Choosing the right type of RESP

> Think about establishing a self-directed RESP to increase your investment options.

If you choose to set up an individual plan rather than enroll in a group plan, the investments can be self-directed. The types of investments that may be held in an RESP are the same as those that may be held by an RRSP—see 3.1.6. However, unlike RRSPs, no foreign content limit applies to RESPs.

You can also choose between a single-beneficiary and a multi-beneficiary plan. Under a single-beneficiary plan, the beneficiary does not have to be related to you — he or she can be anyone you choose. You can also set up a single-beneficiary RESP for yourself if you're planning to pursue post-secondary education in the future.

If you're saving for the education of more than one person, you may want to consider a multi-beneficiary or family plan. The beneficiaries under a multi-beneficiary plan may only include your children, brothers, sisters, grandchildren or great-grandchildren. You cannot contribute to the plan for a beneficiary after he or she reaches age 21. Although you can usually change the beneficiaries after you set up either a single or multi-beneficiary plan if you wish, certain plans may have conditions restricting changing beneficiaries.

Group plans may require that children be enrolled in the plan before they reach a certain age. They generally allow only one beneficiary to be named and may not allow you to change the beneficiary after he or she reaches a certain age.

4.2   Canada Education Savings Grant

In 1998, the government enriched the incentives for RESPs by introducing Canada Education Savings Grants (CESGs). Under the program, the government will provide a direct grant to the RESP of 20% of the first $2,000 of annual contributions made to the RESP in a year. The grant will be worth up to $400 per year for each year the beneficiary is under 18, to a maximum of $7,200 per beneficiary. The grant amount will not be included in the annual and lifetime contribution limits for the beneficiary.

> Contribute $2,000 annually to an RESP and earn a 20% government grant.

If the $2,000 maximum contribution is not made in a year, entitlement to the grant can be carried forward to a later year (within restrictions). The total CESG per beneficiary per year is capped at $800 (20% of the maximum annual $4,000 RESP contribution) or 20% of the unused CESG room, whichever is less.

Example:

Clare contributes $1,000 in 1999 to an RESP for her newborn son. This contribution earns a CESG of $200 (20% of $1,000), leaving $1,000 in CESG contribution room available for carryforward in future years.

In 2000, Clare contributes $3,500 to the plan. In this year, the CESG will be limited to the $2,000 of new contribution arising in the year, plus the $1,000 carried forward. As such, the CESG will be 20% of $3,000, or $600.

Note that only unused CESG contribution *room* can be carried forward; in our example, the extra $500 of contribution could not be carried forward and claimed for CESG purposes in later years. CESGs do not otherwise affect the maximum RESP contribution levels discussed in 4.1.

To qualify for the CESG, the RESP beneficiary must be a resident of Canada under age 18 and must have a Social Insurance Number (SIN) . You can apply for a SIN for your child by contacting Human Resources Development Canada.

If you have already set up an RESP, you may have to amend its terms or open up a new RESP to ensure that your contributions meet the new CESG qualification requirements. Speak to your RESP administrator to determine your best course of action. As a transitional measure, existing RESPs that otherwise do not qualify are eligible for CESGs for 1998 and 1999, so you don't need to change the terms of your existing RESP to qualify for a CESG in 1999.

If you want to receive a CESG for 1999 but you do not have a plan, you'll need to set one up and make a contribution before December 31, 1999. The contributions must be new — money cannot be withdrawn from existing RESPs and recontributed to a new plan to qualify for the grant. If you change the plan's beneficiary, the grant funds can stay in the RESP if both the old and new beneficiaries are under 21 years old and are related to you.

There are special rules for beneficiaries in the years they become 16 or 17. RESPs for beneficiaries aged 16 and 17 will be eligible for CESGs only if :

- Contributions to all RESPs for the child totalled at least $2,000 before the year in which the child turned 16, or
- If there were contributions for the child of at least $100 per year in any four years before the year in which the child turned 16.

If your child chooses not to pursue post-secondary education, you will have to repay the CESG funds received but you will only have to pay back the principal amount of the grant. You do not have to pay back the income earned on the grant funds but the income will be taxed when it is withdrawn from the RESP (see 4.3.2).

4.3   Payments from an RESP

4.3.1   If the beneficiary pursues higher education

Your RESP can begin making educational assistance payments to the plan's beneficiary once he or she becomes a full-time student at a qualifying post-secondary institution. Disabled students can receive educational assistance payments for part-time study. Payments from the plan can be used to cover the student's living expenses and educational expenses such as tuition fees and books, although certain plans may restrict which expenses payments can cover. A beneficiary cannot receive more than $5,000 during the first three months of his or her post-secondary education.

You can decide whether to let the student use the principal amount contributed to the plan or only the income accumulated in the plan. You can also decide how much is paid out of the plan and when the payments are made, subject to what the plan you choose allows. You may want to spread the payments over the duration of the student's program to minimize taxes. If your RESP received CESGs, in most cases, a part of each income payment will be attributed to the CESG funds received by the plan.

If you contributed to a group RESP, the principal you contributed to the plan will be the first year's payment to the student. The plan administrators will determine the student's share of the income from the pooled funds in the plan and start making those payments in the student's second year of post-secondary education.

For an educational program to qualify, generally it must be at least three weeks long, require at least 10 hours per week of instruction, be at a designated educational institution and not be taken while the student is employed as part of the duties of that employment. Correspondence courses and other distanced education courses may also qualify, as well as universities outside Canada if the student is enrolled in a course of at least 13 weeks leading to a degree.

Some group RESP plans may have other restrictions, such as prohibiting the beneficiary from changing schools or requiring the beneficiary to meet a minimum academic standard.

4.3.2　If the beneficiary does not pursue further education

In the past, many parents decided against the use of an RESP because if none of the intended benficiaries go on to post-secondary education, the family would only get back the amounts contributed to the RESP, while the income earned over the years would be forfeited.

> **If your child does not pursue higher education, consider transferring up to $50,000 to your own or your spouse's RRSP.**

The government has partially removed this disincentive for 1998 and later years if none of the RESP's intended beneficiaries are post-secondary students by age 21 and if the plan has been running for at least 10 years. (If a beneficiary is mentally impaired, these prerequisites may be waived.) You will be allowed to transfer up to $50,000 of RESP income during your lifetime to your RRSP (or your spouse's) to the extent you or your spouse has available RRSP contribution room. This allows the RRSP deduction to offset the inclusion of the RESP funds in your taxable income.

If you do not want to contribute the income to an RRSP or you do not have enough RRSP contribution room to do so, you will be subject to an extra tax of 20% of the excess RESP income (plus an additional 20% if you live in Québec), on top of the regular taxes on the amount (the extra tax is designed to make up for the taxes deferred while the funds were in the plan). You must wind up the RESP by March 1 of the year following the year in which you first withdrew income from the RESP.

Family plans are subject to the same contribution limits per beneficiary as single-beneficiary plans but, if one of your children decides against post-secondary school, the funds you have contributed for this child and the income earned on those contributions can be re-directed to benefit your other children who do pursue post-secondary education. If your plan received CESGs, the remaining beneficiaries can use up to $7,200 of CESGs funds each.

Group RESPs will return your contribution, but the income earned will remain in the plan to be distributed to the plan's beneficiaries who go on to post-secondary education.

4.4   References

The following publications can be obtained (in person or by telephone request) from your nearest Revenue Canada District Taxation Office. Some of the brochures and forms are also available from Revenue Canada's Internet site at *www.rc.gc.ca*.

> Information Circular 93-3, "Registered education savings plans"
>
> Guide, "Registered Education Savings Plans"
>
> Form TIE-OVP, "Individual return for RESP overpayments"
>
> Form T1171, "Tax withholding waiver on accumulated income payments from RESPs"

Information on Canada Education Savings Grants and the process for applying for a Social Insurance Number is available from Human Resources Development Canada's website at *www.hrdc-drhc.gc.ca*.

Reducing your family's tax bill through income splitting

- Assess the impact of the new income splitting tax on your tax planning arrangements (5.2.4)
- Beware of the "general anti-avoidance rule" (5.2.6)
- The higher-income spouse should pay household expenses (5.3.1)
- Pay your spouse's tax bills with your own funds (5.3.1)
- Pay the interest on your spouse's investment loans (5.3.1)
- Pay a salary or consulting fee to your spouse and/or children (5.3.2)
- Think about loaning business assets to your spouse or child (5.3.3)
- Consider making spousal investment loans when interest rates are rising (5.3.4)
- Have your spouse or child earn income on income from lent or transferred funds (5.3.5)
- Shelter future gains by transferring property at fair market value (5.3.6)
- Shelter future gains by transferring capital assets to your children (5.3.7)
- Transfer shares that will pay capital dividends (5.3.8)
- Contribute to your spouse's RRSP (5.3.9)
- Make spousal RRSP contributions by December 31 (5.3.9)
- In the year your children turn 17, give them funds they can invest (5.3.10)
- Let your children invest their own earnings (5.3.11)
- Claim baby-sitting wages paid to your adult children as child care expenses (5.3.13)

"Income splitting" is a term used to describe strategies to save taxes by shifting income from the hands of a family member in a higher tax bracket to the hands of a second family member in a lower tax bracket so that the same income is taxed at a lower rate of tax—or not at all if the second family member's income is low enough. In this chapter, we discuss the tax rules that are in place to prevent many forms of income splitting and point out some of the income splitting opportunities that remain available.

5.1   Why income splitting?

The Canadian tax system uses progressive tax rates, whereby the marginal rate of tax (tax on additional income) increases as taxable income increases.

The marginal rate of tax varies from province to province, but is *approximately*:

- 27% on income up to $29,590
- 41% on income from $29,590 to $59,180
- 50% on income over $59,180.

As you can see, the tax payable on two $30,000 incomes will be significantly less than that on one $60,000 income—about $4,500 less, in fact. Taxpayers, therefore, have an incentive to "split" income between, for example, a high-income earner and a non-working spouse or children.

The federal *Income Tax Act* contains a number of measures to prevent the most obvious kinds of income splitting (similar rules apply for Québec purposes). However, some opportunities are available. We'll review the rules, so you understand the context in which to plan, together with a discussion of the planning opportunities that remain.

Note that most of this chapter will be irrelevant to you if you do not have funds invested and earning income that is subject to tax. One of the best tax planning techniques is to channel extra cash into paying off any non-deductible interest such as your mortgage or credit card balances.

5.2 Rules that prevent income splitting

5.2.1 Indirect payments

The *Income Tax Act* provides that a payment or transfer made "pursuant to the direction of, or with the concurrence of" a taxpayer to some other person is to be included in the taxpayer's income to the extent it would have been if paid to the taxpayer. So, for example, if you arrange for your employer to pay part of your salary to your spouse, the income will still be taxed in your hands and you will not have accomplished anything.

5.2.2 Attribution between spouses

Suppose you earn $90,000 per year and your spouse earns $10,000. Your marginal tax rate (tax on any additional income) is 50% and your spouse's is 27%. Assume you have $10,000 in bonds that generate $1,000 per year in interest and decide to give, or lend, the bonds to your spouse. As a result you hope to pay only $270 tax on the income instead of $500.

This is the kind of transaction that the attribution rules cover. These rules attribute income from property (in our example, the $1,000 of investment income each year) back to the person who transferred or loaned the property.

The attribution rules with respect to spouses provide that where property (including money) is *transferred or loaned, directly or indirectly* by you to your spouse (or a person who has since become your spouse), then all *income* or *loss from the property*, and any *capital gain or loss* on the disposition of the property will be *attributed back* to you. So, in our example, the $1,000 income on the $10,000 investment that you gave to your spouse must be reported on your tax return, not your spouse's—and so will be subject to tax of about $500 rather than about $270. This will be true year after year—as long as you and your spouse remain together, any income from the bonds will be taxed in your hands. If you transfer shares, for example, and your spouse sells the shares at some later time, any capital gain or capital loss relative to *your* original cost must be reported as your capital gain or loss, subject to the usual rules for capital gains (see Chapter 6).

Note that common-law spouses who meet the criteria outlined in 2.2.1 are considered spouses for tax purposes, and are therefore subject to these attribution rules as well.

There is an exception to these attribution rules; an exception that applies as well to the rules we will see later. If you transfer for fair market value consideration (e.g., sell the bonds to your spouse for $10,000 cash) and report the resulting gain, the rule will not apply. (If you realize a loss on the transfer, a special rule deems the loss to be zero. However the denied loss can be added to your spouse's cost for tax purposes.) If the consideration includes indebtedness (e.g., you sell the bonds for a $10,000 promissory note), or if you simply lend funds or property to your spouse, then to avoid the attribution rule you must charge (and, of course, report!) interest on the loan. The interest rate must be at least equal to Revenue Canada's prescribed interest rate at that time (see 8.4) or a commercial rate of interest. For this exception to apply, the interest must actually be *paid* in each year, or by the following January 30. If the January 30 deadline ever passes without the interest being paid, that year's income and *all* future income from the loaned property will be attributed back to the lender.

Example:

On January 1, 1999 you lend $10,000 cash to your spouse, who puts the money in the bank and earns $800 interest over the course of the year.

If you do not charge interest, then the $800 will be attributed back to you and taxed in your hands. Suppose you do wish to charge interest. The minimum rate would have to be either:

- the rate that would apply between two arm's length parties (assume 6% for this example); or
- Revenue Canada's rate at the time the loan was granted (assume 4%).

If your spouse is required to pay interest on the anniversary date of the loan and actually pays you at least $400 in interest by January 30, 2000, then the $800 interest will not be attributed back to you. Your spouse can deduct the interest paid to you and the amount will be taxable to you as interest income.

Revenue Canada's (and Revenu Québec's) prescribed rate, which is set quarterly, is 4% lower for this purpose than the rate that applies to late payments of tax (see 8.4).

5.2.3   Attribution between parents and children

Suppose you lend $10,000 in bonds to your daughter, who is in high school and can earn $1,000 in interest without paying any tax at all.

Where property is transferred or loaned to a child, there will be attribution of income (or loss), but not of capital gains or losses. The attribution rules apply only for years in which the child is still under 18 *at the end* of the year.

Not all children under 18 are caught by the rule. It depends on the child's relationship with the taxpayer who transfers or lends the property. Attribution applies where the taxpayer and the child "do not deal at arm's length", a phrase that is defined to include all persons who are "related" as defined in the *Income Tax Act*. Generally, this will cover one's child, grandchild, great-grandchild (including one's spouse's child, one's child's spouse, etc., where "spouse" includes a common-law spouse as outlined in 2.2.1) or brother or sister (including brother-in-[common]-law and sister-in-[common]-law). This rule also specifically applies to nieces and nephews. For other relationships, it is a "question of fact" whether two taxpayers deal at arm's length.

Although the attribution rule with respect to minors does not apply to capital gains and losses, the transfer of the property to the minor itself will generally be deemed to take place at fair market value. So any capital gain or loss accruing up to the time of the transfer will be triggered immediately in the transferor's hands, and it is only the gain or loss accruing *after* the transfer that when realized will be taxed in the child's hands.

The exceptions that we saw in 5.2.2, where the transferred property is acquired for fair market value or where interest is paid on any indebtedness or loan, also apply to this attribution rule.

5.2.4   Income splitting tax on certain income received by minor children

The federal government introduced a new "income splitting tax" in 1999 to curtail certain types of income splitting arrangements with minor children for 2000 and later years. The proposed tax will neutralize the benefits of certain arrangements, including some plans involving the use of family trusts (see 20.4.4), by subjecting certain types of dividend, partnership or trust income received by, or used for the benefit of, minor children to tax at the top marginal tax rate, instead of the lower rate that would usually apply on income received by a minor child.

The types of income that are subject to the new tax include:

- taxable dividends and other shareholder benefits on private Canadian and foreign company shares (received directly by the minor or through a trust or partnership); and

- income from a partnership or trust derived by the partnership or trust from the business of providing goods or services to a business carried on by a relative of the minor or a business in which the relative participates.

Parents will be jointly and severally liable for the tax if they were active in the business from which the income was derived. The only deductions allowed against income subject to the tax are the dividend tax credit and foreign tax credit.

The new tax will not apply to income earned by minors from property acquired on the death of their parent or income earned by minors who have no parent resident in Canada for tax purposes in the year.

> **Assess the impact of the new income splitting tax on your tax planning arrangements.**

Unfortunately, if you have an existing income splitting arrangement affected by the proposals, you may have to pay more tax in 2000 and later years than you did before. This will also be true for trusts that receive any of the above types of income and allocate that income to, or use the income for the benefit of, beneficiaries who are minors.

But don't be in a rush to amend existing arrangements affected by the proposals. Since the new tax does not take effect until 2000, income paid to beneficiaries under age 18 throughout 1999 will be taxed at lower rates. Also bear in mind that the new rules do not apply if a trust's beneficiary is your spouse or child age 18 or older, so income splitting can still be accomplished by allocating the above types of income to older family members.

This new tax is not yet law and aspects of the rules may change before they are enacted. Contact your tax adviser for an update on the status of the proposals or help in minimizing their effect on existing family trust structures.

5.2.5   Attribution on loans to adult family members

One further rule applies to loans (but not transfers) of property to other persons with whom the taxpayer does not deal at arm's length—such as, for example, one's children who are over 18, or one's in-laws or grandparents. If one of the main reasons for the loan was to achieve income splitting and thereby reduce taxes, the income will be attributed back to the lender. So if you lend $10,000 to your adult son who is in university, and the purpose is to allow him to earn the $1,000 interest and pay little or no tax on it (rather than, say, to allow him to use the $10,000 to pay for his tuition), the $1,000 of interest will be attributed back to you. The exception where interest is charged and paid, as outlined in 5.2.2, applies in this case.

5.2.6 Special anti-avoidance rules

If you are creative and devious enough, you may have thought of some possible ways around the rules we have just described. Don't bother. The federal and Québec tax laws contain a number of special rules designed to thwart the loopholes that creative tax planners exploited in years past. We will summarize them only briefly; basically, anything you can think of has probably been thought of before.

Substituted property. If property is substituted for transferred or loaned property, the attribution rules will apply to income or capital gains from the substituted property, and so on *ad infinitum* (to the extent that attribution would have applied to income from the original property). So if you give $10,000 in bonds to your spouse, who then sells them and buys $10,000 in stocks, any dividends and capital gains on the stocks will be attributed back to you.

Transfers to a trust or corporation. In general, transfers to a trust will result in the same application of the attribution rules as if the transfers were made directly to the beneficiaries of the trust. Transfers to a corporation which result in a benefit to a "designated person" (spouse or related minor children, using the same definition we saw in 5.2.3) are also caught in most cases. So, for example, if you and your spouse each own half the shares in a corporation, and you give $10,000 to the corporation so that your spouse will benefit, you will be taxed as though you had received interest from the corporation. This attribution rule does not apply where the corporation is a "small business corporation" (see 6.3.2).

Back-to-back loans and transfers. If you lend or transfer property to a third party, who then lends or transfers it to a "designated person" (your spouse or related minor children), it will be treated as though you had lent or transferred the property directly.

Guarantees. If you arrange for a third party (e.g., a bank) to lend funds to a "designated person" on the strength of your guarantee, it will be treated as though you had lent the funds directly.

Repayment of existing loan. If you lend funds to a "designated person", and they use the funds to pay off another loan that they used to buy property, your loan will effectively be treated as if it had been used to buy that property. (This is the flip side of the "substituted property" case covered above.) So, for example, if your spouse borrows $10,000 to invest in bonds, and you then lend your spouse $10,000 which is used to pay off that loan, the interest from the bonds will be attributed back to you.

Reverse attribution. The attribution rules can be ignored if you try to use them to turn the tables on Revenue Canada and have them apply in the opposite direction from that intended.

> **Beware of the general anti-avoidance rule.**

General anti-avoidance rule. The Act provides a general anti-avoidance rule ("GAAR"), applicable to all transactions. If you come up with a way of avoiding the attribution rules that is not caught by the existing rules but is a misuse or abuse of the *Income Tax Act*, it may be caught by GAAR.

5.3   Income splitting opportunities

In this section we discuss the planning opportunities available to achieve income splitting. For many of these to work, you need to keep careful documentation. Separate bank accounts for spouses will allow you to trace each one's funds properly. (Under provincial family law, this will not normally affect either spouse's rights to the family's funds on marriage breakdown.)

5.3.1   Increasing the lower-income spouse's investment base

> **The higher-income spouse should pay household expenses.**

The simplest technique is to make sure that daily living expenses (groceries, mortgage or rent payments, credit card bills, etc.) are paid by the higher-income spouse. This will allow the lower-income spouse to maintain a larger investment base for earning future income that is taxed at a low rate.

> **Pay your spouse's tax bills with your own funds.**

Another way to effectively transfer funds is for you to directly pay your spouse's income tax liability—both in April and any instalments that are due during the year. Simply make sure that the cheque paying your spouse's taxes is drawn on your own account. Since the amount you pay goes directly to the government and is not invested by your spouse, there is no property from which income can be attributed. The result is that any funds your spouse would otherwise use to pay income taxes can be invested without the income being attributed back to you.

> **Pay the interest on your spouse's investment loans.**

If your spouse has taken out an investment loan from a third party, consider providing him or her with the funds to pay the interest. There will be no attribution provided you do not pay any principal on account of the spousal loan. (Since the amount you pay is not actually invested by your spouse, there is no property from which income can be attributed.) The interest payment will be deductible on your spouse's tax return. This technique will preserve your spouse's assets and thereby increase his or her investment income.

5.3.2 Employing your spouse and children

> **Pay a salary or consulting fee to your spouse and/or children.**

If you carry on a business, either personally or through a corporation, consider paying a salary to your spouse and/or children. The salary must be "reasonable" in light of the services they perform for the business. Such services might include bookkeeping, filing, other administrative work, business development planning and acting as a director of the corporation. Revenue Canada and Revenu Québec auditors are usually fairly flexible in interpreting what constitutes a "reasonable" salary, provided services are genuinely being provided.

The impact of payroll taxes, Canada Pension Plan contributions and Employment Insurance premiums should be weighed against any potential tax savings expected from implementing this strategy.

Consider also whether your spouse can provide services on a contract (consulting) basis rather than as an employee. This would allow your spouse the advantages of self-employment income (see Chapter 10), including writing off expenses. This is an aggressive tactic and should only be implemented with appropriate professional advice.

Another possibility is to bring your spouse into partnership with you. Taxation of partnerships is discussed in 10.3.

5.3.3   Transfers of business assets

> **Think about loaning business assets to your spouse or child.**

The attribution rules, as we have noted, apply to income from *property*—such as interest, dividends, rent and royalties. They do not, however, apply to income earned from a *business*. So if you can transfer or lend business assets in such a way that your spouse or child carries on business on a regular and continuous basis to earn income from business rather than from property, there will be no attribution. Such a step should only be undertaken with proper professional advice, to ensure that the legal steps required to effect the transfer are properly completed and that the possibility of the general anti-avoidance rule applying is minimized.

Note that this generally cannot be done for a passive interest in a partnership (including an interest in a limited partnership). Income from the partnership's business is technically business income, but it is deemed to be property income for purposes of the attribution rules unless the taxpayer is actively engaged in the partnership's business or is carrying on a similar business.

5.3.4   Spousal loans

As we saw in 5.2.2, the attribution rules do not apply where property or funds are loaned and interest is charged at a minimum rate, provided the interest is actually paid. Where assets are expected to produce a return that is well in excess of the minimum rate (the lower of a reasonable commercial rate and the Revenue Canada prescribed rate), it may make sense to lend the funds or assets and charge a rate of interest sufficient to avoid the application of the attribution rules. The excess yield from the assets over the amount of interest charged will then effectively be transferred to the lower-income taxpayer and not attributed back to the lender.

> **Consider making spousal loans when interest rates are rising.**

If interest rates are rising, the current Revenue Canada prescribed rate may be relatively low, since there is a time lag before it is set each quarter. Where such an opportunity arises, consider making a loan to your spouse on which interest is charged, "locking in" at the low prescribed rate, and having your spouse use the funds to invest at current market rates.

5.3.5   Reinvesting attributed income

We have seen that attribution applies to the income from property that is transferred or loaned. But what about the income from that income (secondary income)? Suppose you give $10,000 to your spouse, who earns $1,000 in interest in the first year, and the $1,000 is attributed back to you. In the second year, your spouse invests the $1,000 as well as the $10,000, and the $1,000 generates a further $100 in interest.

> Have your spouse or child earn income on income from lent or transferred funds.

This "secondary income" is not attributed back to you, as it is not income from the property that was transferred. It is thus taxed in your spouse's hands. Over time, a significant stream of such secondary income can be built up. However, accurate records must be maintained. You may wish to have your spouse keep two bank accounts, one for the income that is attributed back to you and one into which all income from the first account is deposited. Only the income from the first account would be reported on your return.

5.3.6   Transfers for fair market value

> Shelter future gains by transferring property at fair market value.

As we have seen, the attribution rules also do not apply where property is transferred in exchange for consideration equal to the property's fair market value. (Where the consideration includes indebtedness, such as a promissory note, interest must be charged as outlined above.) A transfer at fair market value may be beneficial where the assets are expected to produce a high yield or to increase in value in the future.

5.3.7   Transferring capital property to children

> Shelter future gains by transferring capital assets to your children.

As we saw in 5.2.3, the attribution rules with respect to minor children do not apply to capital gains. If you have assets that are expected to increase substantially in value (such as shares of a corporation), consider transferring them to your children or to a trust for your children. Any dividends will be attributed back to you as long as your children are under 18 at the end of the year in which the dividend is paid, but capital gains on sale of the assets will not be.

For example, suppose you own shares in your private business corporation. You invested $10,000 originally, and they are now worth $20,000. But you expect the corporation to do well over the coming years. If you give the shares to your children, you will be deemed to have disposed of them at $20,000, but the capital gain may be shielded by the $500,000 capital gains exemption (see 6.4.1). If, a few years later, your children sell the shares for $100,000, the $80,000 capital gain will be taxed in their hands, not yours, and possibly taxed at a lower marginal rate (or no tax if the capital gains exemption is used).

Other assets that might be appropriate for transfer to children are those which will normally generate capital gains but not income. Examples include jewellery, art and shares in speculative public companies.

Transfers to children should be done with proper professional advice. In some provinces there is a question as to whether minors can legally own property such as shares. You may need to set up a trust for this purpose.

5.3.8   Payment of capital dividends

Normally, dividends that are paid on shares you transfer to your spouse or minor children will be attributed back to you. However, the tax system provides for "capital dividends", which are always tax-free. Such dividends include a distribution of the untaxed 1/4 of a corporation's capital gains. (For an example, see 13.2.4.)

> **Transfer shares that will pay capital dividends.**

If you transfer shares of a corporation, and the shares subsequently pay capital dividends, there will be no attribution of the income because it is not taxed in anyone's hands in the first place. As well, any income earned from reinvesting the dividends will not be attributed. This technique can work well for shares of private holding companies, but must be undertaken with proper professional advice to minimize the application of various anti-avoidance rules which could turn the dividends into taxable dividends.

5.3.9   Spousal RRSP

A contribution to your spouse's RRSP, as we saw in 3.3.1, is specifically allowed for federal and Québec tax purposes. When the funds are turned into an annuity or RRIF on retirement, there will be no attribution of the income back to you.

Contribute to your spouse's RRSP.

A further technique can be used at any time before retirement. Contributions to your spouse's RRSP, if withdrawn by your spouse, are taxed back in your hands to the extent you have made any spousal contributions in the year of withdrawal or in the two previous years. This means that you can split income, provided you can wait 24 to 36 months and not make spousal contributions in the meantime. It also means foregoing the benefits of leaving the funds to grow tax-free in the RRSP (see 3.1.5).

Example:

On December 31, 1999 you contribute $13,500 to an RRSP for your spouse.

This entitles you to a deduction of $13,500 for 1999 (assuming you have adequate contribution room—see 3.1.3—and have made no contributions to your own RRSP for 1999). Any withdrawals of up to $13,500 from your spouse's RRSPs in 2000 or 2001 will be attributed back to you; but on January 1, 2002, your spouse can withdraw the full $13,500, which will be taxed to your spouse as the recipient provided you make no further spousal RRSP contributions in 2000, 2001 or 2002.

Of course, when you contribute to a spousal RRSP you lose your own RRSP contribution room, so the tax advantages of this technique are somewhat limited in scope, but it does achieve income splitting over the long term. You must also consider, however, whether your spouse having a higher income at retirement will affect eligibility for the age credit (see 19.3.4) and will trigger the Old Age Security clawback (see 19.3.2).

Make spousal RRSP contributions by December 31.

Note also that in this example, if you contributed for 1999 on January 1, 2000 rather than December 31, 1999, your spouse would have to wait until January 1, 2003 to withdraw the funds without attribution back to you. Contributions to spousal plans should thus not be put off to January or February, as is often done with one's own contributions.

5.3.10 When your children turn 17

> In the year your children turn 17, give them funds they can invest.

Consider giving your children funds that they can invest. If your child turns 17 in the year you make the gift, the funds can be invested in a one-year (or longer) term deposit or certificate, with the first interest payment being made in the year in which the child turns 18, and no attribution will result. (If the investment is for more than one year with compounding interest, the interest earned must still be reported annually—see 7.2.1.) Do not simply loan the funds without considering the special attribution rule discussed in 5.2.5.

You might also consider a gift of enough funds so that the income earned on the funds will cover the child's university tuition and residence over four (or more) years. Of course, you must be prepared to lose the funds, since they will legally belong to your child and not to you. Consider the use of a trust (with proper legal advice) if this is a concern.

5.3.11 Your children's employment income

> Let your children invest their own earnings.

Consider lending your child, interest-free, an amount equal to what he or she earns over the summer and would otherwise spend. This will allow the child to earn investment income on his or her own earnings, and the investment income will not be attributed back to you.

Suppose you have a daughter who attends university and who earns $10,000 over the summer, and your normal arrangement with her is that she uses her income to pay for her tuition and basic expenses. If you lend her $10,000 interest-free, she can use the funds you lend her to pay her tuition and living expenses, and invest her summer earnings. Since the $10,000 invested represents her own funds, the income earned on that amount will not be attributed back to you and will be taxed at her marginal rate (or not taxed at all if her income is low enough). You could then repeat this process through several years of university, and have your daughter pay back the entire amount of the loan when she graduates, using the funds she has invested from her own earnings. Alternatively, you could lend her less money each year, as she will have her investment income available as an additional source of funds.

5.3.12 Assignment of CPP/QPP benefit payments

You may be able to split income by directing that up to 50% of your Canada or Québec Pension Plan ("CPP/QPP") benefits be paid to your spouse, provided both of you are over 60. If either of you does this, a portion of the other spouse's CPP/QPP is assigned automatically back to the first spouse and the attribution rules will not apply. See 19.3.1 for details.

5.3.13 Paying children over 18 for child care

> **Claim baby-sitting wages paid to your adult children as child care expenses.**

The deduction for child care expenses was discussed in 2.3.2. No deduction is allowed for payments you make to a person related to you who is under 18. Once your older children turn 18, if you are the lower-income spouse you can pay them for child care or baby-sitting services that permit you to earn employment or business income. Your adult child will need to give you a receipt and report the income for tax purposes.

5.4 References

The following publications can be obtained (in person or by telephone request) from your nearest Revenue Canada District Taxation Office. Forms and brochures may also be available from Revenue Canada's Internet site at *www.rc.gc.ca*.

Interpretation Bulletin IT-295R4, "Taxable dividends received after 1987 by a spouse"

Interpretation Bulletin IT-307R3, "Spousal registered retirement savings plans"

Interpretation Bulletin IT-335R, "Indirect payments"

Interpretation Bulletin IT-369R, "Attribution of trust income to settler"

Interpretation Bulletin IT-510, "Transfer and loans of property made after May 22, 1985 to a related minor"

Interpretation Bulletin IT-511R, "Interspousal and certain other transfers and loans of property"

Form T2205, "Calculation of amounts from a spousal RRSP or RRIF to be included in 19___ income"

Capital gains and losses

- Classify your gains as capital gains and your losses as business losses, where possible (6.1)
- Make the Canadian securities election to ensure capital treatment for gains on your stock market trades (6.1)
- Consider delaying the sale of all or part of an asset until after year-end to defer capital gains tax (6.2)
- If you have unused net capital losses, carry them back or forward to offset taxable capital gains (6.3.1)
- Carryover unused "allowable business investment losses" to reduce taxable business income (6.3.2)
- "Purify" your corporation to create qualified small business corporation shares eligible for the $500,000 exemption (6.4.1)
- Plan around your CNIL balance when using the capital gains exemption (6.4.3)
- If you've sold an asset but not received all the proceeds, claim a capital gains reserve (6.5.1)
- Consider changing principal residence ownership to shelter gains on recreation properties (6.5.2)
- Make the election to treat rented-out property as your principal residence (6.5.2)

Capital gains and losses are given special treatment in the federal income tax system. Capital gains are effectively taxed at a lower rate than regular income; and individuals are entitled to an exemption for capital gains on certain kinds of property.

The rules are substantially the same for Québec purposes. In this chapter we'll describe the rules in general and take a look at some of the planning opportunities that are available.

6.1   What is capital?

Before we get into the rules that apply to capital gains and losses, it helps to understand what we mean by "capital". Capital property is property that, if sold, will lead to a capital gain (or capital loss). The alternative is property that, when sold, leads to full income inclusion of any gain as income from business. For example, if you speculate on real estate, and you buy and sell a number of properties, your gains on the sales will probably be business income rather than capital gains.

There are no clear rules defining capital property. The *Income Tax Act's* only comment is to define a "business" as including "an adventure or concern in the nature of trade". The courts have developed guidelines over the years, from which a general picture emerges. If you buy property with the intention of reselling it, and particularly if you sell it quickly and engage in many such transactions, your profit is likely to be considered income from business. If you buy property with the intention of earning income (e.g., rent or dividends) from it, and particularly if this is an isolated transaction and you hold the property for a long time, any gain on a sale is likely to be a capital gain.

> **Classify your gains as capital gains and your losses as business losses, where possible.**

As we'll see in 6.2, most capital gains are only three-quarters taxed (and gains on certain small business shares and farm property are eligible for the $500,000 capital gains exemption—see 6.4), so it is therefore much better to have capital gains than regular income. On the other hand, capital losses are of limited use since they can only be used to offset capital gains (see 6.3), while business losses can be deducted against other income.

To the extent possible within the law, therefore, you should try to classify your gains as capital gains and your losses as business losses. For example, if you buy and sell a commodity on the stock market, how you classify the transaction may depend on whether you have a gain or a loss. Where you are near the borderline between income and capital, you have some leeway to classify the transaction as either. Of course, you should be consistent; you could not take two essentially identical trades and call one a capital gain and the other a business loss.

For example, if you are buying and selling real estate and doing well at it, try to gather data for your files that will support your claim to be engaging in capital transactions. For example, you will want to show that you are purchasing properties purely for their investment value as rental properties, and that any sales were not originally planned but were required by a change in circumstances.

Revenue Canada may well reassess you on your classifications, if you are audited. At that point you would have to decide whether to fight the assessment via a Notice of Objection (see 8.6.1), or to accept it and pay the tax that you would have paid in the first place, plus interest. If you are unsure as to whether property you own is capital property or not, you should consult your professional advisers.

> **Make the Canadian securities election to ensure capital treatment for gains on your stock market trades.**

If you wish to ensure that your trades on the stock market will always result in capital gains rather than business income, you may file an "Election on Disposition of Canadian Securities" (federal Form T123 and Québec form TP-250.1-V) with any year's tax return. This will prevent Revenue Canada or Revenu Québec from claiming that you are buying securities for the purpose of selling them and therefore earning business income rather than capital gains.

Once you do so, *all* "Canadian securities" you ever own will be considered to be capital property for the rest of your life. This includes, generally, shares in Canadian corporations, investments in mutual funds, and bonds, debentures or other debt issued by individuals or corporations resident in Canada (except a corporation related to you). Certain taxpayers, such as traders and dealers, are not allowed to make this election.

The downside of making the election is that you will never be able to claim losses on Canadian securities as business losses in the future. Since this is generally hard to do in respect of shares anyway, this may not be a problem for you. You should consider your entire financial position and possibly obtain professional advice to determine the likely effects of the election.

6.2 Capital gains

Capital gains occur only when property is sold (or deemed to have been disposed of under special rules, which we'll see in 6.5.3 and 6.5.4). So if you own, say, a rental property that has increased in value tenfold, you do not pay any tax on the increase until you actually sell the property. The capital gain is taxed only in the year of the sale.

The basic calculation of a capital gain is easy to understand: proceeds of disposition (normally the sale price), minus any selling expenses (e.g., real estate commissions), minus the "adjusted cost base", equals the capital gain. In most cases the adjusted cost base is simply your cost of the property, but this figure is "adjusted" in various ways. (For the adjusted cost base of an interest in a partnership, see 10.3.5.) Where you have used the election to trigger part of your capital gains exemption (see 6.4), your adjusted cost base will be higher than the actual cost.

Capital gains are, in effect, taxed at a lower rate than regular income. This is done by including in income only the taxable capital gain, which is three-quarters of the capital gain.

Example:

Alison paid $5,000 (including commission) for shares of the TD Bank in 1994. In 1999, she sells the shares for $6,100, of which her broker keeps $100 as commission.

For 1999, Alison has a capital gain of $1,000. The taxable capital gain is three-quarters, or $750, and this amount is included in her income for tax purposes.

We have mentioned in earlier chapters the marginal rates of tax on ordinary income. With three-quarters taxation of capital gains, the effective rates of tax are approximately:

Income level	Salary income	Capital gain (¾)
$0 — $29,590	27%	20%
$29,591 — $59,180	41%	31%
$59,181 and up	50%	37%

The exact rates vary by province.

If you have very large capital gains, minimum tax may apply—see 7.6.

> **Consider delaying all or part of the sale of an asset until after year-end to defer capital gains tax.**

If you sell an asset after the end of the year, any tax on the capital gain will be payable one year later, giving you the use of the funds for an extra year except to the extent you are required to make quarterly tax instalments (see 8.3.2). A sale on December 31, 1999 will require tax to be paid by April 30, 2000; a sale on January 1, 2000 will require tax to be paid by April 30, 2001.

Note that most stock and bond market transactions normally settle three business days after the trade is entered. (This is standard practice in the brokerage industry and is recognized by Revenue Canada.) Because weekends and public holidays may affect the determination of "business days", if you intend to do any last-minute 1999 trades, consider completing all trades before Christmas and be sure to check the settlement date with your broker.

In some circumstances, you may wish to sell half of an asset at the end of December and the other half at the beginning of January. Doing this will split your capital gain across the two years. This can be beneficial for two reasons. First, you may be able to reduce the marginal rate which applies in both years, by keeping your total taxable income below about $59,000 for each year. Second, you may be able to avoid minimum tax, due to the $40,000 minimum tax exemption available for each year ($25,000 for Québec tax purposes).

6.3   Capital losses

6.3.1   Ordinary capital losses

A capital loss occurs when the capital gain calculation produces a negative amount; that is, the adjusted cost base is greater than the proceeds of disposition minus the selling expenses. Just as capital gains are less heavily taxed than regular income, capital losses are less useful to you than regular (business) losses.

An allowable capital loss is *three-quarters* of a capital loss. This amount can be offset against taxable capital gains. In normal circumstances, if you have no taxable capital gains, the loss *cannot* be used against other income.

Example:

Brent earns an annual salary of $40,000. In October 1999, Brent sells some shares of a mining company, which cost him $2,000 several years before, for $6,000 after commission. In November 1999, he sells some bars of gold he bought in 1984 for $18,000, and receives only $10,000 since the price of gold has come down.

Brent has a $4,000 capital gain on the shares, which is a $3,000 taxable capital gain. He also has an $8,000 capital loss on the gold, which is a $6,000 allowable capital loss. This completely wipes out the taxable capital gain, but the extra $3,000 of allowable capital loss cannot be used to reduce his salary income of $40,000. It can only be used against taxable capital gains of other years, as outlined below.

> **If you have unused net capital losses, carry them back or forward to offset taxable capital gains.**

Allowable capital losses that can't be used in any given year, as in this example, can be carried back and applied against taxable capital gains of any of the previous three years, subject to whether the capital gains exemption was used in that prior year. They can also be carried forward indefinitely; this balance is known as "net capital losses" and can be used against taxable capital gains in any future year.

If you have any net capital losses that cannot be used in the current year, look into whether you can carry them back to any of your three prior years' returns. Revenue Canada and Revenu Québec are required to reopen and reassess your return when you make such a claim. Make sure as well that you keep track of any such losses that you can't carry back, and carry them forward to use in future years.

Before May 23, 1985, up to $2,000 per year of allowable capital losses was allowed to be used against other income (such as employment income). If you disposed of any capital property at a loss before that date, you may still use this $2,000 deduction per year. Your unused pre-May 23, 1985 net capital losses less any capital gains exemption claimed since then is called your "pre-1986 capital loss balance".

6.3.2 Allowable business investment losses

There is an exception to the general rule that allowable capital losses cannot be used against ordinary income. It applies to allowable business investment losses. These arise when there is a loss on shares of, or debt owing by, a small business corporation.

The term "small business corporation" has a very specific meaning in the *Income Tax Act*. It need not, in fact, be small. The corporation must meet a number of tests, which are that it be resident in Canada, a private corporation, not controlled in any manner by non-residents or public corporations, not listed on a Canadian or any of about 25 foreign stock exchanges, and, most importantly, that substantially all (taken by Revenue Canada to mean 90% or more of the value) of its assets be used in an active business carried on primarily in Canada. Shares and debts in such small business corporations can qualify as such assets.

A capital loss on the shares or debt of a small business corporation (including, in some cases, simply determining that the debt has gone bad and will not be repaid) is called a "business investment loss". Three-quarters of this amount, the "allowable business investment loss" ("ABIL"), can be deducted against any other income such as employment income or investment income. However the amount of the ABIL that can be deducted against other income must be reduced by any capital gains exemption claimed in prior years. In addition, if an ABIL is deducted against other income, you must realize an equal amount of taxable capital gains in later years before you can use the capital gains exemption again. The availability of an ABIL is an extra incentive to investment in private Canadian businesses.

Example:

Janet carries on business as the proprietor of a clothing store, from which she nets $50,000 per year in business income. In 1989, Janet invests $10,000 in shares in XYZ Jewellery Inc., a corporation run by her brother which meets the definition of "small business corporation." In December 1999, the corporation goes bankrupt and Janet's shares become worthless.

Janet has a $10,000 business investment loss in 1999, resulting in a $7,500 allowable business investment loss. She can use this against her $50,000 business income, and so will be taxed in 1999 as if she had earned only $42,500.

> **Carry over unused ABILs to reduce taxable business income.**

Allowable business investment losses that can't be fully used (because you have already wiped out all of your income) are given the same treatment as business losses (see 10.4.1). That is, they can be carried back and used to offset income in any of the three previous years (even though you have already filed returns and paid tax for those years), or they can be carried forward and used to offset income in any of the next seven years. Any unused balance remaining after the seventh year is reclassified as an allowable capital loss.

6.4   The capital gains exemption

Every individual (but not a trust or corporation) is entitled to a lifetime $500,000 "capital gains exemption" on certain small business shares and farm property.

A general $100,000 capital gains exemption, which applied to all kinds of property, was eliminated as of February 22, 1994. An election was available to use up your exemption for gains accrued to that date. If you made the election in respect of holdings in flow-through entities, your election created an "exempt capital gains balance"—see 6.4.4.

Technically, under the *Income Tax Act* and on Revenue Canada's forms, the exemption is called the capital gains *deduction*. Where it applies, the taxable capital gain is still included in income for tax purposes (see 6.2), but an offsetting deduction from net income is allowed when computing "taxable income", the last step on the tax return before calculating tax and tax credits (see 2.1.1).

Note that your $500,000 exemption is limited to the *total* gains on both small business shares and family farms (plus any other exemption claimed up to February 22, 1994) over your lifetime. If, for example, you have already claimed an exemption in respect of, say, $420,000 of gain on small business shares, the maximum exemption available to you for farm property would be $80,000.

6.4.1   Qualified small business corporation shares

Up to $500,000 of capital gain on "qualified small business corporation shares" can be exempt.

The meaning of "small business corporation" was discussed in 6.3.2. The definition of "qualified small business corporation share" is very complex. In very general terms:

- substantially all (considered by Revenue Canada to mean 90% or more of the value) of the business' assets must be used for carrying on an active business in Canada or be shares and debt in other small business corporations (or any combination thereof);
- nobody but you or a person "related" to you can have owned the shares for the two years before you sell them; and
- throughout the two-year period, more than 50% of the corporation's assets must have been used principally in an active business carried on in Canada or invested in other small business corporations (or any combination thereof).

Consult your tax advisor for the specific details as they apply to any shares you own.

Example:

Arnold has not used any of his capital gains exemption in the past. He owns all the shares of a corporation. The shares, which are "qualified small business corporation shares", originally cost him $30,000. In 1999, Arnold sells the shares for $230,000.

Arnold's capital gain is $200,000. Three-quarters of the gain, or $150,000, goes into Arnold's income for 1999, but an offsetting capital gains deduction of $150,000 is allowed in computing his "taxable income"—so he pays no extra tax, except possibly for minimum tax (see 7.6). Of his $500,000, Arnold still has $300,000 of capital gains ($225,000 of taxable capital gains) that can be exempt in the future.

As you can see from the example, it doesn't matter whether you think of the exemption as covering $500,000 (in the example, $200,000 plus $300,000) of capital gains, or $375,000 ($150,000 plus $225,000) of taxable capital gains. It comes to the same thing.

> **"Purify" your corporation to create qualified small business corporation shares.**

If you own shares in a small business, and are considering selling them, or transferring them to your children, you should investigate whether the corporation's shares qualify for the $500,000 capital gains exemption. There may be steps you can take to "purify" the corporation so that it meets the criteria discussed above.

It is also possible to transfer the assets of a business which you carry on personally (as a proprietor) into a corporation on a tax-free basis in order to take advantage of the $500,000 exemption. This procedure, known as a "section 85 rollover", requires professional advice, as do other mechanisms for "crystallizing" the exemption (see 13.1).

There is also a special election that lets you take advantage of the exemption for qualified small business corporation shares if the corporation goes public, without having to actually sell the shares. (Once the corporation becomes a public corporation, the shares will no longer qualify for the exemption.)

6.4.2 Qualified farm property

The $500,000 exemption generally applies to family farms and farm quotas that meet certain conditions. In general terms, if you acquired the property before June 18, 1987 and it was used in the business of farming by you or a member of your family either in the year you sell it or in any five previous years, it will be qualified farm property. If you acquired it after June 17, 1987, you normally have to have owned it for at least two years, been engaged in farming on a regular and continuous basis, and have earned more gross income from farming than from other sources. Similar rules also apply to allow the exemption to be claimed for gains realized on the sale of shares of a family farm corporation or an interest in a family farm partnership.

If you own farm property that you are considering selling, you should obtain professional advice to determine whether you are eligible for the $500,000 exemption.

6.4.3 Restrictions on use of the exemption

The *Income Tax Act* provides rules to prevent people from taking what is considered unfair advantage of the capital gains exemption. The exemption is supposed to exempt capital gains from being taxed. If, however, you are able to use the system of capital gains taxation to claim capital-related losses against other income, the rules prevent you from getting the exemption as well. We'll look at the details in this section.

Capital losses deducted against other income

There are two kinds of allowable capital losses that can be written off against ordinary income. These are allowable business investment losses (see 6.3.2) and a much rarer bird, pre-1986 capital losses, which can still be used up at $2,000 per year (see 6.3.1).

If you have either of these kinds of losses, you will lose your capital gains exemption to the extent that the losses are or can be written off against your ordinary income. The idea is that such losses should effectively be netted against your taxable capital gains first. In other words, you cannot both have a gain that is sheltered by the capital gains exemption, and also use certain capital losses against your other income.

Cumulative net investment loss ("CNIL")

As discussed in 7.2.3, interest paid on a loan is deductible if you use the loan to invest in shares. Even though your real reason for buying the shares may be to obtain capital gains, the fact that the shares *could* pay dividends (which are income from property) is generally considered enough to make the interest on the loan deductible as interest on funds borrowed to earn income from property.

Tax policy-makers considered it unfair for people to be able to take out large loans, write off the interest, and use the funds to buy shares which would increase in value, giving them a capital gain which was tax-free due to the capital gains exemption. This kind of "double-dipping" was stopped in 1988.

Your capital gains deduction (normally taken, as we have seen, when calculating your "taxable income") is therefore *reduced* by the amount of your cumulative net investment loss, or CNIL (pronounced "see-nile"). The basic idea is that if you borrow money, buy an investment and the investment goes up in value, you shouldn't be able to get both the capital gains exemption and your interest write-off.

The actual calculation is rather more complicated. Your CNIL is the total of your investment expenses minus all your investment income, cumulative since January 1, 1988. "Investment expenses" includes interest you have deducted, investment counsel fees, partnership losses (except where you are an active partner), losses from rental property, and most tax shelter write-offs. Investment income includes interest, dividends ("grossed-up" by one-quarter as explained in 7.1.2), rental income and income from a partnership where you are not an active partner.

> Example:
>
> Arnold has not used any of his capital gains exemption in the past, but has claimed a total of $10,000 in net investment expenses since 1989, so his CNIL balance is $10,000. He owns all the shares of a corporation. The shares, which are "qualified small business corporation shares", originally cost him $30,000. In 1999, Arnold sells the shares for $230,000.
>
> Arnold's capital gain is $200,000. Three-quarters of the gain, or $150,000, goes into Arnold's income for 1999. Because of his $10,000 CNIL balance, the offsetting capital gains deduction is only $140,000, not $150,000.

In effect, Arnold must "eat through" his CNIL balance and pay tax on the $10,000 before he can start to use his capital gains exemption.

Note that the CNIL limitation applies even though the investment expenses and the capital gain are unrelated. However, taxable capital gains that are actually taxed, because you cannot or do not offset them with your capital gains exemption, effectively reduce the impact of the CNIL balance.

> **Plan around your CNIL balance when using the capital gains exemption.**

Note also that the calculation of the exemption (and CNIL) is done at the *end* of the year. It is therefore possible to realize a capital gain that you think is exempt, but for which you cannot claim the exemption because you create a CNIL balance later on in the same year. So if you have a CNIL balance, consider reducing or eliminating it before the end of the year. This can be done by increasing your investment income. For example, if you are the owner-manager of an incorporated business (see Chapter 13), you may be able to reduce your salary and increase your dividends from the corporation to use up your CNIL balance. There may also be situations where you can advance interest receipts to before the end of the year, or defer deductible interest payments until after December 31, to reduce your CNIL.

6.4.4 The $100,000 exemption and exempt capital gains balance

Until 1994, a general $100,000 exemption was available for capital gains on any property (except for investment real estate acquired after February 1992). The federal budget eliminated the regular exemption for gains after that date. An election was available for gains accrued to February 22, 1994. To the extent you would otherwise have been able to claim the exemption, you could have *elected* to treat any property as if you had sold it on February 22, 1994 at a particular price (up to the property's fair market value) and immediately bought it back at the same price. (The exemption was also eliminated for Québec tax purposes and a virtually identical election was introduced.)

Flow-through entities—mutual funds and others

Certain investments can have capital gains calculated at the investment level and then flowed through to you so that you report the capital gain on your personal income tax return. These are called "flow-through entities". They include mutual funds (see 7.1.6), segregated funds (similar to mutual funds, but offered through life insurers), partnerships (see 10.3.3), investment corporations, mortgage investment corporations, employee profit sharing plans and certain other special trusts.

You can have capital gains on flow-through entities in two ways. First, gains incurred in the entity are flowed through to you. Second, you can sell your interest in the entity.

If you made the election in 1994 to trigger your capital gains exemption in respect of holdings in flow-through entities, the effect is very different than for other property. Rather than increasing your cost base in the investment, your election created an "exempt capital gains balance" that you can use until the year 2004 to reduce any capital gain resulting from either the sale of the property or capital gains flowed through to you. Thus, you can shield "flow-through" gains in future years, even though you may not have sold the investment.

Note that you will have to track the "exempt capital gains balance" for each mutual fund or other investment on which you make the election. You cannot use the balance from one fund to shield capital gains distributions from another fund.

If you sell all of the units of a property, any remaining exempt capital gains balance is added to the adjusted cost base of the last units of the flow-through entity to be sold, which will enable you to realize a capital loss at that time. If you still own the units of the flow-through entity at the end of 2004, any remaining exempt capital gains balance is added to the cost base of the units.

6.5   Special cases

6.5.1   Reserves

> **If you've sold an asset but not received all of the proceeds, claim a capital gains reserve.**

If you sell a property for a capital gain but do not receive all of the proceeds right away, you may be able to claim a reserve, to defer recognition of the gain for tax purposes.

Suppose, for example, you sell a house you have been renting out. The house cost you $100,000 and you sell it for $300,000. But you take back a mortgage for $150,000. You can normally claim a reserve on the capital gain, reflecting the fraction of the purchase price that you haven't yet received. In this case, since you haven't received half of the purchase price, you would only have to recognize half of the gain in the year of sale.

Under the reserve rules, you must recognize at least 1/5 of the gain each year (cumulatively), so that the entire capital gain must be accounted for by the fourth year after the year of sale.

Claiming a reserve might not be beneficial where you may be in a higher tax bracket in later years.

6.5.2   Principal residence

As you probably know, a gain on selling your home is normally completely exempt from taxation. The exemption is based on the definition of "principal residence". This term includes, among other things, a house, a condominium and a share in a co-operative housing corporation. It also includes the land around the house, but normally only up to 1/2 hectare (about 1.2 acres).

You, or your spouse or child, must have "ordinarily inhabited" the residence for it to qualify, so you can't use the exemption on property you rent out without ever having lived in it, or for vacant land. However, it need not have been your "principal" residence in a literal sense. It can be a cottage, for example.

Since 1982, each family unit is limited to one "principal residence" at a time. For this purpose, the family unit means you, your spouse (including a common-law spouse as outlined in 2.2.1), and any unmarried children under 18. So if you designate your house as your principal residence for a period of several years, your spouse cannot also designate your cottage as a principal residence over the same period. (The designation is only made when you file your tax return for the year in which you sell the property, so you can decide at that point which property to claim the exemption on.)

> Consider changing principal residence ownership to shelter gains on recreation properties.

Where you and your spouse or another member of your family unit have owned two residences (such as a regular home and a summer cottage) since before 1982, it may be possible to structure your holdings so that the pre-1982 portion of the capital gain on the second residence will be exempt. That is because each taxpayer was entitled to a principal residence exemption before 1982—the "family unit" concept wasn't yet in place. In such a case, the gain accruing to December 31, 1981 may continue to be exempt. Consult a professional advisor on this matter.

If you have adult children, consider giving them the ownership of a second residence. If you own your house and your 19-year-old son owns the cottage, he can designate it as his principal residence when he sells it. However, at the time you transfer it to him you will have to recognize any increase in value since you purchased it (subject to a reduction if you made an election to use your capital gains exemption on it). You should also be sure you are satisfied with the *legal* effect of what you are doing—giving away your cottage—before you embark on such a transaction for tax purposes.

> ## Make the election to treat rented-out property as your principal residence.

An exemption is also available in some cases where you rent the property out, either before or after you use it as your own residence. If you move out of your home and rent it out, you can continue to designate it as your residence for up to four years (provided you do not claim any other property as your principal residence and you file a special election with your tax return for the year in which you begin to rent the property). If you move due to relocation of your or your spouse's employment, the four-year period can normally be extended indefinitely, provided you move back to the home upon leaving that employment.

If you acquire property and rent it out, and then move in at some later date, you can file a special election with your tax return for the year in which you move in, to defer the capital gain that would normally apply when you change the property from income-earning to personal-use. If you do this, you may be able to get an exemption for four years during which you rented the property.

6.5.3 Death

When you die, you are generally deemed for tax purposes to have sold your capital property for its current fair market value, thus triggering a capital gain on all of the increase in value that has accrued since you purchased it. This prevents gains from accruing indefinitely without ever being taxed. In fact, although there are no estate taxes or succession duties in Canada, the taxation of accrued capital gains on death is thought by some to be a close equivalent.

Example:

Morris bought shares in Bell Canada in 1979. When he dies in November 1999, the shares are worth $20,000 more than he paid for them (after all commissions).

Morris will be deemed to have sold the shares before his death for a capital gain of $20,000, three-quarters of which ($15,000) will be included in his income for the year of death.

Where property is left to your spouse, the gain will be put off until your spouse's death, at which point the entire capital gain will be taxed in your spouse's hands. A trust set up for your spouse can also be used to defer the gain, if certain conditions are met. However, your executor in both situations may elect to have this rule not apply to one or more of your properties, so as to use up your unused net capital losses and give your spouse a higher cost base for the assets.

Any net capital losses carried forward from previous years, which as we saw in 6.3.1 can normally be used only against capital gains, can be used against all other income for the year of death and for the immediately preceding year, except to the extent the capital gains exemption has been claimed.

For further details on the treatment of capital gains on death, see 20.1.2.

6.5.4 Other rules

Pre-1972 property—If you have property that you have owned since before 1972, when capital gains were not taxed at all, only the gain accruing since the end of 1971 will be taxed. For publicly-traded shares, valuation is easy; for real estate and shares in private businesses, valuation as of December 31, 1971 may be difficult to accomplish. When you report such a gain, you will need to estimate the value of the property on that date, and use that as the cost of the property (assuming it is higher than your actual cost).

Non-arm's length transfers—When you give or sell property to a member of your family, you are normally deemed to have received fair market value for it, triggering recognition of any accrued capital gain (or loss) for tax purposes. However, if you transfer property to your spouse, it is normally deemed to have been sold at your cost unless you elect to realize a gain. This rule also applies to common-law spouses who meet the criteria outlined in 2.2.1.

Personal-use property—No capital loss is available on personal-use property, except for "listed personal property" (jewellery, works of art, stamps, coins and rare books) losses which can be used only against listed personal property gains. As well, capital gains on personal-use property only apply to the extent the sales price exceeds $1,000.

If you change a property from personal use to income-earning use, you are normally deemed to have sold it at its fair market value, requiring you to recognize for tax purposes any accrued capital gain.

Options—Special rules apply to determine capital gains where you purchase or grant options (e.g., on the stock market).

Superficial loss—If you sell property (e.g., shares) to trigger a capital loss, and you or your spouse or a corporation controlled by either of you acquire identical property within 30 days before or after your sale, the capital loss will be called a "superficial loss" and ignored for tax purposes. The denied loss will be added to the cost of the identical property.

Insurance or expropriation proceeds—If property of yours is lost or destroyed, or expropriated, any insurance settlement or expropriation payment is considered to be proceeds of disposition, for purposes of the calculation described in 6.2.

6.6 References

The following publications can be obtained (in person or by telephone request) from your nearest Revenue Canada District Taxation Office. Forms and brochures may also be available from Revenue Canada's Internet site at *www.rc.gc.ca.*

Interpretation Bulletin IT-78, "Capital property owned on December 31, 1971—Identical properties"

Interpretation Bulletin IT-84, "Capital property owned on December 31, 1971—Median rule (tax-free zone)"

Interpretation Bulletin IT-107, "Costs of disposition of capital property affected by the median rule"

Interpretation Bulletin IT-120R4, "Principal residence"

Interpretation Bulletin IT-133, "Stock exchange transactions—Date of disposition of shares"

Interpretation Bulletin IT-170R, "Sale of property—When included in income computation"

Interpretation Bulletin IT-218R, "Profits, capital gains and losses from the sale of real estate, including farm land and inherited land and conversion of real estate from capital property to inventory and vice versa"

Interpretation Bulletin IT-232R3, "Losses—Their deductibility in the loss year or in other years"

Interpretation Bulletin IT-236R3, "Reserves—Disposition of capital property"

Interpretation Bulletin IT-387R2, "Meaning of identical properties"

Interpretation Bulletin IT-456R, "Capital property—Some adjustments to cost base"

Interpretation Bulletin IT-459, "Adventure or concern in the nature of trade"

Interpretation Bulletin IT-479R, "Transactions in securities"

Interpretation Bulletin IT-484R2, "Business investment losses"

"Capital Gains Election Package"

"Capital Gains Tax Guide"

Form T123, "Election on disposition of Canadian securities"

Form T664, "Election to report a capital gain on property owned at the end of February 22, 1994"

Form T657, "Calculation of capital gains deduction for 19___ on all capital property"

Form T936, "Calculation of cumulative net investment loss to December 31, 19___ "

Form T2091 (IND), "Designation of principal residence"

Form T2091 (IND)-WS, "Principal residence worksheet for 19___"

7

Investments and tax shelters

- Consider acquiring preferred shares to enhance after-tax yield (7.1.2)
- If you're the higher-income spouse, consider electing to report your spouse's dividend income on your own return (7.1.7)
- Defer tax by acquiring investments that mature shortly after year-end (7.2.1)
- Structure your investments to make interest deductible (7.2.3)
- Consider investing in tax shelters—but don't let tax write-offs drive your decision (7.4)
- Before investing in a tax shelter, obtain its Identification Number (7.4.1)
- Look into investing in LSVCC shares—a new $3,500 investment may only cost you $700 after tax (7.4.3)
- Consider the merits of acquiring an exempt life insurance contract (7.5)
- Have 35¢ regular income for each $1 in exempt capital gains to avoid minimum tax (7.6.3)
- Continue generating interest expense and business losses to offset potential minimum tax (7.6.3)
- Watch out for "tainted" tax shelter deductions (7.6.3)

In this chapter we look at how investment income is taxed, how interest expense can be written off, and a few types of tax shelters, along with a number of tax planning ideas that you should keep in mind. For advice on developing an appropriate investment strategy, see 1.1.5.

7.1   Dividends

7.1.1   What is a dividend?

A dividend is a distribution of profits to the shareholders (owners) of a corporation. A corporation may have many classes of shares. Preferred shares are shares on which dividends must generally be paid first, before dividends can be paid on a corporation's common shares.

Preferred shares typically pay a fixed annual or quarterly dividend. In some ways, they are similar to bonds or other debt, since the return is a fixed percentage. However, in certain situations a corporation may not be *required* to pay dividends on its preferred shares as long as it does not pay dividends on its common shares. If the corporation suffers losses, its board of directors may well decide not to pay dividends on preferred shares.

From a tax point of view, for individuals, preferred shares are identical to common shares (which typically pay dividends that bear some relationship to the corporation's profits).

7.1.2　How is a dividend taxed?

Dividends received by individuals from Canadian corporations are taxed in a rather peculiar manner, designed to reflect the fact that the corporation paying the dividend has already paid tax on its profits. The amount included in the individual's income is "grossed-up" to reflect the total amount of pre-tax income that the corporation is presumed to have earned. The individual then receives a credit to offset the tax the corporation is presumed to have paid (at about 20%). In no case, however, is the *actual* income earned or tax paid by the corporation taken into account.

Canadian dividends received are grossed-up by one-quarter. That is, you add 25% to the amount received, and show the total as income from dividends on your tax return. The offsetting federal dividend tax credit is then two-thirds of the amount of the gross-up—two-thirds of that 25%, or, if you like, 13.33% of the total you report as dividend income. For most provinces, this dividend tax credit is then augmented by about half as much again, since the provincial tax is calculated on a reduced federal tax. In Québec a separate dividend tax credit is available for 9.85% of the grossed-up dividend (rising to 10.83% in 2000). (In the example below, we use 50% as the provincial tax rate for illustrative purposes.)

Example:

Melissa earns $35,000 per year. She also owns shares in Canadian Inc., which pay her a dividend of $1,000 in 1999.

Melissa's income for 1999 will be $35,000, plus the $1,000 dividend, plus a gross-up of one-quarter of the dividend, or $250. Her tax will be calculated on this income of $36,250. From the tax, she will deduct her regular credits (see Chapter 2) and a dividend tax credit of $166.67 (two-thirds of the $250 gross-up). When her provincial tax is calculated at 50% of federal tax, her tax will be reduced by a further $83.33, since the federal tax has been reduced by the credit. Melissa's $1,000 dividend is therefore taxed at about 41% of $1,250, but then reduced by a total of about $250 in dividend tax credit and reduced provincial tax. The net result is that the dividend is taxed at about 25% instead of 41%.

(See 13.2.1 for more detail on the dividend tax credit from the perspective of the corporation.) The effect of the dividend tax credit is to tax dividends at *approximately* the following rates:

Income level	Salary income	Dividend income
$0 – $29,590	27%	7%
$29,591 – $59,180	41%	25%
$59,181 and up	50%	33%

The exact numbers vary by province. Remember that these numbers apply only to dividends from Canadian corporations. Dividends on foreign corporations are taxed as ordinary income.

> **Consider acquiring preferred shares to enhance your after-tax yield.**

Since preferred shares pay dividends rather than interest (which is taxed like regular income, as we'll see in 7.2), preferred shares may offer a better after-tax rate of return than many interest-earning investments while still coming close to a guaranteed yield. While the yield is never completely guaranteed, many major public companies will continue to meet preferred share dividend expectations even when they suffer losses.

The yields on preferred shares usually reflect the fact that dividends are less heavily taxed than interest (as well as the fact that dividend payments are not deductible to the corporation). If current interest rates are around 8%, preferred share yields may well be around 6%. You will have to monitor preferred share prices on the market to find the best yields.

7.1.3   Stock dividends

A corporation will sometimes pay a stock dividend by issuing new shares to pay the dividend rather than giving you cash. In such a case, the gross-up and dividend tax credit still apply, and you must pay tax on the stock dividend even though you have received no cash. The amount of the dividend on which the gross-up is calculated is the increase in the paid-up capital resulting from the issue of new shares.

7.1.4   Capital dividends

You may also receive capital dividends from private corporations. They are completely tax-free (see 5.3.8). A capital dividend is generally a distribution of the untaxed one-quarter of capital gains. As we saw in 6.2, that fraction of the capital gain is not taxed at all. The capital dividend mechanism is used to distribute the untaxed portion without any tax consequences to the shareholder. (For an example, see 13.2.4.)

7.1.5 Dividends received by a corporation

Intercorporate dividends are normally tax-free. The assumption is that once a corporation has paid tax on its income, its profits can be distributed through a chain of holding corporations with no further tax consequences until an individual receives a dividend at the end of the chain. However, a special refundable tax—"Part IV tax"—can apply to intercorporate dividends in some circumstances, including most dividends received on investments in public corporations. The Part IV tax is 33 1/3%.

7.1.6 Mutual funds

Mutual funds are pools of assets that are invested by professional managers, either in general investments or in a particular sector (such as real estate or natural resources). A mutual fund corporation will pay dividends, but may designate all or a portion of the dividends as "capital gains dividends", to reflect capital gains earned by the mutual fund. From the taxpayer's point of view, such dividends are treated as capital gains rather than dividends, and subject to the usual capital gains treatment discussed in Chapter 6.

If you own any mutual funds that qualify as "flow-through entities", you may have made the election to trigger the $100,000 capital gains exemption in respect of them and thereby created an exempt capital gains balance—see 6.4.4.

7.1.7 Election to transfer dividends from spouse

Since the dividend tax credit is a credit against tax owing, it is worthless if there is no tax to pay. If your spouse's income is very low, and you claim a credit for your spouse as a dependant (see 2.2.1), a relatively small amount of dividend income, when grossed-up by 25%, can take your spouse over the $538 income threshold and thereby reduce your spousal tax credit. At the same time, since your spouse does not pay any tax, the dividend tax credit is of no use.

> If you're the higher-income spouse, consider electing to report your spouse's dividend income on your own return.

In such a case, you may elect to report all of your spouse's dividend income on your own tax return. While this may result in the income being taxed at a higher rate, it will avoid the erosion of the spousal tax credit. You will have to calculate tax both ways to see which is better. This election is done by including the dividends directly on Schedule 5 (Investment income) on your tax return, not Schedule 2 (Amounts transferred from spouse). If you live in Québec, you can make the same election for Québec tax purposes.

7.2 Interest income

Interest income is taxed at the same rates as employment or business income.

7.2.1 Accruing interest

Suppose you acquire a seven-year term deposit for $1,000 which will return $1,700 after seven years. When do you report the $700 in interest?

The answer depends on when you acquired the investment. If you bought it in 1990 or later, you must declare, each year, the interest accrued to the anniversary date of when you acquired it. Your financial institution should issue you a T5 slip showing the interest accruing on all such long-term investments.

The accrual rules apply to almost all kinds of investments, including stripped bonds (see 7.2.2 below), Canada Savings Bonds, and mortgages or loans to relatives on which interest is allowed to accrue.

Example:

In 1994, Christine lent $10,000 to her cousin, who is attending university and needed the funds for tuition and residence. Her cousin agreed in writing to pay 10% annual interest (not compounded) on the loan, but that he will not pay back the loan or the interest until after he has graduated and secures a job.

Christine is required to report and pay tax on $1,000 of accrued interest income each year beginning in 1995. If in 1999 her cousin pays her $15,000 to cover the loan and all interest, she will only report $1,000 as income in 1999, since she will have already reported $4,000 over the previous four years.

> **Defer tax by acquiring investments that mature shortly after year-end.**

As a general deferral technique, acquire investments that mature shortly after year-end rather than before. For example, if you are investing in T-Bills on July 15, and you can choose between maturity dates of December 29 and January 2, then you should choose January 2 if all else is equal. That way you will defer reporting and paying tax on the income by one year. Of course, tax considerations should not override normal investment considerations, such as the available rates of return and the question of when you will need access to the funds.

7.2.2 Strip bonds and clipped coupons

Strip bonds are long-term government or government-backed (e.g., provincial hydro) bonds which pay interest when their coupons are cashed in. A typical bond might have a 20-year term, have a face value of $100,000 and come with coupons paying $5,000 in interest, cashable every six months. At the end of the 20 years one simply redeems the bond for $100,000.

Brokerage firms often acquire such bonds and split up the bond and its coupons, selling them separately. The $100,000 bond maturing in 20 years, in our example, might be sold for $15,000, while the forty $5,000 coupons would be sold at prices reflecting the length of time until their maturity.

For tax purposes, the difference between the discounted price of the bond (or coupon) and the amount you receive when it is redeemed is considered to be interest. Because of the annual (or three-year, if bought before 1990) accrual rule, such bonds generally are unattractive to many taxpayers—you have to pay tax annually on interest that you will not receive for some time. However, they can be excellent investments for self-directed RRSPs and other tax-deferred plans (see Chapter 3).

One should be cautious when acquiring strip bonds or clipped coupons—or, for that matter, any long-term bond. If you need to sell them before they mature, you will find that their value fluctuates considerably due to trends in interest rates. If interest rates in general have gone up, the resale value of your bond or coupon will likely have gone down.

7.2.3 Deductibility of interest expense

As a general principle, interest is deductible for tax purposes as long as the loan was used for the purpose of earning income from a business or property. So, if you borrow money to buy shares on the stock market, or to invest in a business, the interest you pay is generally deductible. Such expenses are also called carrying charges.

On the other hand, if you buy an investment with a fixed interest rate, you cannot deduct interest on your loan beyond the rate that your investment pays. For example, if you borrow at 15% and lend the funds to a relative at 10%, you can only deduct 10% interest on your loan. Where the investment is in preferred shares, it is the grossed-up amount of the dividend (see 7.1.2) which determines the amount of interest that can be deducted. If the dividend rate is 8%, being effectively 10% when grossed-up by 25%, then once again only the first 10% of interest on the loan can be deducted.

Interest is not deductible where the loan was taken out for some purpose other than to earn income subject to tax. Examples include:

- home mortgage, except to the extent you use a home office for business purposes (see 10.2.10);
- car loan, where the car is used solely for personal use;
- credit cards, except to the extent the charges are for business expenses;
- loan to contribute to an RRSP;
- interest on late income tax or instalment payments.

If you dispose of the property that you borrowed money to acquire, you can continue to deduct the interest in certain cases even though the underlying source of income has been lost. The rules in this respect are complex, and professional advice may be required if you are in this situation.

Interest on a car loan, where the car is used for your employment or business purposes, is limited to the employment or business portion of $250 or $300 per month, depending on when the car was purchased—see 11.3.

Structure investments to make interest deductible.

Since interest on consumer loans and home mortgages is normally not deductible, while interest on loans taken out to purchase income-generating investments is deductible, you should therefore try to ensure that all loans you take out are for a deductible purpose. For example, if you have funds that you could put towards either a home mortgage or investments and you plan to do both, you will probably be better off to use the funds towards the mortgage and take out a loan to purchase the investments.

Revenue Canada often pays special attention to deductions for interest expenses. It is wise to keep on file, along with your tax return, accurate records showing the amount of the loan, the purpose of the loan and the interest paid during the year, along with the relevant financial statements and possibly a confirming letter from your financial institution. It may be appropriate to file this information with your tax return if you have done so in previous years.

For minimum tax purposes, interest expense must be added back to your income if it relates to tax shelters or other "tainted" deductions. See 7.6.2.

7.3   Reporting rules for foreign investment property

You have to file a special annual information return with Revenue Canada if you own or have interests in foreign property where the aggregate original cost is more than $100,000. For these reporting purposes, foreign property includes:

- foreign bank accounts
- rental property outside Canada
- Canadian securities held outside Canada
- investments in foreign corporations, trusts, partnerships or other foreign entities

Excluded from these rules are interests in foreign affiliates (see below), property used in an active business, property held in RPPs, RRSPs and RRIFs, and personal-use property such as a vacation property.

Form T1135, "Foreign Income Verification Statement" is due at the same time as your personal tax return. You must describe each foreign property and disclose its cost and whether any income was earned from the property during the year. (New immigrants to Canada do not have to file this information return in the year in which they become resident.)

Similar reporting rules have applied since 1996 if you own (together with related persons) 10% or more of a foreign corporation, if you transfer or loan property to a non-resident trust (or a corporation controlled by it), and if you receive distributions from, or are indebted to, an offshore trust.

The reporting rules for foreign investment property are complex, the information required is extensive and the penalties for non-compliance are severe. You should seek help from your tax adviser if you own or have an interest in such foreign property.

7.4   Tax shelters

Tax shelters are no longer as important to tax planning as they were some years ago. For a variety of reasons, there are now relatively few publicly-offered vehicles for sheltering your ordinary income from tax.

Contrary to popular perception, tax shelters are generally not "loopholes" in the system. Preferences are given to certain types of investment as a deliberate move by the government to stimulate economic activity in a particular area. Whether it is investment in Cape Breton Island, scientific research or exploration for oil and gas or computer software, the specific write-offs and credits in the *Income Tax Act* are put there to encourage you, the taxpayer, to invest funds in a particular sphere.

> ### Don't let tax write-offs drive your decision to invest in a tax shelter.

One should only invest in a tax shelter if, after taking the tax benefits into account, there is a reasonable expectation of profit from the shelter. The tax benefits alone should rarely control your investment decision. In the past several years, Revenue Canada is extremely aggressive in challenging tax shelter-related deductions on the basis that there is no reasonable expectation of profit from the shelter.

Strict rules were recently enacted that make many tax shelters unattractive. For example, new "at-risk" rules prevent you from writing off more than the original cost of your investment (i.e., in a limited partnership tax shelter—see 7.4.4). Another set of proposals takes aim at certain types of tax shelter investments which have rights to receive future income, such as limited partnership structures involving mutual fund limited partnerships and film production services, curtailing the tax benefits of such investments for 1997 and later years.

When investing in tax shelters, one must be aware of the possible application of the minimum tax (see 7.6). Québec residents should also read Chapter 16. Finally, you must always be aware of the possible application of the general anti-avoidance rule discussed in 5.2.6.

We do not discuss RRSPs and other tax deferral plans in this section. They were dealt with in detail in Chapter 3.

7.4.1   Tax shelter identification number

> ### Before investing in a tax shelter, obtain its Identification Number.

Anyone selling an interest in a tax shelter is required to obtain an identification number from Revenue Canada (and Revenu Québec, in some cases) and provide that number on all documents and financial statements relating to the shelter. *If you do not have the identification number, or if any penalties relating to the identification number are payable by the promoter and have not been paid, you will not be able to claim the benefits of the shelter.*

The identification number does not indicate approval by Revenue Canada or Revenu Québec of the proposed benefits. It merely ensures that the shelter has been registered for administrative purposes, making audit and reassessment easier for Revenue Canada and Revenu Québec if they eventually decide to disallow some or all of the tax benefits.

7.4.2 Resource activities

Two areas that receive special incentives from the federal and Québec tax systems are mining, and oil and gas exploration. Tax shelters in these areas usually involve either limited partnerships (see 7.4.4) or flow-through shares. However, their appeal over the last few years has diminished.

Flow-through shares are special shares issued by a corporation involved in resource exploration. Under the *Income Tax Act*, the corporation can "renounce" some of its resource expenses, and will not be able to claim them for tax purposes. In exchange, it passes the rights to these claims to the owners of the flow-through shares. If the corporation is in its early years and not making a profit anyway, the flowing-through of the deductions allows the shareholders to use write-offs which otherwise could not currently be used by the corporation.

Whether you invest in a limited partnership or flow-through shares, the particular deductions you get will depend on the classification of the partnership or corporation's income and expenses. You will receive a statement and/or an information slip indicating your share of some or all of: business income or loss (partnership only); investment income and dividends (partnership only); Canadian exploration expenses (fully deductible); Canadian development expenses (excluding mining property acquisitions for flow-through shares; 30% deductible on a declining balance basis); Canadian oil and gas property expenses (partnership only; 10% deductible on a declining balance basis); and resource allowance (25% of certain production and processing income).

If the resource activity is in Québec, investors who pay Québec tax may also benefit from the province's special incentives for resource activities. The province allows you to deduct 125% of the amount of resource exploration costs incurred in Québec which are renounced in your favour. The deduction rate jumps to 175% if the expenses are for certain surface mining explorations incurred in Québec, and for certain Québec oil and gas exploration expenses incurred after May 9, 1996. These enhanced deductions are available until the end of 2000.

There is also a special exemption from Québec tax on capital gains resulting from certain flow-through share expenses in the resource sector. Where flow-through shares are sold, any amount received normally gives rise to a capital gain. The details of the exemption are complex, and you should get professional advice if you are selling flow-through shares acquired between May 14, 1992 and the end of 2000.

Before investing in resource funds, be sure to examine the track record of the promoters, the geological and engineering expertise available, the type of exploration to be undertaken and the expected tax effects of the various types of expenditures.

At the time of investment in the shelter you can usually obtain a forecast of the expected expenses and their classification, along with the implications for your tax return.

7.4.3 Labour-sponsored venture capital corporations

> **Look into investing in LSVCC shares.**

A "labour-sponsored venture capital corporation", or LSVCC, is a fund sponsored by organized labour that provides venture capital to start-up businesses. Although the government has curtailed the tax benefits of investments in LSVCC shares, they may still be an investment worth considering.

An investment in an LSVCC of up to $3,500 entitles you to a special federal tax credit of 15% of your investment. Also, depending on the province you live in, you may get a further 15% or 20% credit against your provincial income tax which you claim on your provincial T1C form when filing your tax return (or your Québec tax return). Where the provincial credit is less than 15%, the federal credit will be limited to the lesser amount; if the LSVCC is federally registered, however, the federal credit will not be reduced below 10%. No provincial LSVCC credit is available in Alberta, New Brunswick or Newfoundland.

Like an RRSP contribution, an LSVCC investment can be made up to 60 days after the end of a year and still qualify for the credit for that year.

You may generally redeem your investment whenever you wish, but certain restrictions and charges may apply depending on which fund you invest in. You must repay the special credits you received for your LSVCC investments if you do not keep them for at least eight years. (For LSVCC investments acquired before March 6, 1996, the minimum holding period is at least five years, or two years if you reach age 65, retire or cease to be resident in Canada.)

> **A new $3,500 LSVCC investment may only cost $700 after-tax.**

As we saw in 3.3.5, an investment in an LSVCC can be transferred to your RRSP or bought by your RRSP with "new" funds you have contributed for that purpose. You could also make this arrangement through your spouse's RRSP. In either case, the RRSP must be self-directed (see 3.1.6).

If you live in a province that matches the federal credit and you invest in LSVCC shares after March 5, 1996, you receive 30% of your investment back in credits on your tax return (assuming a 15% provincial credit). If you invest the maximum $3,500 by March 2, 2000 for your 1999 taxation year, your actual cost is $2,450. If you then transfer the investment to your RRSP (or have the RRSP make the investment with "new" funds), you can deduct the full $3,500; if you are in the top marginal tax bracket (about 50%), this will save you a further $1,750.

The result is that the cash cost of a $3,500 investment can be as low as $700, if you have contribution room in your RRSP that you are not otherwise using. However, as previously noted in 3.3.5, you should carefully evaluate the relative investment merits of these funds before cutting the cheque.

7.4.4 Limited partnerships

Tax law changes over the past few years have curtailed the benefits of tax shelters involving the purchase of an interest in a limited partnership.

A limited partnership is a partnership, in that you share the profits of the business with the other partners, and report a percentage of the partnership's income (or loss) directly as your income—whether or not you have received any of the profits. This is in contrast to corporate profits, which are reported only when distributed as dividends, as we saw in 7.1.2 above. However, a limited partnership is similar to a corporation in that you have limited liability—you cannot be sued for the partnership's debts. In general, you can only lose your original investment.

Because you can report partnership losses directly on your own tax return, limited partnerships used to be an attractive investment where the partnership business was expected to have losses in its initial years (either real losses due to start-up costs, or tax-created losses due to high write-offs available on certain kinds of investments).

However, you may not write off more than the original cost of your investment. The *Income Tax Act*'s "at-risk" rules provide that you cannot deduct more than the amount you have at risk in a limited partnership. Other rules severely restrict the use of limited partnerships to create losses where there is "non-recourse" debt (i.e., you are required to contribute amounts to the partnership, but cannot be forced to do so from your own funds, only from the profits from your partnership interest).

Further, losses from limited partnerships must be added back into income for minimum tax purposes. See 7.6.2.

7.5   Exempt life insurance contracts

The life insurance industry has developed attractive and highly sophisticated products that can help you meet two planning objectives at once: having insurance coverage and providing retirement income from tax-sheltered growth.

> Consider the merits of acquiring an exempt life insurance contract.

These policies allow you to pay insurance premiums and make deposits to a tax-sheltered investment account at the same time. You can choose between more conservative investments, such as GICs, or investments that involve more risk, such as equity indices. Unlike RRSP contributions, which are made with before-tax dollars, insurance premiums are not deductible. In both cases, the income earned is tax-sheltered until maturity of the plan or policy. However, all benefits paid out of an RRSP are taxed while benefits out of the insurance policy are tax-free. If you choose not to withdraw the funds from the investment account, they form part of the death benefit that is paid tax-free to the policy's beneficiary on your death. Because premiums paid for life insurance are made with after-tax dollars, some portion of their accumulated cash value can also be withdrawn without tax. Alternatively, funds withdrawn may be treated as a loan against your policy which is repaid from the death benefit.

If you have maximized your RRSP contributions, this type of life insurance policy may provide another opportunity for you to shelter your savings from tax. Most policies today are structured so that if you can commit to a 10-year program, you will probably fare as well as you would by investing the same funds in an unsheltered product.

There are many issues to look at when considering whether to acquire such a contract, such as the underlying mortality costs and administrative expenses, a guaranteed minimum rate of return, compared to a similar return in a non-tax sheltered environment, your required life insurance coverage, your income objectives, the financial reserves and strength of the insurance company and so on. Professional advice is a must when assessing the merits of this type of "investment". They are, however, a substitute for those who cannot otherwise find alternative tax deferral arrangements.

Life insurance is discussed in more detail at 20.6.

7.6 Minimum tax

7.6.1 What is the minimum tax?

The minimum tax was enacted as a political solution to the perception that many high-income taxpayers were paying little tax through the use of tax shelters and other so-called tax preferences. It is relatively narrow in focus, concentrating on specific shelters and credits.

The minimum tax is an alternative tax calculation. You must calculate your tax both normally and under the minimum tax rules, and pay the higher of the two.

In simplest terms, you calculate minimum tax by taking your taxable income, adding back "tainted shelter" deductions (such as resource write-offs and tax shelters) and the untaxed one-quarter of capital gains, taking a $40,000 exemption and then calculating federal tax at 17%. Most personal credits, but not the dividend tax credit or investment tax credits, are then allowed as with regular tax. Once federal surtax and provincial tax are added in, the minimum tax rate comes to about 27%, varying slightly depending on the province. If you live in Québec, see 16.2.24 regarding the Québec minimum tax.

Minimum tax paid can be recovered in the next seven years to the extent your regular tax exceeds your minimum tax (see 7.6.2). Minimum tax does not apply to the year of death.

7.6.2 Calculating the tax

Somewhat simplified, the calculation is as follows:

1. Start with your **taxable income** (after all deductions allowed for regular tax purposes).

2. **Add back the deductions** that you are not allowed to claim for minimum tax purposes:

   - losses from any investment that requires a tax shelter identification number (see 7.4.1)
   - losses from a partnership where you are a limited partner or passive partner (see 7.4.4)
   - resource write-offs (see 7.4.2)
   - carrying charges, such as interest expense, relating to any of the above (see 7.2.3)
   - employee home relocation deduction (see 9.3)
   - employee stock option deduction (see 9.4)

   These are sometimes called "tainted" deductions, since you cannot claim them for minimum tax purposes. Before 1998, you had to add back the amounts of your RRSP or RPP contributions for the year, including the amounts of any retiring allowance transferred to an

RRSP. In 1998, the government eliminated this requirement for 1994 and later years.

3. **Add one-quarter of all capital gains**, whether the other three-quarters was eligible for the capital gains exemption or not. (Note that you don't add back the exemption; that is still allowed for minimum tax purposes. It's the one-quarter which is *never* taxed that you add back no matter what.)

4. **Deduct the gross-up on dividends** (see 7.1.2). Since the dividend tax credit will not be allowed for minimum tax purposes, you are only taxed on the actual dividend received, rather than on the grossed-up amount.

5. **Deduct $40,000** as your basic minimum tax exemption. This gives you your "adjusted taxable income".

6. Calculate federal tax at 17%.

7. **Deduct personal credits** (see Chapter 2), such as your basic credit, other dependants, old age, disability (for self or spouse only), CPP/QPP contributions, EI premiums, tuition, education, medical and charitable. Do not deduct investment tax credits (10.2.14), political contribution credits (2.7.3), pension tax credits (19.3.5), transfer of unused tax credits from spouse (2.1.3), tuition and education credits transferred from a child (2.4), dividend tax credits (7.1.2) or labour-sponsored venture capital credits (7.4.3).

8. If the resulting tax is higher than your federal tax calculated normally, you must pay the minimum tax. **Federal surtax and provincial tax** (other than Québec tax) will be calculated on this figure rather than your regular federal tax figure.

If you find that you have to pay minimum tax in any given year, the excess of your minimum tax over your regular tax becomes a "minimum tax carryover", which can be used in any of the next seven years.

In a future year, you can use the carryover to the extent your regular tax exceeds your minimum tax.

Example:

Miranda's 1999 regular federal tax is $30,000. Her 1999 minimum tax (federal) is $35,000.

Miranda must pay the $35,000 tax, plus surtax and provincial taxes (total about $56,000). However, she has a $5,000 federal minimum tax carryover. If, in 2000, her regular federal tax is $32,000 and her minimum (federal) tax is $22,000, Miranda can deduct the carryover from her regular federal tax and pay only $27,000 basic federal tax (before calculating provincial tax and surtax).

7.6.3   Tips for minimizing minimum tax

Exempt capital gains

The minimum tax can have a serious impact on capital gains, particularly where the $500,000 capital gains exemption would otherwise enable you to avoid regular tax entirely.

Example:

Max sells the shares of his small business corporation for a $480,000 capital gain, which is fully exempt under the $500,000 capital gains exemption (see 6.4.1). Max has no other income in 1999.

Max will pay no regular tax. For minimum tax purposes, however, his adjusted taxable income will be $120,000 (one-quarter of the gain), minus the basic $40,000 exemption. His federal minimum tax will therefore be 17% of $80,000, or $13,600, minus personal credits. Max's total tax for 1999, including surtax and provincial tax, will be about $20,000. This federal minimum tax of $13,600 (net of personal credits) may be carried forward for seven years and applied against regular federal tax payable in those years.

> **Have 35¢ regular income for every $1 in exempt capital gains.**

As a general rule of thumb, minimum tax will not apply if you have at least 35¢ of "regular" income for each $1 in capital gains which are fully exempt due to the capital gains exemption. If your gains are relatively small, they may be shielded by the $40,000 minimum tax exemption anyway.

Interest expense and business losses

> **Continue generating interest expense and business losses.**

Two important deductions are not affected by the minimum tax. The first is deductible interest paid (see 7.2.3) on loans not used for tax shelter purposes. The second is business losses and loss carryforwards (see 10.4) other than loss carryforwards that are attributable to "tainted" shelters (see 7.6.1). Where it otherwise makes sense from a business perspective, you can generate such deductions without triggering any minimum tax liability. Keep in mind, however, that high interest expense may give you a high cumulative net investment loss (see 6.4.3) and thus make the capital gains exemption unavailable to you, to the extent you would otherwise want to use it (see 6.4.1 and 6.4.2).

Tax shelter deductions

> **Limit your tainted tax shelter deductions.**

Be aware of possible minimum tax implications when planning for large tax shelter claims, particularly on resource funds (see 7.4.2) such as drilling funds and flow-through shares. Resource expenses that exceed your total income from such funds (and are therefore claimed as losses) must be added back for minimum tax purposes.

To the extent you have loss carryforwards from previous years that are attributable to "tainted" shelters, they must also be added back to your taxable income for minimum tax purposes.

As a general rule of thumb, you can have "tainted" tax shelter losses equal to about 41% of your other income without being affected by minimum tax.

7.7   References

The following publications can be obtained (in person or by telephone request) from your nearest Revenue Canada District Taxation Office. Forms and guides may also be available from Revenue Canada's Internet site at *www.rc.gc.ca*.

Interpretation Bulletin IT-66R6, "Capital dividends"

Interpretation Bulletin IT-67R3, "Taxable dividends from corporations resident in Canada"

Interpretation Bulletin IT-232R3, "Losses—Their deductibility in the loss year or in other years"

Interpretation Bulletin IT-295R4, "Taxable dividends received after 1987 by a spouse"

Interpretation Bulletin IT-396R, "Interest income"

Interpretation Bulletin IT-445, "The deduction of interest on funds borrowed either to be loaned at less than a reasonable rate of interest or to honour a guarantee given for inadequate consideration in non-arm's length circumstances"

Interpretation Bulletin IT-503, "Exploration and development shares"

Form T691, "Calculation of minimum tax"

Dealing with Revenue Canada and Revenu Québec

8

- File your return on time even if you can't pay your taxes owing (8.2.1)

- Pay your taxes owing by April 30 even if you're filing later (8.2.1)

- EFILE or TELEFILE your return for a quicker refund (8.2.2, 8.2.3)

- Avoid common filing errors that may slow down the processing of your return (8.2.4)

- Consider prepaying instalments to reduce deficient instalment charges (8.3.2)

- Be aware of Revenue Canada's interest rates and compounding of interest (8.4)

- If you know you owe interest on late or deficient instalments, think about paying an estimate with your final payment (8.4)

- Sign a waiver only if necessary (8.5.3)

- File a Notice of Objection to preserve your right to appeal (8.6.1)

- When your return is reopened on reassessment, consider requesting other adjustments (8.6.1)

- Be sure you understand the legal issues when appealing (8.6.2)

- Consider paying the amount owing even if you are going to file an objection (8.6.4)

In this chapter we deal with the administrative side of the tax system—how tax is collected, how your return is assessed and what you can do if you disagree with Revenue Canada or Revenu Québec as to the amount of tax you owe.

8.1   The new Canada Customs and Revenue Agency

Say good-bye to Revenue Canada—as of November 1999, the new Canada Customs and Revenue Agency is scheduled to open for business. This new national tax collection agency will assume Revenue Canada's current tax administration activities, and will be able to administer additional taxes and programs on behalf of the provinces. The agency is being created to reduce overlap and duplication between federal and provincial tax authorities. Some provinces may elect to keep their own tax administrations; Québec has already indicated that Revenu Québec will continue to administer its tax programs.

Though the agency's internal structure will be quite different, it's day-to-day operations will be the same as those of Revenue Canada. Apart from the new name, individual taxpayers are unlikely to notice much of a change. (For simplicity, we continue to refer to the federal tax collector as "Revenue Canada" throughout this book.)

8.2 Tax returns

8.2.1 Filing your return

Most individuals are required to file their federal and Québec tax returns by April 30 each year. The deadline for individuals who have business income and their spouses (including common-law spouses) is June 15 because of the 1995 change requiring individuals and partnerships to use a calendar year for business purposes (see 10.2.1). Even though the return may not be due until June 15, any balance of tax owing for the year is due on April 30.

If you have no tax to pay for the year (as distinguished from no balance owing in April), no return is required unless Revenue Canada or Revenu Québec requests one.

In all provinces except Québec, you file a single return with Revenue Canada to cover both federal and provincial tax. Québec residents and taxpayers with business income from operations in Québec must file a Québec provincial tax return as well (see Chapter 16).

The return must be postmarked (or transmitted electronically) by the due date. If the return is late, an automatic penalty of 5% of any tax still owing applies. This penalty is increased by 1% of the unpaid tax for each full month that the return is late, to a maximum of 12 months. Repeated failures to file a return on time results in higher penalties.

> **File your return on time even if you can't pay your taxes owing.**

To avoid the 5% penalty, you should file your return on time even if you are not able to pay your balance owing. Interest will accrue on the unpaid balance, but the penalty will not apply.

> **Pay your taxes owing by April 30 even if you're filing later.**

Conversely, if you are unable to get your return completed (or your return is not due until June 15), but you do have a rough idea of how much tax you owe, it is a good idea to pay that amount to Revenue Canada or Revenu Québec by April 30. Make sure to have it credited to the correct taxation year (and not as an instalment for the subsequent year, for example).

8.2.2 Electronic filing (EFILE)

Revenue Canada permits most taxpayers to file their returns in electronic form using a personal computer. The system, dubbed EFILE, is available across the country, and allows authorized tax return preparers or transmitters to file returns directly to Revenue Canada using tax return preparation and transmission software. The Québec government also allows electronic filing for Québec provincial tax returns.

Due to the technical requirements and start-up costs involved, most individuals cannot yet file returns on their own using EFILE. However, most professional tax return preparers offer this service in addition to preparing the actual tax returns. If you prepare your own return, most EFILE preparers will charge a small fee to transmit your return.

> **EFILE or TELEFILE your return for a quicker refund.**

The main benefit of EFILE to a taxpayer is the ability to have the return assessed and a refund paid in as little as two to three weeks, as opposed to a somewhat longer wait using the conventional filing method. If you are expecting a refund, EFILE will significantly speed up the processing of your return and the delivery of your refund cheque.

Further, you do not need to file paper returns or receipts with the return. (However, receipts and other supporting documentation still must be retained for any subsequent review by Revenue Canada.) This reduces the paper burden on you, your EFILE preparer and the tax authorities.

If you are concerned about reassessment of your return down the road, filing with EFILE will normally get your return assessed sooner and start the three-year reassessment period (see 8.5) earlier.

8.2.3 Filing by telephone with TELEFILE

Under Revenue Canada's TELEFILE program, certain employees, students or seniors can file their returns by telephone. If you are eligible, Revenue Canada will send you an invitation to use TELEFILE and an access code in your personalized income tax package.

To use TELEFILE, you complete your tax return and then use a touch tone phone to call the service and enter the information as prompted. As with EFILE, you do not have to send supporting documents such as receipts and slips unless Revenue Canada asks for them. Revenue Canada says you will receive your Notice of Assessment and any refund in about two weeks. If you owe money, you can use TELEFILE before the deadline but you have until April 30 to send your payment.

8.2.4 Revenue Canada's top ten filing errors

Avoid common filing errors that may slow down the processing of your return.

Sending in your income tax return free from errors will help ensure that it is processed as fast as possible. Here is a list of items to watch out for—the top ten mistakes people make on their tax returns, according to Revenue Canada:

1. Mathematical errors, such as adding or subtracting amounts incorrectly.

2. Forgetting to reduce income by identifying Worker's Compensation, social assistance payments and net federal supplements.

3. Calculating and claiming provincial tax credits incorrectly.

4. Not including pension adjustments, which affect RRSP contribution room for the coming year (see 3.1.3).

5. Claiming GST/HST credits (see 2.9.3) incorrectly by using incorrect spousal income amounts.

6. Entering the wrong amounts on lines referring to Canada Pension Plan, Québec Pension Plan and Employment Insurance contributions and overpayments (see 2.9.1 and 2.9.2).

7. Claiming incorrect amounts as RRSP contributions (see 3.1.3).

8. Forgetting to claim the basic personal amount (see 2.2).

9. Claiming the spousal amount incorrectly (see 2.2.1).

10. Forgetting to claim the age amount, or claiming it incorrectly (see 19.3.4).

Revenue Canada recommends checking your math and following the income tax guide carefully to avoid making these errors.

8.3 Payment of tax

8.3.1 Source withholdings

Tax is withheld at source and remitted to Revenue Canada and Revenu Québec by employers and others. Tax withheld from a payment to you is considered to have been paid by you to the tax authorities, even if your employer never remits it. It is also considered to have been paid to you in the sense that it forms part of your income.

Source withholding applies to the following kinds of payments, among others:

- employment income
- pension benefits
- unemployment insurance benefits
- withdrawals from an RRSP
- annuity payments
- Old Age Security benefits
- payments of passive income to non-residents (interest, dividends, rent, royalties, etc.)
- purchase of real estate from a non-resident (unless the non-resident has a certificate from Revenue Canada and Revenu Québec, where applicable)

Note that there is no withholding of tax on interest, dividends, rent or royalties paid to Canadian residents. Self-employment income such as consulting fees (see 10.1) is also paid without source deductions.

8.3.2 Instalments

You must pay instalments if the difference between your tax payable (including provincial tax except Québec tax) and amounts withheld at source is more than $2,000 in both the current year and either of the two preceding years. For Québec residents, since provincial tax is not collected by Revenue Canada, the threshold is $1,200 of federal tax instead of $2,000—see 16.2.25.

Quarterly instalments are due on the 15th of March, June, September and December.

There are three possible ways to calculate your instalment obligations.

The first method is for your total instalments, paid in four equal payments, to equal the tax owing for the year on your sources of income from which tax is not withheld. In other words, your instalments should equal the balance owing at the end of the year.

The second method is for your quarterly instalments to equal the tax owing on your previous year's sources of income for which tax was not withheld. In other words, take the balance you had to pay last year after accounting for source withholdings, and pay that amount over the year in instalments.

The first method requires you to estimate your current year's income. If you guess low, you will end up not paying enough. The second method lets you use the previous year's income, but on March 15, when the first instalment is due, you might not yet have calculated your previous year's total tax. For this reason the third method was introduced.

Under the third method, your March and June instalments are each one-quarter of the total tax owing on income from which tax was not withheld for two years ago. Your *total* instalments for the year must still equal the total amount for one year ago, as with the second method. Therefore, the September and December instalments must be enough to reach this total. Revenue Canada and Revenu Québec will mail you a statement twice a year advising you of your quarterly instalment obligations under the third method.

Example:

Chris is self-employed as a consultant. Her 1998 tax payable (combined federal/provincial) was $20,000. Her 1999 tax payable was $24,000. She expects her total 2000 tax bill to be $27,000.

Chris should pay quarterly instalments on March 15, June 15, September 15 and December 15, 2000, totalling $24,000, her tax payable for the previous year. If she wishes, she may pay four instalments of $6,000 each.

Revenue Canada will advise Chris in February 2000, however, that her March and June payments should be $5,000 each—one-quarter of her 1998 tax payable, since her 1999 figures are not yet available. If she makes these payments, and then pays $7,000 on each of September 15 and December 15, she will have paid the required $24,000 and met her instalment obligations under the "third method."

The $3,000 balance (assuming Chris' estimate of income for 2000 turns out to be correct) will then be due on April 30, 2001, although her return need not be filed until June 15.

> **Consider prepaying instalments to reduce deficient instalment charges.**

If instalments are made on time and in the correct amount as per any of the three methods, no interest is payable. If instalments are not made when required or are deficient, interest is assessed at Revenue Canada's and Revenue Québec's current high "prescribed rate" (see 8.4), compounded daily.

You cannot *earn* interest by paying instalments early, but you can earn "contra-interest" at the same rate as applies to late payments, to offset interest that would otherwise be assessed on late instalments. If you've fallen behind in your instalments, consider making an extra or early payment to offset the (non-deductible) interest that will otherwise be assessed.

Example:

Chris, from the above example, does not make any instalment payments until June 15, 2000. On that day she makes a single payment of $15,000. She then makes a $2,000 payment on September 15, 2000 and a $7,000 payment on December 15, 2000.

Chris should not owe any interest on instalments, assuming the prescribed interest rate stays constant through 2000. Her June 15 payment can be thought of as three parts: $5,000 due in March, paid three months late; $5,000 paid on time; and $5,000 of the $7,000 not due until September, paid three months early. The payment that is early will generate "contra-interest" to offset the interest that Chris would otherwise have to pay due to her being late with her March payment.

For federal purposes, if the interest owing on late instalments is greater than $1,000, you may be subject to an additional penalty of up to 50% of the interest.

8.3.3 "Direct Deposit" of refunds

The federal government offers a "Direct Deposit" service whereby tax refunds, GST credits and Child Tax Benefit payments can be deposited directly into your account at any financial institution in Canada. To take advantage of this service, which saves the time it takes to print and mail the cheques and avoids the problem of cheques lost in the mail, complete Form T1-DD if you are filing a paper return or Form T183 if you are filing electronically. For other government payments, such as monthly Old Age Security or Canada Pension Plan payments, contact your financial institution for the appropriate forms.

8.4 Interest

Interest that you owe on late payments of tax and instalments and on refunds is calculated at a prescribed rate, which varies quarterly based on the Bank of Canada rate. The new rate for each quarter is announced by Revenue Canada in a news release about three weeks before the quarter begins.

> **Be aware of Revenue Canada's interest rates and compounding of interest.**

There are three different "prescribed" interest rates each quarter. The lowest rate, which is roughly the Bank of Canada rate for the previous quarter, applies for purposes of applying the attribution rules (see 5.2.2) and the employee and shareholder loan rules (see 9.3 and 13.2.6). The middle rate, which is two percentage points higher, applies to refunds paid by Revenue Canada. The highest rate, which is a further two points higher, applies to late payments of tax and instalments owing by taxpayers.

Although the rate is expressed as an annual rate, it is in fact compounded daily, so the effective rate is somewhat higher than shown. A 10% interest rate, for example, is equivalent to a rate of about 10.52% in simple annual interest.

Interest that you owe on late payments runs from when the payment was due. Interest on refunds generally runs from 45 days after the due date for the return, or from the day on which you file your return, whichever is later. However, if you have a June 15 filing deadline because you have self-employment income (see 10.2.1), interest will not be paid until 45 days after April 30 or 45 days after the date that the return is actually filed, whichever is later.

Interest that you are required to pay to Revenue Canada, such as on late payments of tax or instalments, is not deductible.

Interest paid to you on a refund is taxable in the year in which you receive it. Thus, if you file your 1999 return when it is due in April 2000 and receive a refund in August, the interest from June 14 included in that cheque must be reported on your 2000 return.

> **If you know you owe interest on late or deficient instalments, think about paying an estimate with your final payment.**

Since interest paid to Revenue Canada is not deductible, but interest you receive is taxable, the interest you pay costs up to twice as much. For example, if you receive $200 in interest on your 1998 refund, but are assessed $200 in interest owing on your 1999 return, and are in a 41% tax bracket, you are out of pocket $82, which is the tax owing on the refund.

If you have tax owing at April 30 and you know interest will be charged because of late or deficient instalment payments, consider paying an estimate of the interest with your April 30 payment to stop any further interest from accruing.

The federal prescribed interest rates are announced each quarter, but have been relatively stable for the past year or so. Prescribed interest rates from April 1, 1998 to September 30, 1999 are as follows:

Low rate: 5% — This rate applies for the purposes of the attribution rules and shareholder and employee loans.

Middle rate: 7% — This rate applies to tax refunds.

High rate: 9% — This rate applies to late tax and instalment payments.

For Québec purposes, the low rate is the same as the federal rate and the middle rate is slightly lower (so less interest is paid to you on refunds). For late taxes, the Québec high rate is the same as the federal rate, but a whopping 10% higher for late Québec tax instalments.

8.5 Assessment, audit and reassessment

8.5.1 "Quick" assessment

When you file a conventional (paper) return, it is processed over a period of typically three to six weeks, after which you receive a "Notice of Assessment" and any refund owing to you. The processing includes a review of the numbers on your return to make sure they are consistent (e.g., that your arithmetic is correct and that any numbers that need to be supported by receipts or information slips are consistent with them).

Most EFILE and TELEFILE users can expect their returns to be assessed in two to three weeks.

The assessment is normally not based on any investigation beyond what is on your return. It is sometimes referred to as a "quick assessment". The fact that a particular claim is allowed at this point does not mean that Revenue Canada or Revenu Québec is "letting" you claim it; it merely means that Revenue Canada has not addressed the issue in any detail.

For a partnership, the tax authorities may issue a determination of the partnership's income or loss, which is effectively an assessment of each partner's portion of the income or loss. See 10.3.6.

8.5.2 Audit

Some time after the initial assessment, your return may be selected for audit. Most audits of individual taxpayers (as opposed to corporations) are "desk audits", in which the auditor will ask you to supply supporting material for claims you have made. Some audits are "field audits", in which the auditor will come to your place of business to look at your records.

If you use EFILE or TELEFILE, you will not have to file any receipts with your return. However, Revenue Canada or Revenu Québec may later "spot-check" your return to verify certain claims, such as donations, RRSP contributions or tuition fees. This is normally just a formality, designed to maintain the integrity of the electronic filing systems.

You should be aware of your rights on an audit. The auditor is not entitled to go on a "fishing expedition" through your books. He or she may request specific information, and you may ask why that information is needed. You may wish assistance from your professional advisers in dealing with the auditor, if you anticipate problems.

If you have not engaged in tax evasion, an audit should not normally be cause for concern.

8.5.3 Reassessment

If the audit (or an audit of another taxpayer) turns up an indication that your tax payable should be other than what was initially assessed, Revenue Canada will issue a reassessment. If the reassessment results in more tax payable by you, this will not normally be done without you first being consulted and given an opportunity to explain your position.

> **Sign a waiver only if necessary.**

A reassessment cannot normally be issued more than three years after the date of the original assessment. However, in cases of fraud, or misrepresentation attributable to "neglect, carelessness or wilful default", the reassessment may be issued at any time.

There are several other situations where the three-year limitation does not apply. The most important is where you have filed a waiver. The waiver, which is directed to a specific issue that is in dispute, will allow Revenue Canada to reassess you on that issue at any time. You can revoke a waiver on six months' notice to Revenue Canada. If you are asked by a Revenue Canada auditor to sign a waiver, consider the request carefully and obtain professional advice before agreeing.

First, consider the auditor's alternative if you do not sign the waiver. You are under no obligation to file a waiver simply to be "nice". If the three-year reassessment period is about to expire, and the auditor does not yet have enough information to justify a reassessment, it may be to your advantage not to sign the waiver. Bear in mind that a reassessment normally takes some time to work its way through Revenue Canada's internal system, although it can be rushed through in a couple of days in extreme cases.

Second, make sure that the waiver is very specific and waives the three-year period only in respect of the specific issues that are under investigation or dispute.

Similar rules apply for Québec tax purposes.

8.5.4   Requests under the "Fairness" rules

What happens if you can't pay your taxes or make a tax filing on time because of a natural or human-made disaster, serious illness or accident? The *Income Tax Act's* "Fairness" rules give Revenue Canada the discretion to waive penalties and interest on overdue taxes if you were unable to pay on time because of circumstances beyond your control. (In the case of large natural disasters such as floods, Revenue Canada may extend tax-related deadlines for everyone in the affected area.)

Under the Fairness rules, Revenue Canada may also issue tax refunds even where the return is filed after the late-filing deadline (i.e., generally three years from the original due date) and accept late-filed elections, or allow you to amend or revoke an election after the applicable deadline.

Aside from natural disaster or personal misfortune, the Fairness rules can apply if you could not make a tax payment or file an election on time for more mundane reasons such as incorrect information provided in writing by Revenue Canada or service disruptions such as strikes. But if you were simply negligent or unaware of the rules, you will still have to pay the usual penalties and interest on your overdue taxes.

In weighing your Fairness request, Revenue Canada may consider your previous compliance record and your promptness in bringing the matter to Revenue Canada's attention.

Although the provinces generally do not have formal Fairness legislation, this should not stop you from applying for similar relief provincially. Ontario, for example, has internal guidelines for waiving interest and penalties that have not been released to the public.

8.6   Objections and appeals

8.6.1   Notice of Objection

If you cannot come to an understanding with the auditor and a reassessment is issued, or if you disagree with the original assessment, you may file a Notice of Objection. This is done by writing to the Chief of Appeals of your local district taxation office. It begins the formal administrative appeal process. The notice should set out the specific issue(s) that you are objecting to.

When you file a Notice of Objection, your objection is reviewed by an Appeals Officer within Revenue Canada. The Appeals Officer is independent of the Audit Branch, and he or she should conduct the review impartially and objectively.

> **File a Notice of Objection to preserve your right to appeal.**

To be valid, a Notice of Objection must be filed either within 90 days of the date of the assessment or reassessment to which you are objecting, or within one year of the original due date for the return. For example, an objection to an assessment of your 1998 return would have to be filed by April 30, 1999 or 90 days after the (re)assessment you are objecting to, whichever is later. The same deadlines apply for Québec purposes.

Filing your Notice of Objection before the deadline is vital—even if you are in the midst of discussions with Revenue Canada authorities, and even if you have been assured that a reassessment in your favour will be issued. Otherwise your right to appeal vanishes, and any reassessment will be entirely up to Revenue Canada.

Even if the period for objecting has expired, you may request a reassessment of your return. In this case, you have no legal right to force a reassessment, but in many cases the reassessment will be issued anyway. Revenue Canada will allow a reassessment of a return for any year back to 1985, if the request meets the guidelines issued under the government's "Fairness Package".

In some cases you can also apply to Revenue Canada or the Tax Court of Canada for extension of the time for filing a Notice of Objection.

> **When your return is reopened on reassessment, consider requesting other adjustments.**

If Revenue Canada issues you a routine reassessment for some reason after your own right to force a reconsideration of your return has expired, bear in mind that the reassessment reopens your return for 90 days. If this happens and there are other issues that you want to contest or change, you can raise them within the 90-day period and file a Notice of Objection to preserve your rights of appeal. However, you cannot do this where the return was reopened for any of a number of special reasons (such as a carryback of losses from a later year).

Similar rules and deadlines apply for Québec tax purposes.

8.6.2 Appeal to the Tax Court

The Appeals Officer is normally your last level of appeal within Revenue Canada. A further appeal is available to the Tax Court of Canada (or the Court of Québec if Québec taxes are in dispute).

You have a choice between the Court's "informal" and "general" procedures for making an appeal.

The general procedure normally requires you to retain a lawyer. It is similar to higher court proceedings in provincial courts. If the amount of tax in dispute for any one taxation year is more than $12,000 of federal tax (about $19,000 including provincial tax other than Québec tax), you must follow the general procedure. In certain "test cases", Revenue Canada may also force a case below the threshold into the general procedure, in which case Revenue Canada will be required to reimburse you for most or all of your legal fees.

The informal procedure, as its name suggests, is much less complicated. You may appear on your own, or have someone else (such as a lawyer, accountant, consultant or friend) there to assist you. No specific form needs to be filed to launch the appeal. The formal rules of evidence that normally apply to court proceedings will not necessarily apply. Under the informal procedure, your case will normally be heard fairly quickly, and a judgment given within a year of when you first file the appeal. The decision given is not binding as a precedent for future cases, whether yours or another taxpayer's.

> **Be sure you understand the legal issues when appealing.**

If you are taking an appeal to the Tax Court of Canada, make sure you understand the legal issues involved. Even if you wish to represent yourself or be represented by a friend or relative, consult with a qualified tax professional before the appeal. Many issues in tax law have answers on which all the experts (and the judge!) will agree, yet which will not be obvious to the non-expert.

8.6.3   Appeal beyond the Tax Court

A decision of the Tax Court of Canada under its informal procedure can be appealed, on a question of law only, in the form of a "judicial review" by the Federal Court of Appeal. A decision under the general procedure can be appealed directly to the Federal Court of Appeal. In either case you would need a lawyer for such an appeal, which would typically take about two years from time of filing until judgment is given. Court of Québec decisions may be appealed to the Québec Court of Appeal.

Once a decision is given by the federal or Québec appeals courts, either you or the tax authority may seek "leave to appeal" from the Supreme Court of Canada. Only if a panel of three justices of the Supreme Court grants the application for leave to appeal can an appeal be made. The Supreme Court rarely grants leave to appeal in tax cases; typically only three or four tax cases a year reach the Supreme Court.

8.6.4   Amounts in dispute—should you pay up?

Suppose you are contesting an amount of $5,000, but you are not sure whether you will win or not. Although you have filed a Notice of Objection or perhaps an appeal, you are receiving notices from Revenue Canada Collections asking you to pay even though Revenue Canada cannot start collection action as long as you have an objection or appeal outstanding.

> **Consider paying the amount owing even if you're filing an objection.**

It may be a good idea to pay the balance anyway. The interest rate charged on late payments (see 8.4) is likely higher than the rate you would otherwise earn with your money, or higher than the rate at which you must borrow from the bank. If you ultimately succeed in your appeal, you will recover all the funds you paid, plus interest (at the middle rate shown in 8.4).

Note also that when you receive a statement from Revenue Canada, you normally have 20 days to pay without further interest charges applying. If you are going to have to pay anyway, you may as well take advantage of this "interest-free" period and pay the balance on the 20th day.

Taxpayers sometimes think they should not pay an amount in dispute because "that would be an admission of guilt", or because Revenue Canada would then have no incentive to settle the case. Such reasoning is misplaced. You cannot prejudice your case by paying the tax. The determination as to your legal rights is not affected by whether or not the tax has been paid.

The only circumstance where you are better not to have paid your account is where you are applying for a waiver of interest and penalty, at Revenue Canada's discretion, on the grounds of "inability to pay". Once you have paid, it is difficult to argue that you cannot find the money to pay your tax bill and require a waiver of interest to be able to meet the requested payments.

8.7   References

The following publications can be obtained (in person or by telephone request) from your nearest Revenue Canada District Taxation Office. Forms and guides may also be available from Revenue Canada's Internet site at *www.rc.gc.ca*.

> Interpretation Bulletin IT-241, "Reassessments made after the four-year limit"
>
> Information Circular 75-7R3, "Reassessment of a return of income"
>
> Information Circular 92-1, "Guidelines for accepting late, amended or revoked elections"
>
> Information Circular 92-2, "Guidelines for cancellation and waiver of interest and penalties"
>
> Information Circular 92-3, "Guidelines for refunds beyond the normal three-year period"

Form T1, "General individual income tax return"

Form T1-DD, "Direct deposit request form for individuals"

Form T183, "Information return for electronic filing"

Form T400A, "Notice of objection"

Form T1013, "Consent Form"

Form T1033-WS, "Worksheet for calculating 19___ instalments"

Form T2029, "Waiver in respect of the normal reassessment period"

Brochure, "EFILE: Electronic Filing for Individuals"

Brochure, "Frequently Asked Questions About Electronic Filing (EFILE) for T1 Returns"

Brochure, "Paying Your Tax by Instalments"

Brochure, "Your Appeal Rights: Under the *Income Tax Act*"

If you are employed

9

- Arrange to get non-taxable benefits (9.1.1)
- Ask to have your source withholdings reduced where possible (9.2)
- Pay interest owing on loan from employer by January 30 of the following year (9.3)
- Encourage your employer to set up a stock option plan (9.4.1)
- Consider employees' profit-sharing plan for cash-flow purposes (9.5.2)
- Transfer retiring allowances to an RRSP (9.6)
- Claim rebate for GST paid on expenses deductible from your employment income (9.10)
- Arrange to be a consultant rather than employed (10.1)

As a general principle, all income (including tips) and benefits from or related to your employment are taxed, except where the federal or Québec rules specifically provide otherwise. Also as a general principle, you cannot claim any deductions against employment income, except for those that are specifically allowed by the system. There are, however, many special rules, and we examine some of them in this chapter.

9.1　Employment benefits

9.1.1　Non-taxable employment benefits

Certain employment benefits are not taxable, even though many of them are deductible expenses to the employer. The government is therefore providing an incentive to employers to provide these benefits, since the after-tax returns are greater than straight salary. Non-taxable benefits include:

- Contributions to a registered pension plan (the pension is taxable when received—see 3.4.1).
- Contributions to a group sickness or accident insurance plan.
- Contributions to a "private health services plan", such as those covering drugs, medical expenses and hospital charges not covered by public health insurance, and dental fees (except for Québec purposes—see 16.2.17).
- All or a portion of the cost of free or subsidized school services for your children (for example, if the services are provided in a remote area).
- Contributions to a supplementary unemployment benefit plan.
- Contributions to a deferred profit-sharing plan.

- Reimbursement of certain moving expenses on work-related relocation (excluding any reimbursement or compensation to help finance the new residence—see 12.1.4).
- Payment of club dues if your membership in the club may potentially benefit the employer's business (however, these dues are normally not deductible to the employer).
- Employee discounts, where such discounts are commonly available to other employees (but not below the employer's cost).
- One Christmas gift, wedding gift or similar gift of up to $100, where the employer does not deduct the cost for tax purposes.
- Tuition fees for courses taken to maintain or improve your skills in an area related to your current or future employment responsibilities.
- Costs of other business-related courses such as stress management, employment equity and language skills.
- Counselling services related to mental or physical health, employment termination, or retirement.
- Subsidized meals, where you are required to pay a reasonable charge covering the cost of the food.
- Uniforms or special clothing you need for your job.
- Transportation to the job, if provided directly by the employer.
- Board and lodging at, and transportation to, a "special work site" where you work temporarily or a "remote work site" that is remote from any established community.
- Use of your employer's recreational facilities.
- Transportation passes given to bus, rail and airline employees, except for airline employees travelling on a space-confirmed basis.
- Transportation and parking costs, whether paid directly by the employer or reimbursed to you, if you are blind or are disabled due to a mobility impairment.
- The cost of an attendant to assist you at work if you are disabled.

Note that where your employer deducts its contributions to a sickness or accident insurance plan, a disability insurance plan or an income maintenance insurance plan, any benefits you receive from the insurance will be taxable (but reduced by your own premium payments to the plan).

In the 1998 federal budget, the government announced that relocated employees will have to start paying tax on any extra compensation that helps defray their increased home financing costs resulting from the relocation—see 12.1.4.

> ### Arrange to get non-taxable benefits.

Ask your employer to make use of the non-taxable benefits outlined above as much as possible. If you have an employment benefit package where you and the employer share the costs, try to have the cost-sharing reallocated so your employer pays for all the non-taxable benefits and you pay for the benefits that are taxable if your employer pays them. In many cases, without changing the cost to your employer, you can reduce your tax burden this way.

One non-taxable benefit that is often overlooked is that of board and lodging at a "special work site". Unlike a "remote work location", a special work site need not be far from an established community; as long as the duties you perform at that location are of a temporary nature, and you maintain another residence, the board (i.e., food) and lodging paid by your employer are a non-taxable benefit. This could apply, for example, if you spend several months in another city working on a project for your employer.

9.1.2   Taxable employment benefits

In general, employment benefits other than those listed above are taxed as though you had received an equivalent amount of income. Examples include:

- Tips (gratuities) that you receive from customers.
- Board, lodging, and rent-free or low-rent housing (with some exceptions for remote or special work sites).
- Travelling expenses for personal travel, including expenses for your spouse to travel on a business trip of yours, unless your spouse was engaged primarily in business activities on behalf of the employer during the trip.
- Personal use of employer's automobile (see 11.2).
- Gifts, except for $100 per year as noted above.
- Allowing you and/or your family to use a vacation property.
- Holiday trips, prizes and incentive awards.
- Use of frequent-flyer credits that you earn through employer-paid trips used for personal trips.
- Cost of employer-paid courses for personal interest or technical skills not related to your employer's business.
- Payment of provincial (public) health insurance premiums (note that most provinces no longer charge such premiums).

- Life insurance premiums.
- Reimbursement for the cost of tools used in employment duties.
- Loans to employees (see 9.3 below).
- Tax equalization payments to relocated employees to offset higher taxes in their new work location.
- Stock option plans (taxed only when you exercise the option—see 9.4.1 below).
- Income tax return preparation and financial counselling (but not retirement or re-employment counselling).

In general, where the employer pays sales tax on goods or services, and then provides those goods or services to you as a taxable benefit, the calculation of the taxable benefit will require an additional 7% to account for the GST. This applies, for example, to automobiles. If you live in Nova Scotia, New Brunswick or Newfoundland, the 15% HST rate will apply (see 10.2.5); for Québec, the benefit is increased by the 7% GST and 7.5% QST.

9.2   Reductions of source withholdings

As we saw in 8.3.1, your employer and others are required to withhold tax at source and remit it to Revenue Canada. The same rules generally apply for Québec purposes.

> **Ask to have your source withholdings reduced where possible.**

In any situation where you expect to receive a refund after filing your return (e.g., due to personal tax credits, RRSP contributions, medical expenses or charitable donations, alimony and maintenance payments), you should review the TD1 form (and MR-19 in Québec) you file with your employer and seek to have source withholdings reduced. You can ask your local Revenue Canada district office to permit your employer to reduce your source withholdings for deductions not normally provided for on the TD1 form, such as RRSP contributions and alimony and maintenance.

However, if your employer withholds from your remuneration RRSP contributions, union and professional dues and alimony and maintenance payments for direct remittance to the intended recipient, the employer can take these withholdings into account in calculating your tax withheld at source without requesting permission from Revenue Canada.

If you have a loan from your employer on which imputed interest is assessed as a taxable benefit (see 9.3 below), your source deductions of income tax will reflect that taxable benefit. If, however, you are using the funds for a purpose that allows you an offsetting deduction, you may write to Revenue Canada, setting out that fact, and request that your employer be permitted to reduce the source withholding. An example of this is where you use the loan proceeds for investment purposes.

Many people look forward to receiving a tax refund, but it's not good tax planning to get one. If you get a refund, that means Revenue Canada has been holding your money and not paying you interest on it for many months. Although fiscal responsibility is needed to make sure you can pay your tax when it is due, it is better to be required to send a cheque to Revenue Canada at filing time, since it means that you have had use of the funds (for investment or other purposes) in the meantime. However, you must pay instalments if the difference between your tax payable and amounts withheld at source is more than $2,000 ($1,200 in Québec—see 16.2.25) in both the current year and either of the two preceding years. (See 8.2.2.)

Note that interest is not paid on refunds for the first 45 days of processing after the filing deadline—i.e., until after June 14 for most employees. If you have a June 15 filing deadline because you have self-employment income (see 8.2.1), interest will not be paid until 45 days after April 30 or 45 days after the date that the return is actually filed, whichever is later. (See 8.2.1 and 8.4.)

9.3 Loans to employees

If you receive a low-interest or interest-free loan from your employer (or past or future employer), you are considered to have received a benefit from employment. The benefit is set at Revenue Canada's (and Revenu Québec's) current prescribed rate of interest, which varies quarterly, minus any interest you actually pay during the year or within 30 days after the end of the year. The prescribed rate is 4% lower (3% in Québec) than the rate charged on late payments of tax—see 8.4. (There may be an offsetting deemed interest deduction, as we shall see.)

Example:

Rebecca receives a loan of $10,000 from her employer on January 1, 1999. She is required to pay it back one year later, without interest. Assume the prescribed rate throughout the entire year is 4%.

Rebecca is considered to have an employment benefit of $400, and will be required to include this amount in her employment income.

But if instead the loan bore interest at 2%, and Rebecca made an interest payment before January 30, 2000, her taxable benefit would be calculated as 2% (the prescribed rate of 4% minus her employer's 2% rate) of $10,000, or $200.

> ### Pay interest owing on loan from employer by January 30 of the following year.

If you have received an interest-bearing loan from your employer, consider deferring the payment of interest on the loan until January 30 of the next calendar year. This will provide you with a cash flow advantage. Make sure you do pay the interest by that date, however.

Exceptions

A home purchase loan is taxed on the same basis as other employee loans, but the rate applied in calculating the imputed interest for the first five years of the loan will not be greater than the prescribed rate in effect at the time the loan was made. At the end of the five-year period, it is considered a new loan, and the prescribed rate at that time will be the maximum for the next five years.

Example:

Keith receives an interest-free loan from his employer to help him buy a house. (He is not relocating, just moving from an apartment to a house.) At the time, the prescribed interest rate is 4%. Two years later, interest rates have gone up, and the prescribed rate increases to 8%.

Keith will still pay tax on the interest benefit calculated at only 4% of the amount of the loan. If the prescribed rate had gone below 4%, he would, however, pay tax on imputed interest at the lower rate as long as it stayed below 4%.

If you relocate, and receive a home purchase loan to acquire a residence at least 40 km closer to your new work location, then a special deduction in computing your taxable income is available to you for the first five years of the loan equal to the interest imputed on $25,000. Note that you must still report the entire interest amount as a taxable benefit, and claim this special deduction as a separate item on your tax return.

Where you use funds borrowed from your employer to purchase investments or to purchase an automobile (or aircraft) to be used for your employment, you can obtain an offsetting deduction. The amount of imputed interest that you include in your income as a taxable benefit is deemed to have been *interest paid by you*. As a result, if such interest would otherwise have been deductible, you can deduct it. (As we saw in 7.2.3, interest paid on loans to acquire investments is deductible, and as we'll see in 11.3.1, interest paid on loans to acquire a car is deductible if the car is required by your terms of employment.) The effect is to eliminate the tax cost of the taxable benefit.

If you are a shareholder of the company as well as an employee, or if a member of your family is a shareholder, you must be especially cautious. It is possible for the *entire* amount of the loan, rather than the imputed interest, to be included in your income for tax purposes, unless stringent conditions are met. In general, you can avoid this rule if the loan is made for certain specific purposes and with arrangements for repayment within a reasonable time, provided the loan was made because of your employment relationship. Alternatively, the entire loan must be repaid within one year, and not be part of a series of loans and repayments (see 13.2.6).

9.4   Stock option plans

9.4.1   Regular stock option plans

A stock option plan is an arrangement whereby a corporation gives an employee the right (an option) to invest in its shares at a given price. The price may or may not be less than the market price at the time the option is granted. For example, suppose you work for a corporation whose stock trades at $20. In 1999, you are given an option to buy up to 1,000 shares at $20, good until 2001. If, in 2000, the stock is trading at $30, you can exercise the option, buy 1,000 shares for $20,000, and then, if you wish, turn around and sell the shares on the market for $30,000.

The general rule is that you are considered to receive a benefit from employment, not when the option is granted (1999 in the above example), but when you exercise it (2000). The taxable benefit is the difference between the price you pay ($20,000) and the value of the shares when you exercise the option ($30,000). You would, therefore, report a taxable benefit of $10,000 in your employment income for 2000. (The adjusted cost base of the shares to you will be $30,000, so you will not be doubly taxed when you subsequently sell them.)

An offsetting partial deduction is available if certain requirements are met. The first requirement is that the shares be normal common shares (not preferred shares). Second, the exercise price must be no less than the fair market value of the shares at the time the option was granted. (Otherwise you could simply exercise the option the day you received it, so the benefit would be just like cash.) Third, you must deal at arm's length with the corporation (meaning essentially that you or members of your family do not control it). If these conditions are met, you can claim a deduction from income of one-quarter of the amount of the taxable benefit. The effect of this deduction is to make the taxable benefit taxed at the same three-quarters rate as a capital gain.

> ## Encourage your employer to set up a stock option plan.

You may wish to approach your employer about establishing a stock option plan as an employment benefit. It may cost your employer very little, and can even bring investment funds into the corporation to some extent. (The cost is the dilution of the existing shareholders' interests.)

9.4.2 Stock options in Canadian-controlled private corporations

If your employer is a Canadian-controlled private corporation ("CCPC") with which you deal at arm's length, stock options are particularly attractive since you do not record the taxable benefit until you *sell* the shares, rather than when you exercise the option and acquire them. And, if you have held them for at least two years at the date of sale, you can claim a deduction when computing your taxable income for one-quarter of the benefit realized in the year the shares were sold without having to meet the first two requirements outlined in 9.4.1 above. This exception is designed to stimulate employee participation in ownership of small businesses. It also recognizes that valuation of shares in a private company at the time you exercise the option may be difficult.

Be cautious about relying on CCPC shares too much for your future, however; shares in private corporations are not liquid, and can become worthless very easily if the corporation runs into trouble.

If you receive shares in a CCPC through a stock option plan, consider contributing some of them to your RRSP if the shares qualify for that purpose (see 3.1.6).

9.4.3 Share appreciation rights

The terms of some stock option plans may allow you to receive a cash payment equal to the value of the options instead of the shares. Where the plan allows the employee to make the choice, the same tax consequences apply to the cash payment as would apply to the issuance of shares—the employment benefit is included in income and the related 25% deduction is available if the required conditions are met. But if the decision is the employer's, the stock option rules will not apply and the cash payment will be treated as regular employment income.

9.4.4 Stock purchase plans

A stock purchase plan is a possible alternative to a stock option plan. In a typical stock purchase plan arrangement, a defined group of employees (which could be all employees) may purchase a limited number of shares of the company at their fair market value or at a slight discount. The plan is usually administered by a trust. You contribute a portion of your salary to the trust and in many cases your employer will make matching contributions. The trustee then uses the funds to purchase the shares at their current fair market value.

Since you make your contribution from after-tax dollars, no additional tax arises. If your company does not contribute to the plan and your contributions are simply used to purchase the shares, there will be no tax consequences. However, if the shares are issued at a discount, you will be assessed a taxable benefit on the difference between the shares' purchase price and their fair market value.

If your company contributes to the plan, the tax consequences to you will depend on how the shares are purchased. If the shares are issued from treasury, the stock option rules will apply. If the shares are purchased on the open market, you will be assessed a taxable benefit equal to the value of the shares at the time they vest.

9.4.5 Stock bonus plans

Stock bonus plans reward employees with shares of the corporation instead of cash. In most cases, the same rules apply as those outlined in 9.4.1 for stock options.

9.4.6 Phantom stock plans

A phantom stock plan avoids the requirement that you acquire shares in the corporation, and thus may be more attractive to your employer's controlling shareholders. Under such a plan, you receive bonuses based on the increase in value of your employer's shares. Such bonuses are simply taxed as employment income when they are paid to you. If they are not paid to you on an ongoing basis, you will need to determine whether they constitute a salary deferral arrangement (see 9.5.1), in which case they will be taxed in your hands even if not received. This type of plan allows you to benefit from the potential appreciation in value of your company's shares without a cash outlay and with no risk of any loss in the value of the shares.

9.5 Deferred compensation

Various techniques have been tried over the years to avoid paying tax on employment income by having some of it held back in one way or another. (In general, employment income is taxed when received.)

Registered pension plans and deferred profit-sharing plans were discussed in 3.4 and 3.5. They are accepted mechanisms for deferring employment income.

9.5.1 Salary deferral arrangements

The rules for salary deferral arrangements catch most arrangements for deferred compensation. For example, if you agree with your employer that your salary for 1999 will be $50,000, plus a further $10,000 to be paid in 2003, you will be taxed on the whole $60,000 in 1999. You can generally only escape this taxation if there is a substantial risk of forfeiting the future income.

The salary deferral arrangement rules allow certain exceptions. One is a self-funded leave of absence program, sometimes used by teachers, academics and others to fund sabbatical leaves. Provided you meet all of the conditions, you can arrange for your employer or a trustee to hold back a portion of your salary every year for up to six years, not recognize that portion as employment income each year, and receive it in the sabbatical year, paying tax on it then. Another exception is an arrangement whereby you have a right to receive a bonus to be paid within three years.

9.5.2   Profit-sharing plans

> **Consider employees' profit-sharing plans for cash flow purposes.**

Employee profit-sharing plans do not defer the taxation of employment income. Rather, contributions are made by the employer, based on profits for the year. Although the contributions are paid to the plan, the amounts contributed are treated as income of the employees for tax purposes. Such plans can therefore operate as forced savings plans for bonuses. Income (such as interest income) earned within the plan must be allocated to specific employees, who pay tax on it as it is allocated (even if it is not paid to them).

Though these plans are not widely used, one of their tax advantages is that there is no source withholding on the amounts paid into the plan, or on the amounts paid by the plan to you. Careful timing of the employer's contributions and the plan's disbursements can give you better cash flow than would a straight bonus payment.

9.5.3   Supplemental ("top-hat") retirement plans

Supplemental retirement plans are usually designed to provide retirement benefits similar to those offered under registered pension plans (see 3.4) but they are not subject to the same contribution limits. As a result, they are often used to enhance the retirement compensation packages of higher-income executives and employees (which is why they are also known as "top-hat plans"). Supplementary plans may be unfunded or funded. If they are funded, they will be treated as a retirement compensation arrangement (see 9.5.4).

Under the most common type of unfunded supplemental retirement plan, the employer simply makes a promise in a letter or a more formal agreement to pay an additional amount to the employee on retirement. Because no funds are set aside, there is no immediate tax liability for either the employee or the employer. However, because the retirement benefits are not secured, their payment will ultimately depend on the employer's ability to pay on the employee's retirement.

If the payments from the supplementary retirement plan are arranged to qualify as retiring allowance payments (see 9.6), you may be able to transfer part or all the payments to your RRSP.

9.5.4 Retirement Compensation Arrangements—RCAs

RCAs are arrangements made outside the registered pension plan system, whereby a custodian will receive funds from an employer and make payments after the employee's retirement or termination. The employer receives a deduction for contributions to such plans, but a 50% refundable tax applies to the payments made to the custodian. The tax is refunded when the payments are made to the employee. The employee does not report the income for tax purposes until he or she receives the payments from the custodian.

RCAs may also be funded through a letter of credit or through a life insurance policy. The letter of credit's terms usually allow it to be called upon if the employer does fulfill its obligations under the RCA. The contribution to the RCA is equal to the amount charged by the financial institution for issuing the letter of credit. A letter of credit is often viewed as a compromise between an unsecured arrangement and a fully funded RCA.

In recent years a variety of new methods have been developed for funding supplemental plans through exempt life insurance products—these are discussed at 7.5.

9.6 Retiring allowances, wrongful dismissal payments and severance pay

A "retiring allowance", as defined for tax purposes, includes what one would normally call severance pay or termination pay, as well as a court award or settlement for wrongful dismissal. It also includes, of course, a payment by an employer for long service on retirement.

Transfer retiring allowances to an RRSP.

A retiring allowance, like ordinary employment income, is included in your income in the year you receive it. If you receive your retiring allowance in a year after the year you terminated employment, a 1999 budget proposal will allow you to ask Revenue Canada to determine whether it is more advantageous to you to recalculate the tax on that income as if you received it in the prior year to which the payment relates. This change is intended to relieve the higher tax liability that may result if the entire lump-sum is taxed in the year of receipt, rather than year by year as right to receive the income arose. Eligible payments must total at least $3,000 in the year and include superannuation or pension benefits (other than non-periodic benefits), wrongful dismissal and other employment-related payments arising from a court order or similar judgment, and certain other amounts. (This change was introduced in the 1999 federal budget, but will apply to qualifying lump-sum payments received after 1994. At the time of writing, the details of the computation have not yet been released.)

Though damages awarded for wrongful dismissal are usually taxable as a retiring allowance, the amounts may not be taxable if the settlement includes damages related to mental anguish, humiliation, hurt feelings or loss of self-respect suffered on the job rather than as a result of losing the job. If you are suing for wrongful dismissal including damages for mental distress, ensure that any settlement contains a detailed breakdown of its components to show that it includes non-taxable general damages.

As we saw in 3.3.2, part or all of a retiring allowance can be transferred to an RRSP and thus sheltered from immediate tax. The amount that can be transferred is $2,000 for each calendar year (or part year) of service before 1996, plus $1,500 for each year (or part year) before 1989 for which employer contributions to your pension plan have not vested. (Vested pension rights are those that you can take with you on retirement or termination—see 3.4.1.)

Legal fees incurred in establishing your retiring allowance are deductible against the retiring allowance—see 9.9.5. Note that you should probably not transfer the maximum amount to an RRSP if you have incurred legal fees in obtaining your award (even if the case was settled without going to court). If you transfer the entire retiring allowance into an RRSP, the legal fees will never become deductible. (When you take payments *out* of the RRSP, they are no longer considered a "retiring allowance".) However, if you intend to leave the funds to grow tax-free in the RRSP for many years, you may want to consider transferring the maximum anyway. Legal fees can be carried forward for up to seven years and deducted against the "retiring allowance" income.

9.7 Death benefits

A death benefit is an amount paid in recognition of a deceased employee's service. It is usually paid to the deceased's spouse or children. Subject to the $10,000 exemption outlined below, it is taxable.

The first $10,000 of death benefits paid in respect of any one employee is exempt from tax. The employee's spouse gets the exemption; to the extent there is no spouse or the spouse receives less than $10,000 and other taxpayers receive such funds, any remaining amount of exemption can be split among the other recipients. "Spouse" includes a common-law spouse who meets the criteria outlined in 2.2.1.

Note that life insurance proceeds are completely different from death benefits, and are not taxed at all when received.

9.8 Overseas employment tax credit

If you are resident in Canada but you work outside Canada for a period of six months or more, a special tax credit may be available (if you live in Québec, see 16.2.20). To be eligible, you must be working for a Canadian employer (or its foreign affiliate) on certain kinds of projects, such as mining, oil and gas exploration or production, agriculture, construction or engineering.

The credit effectively allows you to offset the tax payable on up to $100,000 of overseas employment income per year, but is limited to 80% of that income. The details are very complicated—see the reference information in 9.11 below.

9.9 Deductions from employment income

The only deductions allowed against employment income are those specifically provided for in the federal and Québec tax rules. We look at some of them below.

9.9.1 Travelling expenses

If you are required by your employment to spend funds on employment-related travel, the amounts you pay will normally be deductible. Examples might include parking, taxis and train fares. You cannot deduct the costs of travelling between your home to your workplace. If you use your own automobile for employment-related travel, see 11.2.

If you travel for a transportation company (e.g., as a bus or truck driver or a flight attendant), you can also deduct costs of meals and lodging to the extent you are not entitled to be reimbursed. The deduction for meals will be further restricted to 50% of your cost (see 10.2.9).

9.9.2 Commission sales person's expenses

If you are employed as a sales person under a contract that requires you to pay your own expenses, and you earn commissions, you may be able to deduct the costs of your employment-related expenditures—the same kinds of costs as could be claimed if you were self-employed (see 10.2.2). To do so, you must be required by your contract of employment to pay your own expenses, and you must be ordinarily required to carry on your duties of employment away from your employer's place of business. The total expenses you claim this way cannot exceed your total commission income.

9.9.3 Supplies, assistant's salary and home office

If you are required by your contract of employment to pay for any supplies or to pay for an assistant or substitute, you can deduct the cost of the supplies or the assistant's salary.

You can also deduct expenses relating to a home office, in limited circumstances. First, you must be required by your employment contract to maintain the office, and your employer must sign a certificate (federal Form T2200 and Québec Form TP-64.3-V) that you file with your return. Second, either the home office must be the place where you "principally perform the duties of employment", or you must use it on a regular and continuous basis for *meeting* people (such as your employer's customers) in the ordinary course of your employment. The second restriction is parallel to that which applies to self-employed people, as outlined in more detail in 10.2.10. The effect is that the deduction is rarely available to employed individuals. You will normally only be able to claim it if you spend more of your time working at home than at your employer's premises.

9.9.4 Union and professional dues

Union dues are deductible for federal tax purposes (see 16.2.18 if you live in Québec). These are normally withheld at source and reported on the T4 and Québec Relevé 1 you receive from your employer.

Dues required to maintain a legally recognized professional status are deductible, even if you do not need to maintain that status for your current job. Your status as a lawyer, engineer, accountant, physician, architect, nurse, dentist, etc., will qualify for this purpose. Dues to voluntary associations are not deductible, unless you are self-employed (see 10.2.2).

9.9.5 Legal fees

If you spend money on a lawyer to recover unpaid wages, you can deduct the legal fees.

Legal fees you incur to establish your right to a "retiring allowance" (which includes severance pay), or to private pension plan benefits, are deductible. Under the current rules, you can only deduct the legal fees *against the income from the retiring allowance or pension benefits in that year*. To the extent you have not yet received that income, you can "carry forward" the expenses for up to seven years and claim them against such income in those later years. (See 9.6 if you transfer your retiring allowance to an RRSP.)

> Example:
>
> Lewis was fired from his job in 1997. He retained a lawyer and sued for wrongful dismissal, spending $3,000 in 1997 and $5,000 in 1998 in legal fees. In 1999, the case is settled and his former employer pays him $50,000.
>
> Lewis can deduct his $8,000 in legal fees only in 1999 against his $50,000 "retiring allowance" income, thus recognizing only $42,000 as income in that year.

Note that under a 1999 budget proposal, Lewis could ask Revenue Canada to recalculate his tax on the retiring allowance income as if it had been received in the year to which the payment relates—see 9.6.

See also 2.8.1 regarding the deductibility of legal fees that are not related to employment.

9.9.6 Musicians' instruments

If you are employed as a musician and required to supply your own instrument, you may deduct any maintenance, rental and insurance costs. If you have purchased the instrument, you may claim capital cost allowance (depreciation), at a rate of 10% for the first year, and 20% of the remaining balance in each subsequent year. All of these deductions can only be used to offset your income from employment as a musician, not against other income.

9.9.7 Artists' expenses

If you are employed as an artist (including, for example, a painter, sculptor, playwright, literary author, composer, actor, dancer, singer or musician), you may deduct up to $1,000 of your actual expenses incurred in order to earn income from such activities. This deduction is limited to 20% of your income from artistic employment, and the $1,000 limit is reduced by any amounts you claim as automobile expenses (see 11.3.1) and musical instrument costs (9.9.6). (No parallel deduction is allowed for Québec tax purposes.)

Of course, if you earn income from your artistic activities that is not employment income, you are self-employed, in which case all your expenses are normally deductible (see 10.2.2).

9.9.8 Northern employees

If your employer pays for you to take a vacation trip, with or without your family, the value of the taxable benefit is included in your income (see 9.1.2). If you live in northern Canada, a federal deduction is available to offset all or part of this benefit (a similar deduction is available for Québec purposes). Provided you meet certain residency requirements, the deduction can eliminate the taxable benefit associated with up to two trips per year, based on the cost of airfare to the nearest large Canadian city. (There is no limit to the number of such trips if they are taken to obtain medical services not available locally.)

See also 2.8.2, regarding the special deduction for residents of northern Canada, and 9.1.1, regarding the non-taxability of benefits relating to a remote work site.

9.10 GST rebate for employees

> Claim rebate for GST paid on expenses deductible from your employment income.

In general, where you can deduct expenses from your employment income, such as those discussed in 9.9, you can also claim a rebate of GST or HST paid on those expenses. A QST rebate is available for Québec taxpayers. Documentation must be kept to support the claim for the rebate. The rebate claim is filed with your personal income tax return. That rebate will itself be considered income from employment in the year in which you receive it, except where it relates to capital cost allowance (see 11.3.1). If you drive your own car for employment-related travel, see 11.3.1.

9.11 References

The following publications can be obtained (in person or by telephone request) from your nearest Revenue Canada District Taxation Office. Forms and guides may also be available from Revenue Canada's Internet site at *www.rc.gc.ca*.

Interpretation Bulletin IT-63R5, "Benefits, including standby charge for an automobile, from the personal use of a motor vehicle supplied by an employer after 1992"

Interpretation Bulletin IT-113R4, "Benefits to employees—stock options"

Interpretation Bulletin IT-148R3, "Recreational properties and club dues"

Interpretation Bulletin IT-158R2, "Employees' professional membership dues"

Interpretation Bulletin IT-196R2, "Payments by employer to employee"

Interpretation Bulletin IT-337R3, "Retiring allowances"

Interpretation Bulletin IT-352R2, "Employees' expenses, including work space in home expenses"

Interpretation Bulletin IT-421R2, "Benefits to individuals, corporations and shareholders from loans or debt"

Interpretation Bulletin IT-470R, "Employees' fringe benefits"

Interpretation Bulletin IT-497R3, "Overseas employment tax credit"

Interpretation Bulletin IT-508R, "Death benefits—calculation"

Interpretation Bulletin IT-522R, "Vehicle, travel and sales expenses of employees"

Interpretation Bulletin IT-529, "Flexible employee benefit programs"

Information Circular 73-21R7, "Away from home expenses"

Information Circular 77-1R4, "Deferred profit sharing plans"

"Completion Guide and Form for Employee and Partner GST Rebate"

"Employment Expenses Tax Guide"

Form TD1, "19__ Personal tax credit return"

Form T626, "Overseas employment tax credit"

Form T777, "Statement of employment expenses"

Form T2200, "Declaration of conditions of employment applicable to expense claims"

Form GST 370, "Employee and partner GST rebate"

10

If you are self-employed

- Arrange to be a consultant rather than employed (10.1)

- Recover GST (or HST) and QST that you've paid by claiming input tax credits for your business (10.2.4)

- If you're a residential landlord, account for sales tax when setting rents (10.2.4)

- Be aware of your HST obligations for sales to customers in Nova Scotia, New Brunswick and Newfoundland (10.2.5)

- Simplify your paperwork by using the "Quick Method" for GST and QST reporting (10.2.6)

- Acquire depreciable assets before year-end (10.2.7)

- Consider claiming less CCA than the maximum (10.2.7)

- Claim accelerated CCA on computer hardware and software purchased to correct the year 2000 problem (10.2.7)

- Deduct public transit fares, taxis and other business travel costs (10.2.8)

- Document and claim your business meals and entertainment expenses (10.2.9)

- Write off your eligible home office expenses (10.2.10)

- If you're a partner, claim sales tax rebates on your unreimbursed partnership expenses (10.3.7)

- Use your loss carryovers to maximum advantage (10.4.1)

- Keep detailed documentation to support your write-offs for losses from rental properties (10.4.2)

- Consider the potential benefits of incorporating your business (10.5)

In this chapter we highlight some of the major topics in the taxation of business income. If you are a professional, see Chapter 15 for additional planning ideas. If you are in a partnership, see also 15.2; if you are in Québec, see also Chapter 16. It goes without saying that anyone with a substantial amount of business income should obtain proper professional advice due to the large potential for planning legitimate deductions.

10.1   Employee or independent contractor?

As you will see in this chapter, people who are self-employed, carrying on business for themselves, generally have wider scope for tax planning than do employees.

Carrying on a business has nothing to do with setting up a corporation (which is discussed in 10.5 and Chapter 13). Any taxpayer can carry on business. If you set up a second-hand clothing-for-cash exchange in your basement, you are carrying on business. If you decide to put a name to your business (say, "XYZ Second-Hand Clothing"), that is just you carrying on business under that name. You have not created a new entity. You simply have a proprietorship, which means you are the proprietor of a business.

The distinction between employee and independent contractor (i.e., self-employed) is not always clear in cases where you receive most or all of your "work" income from one source. If you provide services to an organization, you can be classed in either group, depending on the facts.

Example:

Lisa is a computer programmer. She develops software under contract for ABC Corporation, and is paid for each hour she works. She does a lot of her work at home, though she goes to ABC's offices for regular meetings.

Is Lisa an employee of ABC, or an independent consultant who carries on business and whose major (or only) client is ABC?

In cases like this, one must look at all the facts to determine the person's status. There are no hard and fast rules. In general, you are more likely to be considered an employee if you:

- work a set number of hours per day
- have to account for your time to the company
- are told what to do each step of the way
- are a member of the company's group life, drug, dental and pension plans and receive other "benefits"
- use the company's computer equipment and supplies and have an office at the company.

At the other extreme, you would likely be considered an independent contractor carrying on your own business as a proprietor if you:

- agree to get the job done, but you don't make a commitment for any particular number of hours on any particular day
- work on your own with no supervision, and simply report back to the company periodically on progress
- issue invoices and receive cheques (with no source deductions for income tax, EI or CPP/QPP) and receive no employee benefits
- use your own equipment and work at home, going to the company for planning meetings only
- provide services to more than one company.

These examples are fairly extreme. Between them is a large fuzzy area, where each case will depend on its facts. It doesn't matter very much what you and the company *call* your relationship; more specifically, calling it independent contracting doesn't make it independent contracting unless the facts support such a claim.

One case where Revenue Canada has a clear administrative policy is that of real estate agents. You will be considered self-employed if you are entitled to the full amount of commissions, and either (a) you pay only a fixed amount to your broker for administrative operating costs, or (b) you pay a percentage of your gross commissions to your broker to cover such costs, and you set your own commission rate for sales on your listings.

> **Arrange to be a consultant rather than employed.**

If you are currently employed in a position where you maintain a fair amount of independence from your employer, investigate whether you can change your relationship so that you become an independent consultant rather than an employee. You will need to document the details of your relationship carefully, in case Revenue Canada or Revenu Québec challenges you in the future.

If you succeed in becoming independent, you will be able to take advantage of all of the planning tips throughout this chapter. You will lose certain advantages, however, including the right to Employment Insurance benefits, the employer's contribution to the Canada Pension Plan for you, and possibly all of the employment benefits you now have (pension plan, drug plan, etc.). You may wish to negotiate to have your cash compensation increased in exchange for any employment benefits you are giving up.

Revenue Canada has a questionnaire, Form CPT-1, through which your employer can supply the details of its relationship with you and ask for a ruling as to whether you are an employee or not for CPP purposes (and, by extension, for income tax purposes). However, there is no requirement to apply for such a ruling, and you and your employer/client are not bound by Revenue Canada's administrative decisions. If, after receiving professional advice, you believe that you are legally an independent contractor, then you are quite entitled to proceed on that basis. (Of course, your employer/client may not be willing to risk not withholding tax at source, if Revenue Canada has expressed the view that you are an employee.)

10.2 Taxation of the business

In this section we review how your business income is taxed. If you are a professional, see also Chapter 15.

10.2.1 Business year-end

Until 1995, you could pick a year-end for any business when you started the business. The income was then taxed only in the taxation year in which the business year *ended*, which allowed individuals and partnerships carrying on business to defer paying tax by up to a year. This option was eliminated by the 1995 federal and Québec budgets. Since 1995, all individuals, and all partnerships which have any individuals as members, have had to use a calendar year for reporting their income.

If you have been in business since before January 1, 1995 and were not already using a calendar year-end, you had to report two business "years" on your 1995 return: one ending on your normal year-end and the other ending on December 31. Since you probably would have ended up with much higher income for 1995, you are allowed to spread the "extra" income (for the "stub period" ending December 31, 1995) over 10 years, reporting at least 5% in 1995, 10% more by each of the next eight years, and the final 15% in 2004.

> Example:
>
> Andy is a lawyer who earns $120,000 per year. Before 1995, his business year-end was January 31.
>
> For the 12-month year ending January 31, 1995, Andy's income was $120,000. As well, he had to recognize the income for the 11 months running from February 1 to December 31, 1995 ($110,000). For this "stub period", Andy reported 5% of the income, or $5,500, in 1995.
>
> In 1996, and for each year from 1997 through 2003, Andy must include a further 10% ($11,000) of his 1995 "stub period" income. The final 15% ($16,500) must be included by 2004.

In 1995, the income inclusion was done by reporting the full amount of the stub period income, and claiming a "reserve" (deduction) against that income of up to 95% in 1995. The amount of the reserve was then included in 1996 income, and a new reserve could be taken for 1996 of up to 85% of the original stub period income. You can claim a deduction for up to 55% of your stub period income on your 1999 return. You may choose to report (and pay tax on) more than the minimum in any given year.

If you are a proprietor or an individual who is a member of a partnership composed of individuals, you or your partnership may have elected to keep the off-calendar year-end by using an "alternative method" of eliminating the tax deferral. Under the alternative method, you or the partnership were required to add to the business income for the actual off-calendar fiscal period an estimate of income earned between the end of the 1995 fiscal period and December 31, 1995. The adjustment is determined by prorating the actual off-calendar fiscal period. For example, if your traditional fiscal year-end is January 31, 1995, the additional amount taxable in 1995 under the alternative method was 11/12 of your actual income for the fiscal period ended January 31, 1995. Similar adjustments must be made for later years. You can then claim a reserve for the 1995 adjustment amount in the years 1995 through 2004 similar to the reserve described above.

If you had a non-calendar fiscal period and initially adopted the alternative method, you may later change to a December 31 year-end, but once you do, you will not be able to go back to an off-calendar year-end. (The election to use the alternative method must have been made by June 15, 1996.)

10.2.2 Business income and expenses

As a general rule, business income for tax purposes is based on generally accepted accounting principles. (Among other things, this means operating on the accrual basis: you record your income when you have billed your clients, whether or not you have been paid.) However, there are many adjustments required for tax purposes. Some of them are discussed in the sections below.

When you earn business income, there is normally no withholding of tax at source. If you are providing services to a single organization, and are able to classify your relationship as one of independent consultant rather than employee (see 10.1), you can submit invoices that will be paid in full, without tax (or UIC premiums or CPP/QPP contributions) being taken off and remitted to Revenue Canada. You may, however, be required to pay instalments of income tax. Instalments are discussed in 8.3.2.

In general, expenses are deductible if they are laid out to earn income from the business and are in reasonable amounts. There are certainly exceptions, as we shall see in the following sections. However, the underlying principle is the reverse of that for employees. *Employees can only deduct expenses that are specifically permitted under the federal* Income Tax Act *and the* Québec Taxation Act. *Someone carrying on business can deduct any expenses that are not specifically prohibited by these statutes, provided such expenses relate to the earning of business income.*

10.2.3 EI, CPP and other payroll taxes

Employment insurance is available only to those who are employed. If you carry on business for yourself, you are neither required nor permitted to pay EI premiums. This will save you up to $2,387 in 1999 when taking into account both the employee and employer's portions; on the other hand, it means that if your consulting contracts terminate and you are left without work, you cannot benefit from EI.

Canada and Québec Pension Plan contributions are split equally between employees and their employers. If you are self-employed, you are required to pay the "employer's share" to make up what is not being paid for you, as well as your own share. Since you are not employed, no CPP/QPP contributions are withheld from your income. As a result, you will find yourself required to pay up to $2,373 for 1999 in mandatory CPP/QPP contributions when you file your return, offset by a 17% federal tax credit (worth about 27% of these amounts when provincial tax and surtax are factored in). If it's any consolation, you'll get your CPP/QPP contributions back in the form of a pension after you turn 65, or optionally as early as age 60 at a reduced amount (see 19.3.1).

Many provinces also have payroll taxes that apply to employment income. In some cases, they apply to self-employed income as well.

10.2.4 Recovering GST by claiming input tax credits

> **Recover GST (or HST) and QST that you've paid by claiming input tax credits.**

If you are self-employed (or the owner-manager of an incorporated business), the business can normally claim a full refund (an "input tax credit") of the 7% Goods and Services Tax ("GST") or 15% Harmonized Sales Tax ("HST"; see 10.2.5) paid on most purchases. To be eligible for input tax credits, you must register with Revenue Canada to collect GST even though you are not specifically obliged to unless your annual sales are more than $30,000. As is the case for income tax purposes, "personal or living expenses" are not eligible for input tax credits. Once you are registered, you must charge GST on all your taxable sales (or HST on taxable sales made to customers in Nova Scotia, New Brunswick and Newfoundland). You can build the tax into your prices if you wish.

Make sure to keep accurate records so you can claim credits where possible. Claims for input tax credits must generally be supported by receipts or other documentation, not submitted with the GST return but held on file in case of audit. All documentation must show the vendor's name, the date (or, for a contract, the date amounts are payable), and the total amount payable. Where the total (including all taxes) is $30 or over, the receipt must also show:

- the amount of GST, or a statement that the total includes GST, and a clear indication of which items are taxable; and
- the supplier's GST nine-digit registration number.

Where the total is $150 or over, the receipt must also show:

- the purchaser's name;
- the terms of payment; and
- a description sufficient to identify each item supplied.

Failure to have this documentation will normally lead to a disallowance of any input tax credit claim if the return is audited.

Input tax credits can only be claimed where the expenses were incurred in the course of providing "taxable supplies". A business engaged in providing supplies that are GST exempt—such as a doctor, dentist, life insurance agent or financial institution—cannot claim input tax credits in respect of the costs of making those supplies.

> **If you're a residential landlord, account for sales tax when setting rents.**

If you rent out residential real estate (whether a house or an apartment building), no GST will apply to the rent since it is GST-exempt. As a result, you cannot use the input tax credit system to recover any of the GST that you pay on utilities, property management fees and other costs. You must set the rent high enough to cover your costs.

Rental of commercial real estate is subject to GST, unless your total revenue (including from any businesses you operate) is under $30,000 and you decide not to register for GST. If you are renting to a business that makes taxable supplies (that is, just about any business other than a financial institution, health care professional, school or day care), you are likely better off to register, collect GST (which your tenant will recover in the form of an input tax credit), and claim input tax credits for GST paid on your costs, such as utilities and property management fees.

In Québec, similar rules apply for QST purposes.

10.2.5 Harmonized Sales Tax

> **Be aware of your HST obligations for sales to customers in Nova Scotia, New Brunswick and Newfoundland.**

No matter where in Canada your business is located, you should be aware of your obligations under the new Harmonized Sales Tax. In 1997, the provincial sales taxes in Nova Scotia, New Brunswick and Newfoundland and Labrador were repealed and the GST rate that applies in those provinces increased to 15% (comprised of a 7% federal component and an 8% provincial component). The HST and the GST are the same tax and apply to the same goods and services. The only major difference is that the tax applies at the rate of 15% on goods and services supplied in the three Atlantic provinces, instead of the 7% rate that applies in the rest of the country. As a general rule, our comments with respect to the GST throughout this book apply equally well to the HST, although there are some exceptions.

All GST registrants in Canada must collect HST on taxable supplies made to or in the above three Atlantic provinces. If you're registered for the GST, you are already in the HST system. Collection, reporting and remittance of the HST is done through the existing GST system.

The HST could complicate your recordkeeping and sales tax reporting if you make taxable sales to customers both inside and outside Nova Scotia, New Brunswick and Newfoundland. Depending on the province to which the goods or services are delivered, you will have to determine whether you should charge GST only, HST only, or the GST and the appropriate provincial sales tax.

10.2.6 GST—the "Quick Method" and simplified accounting

> **Simplify your paperwork by using the "Quick Method" for GST and QST reporting.**

Self-employed individuals and small businesses may elect to use the "Quick Method" to simplify recordkeeping for GST. It can be used by any business with annual sales under $200,000 (excluding sales of basic groceries). This method can be particularly useful for certain consultants. However, the Quick Method may not be used by anyone providing legal, accounting, actuarial, bookkeeping, financial consulting, tax consulting or tax return preparation services.

Under the Quick Method, instead of remitting total GST collected minus total GST paid, the business remits to Revenue Canada a flat percentage of sales (including GST). The percentages vary depending on whether your business operates exclusively outside of Nova Scotia, New Brunswick and Newfoundland, exclusively in those provinces, or both in and out of those provinces. The rates also vary depending on whether your business is primarily selling goods (other than basic groceries) or services.

For businesses operating exclusively outside those provinces, where sales are mostly services rather than goods, the flat percentage is 5% (but only 4% on the first $30,000 of sales). For qualifying suppliers whose purchases of taxable personal property (other than basic groceries) for resale are at least 40% of sales (excluding basic groceries), the flat percentage is 2 1/2% (but only 1 1/2% on the first $30,000 of sales). Input tax credits can only be claimed for capital purchases.

For businesses operating exclusively in Nova Scotia, New Brunswick and/or Newfoundland and selling primarily services, the flat percentage is

10% (9% on the first $30,000 of sales). For businesses selling goods, the flat percentage is 5% (4% on the first $30,000 of sales). Special rules apply for businesses operating both inside and outside of these provinces.

Example:

John is a computer consultant who works exclusively in Alberta. He bills his clients $100,000 in 1999, plus $7,000 GST, for his consulting services. Because he is able to use his clients' equipment and facilities, his cost of doing business is very low. He pays a total of $70 GST on $1,000 of business expenses during the year.

Normally, John would remit his GST collected minus his GST paid to Revenue Canada for the year. This would be $7,000 minus $70, or $6,930.

By electing to use the Quick Method, however, John will be required to remit a flat 4% of the first $30,000 of his GST-included sales and 5% on the remaining $77,000 (or, to put it another way, 5% of his total sales of $107,000, minus $300). He thus remits $5,050 instead of $6,930.

Clearly, the Quick Method can be useful for businesses that have few taxable expenses. If the business' taxable expenses are high, however, the loss of the ability to claim input tax credits will offset the benefit of the Quick Method's reduced remittance rate.

As an alternative to the Quick Method, you can total up your GST-bearing purchases—including GST, provincial sales tax, late payment penalties and tips—and claim 7/107 of the total for input tax credit purposes (or 15/115 for expenditures on which HST was paid). Your business' annual sales must not exceed $500,000 for you to use this method. Not only does it make accounting for input tax credits simpler, but it gives you a slightly larger claim than you can make by totalling up individual amounts of GST paid.

For QST reporting in Québec, you can use a similar "Quick Method" and simplified accounting (however, the percentage rates under the QST system are somewhat different).

10.2.7 Capital cost allowance

The treatment of capital expenses is one of the major differences between business income based on accounting principles and income calculated for income tax purposes. In both cases, you cannot simply write off the cost of purchasing major capital assets (furniture, buildings, computers, automobiles, etc.). You must spread the cost over several years.

For accounting (not tax) purposes, a professional will make a judgment call as to the appropriate depreciation to claim. Various methods of depreciation can be used.

For tax purposes, depreciation is subject to strict rules and limitations, since it reduces your income (and thus the tax you pay). The income tax system of depreciation is called capital cost allowance ("CCA"); the rules are numerous and complex.

In very general terms, your capital assets are grouped into classes, and capital cost allowance can be claimed annually against each class. The "declining balance" method is used for most classes; the maximum you can claim against each class is a fixed percentage of the "undepreciated capital cost". What you claim then reduces that balance for next year's claim.

Some common CCA rates	
Buildings acquired after 1987 (class 1)	7%
Buildings acquired in 1979 – 1987 (class 3)	5%
Furniture and fixtures (class 8)	20%
Computer hardware (class 10)	30%
Automobiles (class 10 or 10.1)	30%
Most computer software (class 12)	100%
Tools costing less than $200 (class 12)	100%

Acquire depreciable assets before year-end.

For most acquisitions, only one-half of the CCA you could otherwise claim for the asset will be allowed in the year of acquisition. As a result, acquiring an asset just before your year-end will accelerate the timing of your tax write-off, while acquiring the asset at the beginning of the year will delay your CCA claim. Assets are normally required to be available for use and not simply "on the books" to be eligible for CCA, unless you have owned them for at least two years. (The term "available for use" has a specific and complex definition, and professional advice should be sought if you are unsure as to how it applies in your case.)

Consider claiming less CCA than the maximum.

Note that you are never required to claim the maximum CCA. You may in any year choose to claim less than the maximum, or nothing at all, for any given class of assets. The undepreciated capital cost for that class will remain intact, so you can make claims in later years based on that carried-forward balance.

In some circumstances you may wish to claim less CCA than you are entitled to. For example, if you have old non-capital losses or investment tax credits that will otherwise expire, you are better off to not claim CCA, use up the losses or credits, and save your "undepreciated capital cost" balances for CCA claims in future years.

You might also choose not to claim CCA if you are in a low-income year and expect your income to be much higher (and thus taxed at higher marginal rates) in subsequent years. Such a decision should only be made after careful analysis of the present value of the future tax savings, including the impact on your ability to make an RRSP contribution in the subsequent year.

> **Claim accelerated CCA on computer hardware and software purchased to correct the year 2000 problem.**

You may be entitled to an accelerated CCA deduction of up to $50,000 for computer hardware and software acquired between January 1, 1998 and October 31, 1999 to replace systems acquired before 1998 that are not Year 2000-compliant. For eligible computer hardware and systems software, the accelerated CCA deduction is 85% of the cost. For eligible application software, the accelerated CCA deduction is 50% of the cost. Combined with your regular CCA claim, the accelerated CCA can result in a deduction of 100% of the cost of eligible expenditures in the year acquired. (Note that only unincorporated businesses and corporations not subject to Large Corporations Tax are eligible for this tax relief. There are special rules for corporate groups and partnerships that have corporate members.)

10.2.8 Transportation expenses

> **Deduct public transit fares, taxis and other business-related travel costs.**

If you rely on modes of travel other than an automobile for your business travel, you can generally deduct the related expenses. Keep records of all such business trips, and deduct the appropriate costs of public transit, taxicabs, and so on. (If you use your own car, see 11.3.)

You cannot consider transportation from your home to your own office as a business expense. However, if you have an office in your home, and you travel from there to your major client (who might happen to provide you with an office on its premises), you are engaging in business travel.

10.2.9   Meals and entertainment

> **Document and claim your business meals and entertainment expenses.**

If you take a client or potential client (or a group of such people) to lunch or dinner, you can normally consider the cost of the meal as a business expense. The tax rules restrict the amount you can claim to 50% of the amount paid; the restriction is designed to deny a deduction for some of the personal benefit you receive (since you would need to eat anyway). The same 50% limitation applies to entertainment expenses, such as taking a client to a sports event. (If you pay Québec tax, see 16.2.21.)

Similarly, if you are registered for GST purposes, you can only claim input tax credits for half of the GST paid on such expenses (see 10.2.4).

Make sure you claim all lunches and dinners that you can justifiably relate to your business. For audit purposes, you should make a notation on your receipt of the individual(s) entertained and the reason for the meeting.

10.2.10   Home office expenses

If you have an office in your home, you can claim a portion of your ongoing home expenses as business expenses, subject to the restrictions discussed below. The portion will normally be based on the fraction of the home that is used for your office (you can usually exclude common areas, such as hallways, kitchen and washrooms, when making the calculation).

Example:

Mary is a computer programmer and works as a consultant to various companies. She works in her home, where her office is a room that is 200 square feet. The total area of the rooms in her house (bedrooms, living room, dining room and the office) is 2,000 square feet.

Provided her home office qualifies (see below), Mary can claim 10% of her costs such as mortgage interest, property taxes, house insurance and utilities as expenses for tax purposes.

The expenses you can claim include:

- rent, if you are a tenant
- mortgage interest (but not the principal portion of blended mortgage payments)
- property taxes

- utilities, such as electricity, heat, water, gas
- telephone (if you have a separate business telephone which is fully deductible, consider whether you also use your personal phone for business calls)
- home insurance.

Also make sure to claim your business portion of some of the less obvious expenses, such as garden service, driveway snowplowing, and minor repairs. You will need to keep receipts on file; do not simply estimate your expenses.

You may also claim capital cost allowance on the appropriate fraction of your home, but this is often not advisable. If you claim CCA, Revenue Canada will take the position that that fraction of your home is not part of your principal residence, and will disallow your claim for the principal residence exemption (see 6.5.2) in respect of that portion of the home. Any CCA you claimed can also be "recaptured" into income when you sell your home. (If you bought your home at the top of the housing market and do not expect to recover your costs when you sell, claiming CCA may be a good idea, however.)

The home office expenses are subject to restrictions. First, you can only claim the expenses against your income from the business. You therefore cannot use home office expenses to produce an overall business loss that is applied against other income. However, losses disallowed because of this rule can be carried forward and used in any later year against income generated from the same business.

Second, the home office will only be allowed if:

- your home is your principal place of business—that is, you do not have an office elsewhere. Note that if you have one major client and that client provides you with an office on its premises, it is still the client's premises and it will not disentitle you to your claim for a home office; or
- the home office is used exclusively for your business, and is used "on a regular and continuous basis for meeting clients, customers or patients".

Example:

Les is a optometrist and has an office outside his home. He also has an office in his basement, where he does a lot of his business' paperwork and occasionally sees patients (usually neighbours who come over for treatment in the evening).

Les will not be able to claim any expenses in respect of his home office unless he can show that he uses it "on a regular and continuous basis" to see patients.

Of course, *supplies* that relate exclusively to your home office are fully deductible and not subject to the above restrictions. Fully deductible expenses would normally include a separate business phone line; fax and printer paper; laser printer or photocopier toner cartridges; computer repairs (assuming your computer is used only for your business); and so on.

If you pay Québec tax, see also 16.2.22.

10.2.11 Health and dental premiums

Self-employed individuals may write-off premiums paid for supplementary health care coverage against their business income. For the premiums to be deductible, your coverage must be no greater than the benefits provided to your arm's length employees. If you have no such employees, your deductible premiums are limited to $1,500 for yourself, $1,500 for your spouse and $750 for each child.

10.2.12 Convention expenses

Revenue Canada will allow you to deduct the costs of attending two conventions a year in connection with your business or profession. A portion of your expenses may be subject to the limitation on the deductibility of meals and entertainment expenses discussed at 10.2.9.

For the expenses to be deductible, the convention must be held at a location that can reasonably be considered to be within the scope of the host organization. For example, if the convention's sponsor is a business or professional body that is provincial in scope, the convention must be held in that province. Under the Canada-U.S. tax treaty, expenses to attend a Canadian-sponsored convention in the U.S. are deductible, but only if the Canadian organization is a national one. (Revenue Canada will not allow you to deduct any costs for attending a convention held during an ocean cruise, no matter who sponsors it.)

10.2.13 Capital gains

Any capital gains that you realize are accounted for directly, through the capital gains system discussed in Chapter 6. They are not counted within the business' income.

10.2.14 Investment tax credits

Federal investment tax credits ("ITCs") are available for investment in certain regions of the country (e.g., the Maritimes) and for investment in scientific research and experimental development.

ITCs are claimed in the return for the calendar year in which they are generated. Unused ITCs can be carried back three years or carried forward for up to 10 years.

10.3 Partnerships

If you join together to carry on business with one or more other people—which could include your spouse—you will be in partnership. You are still, for tax purposes, carrying on business. (As well as the discussion below, see 15.2, where some special rules applying to partnerships are discussed.)

10.3.1 How partnership income is taxed

Partnerships do not pay tax. Partnerships with more than five partners are required to file "information returns" with Revenue Canada, reporting partnership income, but these are not tax returns.

The individual partners must each report their share of the partnership's income (or loss) as their own, *whether or not they have taken any of the profits out of the partnership*. The partnership is required to report income on a December 31 year-end basis. Resource allowances and various other resource-related expenses (see 7.4.2) are claimed by the individual partner rather than at the partnership level.

Note that a partnership cannot pay a "salary" to a partner. Even if you, as a partner, receive something called a "salary", it is really partnership drawings (withdrawal of profits or capital from the partnership). You are *not* taxed on your partnership drawings, but on your share of the partnership's income, which may be very different.

If the partnership suffers losses, you can normally claim your share of those losses against your other sources of income. (This may not be the case where the partnership is a limited partnership.)

10.3.2 Adjustment of partnership allocation

The allocation of partnership income (or losses) among the partners is normally left up to the partners to resolve. If you set up an unreasonable allocation for income-splitting purposes, however, Revenue Canada may disallow your allocation and substitute a reasonable one.

For example, if you and your spouse are in partnership together and you supply all of the capital and do almost all of the work in your business, while your spouse does almost nothing, Revenue Canada could be expected to disallow a 50/50 allocation of the business' income between the two of you.

10.3.3 Capital gains

Capital gains or losses realized by a partnership are allocated to the individual partners at the end of the partnership's taxation year. This will continue to be the case where the partnership has elected to follow the alternative method and keeps its off-calendar year-end (see 10.2.1). However, for partnerships that must use a December 31 year-end, such gains or losses will always be reported by the individual partners in the calendar year in which they are realized.

10.3.4 Allocation of investment tax credits

Investment tax credits (see 10.2.14) earned by a partnership are allocated to the individual partners and claimed in the year in which the partnership's year ends.

10.3.5 Gain or loss on partnership interest

When you are a member of a partnership you own a "partnership interest", which has an adjusted cost base for capital gains calculation purposes (see 6.2). If you sell your interest in the partnership (or are deemed to dispose of it at fair market value on death or emigration—see 6.5.3 and 12.3.2), the adjusted cost base will determine whether you have a capital gain or capital loss.

Your initial cost base is the capital you put into the partnership. Each year, when you report your share of the partnership's income, that amount is added to your cost base (since you have already been taxed on it, it should not be taxed again if you sell your interest without withdrawing the profits). When you withdraw profits from the partnership (see 10.3.1), the amount you withdraw reduces your adjusted cost base. Thus, in simplified terms, your adjusted cost base is your contributions, plus all partnership profits, minus all partnership losses and your withdrawals. (The details are much more complicated and there are many special rules, but that is the essence of it.)

A partnership is a "flow-through entity" for purposes of the 1994 capital gain election, so you may have an "exempt capital gain balance" that you can use until the year 2004 against the capital gain on a partnership interest (see 6.4.4).

10.3.6 Assessment of partnership

Under new rules, Revenue Canada is able to issue a "determination" of a partnership's income or loss. This "determination" will be much like an assessment of a taxpayer's tax (see 8.5.1), in that it will be binding on the partners unless a Notice of Objection is filed. One partner will have to be designated by the partnership to file any such Notice of Objection, and the other partners will not be able to object directly to the determination. These rules took effect on June 18, 1998. The Québec government has said it will be adopting similar rules.

10.3.7 Partners' sales tax rebates

> If you're a partner, claim sales tax rebates on your unreimbursed partnership expenses.

Like employees, partners who are not registered for GST purposes and who have unreimbursed expenses such as automobile expenses that are deductible for income tax purposes can generally claim a rebate for the GST, HST or QST paid on those expenses (see 11.3.2 for an example).

Make sure to keep records through the year and obtain invoices that indicate the amount of tax paid. The rebate is claimed with your individual income tax return.

10.4 Losses

10.4.1 Business losses

If your business expenses claimed for tax purposes exceed the revenues from the business, you have a loss. You also have a loss for tax purposes if you share in a portion of a partnership's loss.

You can only claim a business loss against other income if your business has a "reasonable expectation of profit". As well, if your loss arises from a limited partnership, you may not be able to claim it.

A business loss must first be used in the year in which it arises, to offset income from other businesses and other types of income, such as employment income, interest, (grossed-up) dividends and taxable capital gains. You do not have any choice in this matter; even if, for example, the tax on your dividend income could be offset by the dividend tax credit anyway, you must apply your business losses against any income you have in that year.

> Use your loss carryovers to maximum advantage.

Business losses not deductible in the year they arise are called non-capital losses. They can be applied to other years' income. They can be carried back for up to three years and forward for up to seven years. They can be applied against any source of income in those years. All such claims are optional.

Example:

Judy earned $40,000 in 1997 and $50,000 in 1998 as an employee. In 1999 she goes into business for herself , and for her 1999 business year she suffers a loss for tax purposes of $100,000.

Judy can file a form requesting that her non-capital loss from 1999 be applied against any amount of her 1997 and 1998 income. She will then receive a refund for the tax she paid in those years. If she wipes out all of her 1997 and 1998 income, she will still have a $10,000 non-capital loss, which can be carried forward to future years.

Judy should not, however, use up $90,000 of her loss. She only needs to use enough to bring her 1997 and 1998 income so low that she pays no tax at all ($6,500 or so). If she wishes, she may choose to use even less, and leave some of the 1997 and 1998 income taxed at relatively low rates.

This example shows the need to use any non-capital losses carefully. When using non-capital losses against income for any given year, consider whether you want to keep some of the income taxed at a low rate. For example, if you have a loss in 1999 and are carrying it back to 1998, any taxable income below $29,590 was taxed at only about 27%. If you (confidently) expect to have a large income within the next few years, so that you can apply the loss against income which will otherwise be taxed at approximately 50%, you are probably better off not to bring your 1998 taxable income below the $29,590 level.

Of course, you should never use loss carryovers to reduce your taxable income below the level (about $6,500, or more depending on the credits you can claim—see Chapter 2) where no tax is payable anyway.

10.4.2 Losses from rental properties

If you are a residential landlord, your losses from your rental property are deductible in the same way as other business losses as long as your rental business meets the general tax law requirements for business deductions. Lately, Revenue Canada has been aggressively targeting rental loss deductions, so you should be sure to have adequate supporting documentation on hand to support your rental loss deductions.

> **Keep detailed documentation to support your write-offs for losses from rental properties.**

Revenue Canada is likely to question your rental losses if your ownership of the property has a personal-use element, for example, if you or one of your relatives live there rent-free, or if you plan to live there in the future. Revenue Canada may ask for detailed documentation such as a floor plan of the building showing which areas you use, rent out and share with your tenants. You should also be prepared to show which of your expenses relate to the whole property as opposed to the rental portion only. If you rent to a relative, your losses may be disallowed if you charge a lower rent than you would charge another tenant.

Revenue Canada may also challenge your rental losses on the grounds that you had no reasonable expectation of profit. Where possible, you should keep complete records to show that you did thorough research on rental properties before you chose one to buy and complete records of the information that led you to believe your rental property would be a profitable investment. The tax courts have ruled that rental businesses may take several years—up to eight years in one case—to turn a profit. An explanation for your losses and description of steps taken to increase revenue or reduce expenses would also help support your case.

In another case involving rental losses, the tax courts found in the taxpayer's favour on the basis that the tax system should not penalize taxpayers for making bad business decisions. Even if you do not have detailed profit projections and market research on hand, you should seek professional tax advice if Revenue Canada seeks to deny your rental losses.

10.5 Should you incorporate your small business?

If you have an unincorporated business, you may be considering incorporation to save on taxes. But whether you and your business will gain a tax benefit from incorporation will depend on your personal cash flow needs, the personal and corporate tax rates in your province and the status of your business. (If you are considering setting up a corporation for the sole purpose of holding your investments, see 13.6.)

If you rely on all of your business' profits to support your personal cash flow needs, incorporation may not be a good idea—the cost of setting up and maintaining the corporation could outweigh the tax benefits. But if you can leave some of your profits in the corporation to be reinvested, incorporation could result in significant tax savings.

The taxation of corporations is discussed in 13.1. Generally, if you earn income through a corporation, the income will be taxed at the corporation level and then again at the personal level when the corporation distributes its after-tax income to you as a shareholder in the form of a dividend. Theoretically, the total corporate and personal income tax incurred by using a corporation to earn income should be the same as the personal tax that would result if the income were earned directly by an individual who was taxable at the top marginal rate. But in practice, this is not always the case. Before you incorporate your business, ask a professional tax adviser to help you compare the total amount of tax you will pay if you earn your business income directly or through a corporation.

> ## Consider the potential benefits of incorporating your business.

Some advantages of incorporating your business include the following:

Creditor-proofing your personal assets—Incorporation can limit your liability by keeping your personal and corporate assets separate. But since banks often ask small business owners for personal guarantees before they'll provide financing, incorporation may not protect you from all creditors.

Deferring expenses—You may be able to defer certain expenses if you incorporate. For example, if you report a bonus paid to an employee for tax purposes, you do not have to pay out the money until six months later.

Fiscal year flexibility — As we saw in 10.2.1, an unincorporated business must use the calendar year for tax purposes. An incorporated business can choose a non-calendar fiscal year, which may work better for your business cycle. If the fiscal year-end is in the later part of the calendar year, the payment of a bonus six months after the end of the year would put the payment into the next calendar year.

Access to the small business deduction and manufacturing and processing credit—With a corporation, you may be able to take advantage of the special lower tax rates for the first $200,000 of active business income of small "Canadian-controlled private corporations" and for income from manufacturing and processing (see 13.1).

Income splitting — If your spouse and adult children are shareholders in the corporation, any dividends they receive will be taxed in their hands. Your corporation can also employ your family members as long as the amount paid is reasonable for the work performed (see 5.3.2).

Capital gains exemption — If your corporation is a qualifying small business corporation, the $500,000 capital gains exemption discussed in 6.4.1 is available to shelter your gain and the gains of each of your family members that will arise when the shares of the corporation are sold or transferred through a will.

Group insurance and retirement benefits—Once you incorporate, you can create a registered pension plan and obtain tax-deductible group health and life insurance for yourself and your employees, which could include family members. (Unincorporated businesses can also deduct group health insurance premiums if certain conditions are met and within certain limits—see 10.2.11.)

Against these potential advantages, you will need to weigh the substantial legal and administrative costs of setting up and maintaining the corporation, keeping separate books and filing corporate federal and provincial tax returns. Also bear in mind that once you incorporate you will no longer be able to deduct business and capital losses against your other sources of income. Your decision about whether and when you should incorporate your business should be made with appropriate professional advice.

10.6 References

The following publications can be obtained (in person or by telephone request) from your nearest Revenue Canada District Taxation Office. Forms and guides may also be available from Revenue Canada's Internet site at *www.rc.gc.ca*.

Interpretation Bulletin IT-79R3, "Capital cost allowance—Buildings or other structures"

Interpretation Bulletin IT-131R2, "Convention expenses"

Interpretation Bulletin IT-232R3, "Losses—Their deductibility in the loss year or in other years"

Interpretation Bulletin IT-514, "Work space in home expenses"

Interpretation Bulletin IT-518R, "Food, beverages and entertainment expenses"

Interpretation Bulletin IT-521R, "Motor vehicle expenses claimed by self-employed individuals"

Interpretation Bulletin IT-525R, "Performing artists"

Guide, "Business and Professional Income Tax Guide"

Guide, "Employee and Partner GST/HST Rebate"

Guide, "Employee or Self-Employed?"

Guide, "General Information for GST Registrants"

Guide, "Guide for Canadian Small Businesses"

Guide, "Guide for the Partnership Information Return"

Guide, "GST/HST Calculation Guide"

Guide, "GST/HST General Rebate Application"

Guide, "The Quick Method of Accounting for GST/HST"

Guide, "Rental Income Tax Guide"

Brochure, "Paying Your Tax by Instalments"

Form CPT1, "Request for a ruling as to the status of a worker"

Form T1A, "Request for loss carry-back"

Form T776, "Statement of real estate rentals"

Form T2038, "Investment tax credit (Individuals)"

11

If you use an automobile for business

- Keep track of—and maximize—business use of car (11.1, 11.2.1, 11.3.1)
- Avoid employer-owned vehicles costing over $26,000 (11.2.1)
- Reduce the amount of time your company car is available for personal use (11.2.1)
- Take steps to minimize the taxable benefit from car operating costs (11.2.2)
- Claim rebate for GST paid on expenses deductible from your employment income (11.3.2)

If your employer provides you with an automobile, you may be assessed a taxable benefit for your personal use of the car. If you drive your own car in the course of your job or your business, you may be able to write off your work-related automobile costs against your employment or business income. In this chapter, we map out the complex rules that Revenue Canada uses to arrive at your automobile-related taxable benefit or deduction. Along the way, we also point out some tax-saving opportunities.

11.1   Keeping a log

Whether you drive your employer's car or your own in the course of your work, keep careful track of the distance you drive for work-related purposes to verify your automobile-related tax claims with Revenue Canada. You may wish to keep a log book on the dashboard, or record your business driving in your daily appointment calendar. The log must show the total number of kilometres driven and total business kilometres for the year. It should also include the date, destination and distance driven for each business trip.

11.2   Using a company automobile

Special rules apply for determining the taxable benefit when your employer provides you with an automobile. (If you use your own car for employment purposes, see 11.3.1.)

There are two elements to the benefit that must be reported for tax purposes: a standby charge, and the benefit in respect of operating costs. These will normally be reported together on your T4 (and Québec Relevé 1) statement from your employer as a single amount, and included in your total "income from employment" for tax purposes.

11.2.1   Standby charge

The standby charge is, essentially, 2% of the original cost of the car for each month that it is available to you—i.e., 24% per year. (For automobile sales persons, it can instead be 1.5% per month of the average cost of the dealer's cars acquired in the year.) You can have this amount reduced only if you can show both (a) that your business use of the car is 90% or more of the kilometres driven, and (b) that your personal use of the car is less than 1,000 km per month in the year.

Note that driving between your home and your place of employment is normally *not* considered business use. It can thus be very difficult to satisfy the above tests for a reduction in the standby charge.

Where the car is leased, the standby charge is two-thirds of the monthly leasing cost instead of 2% of the purchase price. Up-front, lump-sum leasing charges (or "balloon" payments) are pro-rated over the term of the lease for purposes of the calculation.

Lease termination charges are normally considered a lease payment in the year paid. If you and your employer agree, a lease termination payment may be retroactively spread over the term of the lease for purposes of the standby charge, as long as the years are not statute-barred and your employer issues amended T4 slips (Relevé 1 for Québec) for those years. This will generally be advantageous if your income in the year that the lease is terminated is taxed at a higher rate than in previous years, although you will need to factor in the non-deductible interest that will be payable on the increase in your taxes for the prior years.

An extra 7% (15% in Nova Scotia, New Brunswick and Newfoundland) must be added to the employee's taxable benefit to reflect the GST or HST embedded in the value of the automobile to you (7% GST plus an extra 7.5% QST if you live in Québec).

> **Reduce the amount of time your company car is available for personal use.**

The standby charge is based on the number of 30-day periods in the year that a company car is "made available" to you or a member of your family. However, the actual calculation is based on the number of *days* during which the car is available. This number is divided by 30 and rounded to the nearest whole number, and rounded down if it is exactly in the middle.

If you can get the number of "available days" down to 345, which is 11.5 30-day periods, the standby charge will therefore be reduced to only 11 times 2% of the automobile cost instead of 12 times 2%.

If you take three weeks or more of vacations or business trips during the year, leave the car at the company's premises during those times. If the car cost $26,000 new in 1999, you can thus reduce your taxable income for the year by $520 (and save about $210 to $260 in tax) by getting the number of "available days" down to 345. Note, however, that Revenue

Canada holds the view that the car is still made available to you during this time unless you are *required* to return the car and control over its use to your employer. You might wish to arrange for your employer to impose this requirement on you.

> **Avoid employer-owned vehicles costing over $26,000.**

There is an element of double taxation if you drive a company car that was purchased in 1998 or 1999 and cost more than $26,000 ($25,000 for cars purchased in 1997 and $24,000 for cars purchased in 1991 – 1996). Your taxable "standby charge" benefit is 2% per month of the actual cost of the car. However, only $26,000 can be written off (over time) as capital cost allowance by your employer. For cars purchased in 1998 and later, the purchase limit is increased by both the GST and PST paid on the first $26,000. It may be more economical for you to purchase the car yourself and arrange for an appropriate increase in remuneration from your employer.

11.2.2 Operating cost benefit

The taxable benefit for operating costs is 14¢/km of personal use for 1999. If your employer pays any operating costs during the year in respect of your personal use of an employer-provided car (and you don't fully reimburse your employer by the following February 14), the 14¢ rate applies. If you are employed principally in selling or leasing automobiles this rate is 11¢.

An alternative calculation is available for the operating expenses where your business use of the car exceeds 50%. If you notify your employer in writing *by December 31* that you wish this option, the operating costs benefit will be a flat 50% of the standby charge. A benefit of one-half of the standby charge will be to your advantage where the cost of the car is relatively low (for a small car, or a car that was purchased used), and the number of personal kilometres is relatively high even though it is used personally less than 50% of the time.

> **Take steps to minimize the taxable benefit from car operating costs.**

If your employer pays only part of the operating costs of an employer-owned car that you use, the taxable benefit from operating costs can cost you more than the amount the employer pays. Sometimes the employer pays only the insurance and the employee pays for all gas and repairs, or the employer does not pay most operating expenses but might cover an occasional major repair bill.

For example, suppose you put 20,000 km on your company car over the year, all of which is personal use (including driving to work and back). Your employer pays the insurance ($500 per year) and you pay the rest of the operating expenses. Your taxable benefit for operating costs will be 14¢ per personal-use kilometre, or $2,800, which will typically cost you about $1,200 to $1,400 in tax. So having the employer pay for the insurance is very disadvantageous.

In such a case you should repay the $500 to the employer *by February 14* of the following year, so that the "14¢ per kilometre" rule will not apply. Of course, your employer can pay you sufficient additional salary so that the after-tax amount will be enough to offset your repayment of the insurance costs.

11.2.3 Allowances and advances for automobile expenses

If you receive a reasonable allowance for automobile expenses, the allowance will not be included in your income if it is based solely on the number of kilometres driven in the performance of your employment duties. If it is a flat amount not calculated in terms of your employment-related driving, it will be taxable (though you may be able to claim offsetting automobile expenses—see 11.3.1).

Revenue Canada will agree to consider a flat periodic amount to be an accountable advance (rather than a taxable allowance) if you and your employer agree at the beginning of the year that you will receive a reasonable stated amount for each employment-related kilometre driven and you and your employer settle up at the end of the year regarding the difference between your actual business-related kilometres and the stated amount.

For 1999, Revenue Canada and Revenu Québec accept as a "reasonable allowance" 35¢/km for the first 5,000 km and 29¢/km thereafter (4¢ more in the Yukon and Northwest Territories); in some cases you may be able to justify a higher amount as "reasonable".

11.3 Using your own automobile for business use

11.3.1 Automobile expense deductions for employees

If you are required by the terms of your employment to use your own automobile and are not receiving a (non-taxable) reasonable allowance based on the number of kilometres you drive for employment purposes (see 11.2), you can deduct a portion of your automobile expenses from your employment income. (You must file with your tax return the federal Form T2200 and Québec Form TP-64.3-V on which your employer certifies that you were required to use your own vehicle.)

You can deduct operating costs, such as gas, repairs and car washes, to the extent they relate to your employment. As noted in 11.1, you will need to keep a detailed log of your driving to track your employment-related use as opposed to your personal use.

You can also deduct capital cost allowance (depreciation), or your monthly lease payments for the proportion of employment-related use. The allowable rate of capital cost allowance is 15% in the year of acquisition of the car, followed by 30% *on the remaining balance* in each subsequent year. However, there is a cap on the cost of the car for this purpose:

Year car purchased	Limit
1991 – 1996	$24,000*
1997	$25,000*
1998 – 1999	$26,000*

plus GST and PST on this amount

Example:

Michelle buys a new car in Ontario in January 1999 for $30,000 plus 7% GST and 8% Ontario sales tax. She is required to drive 10,000 km for employment-related purposes during the year. She also drives 10,000 km on personal trips.

Since half of her driving is employment-related, Michelle can claim half of the capital cost allowance normally allowed for a car. Although she spent $30,000, the cost is capped at $26,000, plus $2,080 Ontario sales tax and 7% GST (total of $29,900), for tax purposes. The maximum capital cost allowance for the year of acquisition is 15%. Fifteen per cent of $29,900 is $4,485. Michelle can therefore claim $2,243 as a deduction against her employment income for 1999.

Further, because she uses her car partly for business, Michelle can claim a GST rebate in 1999 from Revenue Canada equal to 7/107 of her capital cost allowance claim—see 11.3.2. (If she had purchased the car in Nova Scotia, New Brunswick or Newfoundland, the rebate would be equal to 15/115 of her capital cost allowance claim.)

If you lease the car, your deduction in respect of the lease payments is restricted to parallel the dollar limit on purchases:

Year lease entered into	Limit
1991 – 1996	$650*
1997	$550*
1998 – 1999	$650*

plus GST and PST

Your maximum deductible monthly lease charge is the lesser of the maximum lease limit set out above and an amount determined through a complex formula that takes into account your leasing charges and cumulative payments, the manufacturer's suggested list price, the prescribed purchase limit for CCA purposes and refundable deposits.

If you lease the car and you make an up-front lump-sum payment (or "balloon" payment), Revenue Canada will normally consider the amount to be part of your normal lease charge in the year paid and your deduction may be restricted by the lease deduction limit—see 11.3.3.

You can also deduct interest on any loan you have taken out to purchase the car (including financing on the purchase itself, where you make monthly payments that combine interest and capital). Your monthly interest is limited to $250 for cars purchased in 1997 and after ($300 per month for cars purchased in 1989 through 1996).

Example:

Michelle, who bought a new car in January 1999 for $30,000, is paying $700 per month on her car loan. She paid $2,000 down and the loan interest rate is 15%.

Calculations show that Michelle pays $350 per month in interest for the first month, and slightly less over the following months. Her interest for tax purposes over the year will be limited to $250 per month, or $3,000. Of this, she can deduct half, or $1,500, to reflect the proportion of her driving which was employment-related.

If you are reimbursed by your employer for employment-related use of your automobile, the reimbursement payments are not taxed. Of course, you cannot deduct your own expenses to the extent you have been reimbursed for them.

Driving between home and work is normally considered personal use. If, however, you travel from your home to a business call (to visit a client or supplier, for example), that will constitute business use. You can maximize your employment-related travel by making all of your business calls at the beginning and end of your day, before you go to work and after you leave work. You can thus make your entire trip from home to work count as travel for employment purposes.

11.3.2   GST rebate for employees' auto expenses

> Claim rebate for GST paid on expenses deductible
> from your employment income.

Where you can deduct expenses from your employment income, you can also generally claim a rebate of GST or HST paid on those expenses (see 9.10). If you have auto expenses you're deducting from your employment income, you may be entitled to a GST or HST rebate, as the following example shows.

Example:

Continuing our example in 11.3.1, Michelle is required to drive 10,000 km for employment-related purposes during the year. She also drives 10,000 km on personal trips. She spends $2,140 (including GST) over the course of the year on gas and repairs for her car, and does not receive any reimbursement from her employer. All the expenses are paid in Ontario.

Since one-half of Michelle's expenses are required by her employment, she can claim $1,070 as a deduction from employment income. That figure, however, already includes $70 in GST that applied to the gas and repairs. Michelle can claim a rebate of the $70 on a form filed with her income tax return. The $70 rebate is taxable in the year she receives it.

Further, because she uses her car partly for business, Michelle can claim a GST rebate in 1999 from Revenue Canada equal to 7/107 of her capital cost allowance claim. That is, 7/107 of the $2,243 Michelle can deduct as capital cost allowance, or $147, is refunded to her. This $147 is deducted from the undepreciated capital cost of the car at the beginning of 2000.

Note that a rebate is only available where GST was paid on the purchase. Michelle cannot receive a rebate in respect of the deductible portion of her car insurance, since insurance is not subject to GST. Similarly, there is no rebate for GST paid on gas purchased in the United States, because there is no GST included in the price of such gas.

In the above example, we have assumed that Michelle's employer is a GST registrant and is not a financial institution. If, instead, she was employed by a financial institution or by a non-GST registrant, she would not be entitled to the employee GST rebate which, as shown, amounts to $217 in the first year.

We have also assumed that Michelle did not receive a per kilometre allowance from her employer. If she had, she would not be able to claim a GST rebate on any of her automobile expenses unless her employer certified on her Form GST 370 that the allowance was "unreasonable" and that her employer would not be claiming a GST tax credit with respect to her allowance. However, in the unlikely case that Michelle's employer certifies that her per kilometre allowance is unreasonable, the amount will be included in her income and her employer must withhold income tax and other source deductions on the amount.

Finally, note also that if Michelle's expenses were incurred in Nova Scotia, New Brunswick or Newfoundland, she would have paid the 15% HST (instead of the 7% GST) and would be entitled to claim a rebate of 15/115 of her HST-included expenses.

11.3.3 Automobile expense deductions for the self-employed

If you're self-employed, you can generally deduct the proportion of your automobile expenses that represents your business use of the vehicle, normally based on kilometres driven.

If half of your driving is done for your business (excluding driving from your home to your own place of business) and half is personal use, you can deduct one-half of the expenses of the car for that year. The expenses would include gas, washes, repairs, insurance, interest on financing the vehicle, leasing costs if the car is leased, and capital cost allowance if you own it.

However, there are limits to how expensive a vehicle you can write off. Your claims for CCA and leasing costs will be based on a maximum cost:

Year car purchased	Purchase limit	Lease limit
1991 – 1996	$24,000*	$650*
1997	$25,000*	$550*
1998 – 1999	$26,000*	$650*

before GST/HST and PST

For most businesses, since you get back all GST paid as an input tax credit (see 10.2.4), "before GST and PST" effectively means "plus PST". (However, if you are a sole proprietor, you can only claim an input tax credit for the GST portion of your CCA. For other businesses, no input tax credits are available if the vehicle is driven 90% or more of the time for personal use.)

Where you have financed the purchase of a car, your monthly interest expense before determining the business portion will be limited to $250 for cars purchased in 1997 and after ($300 per month for cars purchased in 1989 through 1996).

These rules are identical to those for employees' use of a vehicle for employment purposes (see 11.3.1).

If you lease the car and you make an up-front lump sum payment (or "balloon" payment), Revenue Canada will normally consider the amount to be part of your normal lease charge in the year paid and your deduction may be restricted by the lease deduction limit. However, the full balloon payment amount may be deductible if the sum of:

- the amount of the balloon payment divided by the number of months in the term of the lease, plus
- your monthly lease payment

does not exceed your maximum monthly lease deduction limit.

Revenue Canada counts lease termination payments as normal lease payments in the year paid, and their deductibility is also subject to your lease limit for the year. However, Revenue Canada will make the adjustment at your request over the term of the lease (instead of just in the year of sale), provided none of the years to be adjusted are statute-barred.

The $26,000 purchase limit also applies for purposes of calculating your GST input tax credit (see 10.2.4) and Québec input tax refund.

See the planning tips suggested for employees in 11.3.1—the same considerations apply to business use of your own car.

11.4 References

The following publications can be obtained (in person or by telephone request) from your nearest Revenue Canada District Taxation Office. Forms, guides and interpretation bulletins may also be available from Revenue Canada's Internet site at *www.rc.gc.ca*.

Interpretation Bulletin IT-521R, "Motor vehicle expenses claimed by self-employed individuals"

Interpretation Bulletin IT-63R5, "Benefits, including standby charge for an automobile, from the personal use of a motor vehicle supplied by an employer after 1992"

Interpretation Bulletin IT-522R, "Vehicle, travel and sales expenses of employees"

Form T2200, "Declaration of conditions of employment applicable to expense claims"

Form GST 370, "Employee and partner GST rebate"

If you are moving

12

- If you're planning to move, arrange to meet the tests for deducting your moving expenses where practical (12.1.1)

- Arrange to avoid a taxable benefit on your employer-paid moving expenses where possible (12.1.3)

- Before moving to Canada, consider setting up a foreign trust to hold your non-Canadian investments (12.2)

- Take steps to cease Canadian residency if you are moving abroad (12.3.1)

- Beware of Canadian departure tax on emigration (12.3.2)

- Obtain a clearance certificate from Revenue Canada if you sell your Canadian home after you emigrate (12.3.5)

- If you wish to wind up your RRSP, consider waiting until after you become non-resident (12.3.6)

- Repay Home Buyers' Plan withdrawals within 60 days of becoming non-resident (12.3.6)

Moving expenses are often overlooked as a deduction. Depending on your circumstances, many of your expenses may be tax-deductible if you're moving within Canada to start a new job or business or attend school. If you're immigrating to or emigrating from Canada, there are complex tax rules that you'll need to consider before and after your move. In this chapter we discuss the tax treatment of moving expenses and other tax rules related to moving, including some planning opportunities to help make your move as tax-efficient as possible.

12.1 Moving within Canada

12.1.1 Work-related moving expenses

If you start working at a new location of employment, or start a new business, and you move to a home that is 40 km closer to your new work location than your old home was, you can deduct substantial amounts for tax purposes. The 40 km distance is measured by the shortest normal route of travel, including roads, bridges and ferries, rather than "as the crow flies". Expenses incurred in moving from another country to Canada, or from Canada to another country, are not deductible for Canadian tax purposes (unless you are a student receiving scholarship or grant income—see 12.1.2).

Except to the extent you are reimbursed by your employer, you can deduct the following:

- Reasonable travelling costs, including meals and lodging, to move you and the members of your household

- The moving costs for your household effects, including storage charges
- The cost of meals and lodging near either the old or the new home for up to 15 days
- Lease cancellation costs
- The costs of revising legal documents to reflect your new address, replacing driver's licences and automobile permits, and connecting and disconnecting utilities
- Selling costs in respect of your old home, including real estate commissions
- Where you are selling your old home, the legal fees and land transfer tax payable when you buy a new home (but not GST and QST)
- Mortgage interest, property taxes, insurance premiums and utility costs related to your old residence (provided it remains unoccupied), to a maximum of the actual costs for three months, or $5,000, whichever is less.

The real estate commissions alone can easily run into many thousands of dollars.

> **The higher-income spouse should claim credits to reduce high-income surtax.**

So when considering a move, ensure if possible that your move coincides with a new employment location or a new place of business, and that your move meets the 40 km test.

12.1.2 Students' moving expenses

If you are a student, you can claim moving expenses if you move when you begin a job (including a summer job) or start a business. If you are moving to attend full-time post-secondary education (in Canada or abroad), you can deduct the expenses but only to the extent you have scholarship or research grant income.

12.1.3 Moving allowances and reimbursements paid by your employer

If your employer is paying your moving expenses, you may be assessed a taxable benefit for the payments, depending on how they are structured. Generally, if your employer pays you an allowance related to relocation expenses without asking you to account for the use of the money, Revenue Canada considers it to be a taxable benefit but you will be able to deduct your actual qualifying expenses incurred (as listed in 12.1.1). If your employer reimburses you for your documented expenses or pays you an accountable advance, the payment is usually not considered a taxable benefit. Your employer can reimburse you for certain moving expenses for you and your family without conferring a taxable benefit, including:

- The cost of house-hunting trips to the new location
- Travelling costs, including meals and lodging, while you and members of your household are moving from old to new homes
- The cost of transporting or storing your household effects and other personal property such as cars and boats while moving from old to new homes
- The costs of revising legal documents to reflect your new address, replacing driver's licences and automobile permits and connecting and disconnecting utilities
- Selling costs of the old residence (advertising, legal fees, real estate commissions and mortgage prepayment or discharge fees)
- Where the old residence has been sold, legal fees to purchase the new residence and any taxes on the transfer or registration of title on the new residence
- Mortgage interest, property taxes, insurance premiums and utility costs related to the former residence (provided it remains unoccupied), to a maximum of the actual costs for three months or $5,000, whichever is less.

If your employer pays a non-accountable moving expenses allowance of up to $650, it is not a taxable benefit as long as you certify in writing that you used the allowance for moving expenses. Any amount over $650 paid as a non-accountable moving allowance is considered a taxable benefit and you can deduct your actual moving expenses.

> **Arrange to avoid a taxable benefit for employer-paid moving expenses where possible.**

Where possible, you should try to avoid being assessed a taxable benefit by arranging for your employer to reimburse you for your moving costs or pay you an accountable advance or a non-accountable moving allowance that does not exceed $650, rather than paying you a non-accountable allowance over $650.

Moving allowances are treated differently for Québec tax purposes. If you are relocated by your employer and receive a moving allowance, you do not have to include in your Québec income an amount equal to two weeks' worth of your salary (based on your new salary after your relocation).

If you relocate and receive a home purchase loan from your employer, a special deduction is available for the imputed interest on the loan—see 7.2.3.

12.1.4 Other relocation payments

Your employer may make certain types of relocation payments to help you defray higher home financing costs in your new location. As of September 30, 1998, most direct or indirect financing support payments are considered taxable benefits. These payments include:

- *Mortgage interest differential payments* made by your employer to compensate you if the interest rate on your new mortgage is higher than the interest rate on the old one.
- *Mortgage subsidy payments* to offset the larger mortgage interest payments created by a higher mortgage principal amount due to higher housing prices in the new location for homes of the same size as your previous one.
- *One-half of the excess of reimbursements over $15,000 for a loss on the sale of a former residence*, calculated as the difference between the employee's cost of the home and the selling price, or the difference between the selling price of the home and its fair market value, as determined by an independent appraisal.
- *Tax equalization payments and cost-of-living payments* made to compensate you for higher taxes and higher living costs in your new location.

Such payments related to pre-October 1998 relocations will become taxable in 2001.

12.2 Moving to Canada

When you immigrate to Canada, most property you own is deemed to be acquired by you at its fair market value as of your date of immigration. This means that Canada will tax only the capital gain that accrues while you are resident in Canada.

> Before moving to Canada, consider setting up a foreign trust to hold your non-Canadian investments.

If you have significant non-Canadian investments, it may be worthwhile to set up a foreign trust before you become resident in Canada. A foreign trust can be exempt from Canadian tax for up to five years after you become resident. This may be a useful strategy where the tax rate in your former country of residence is lower than your Canadian rate.

If you are being relocated to Canada by your employer, you may wish to negotiate for a payment to cover the higher taxes imposed in Canada. Note, however, that "tax equalization payments" are considered a taxable benefit for Canadian tax purposes.

If you are moving to Canada, you should obtain professional advice regarding strategies for minimizing your tax burden. There may be steps you should take before you arrive in Canada.

12.2.1 Moving to Canada from the U.S.

If you're a U.S. citizen moving to Canada, moving expenses can present particular difficulties. If you are posted to Canada and move to Canada, reimbursement by your employer of your moving expenses will normally be considered Canadian-source income for purposes of the U.S. foreign earned income exclusion (see 17.2.1) and foreign tax credit (see 17.2.2). You may be able to claim certain moving expenses as a separate deduction on your U.S. tax return, but only if you have not used the foreign earned income exclusion to eliminate your Canadian-source employment income for tax purposes. Numerous special rules and restrictions apply to moving expenses claimed on a "foreign move" (a move to a non-U.S. home).

For U.S. purposes, your move must be employment or business related and you must work in the new location for 39 weeks for your moving expenses to be deductible (unless you are retiring and returning to the U.S. from a foreign assignment). The deduction is limited to the costs of moving household goods and personal effects to the new residence and travel and lodging costs during the move. No deduction is allowed for meal expenses, expenses incurred while searching for a new home after obtaining employment, costs of selling the old residence or temporary lodging after obtaining employment. Reimbursement of moving costs by your employer is taxable income to you.

12.3 Moving from Canada

12.3.1 Ceasing Canadian residence

Generally, Canada imposes tax on the worldwide income of its residents but only on the Canadian-source income of non-residents. So whether you are considered resident in Canada can make a significant difference to your potential Canadian tax liability after you move.

> **Take steps to cease Canadian residency if you're moving abroad.**

If you move to another country, you may still be considered a Canadian resident for tax purposes if you keep certain ties with Canada such as maintaining a home, club memberships, credit cards or medical plans or if your spouse or dependants remain in Canada. If you're moving to another country permanently or for an extended period, you may want to take steps to cease Canadian residency.

Revenue Canada has no hard and fast rules for determining residency. Each situation is assessed on its own merits. Generally you will be considered a non-resident of Canada if your stay abroad has a degree of permanence, you sever your residential ties to Canada and establish new ties elsewhere, and your visits to Canada after your departure are occasional and sporadic.

Starting in the year of your departure, you should spend significantly less than 183 days in Canada per year. Days during any portion of which you are physically present in Canada count as full days.

Other steps that will show you have ceased Canadian residency include:

- Selling your personal property such as furniture or cars or taking it with you to your new country
- Cancelling or suspending club memberships
- Cancelling your Canadian driver's licence and plate (you may want to obtain a driver's licence in your new country before you give up your Canadian licence)
- Closing your Canadian bank accounts or putting them on non-resident status
- Cancelling credits cards issued in Canada and having them re-issued in your new country
- Changing your mailing address for all correspondence
- Cancelling your Canadian medical plans and taking out new ones in your new country
- Situating your primary place of business outside Canada.

As a non-resident of Canada, you will still be subject to Canadian tax if at any time during a calendar year you:

- Are employed or perform services in Canada;
- Carry on business in Canada;
- Dispose of property not subject to Canadian departure tax (see 12.3.2) such as rental property;
- Receive Canadian sourced dividend or interest income related to a property or company in Canada; or
- Receive rental income from rental properties in Canada.

A tax treaty between Canada and your new country may reduce or eliminate your Canadian tax liability in many circumstances.

12.3.2 Canadian departure tax

If you leave Canada and become non-resident, you are deemed to have sold most of your assets at fair market value, and will have to recognize any resulting income or capital gains. As of October 2, 1996, the range of assets treated as having been sold for fair market value on emigration now includes *all* property, except for:

- Canadian real estate

- Property that you already owned when you became resident in Canada, if your residence in Canada totalled no more than five years out of the last 10
- Pension entitlements, including RRSPs or RRIFs
- Property used in a business in Canada
- Certain stock options.

> **Beware of Canadian departure tax on emigration.**

For other property, the deemed disposition will result in an immediate tax liability on the resulting income or gains, although Revenue Canada will allow you to defer paying the tax on gains as long as you post acceptable security. Acceptable security could be a letter of credit, a mortgage or a bank guarantee. You will not have to post security for the first $25,000 of departure tax (representing about $70,000 in gains). The tax will still be due when the assets are sold.

If you decide to post the security, interest will not be charged for the period up to the actual disposition of the property or death of the owner (whichever occurs first). If the security subsequently becomes deficient (e.g., due to a decline in value of the assets posted), you will have 90 days after you're notified by Revenue Canada to make up the deficiency.

Security for private Canadian company shares

If you're a private Canadian company shareholder and you give up your Canadian residency status but retain your shares, the new rules may create valuation and financing problems if your shares have significantly appreciated in value. For example, determining the fair market value of your shares will generally require professional assistance, possibly resulting in significant valuation costs. If you don't have your shares valued, Revenue Canada will fix the value. Financing your tax liability may also pose a problem if it is not advisable or possible to use the business's banking facilities and you do not have other liquid resources available to satisfy the debt.

In the past, Revenue Canada has not normally accepted non-liquid assets such as shares of private corporations as security for future tax liabilities. However, recognizing the dilemma many taxpayers will face, Revenue Canada officials say that they may accept such shares as security for the debt. Revenue will act as any other commercial lender and expect the normal representations, warranties and covenants to ensure that the shares retain their value. To satisfy Revenue Canada, you may have to change existing collateral arrangements and shareholder agreements.

12.3.3 Capital gains exemption on emigration

Once you are non-resident, you cannot use the $500,000 capital gains exemption discussed in 6.4. So if you still have room in your exemption, and you own qualifying farm property (which includes Canadian real estate), you may wish to take steps to "crystallize" your gain before you emigrate. That way, you will trigger a gain that is absorbed by the $500,000 exemption which would not otherwise be available after you have emigrated, and only the increase from the current fair market value will be taxed in Canada when you, as a non-resident, eventually dispose of the property.

Alternatively, if you realize gains on the deemed disposition of qualified farm property or shares in a qualified small business corporation, you will want to make sure you apply any of your remaining $500,000 exemption against these gains.

For small business shares and certain qualifying farm property, the deemed disposition on emigration will occur automatically. You will not need to make a special election and you can claim the exemption on your return in the year of your emigration.

12.3.4 Reporting rules for emigrants with property worth over $25,000

If you emigrate from Canada in 1996 or later and you own property with a total value of $25,000 or more, you are required to file an information form (T1161) listing all your significant assets with your final Canadian tax return in the year of emigration. In determining whether your property exceeds the $25,000 reporting threshold, the following assets are not included:

- Cash, including bank deposits;
- RRSPs, private company pension plans (RPPs), RRIFs, retirement compensation arrangements (RCA), employee benefit plans and deferred profit sharing plans (DPSPs); and
- Items for personal use (such as household effects, clothing, cars, collectibles) whose fair market value is less than $10,000.

12.3.5 If you rent or sell your Canadian home after emigration

Real property that you own in Canada will not be subject to the deemed disposition rules discussed above when you emigrate. If you decide to rent your property, you will generally have to remit a 25% non-resident withholding tax on your gross rental income. If you will be incurring expenses to earn your rental income, you can file form NR6 before your first non-resident tax payment is due and the withholding tax will be assessed on your net rental income. If you file the form, you will have to file an annual rental return by June 30 of each following year.

> **Obtain a clearance certificate from Revenue Canada if you sell your Canadian home after you emigrate.**

Generally, there is no Canadian income tax levied on the gain from selling a principal residence (see 6.5.2). If you sell your former principal residence while you are a non-resident of Canada, you must notify Revenue Canada (and Revenu Québec if the property is in Québec) of the disposition and request a clearance certificate. If you don't obtain a clearance certificate before the disposition, the purchaser must withhold and remit one-third of the gross proceeds to Revenue Canada (and a further 18% to Revenu Québec, where applicable). You should file Revenue Canada's Form T2062 at least 30 days before the property is sold or within 10 days of the sale to obtain the clearance certificate. (You must also file Revenu Québec form TP-1097-v if the property is located in Québec.)

If you sell your former principal residence more than one year after the year of your move, only a portion of the gain would be exempt under the principal residence exemption. As we saw in 6.5.2, the principal residence exemption calculation is based on the fraction of one plus the number of taxation years ending after 1971 for which the property was a principal residence and during which you are a resident of Canada over the total number of years (after 1971) it was owned by you. So for each additional year that you do not sell your principal residence after you cease Canadian residency, the denominator increases while the numerator stays constant and a smaller portion of the gain is exempt from Canadian tax.

If you plan to rent out your former principal residence, the property's use will change from personal to income-producing and will be subject to a deemed disposition at fair market value. Any gain accruing up to the date of the change in use will be taxable but the tax may be completely reduced or eliminated by the principal residence exemption.

You may be able to make an election not to deem a change in use of the property. You will not be able to claim depreciation on the property while the election is in effect. However, the election could be beneficial if you expect the property to increase significantly in value since you will be able shelter some of the resulting capital gain with the principal residence exemption.

12.3.6 If you have RRSPs

As noted in 12.3.2, your RRSPs are not subject to the deemed disposition rules when you leave Canada. For Canadian tax purposes, you can continue to make deductible contributions to your RRSP as long as you have contribution room available.

> **If you wish to wind up your RRSP, consider waiting until after you become non-resident.**

If you wish to collapse your RRSP, you may want to wait until you are a non-resident of Canada to do so. As a non-resident, you will be subject to a 25% withholding tax on the proceeds received from the plan. If you collapse the plan while you're a resident of Canada, the proceeds will be taxed at your marginal tax rate, which will be about 50% if you are in the top tax bracket, depending on the province you live in.

> **Repay Home Buyers' Plan withdrawals within 60 days of becoming non-resident.**

If you withdrew funds from your RRSP under the Home Buyers' Plan (see 3.3.6) to purchase your Canadian home and you become a non-resident, you should repay the entire withdrawal within 60 days of becoming non-resident. To the extent you do not make the repayment within 60 days, the unpaid balance will be included in your income on your Canadian income tax return for the year of your departure.

If you move to the U.S., your RRSP contributions will not be deductible for U.S. tax purposes and the income earned inside your RRSP is technically subject to U.S. taxation in the year it is earned. However, the Canada-U.S. tax treaty provides an election to defer the U.S. taxation until an actual distribution is made.

12.4 References

The following publications can be obtained (in person or by telephone request) from your nearest Revenue Canada District Taxation Office. Forms and guides may also be available from Revenue Canada's Internet site at *www.rc.gc.ca*.

Interpretation Bulletin IT-178R3, "Moving expenses"

Form T1-M "Claim for moving expenses"

Form NR6, "Undertaking to File an Income Tax Return by a Non-Resident Receiving Rent from Real Property or Receiving a Timber Royalty"

Form T2062, "Notice by a Non-Resident of Canada Concerning the Disposition or Proposed Disposition of Canadian Taxable Property"

The following may be obtained from any office of the Internal Revenue Service, and are generally available at U.S. embassy and consular offices, or from the IRS' Internet site at *www.irs.ustreas.gov.*

Publication 521, "Moving expenses"

Form 3903, "Moving expenses"

Form 3903F, "Foreign moving expenses"

If you have your own corporation

13

- Consider the potential benefits of incorporating your business (10.5)
- Keep the corporation a small business corporation at all times (13.1)
- Consider crystallizing your $500,000 capital gains exemption (13.1)
- Multiply your access to the capital gains exemption (13.1)
- Defer income to the next calendar year by accruing bonuses (13.2.2)
- Maximize capital dividend payments (13.2.4)
- Consider a tax-free repayment of capital (13.2.5)
- Crunch the numbers to calculate your optimum salary/dividend mix (13.3)
- Consider the tax benefits of setting up a holding corporation (13.3)
- Look into the potential advantages of a corporate partnership (13.3.1)
- Weigh the potential advantages of incorporating your investments (13.6)
- Be cautious about having investment income in your corporation that carries on an active business (13.6)

In this chapter we suggest some tax planning techniques that are available if you are an owner/manager—that is, you carry on your business through a corporation. We will not discuss tax planning for the corporation itself, except in relation to how to most effectively get its profits into your hands. If you are thinking about setting up a corporation for running your business, see 10.5 for a discussion of some of the pros and cons. The tax rules in this area are substantially the same for both federal and Québec tax purposes.

13.1 Taxation of the corporation

A corporation is a distinct legal entity, and if you have an incorporated business, the corporation's profits are not yours simply to take. You, as a director of the corporation (even if you are the sole director), act in a different capacity from yourself as a shareholder of the corporation. Legally, as a shareholder your only right is to elect the board of directors, who then cause the corporation to take specific actions.

To extract funds from the corporation you must follow one of the "correct" methods we discuss in 13.2 below. If you do not, the tax system will penalize you.

For tax purposes, the corporation's business and investment income will be calculated in much the same way as your own. (See 10.2 regarding the calculation of business income.) As with individuals, certain deductions (such as loss carryforwards) are available in computing taxable income.

The corporation then pays federal tax and provincial tax on its taxable income.

The federal corporate tax rate (including federal surtax) is currently 29.12%, but can be as low as 22.12% for income from manufacturing and processing. However, for small "Canadian-controlled private corporations", the federal rate on the first $200,000 of "active business income" is 13.12%. (A Canadian-controlled private corporation is a corporation that is resident in Canada and is not controlled in any manner by any combination of non-residents or public corporations.) The federal small business rate is not available for large corporations. It begins to be phased out once the corporation's capital exceeds $10 million.

Provincial tax varies, but is typically around 16% of taxable income. Most provinces have reduced rates for the first $200,000 of business income; they range from 5–10%. Québec eliminated its reduced small business rate as of July 1, 1999. The combined tax burden is thus about 23% on the first $200,000 of a small business corporation's income, and about 45% on the remainder, unless the corporation earns income from manufacturing and processing, in which case the combined tax burden can be as low as 27%.

Keep the corporation a small business corporation at all times.

If possible, ensure that your corporation remains a "small business corporation" (see 6.3.2) and that your shares are "qualified small business corporation shares" (see 6.4.1) at all times. This will preserve, respectively, your ability to claim allowable business investment losses in respect of any loss on the corporation's shares, and the $500,000 capital gains exemption on any gain.

Note that you cannot always predict when the sale of the shares will be triggered for tax purposes. On the death of any shareholder, there will be a deemed disposition of that shareholder's shares at their fair market value unless the shares are transferred to a spouse or a qualifying "spousal trust" (see 20.4.2).

Consider crystallizing your $500,000 capital gains exemption.

As an alternative, you may wish to "crystallize" your capital gains exemption. "Crystallizing" means triggering a capital gain on your shares of a qualified small business corporation, while continuing to own (or at least control) the corporation. This will permanently increase your adjusted cost base of the shares and possibly eliminate the need for the corporation to retain its qualified small business corporation status. Several techniques (such as selling shares to a family member) can be used to crystallize an exemption; professional advice should be sought. Crystallization may be a good idea given that the federal and Québec governments could eliminate the $500,000 exemption at some point in the future.

> **Multiply your access to the capital gains exemption.**

If you arrange for your spouse to invest in common shares of your corporation, you can effectively double the available exemption by each claiming $500,000. Your spouse's own funds must be used for the investment, to avoid the attribution rules discussed in 5.2.2. You may also be able to multiply the exemption by transferring shares to your children.

On death, it is possible to double the available capital gains exemption by leaving shares to your spouse or to a trust for your spouse. See 20.1.2 and 20.4.2.

13.2 Ways of extracting funds from the corporation

Since the corporation is legally a separate "person", you must follow one of the methods described below to get your hands on the corporation's income.

13.2.1 Dividends

Dividends are the distribution of a corporation's profits to its shareholders. They are not deductible to the corporation. In your hands, dividends will be grossed up by one-quarter and eligible for a dividend tax credit worth approximately the same amount (one-quarter of the actual dividend). See 7.1.2 for details.

If the corporation earns income, pays tax on it and pays what is left to you as a dividend, the combined effect of the corporation's tax and your personal tax will be about the same as if you had earned the income directly, if the corporation's tax rate is 20%. This is called "integration".

Where the corporate rate (federal plus provincial) is more than 20%, the combined effect of the two levels of tax will normally be that more tax is paid than if you had earned the same income directly. Conversely, where the corporate tax rate is less than 20%, paying dividends results in less tax than if you were to pay tax directly on the business income.

Example:

Ken owns all the shares of Ken Ltd. Ken Ltd. earns $100,000 in small business income, which is taxed at a combined federal/provincial rate of 20%. Ken Ltd. then pays the remaining $80,000 as a dividend to Ken.

Ken will "gross up" the $80,000 dividend by one-quarter, or $20,000, and will pay tax on $100,000, which conceptually represents the corporation's original income. He will then receive a combined federal/provincial dividend tax credit worth about $20,000, equal to the amount of tax the corporation paid. So Ken and the corporation will together be taxed as if Ken had earned the $100,000 on his own.

Note that Ken's gross-up and dividend tax credit will be 25% of the dividend regardless of the rate of tax that Ken Ltd. actually paid.

13.2.2 Salary

Where the corporation pays you a salary, the amount paid is deductible to the corporation and taxable to you as employment income. If the corporation pays all of its profits to you as salary, you are therefore in much the same position as you would be if you earned the income directly, without having a corporation.

Although your salary may become quite high in such situations, Revenue Canada's general policy is not to consider it an unreasonable deduction (for the corporation) where you are the owner/manager of the corporation. It is usually acceptable to consider the corporation's income is due to your efforts, and therefore a salary equal to that income is a reasonable one. Of course, you are paying tax on the salary anyway.

You may decide on a base salary followed by a bonus, to be paid to you after the corporation has calculated its income at the end of the year. In general, you are taxed on employment income only when you receive it, while the corporation can accrue salary or bonus, counting it as deductible in the year even though it is paid after year-end.

However, any salary or bonus that is deducted by the corporation must actually be *paid* to you no later than 179 days after the end of the year. (As an administrative concession, Revenue Canada actually allows you 180 days instead of 179.) Otherwise, it is not deductible by the corporation until the year in which it is actually paid.

> **Defer income into the next calendar year by accruing bonuses.**

If the corporation's year-end occurs after early July, it can declare a bonus to you as of its year-end, but pay the bonus within 180 days which will be after December 31. The corporation can thus get a deduction from its income, but you do not have to recognize the income personally for tax purposes until the next calendar year.

13.2.3 Payments on loans from shareholders

If you lend funds to the corporation (or if you did so when originally setting up the business), the corporation can repay any amount of the loan without tax consequences. Such a repayment is neither deductible to the corporation nor taxable to you.

You could arrange to have the corporation pay you interest on your loan. The interest paid will normally be taxable to you as investment income. The tax effect would be about the same as if the corporation paid you that amount in salary. However, if your loan to the corporation does not *require* that interest be paid or there is no formal loan document, there is a danger that the interest will not be deductible to the corporation since it has not been paid pursuant to a legal obligation to pay interest. (Conversely, if you arrange for documentation requiring that interest be paid, the annual interest accrual rule discussed in 7.2.1 may require you to include interest in your income even in years when it is not paid!)

13.2.4 Capital dividends

We mentioned capital dividends in 5.3.8 and 7.1.4. As you will recall from Chapter 6, only three-quarters of capital gains are taxed. When a "private" (i.e., non-public) corporation realizes a capital gain, the untaxed portion is added to its "capital dividend account". Similarly, one-quarter of capital losses reduce the capital dividend account.

> **Maximize capital dividend payments.**

Any amount in the corporation's capital dividend account may be paid out entirely tax-free to its shareholders. This preserves the non-taxability of the appropriate fraction of the capital gain. So if the corporation has realized any capital gains, you should cause it to pay out capital dividends as your first choice for extracting funds.

Example:

Tod owns all the shares of Todcorp Inc. In 1999, Todcorp Inc. sells some land for a capital gain of $120,000, three-quarters of which is brought into Todcorp's income and taxed as a taxable capital gain.

Todcorp can pay a dividend of up to $30,000 (one-quarter of the capital gain) to Tod in 1999 or any later year, provided he elects beforehand to make the dividend a "capital dividend." The capital dividend will then be completely tax-free to Tod. (Of course, because it is a dividend, it is not deductible to Todcorp.)

Note also that if you allow a capital dividend account to build up in the corporation without paying capital dividends, the account can be reduced or wiped out by future capital losses. Once you have paid out capital dividends, however, they are safely out of the corporation, and subsequent capital losses will have no effect on them.

13.2.5 Repayment of capital

> **Consider a tax-free repayment of capital.**

Any amount that is less than the corporation's "paid-up capital" may be paid out to the shareholders as a repayment of capital, generally with no tax consequences, if the paid-up capital is reduced by that amount.

Paid-up capital is essentially the amount of capital contributed to the corporation in exchange for its shares. However, the figure can be adjusted in various ways for tax purposes, as a result of transactions involving the corporation. As such, the legal PUC often differs from the tax PUC.

Example:

ABC Corp. was capitalized with $50,000, the amount that the original shareholders contributed when subscribing for 1,000 common shares.

If the directors of ABC approve a reduction in paid-up capital to $20,000 and a simultaneous repayment of $30,000 in capital to the shareholders, there will be no adverse tax consequences for either ABC or its shareholders. The $30,000 simply comes out tax-free. ABC then has 1,000 common shares issued with a paid-up capital of $20,000 and an adjusted cost base to its shareholders of $20,000.

If the corporation was originally funded with a substantial amount of capital, consider extracting funds by a reduction of the paid-up capital of the corporation. Make sure the corporation remains sufficiently capitalized to satisfy any requirements of its creditors or bankers.

13.2.6 Loan to shareholder

All of the mechanisms we have looked at so far—dividend, salary, repayment of a shareholder loan, capital dividend and repayment of capital—are legitimate ways to get your hands on the corporation's income or funds. We now turn to some of the rules designed to prevent you from doing so without following the normal routes.

Suppose the corporation simply lends you its funds? If you do not fit within certain exceptions, the entire amount of the loan will simply be included in your income. This is a very serious penalty, because the corporation receives no deduction for the amount of the loan, and you do not benefit from the dividend tax credit. The same rule applies if you become indebted to the corporation in some other way (e.g., you buy property from it, but pay for the property with a promissory note rather than cash). However, where a loan has been included in your income and you subsequently repay it, you will be allowed a deduction from your income.

To avoid this provision, bona fide repayment arrangements must be made at the time the loan is made and the loan must fall into one of the following exceptions:

- a loan to an employee who (along with family members) does not own 10% of the shares of any class of the corporation, where the reason for the loan is the individual's employment rather than the shareholding
- a loan to an employee, where the reason for the loan is the individual's employment rather than the shareholding, to help the employee purchase (a) a home, (b) shares in the employer or a related corporation, or (c) a car to be used in employment duties (note that the rules do not specify a threshold for the percentage interest owned in the corporation for purposes of determining the reason for the loan)
- a loan that is repaid within one year of the end of the corporation's taxation year in which the loan was made, and which is not part of a series of loans and repayments.

If the loan falls into one of the above exceptions, but is made at no interest or at a low rate of interest, you will be considered to be receiving a taxable benefit from the corporation based on the difference between Revenue Canada's current "low rate" prescribed rate of interest (see 8.4) and the rate that you are paying. This rule is exactly the same as for loans to employees, which we saw in 9.3. As in the case of employees, you may be allowed an offsetting deduction as a notional interest expense (which affects your entitlement to the capital gains exemption—see 6.4.3) if such expense would otherwise meet the rules concerning the deductibility of interest.

13.2.7 Deemed dividends

Certain types of actions that involve changes to a corporation's capital structure will deem you to have received a dividend from the corporation. Generally, this happens when the corporation takes actions that would otherwise allow you to extract profits as a repayment of capital.

For example, if the corporation redeems shares that you own, any amount paid by the corporation in excess of the paid-up capital of the shares is deemed to be a dividend (and not part of your proceeds of disposition for capital gains purposes). The return of the paid-up capital on the redemption is generally tax-free.

13.2.8 Shareholder appropriations

We have covered all of the "proper" mechanisms for extracting funds from a corporation. Suppose you don't follow any of the legalities and you simply take the corporation's funds or property, and use them as your own? If you are the sole shareholder, there will be no one to object to you doing this.

In such cases, the *Income Tax Act* deems that any benefit the corporation confers on you will be brought into your income for tax purposes. So, for example, if you simply take $10,000 out of the corporation's bank account without declaring a dividend, that $10,000 will be added to your income (without you benefitting from the dividend tax credit).

Clearly, it is to your advantage to follow the more conventional mechanisms for extracting funds. In the next section, we explore some of the considerations that will affect your decision as to the appropriate mix between salary, dividend and other forms of remuneration for yourself.

13.2.9 Determining your salary/dividend mix

> Crunch the numbers to determine your optimum salary/dividend mix.

Careful analysis will be needed to calculate the best mix of salary and dividends for your case. It will depend on your cash flow needs, your income level, the corporation's income level, the corporation's status for tax purposes, and many other factors. Computer spreadsheets and planning tools are available to assist in this task.

In many cases, the best strategy for a small business corporation is to pay enough salary to reduce the corporation's income to $200,000. This maximizes the amount of income that is taxed at the low small business rate, without having corporate income taxed at the high rate that applies to income beyond $200,000.

However, you will usually want to pay yourself enough salary to allow the maximum possible contribution to an RRSP (see 3.1.3). The same goes for any family members you've employed for income splitting purposes (see 5.3.2).

Note also that if you are in a business that can suffer a downturn, paying out a large salary can prevent you from carrying back a later year's loss. Suppose, for example, your business earns $1 million in 1999, and you pay out $800,000 to yourself as a salary, leaving $200,000 as the business' income. If in 2000 the business loses $1 million, you will have no way of carrying back the loss against your personal income. If you had left the funds as business income and paid out dividends, you would be able to carry back the 2000 loss to 1999 retroactively wiping out the business' 1999 corporate tax, and obtain a refund of that tax from Revenue Canada.

13.3 Effect of having a holding company

> Consider the tax benefits of setting up a holding corporation.

You may choose to interpose a holding company between yourself and your corporation for various reasons. One reason for doing this is to pay out dividends from the operating business to make the funds harder for creditors to reach, while keeping the income subject to a lower level of taxation than would apply if it were paid out to you personally.

For example, you own 100% of the shares of Yourname Holdings Ltd., which owns 100% of the shares of Yourname Manufacturing Ltd. In general, dividends can be paid from the manufacturing company to the holding company without any tax effects.

If your children do not have any ownership in the business, you can consider bringing them in as shareholders at the time you set up the holding corporation. (See the estate planning example in 20.5.2 for one way of doing this.) This may be desirable for several reasons including income splitting as well as planning for your succession. However, if your children are under 18 you must be particularly careful about the attribution rules (see 5.2.3 and 5.2.4).

A holding company is often appropriate where you have family members involved in ownership of your share of the business (perhaps for income-splitting purposes), and there are other shareholders not related to you. If you and your family members own shares in the holding corporation, and the holding corporation owns all of your family's interest in the operating company, the other shareholders of the operating company need not be concerned with your internal family arrangements.

You should be cautious about accumulating funds in a holding company, however. If you intend to treat the holding corporation as qualifying for the $500,000 capital gains exemption (see 6.4.1), you can run into trouble if the corporation begins to have a substantial amount of funds that are used for generating investment income, rather than owning only the shares in the operating corporation. You may also be caught by the attribution rules or the new income splitting tax on certain income received by minor children (see Chapter 5), depending on when and how you introduced family members as shareholders of the corporation. Note also that investment income in a corporation is subject to an extra refundable tax that makes the up-front cost of earning the income very high (see 13.6).

13.3.1 Corporate partnerships

> Look into the potential advantages of a corporate partnership.

An alternative to the use of holding companies is a corporate partnership. This is a partnership between your corporation and one or more other corporations (owned by other people).

There are a number of advantages to this form of corporate structure, including the deferral of tax in the initial years and increased flexibility concerning remuneration. Professional advice should be obtained to determine whether this structure is appropriate.

13.4 Shareholders' agreements

Where you share the ownership of a private corporation, it is usually wise to have a shareholders' agreement. Such an agreement can set out rights and obligations of the shareholders that go beyond the basic ownership of shares.

Typically, a shareholders' agreement will provide for the orderly termination of the relationship between the shareholders if there is a future disagreement, or death or disability of one of the key shareholders.

Example:

Euan and Jonathan start a small manufacturing business together. Each owns 50% of the shares of the corporation. Over the years, the business becomes very successful, but Euan and Jonathan cannot get along and decide that one of them must leave.

Euan and Jonathan signed a shareholders' agreement that contains a "shotgun" clause. Euan now offers Jonathan $500,000 for Jonathan's shares in the corporation. If Jonathan refuses to sell, the agreement provides that Jonathan must buy Euan's shares for the price Euan is offering ($500,000).

The "shotgun" clause is just one example of a provision that can resolve (or prevent) major disputes between key shareholders. Typical provisions in a shareholders' agreement deal with:

- desire of a shareholder to sell his or her shares
- dissension among shareholders
- death or disability of a shareholder
- agreement as to who the directors and/or officers of the corporation will be
- agreement to vote the shares in a particular way on certain issues
- what will happen if the corporation's shares are awarded to a key shareholder's spouse on separation or divorce.

Tax considerations play a major part of planning for shareholder agreements. The tax treatment of life insurance payments, the availability of the $500,000 capital gains exemption, the valuation of shares, and many other issues must be considered. Clearly, shareholder agreements should always be drafted with proper professional advice as to both the legal and the tax issues.

13.5 Pension plans for small business owners

Registered pension plans were discussed in 3.4.1. Both "money-purchase" and "defined-benefit" pension plans can be used to accrue benefits for major shareholders (see also 3.4.2, regarding individual pension plans). As an alternative to saving for retirement exclusively through an RRSP, consider having your company establish an individual pension plan, which we discussed in 3.4.2. However, this is a complex area and professional advice is essential.

If you are a small business owner and you don't want the trouble of administering a pension plan, you may simply want to set up an RRSP for yourself and ensure that you have sufficient "earned income" (i.e., salary from the corporation) to be able to make adequate contributions (see 3.1.3).

13.6 Investment income earned in a corporation

In the past, it was generally advantageous to have investment income earned in a corporation. Since the regular 44% corporate tax rate (combined federal/provincial) was substantially lower than the rate that applies to high levels of personal income, you could often achieve a significant tax deferral in the current year, assuming you were already paying tax at the top personal rate.

But since 1995, a federal 6 2/3% refundable tax has applied to interest and other investment income in a Canadian-controlled private corporation. Most dividends received by a private corporation from public companies are also subject to a 33 1/3% refundable tax (Part IV tax). These refundable taxes are paid back to the corporation only when it has paid out sufficient taxable dividends (resulting in tax being paid by the shareholders). The combined corporate tax rate has thus risen to about 51% (combined federal and provincial).

As a result of this increase and provincial personal tax rate cuts over the past several years, there is generally no tax deferral advantage to earning investment income in a corporation. In some cases a tax prepayment results. The precise calculation depends on your province of residence, your level of personal income, the extent to which you need to extract the funds from the corporation, and the way in which you extract those funds. It may well be cheaper to hold your investments personally.

> ## Weigh the potential advantages of incorporating your investments.

Looking beyond the potential tax deferral advantages and absolute costs, there are other possible benefits of holding investments in a corporation. For example, incorporating your investments can help you to shield your investments from creditors, reduce probate fees on your death (see 20.1.3), and protect your assets from U.S. estate tax (see 18.4). Incorporation will also give you control over the timing of dividend payments and thus the timing of income receipts in your own hands, allowing you to:

- maximize Old Age Security (OAS) benefits (if your income from sources other than investments is less than $53,215) (see 19.3.2);
- reduce your exposure to alternative minimum tax (see 7.6);
- manage the timing of dividend payments in order to manage your cumulative net investment loss (CNIL) account balance (see 6.4.3); and
- increase your earned income and RRSP contribution room (see 3.1.3) through the payment of directors' fees and/or salaries.

Against the potential benefits, you'll also need to weigh the incremental costs of forming and maintaining the corporation, including substantial start-up and ongoing legal and administrative costs and the corporation's potential liability for federal Large Corporations Tax and provincial capital taxes.

> ## Be cautious about keeping investments in a corporation that carries on an active business.

Be particularly wary of moving investments into a corporation carrying on an active business. You will likely jeopardize the status of the corporation's shares from being eligible for the $500,000 capital gains exemption (see 6.4.1 and 13.1). In addition, the creditors of the active business will have access to the investments.

13.7 Selling the business

If you decide to sell your incorporated business, there are two general approaches that can be taken. One is for the corporation to sell the assets of the business. The other is for you to sell the shares of the corporation.

If your shares are "qualified small business corporation shares" (see 6.4.1), you may be able to claim an exemption for up to $500,000 of your gain on the sale. No capital gains exemption is available to the corporation if it sells the assets. From your point of view, it may therefore be preferable to sell the shares.

The buyer of your business, however, will often prefer to purchase the assets. One reason is that this will normally allow the buyer to claim higher capital cost allowance on the cost of depreciable assets (see 10.2.7).

No GST or other sales tax applies on a sale of shares. On a sale of assets, GST (or HST) and QST will usually apply, but can almost always be recovered by the purchaser in the form of an input tax credit (see 10.2.4). Alternatively, in many cases on the sale of part or all of a business an election can be made to have no GST (or HST) or QST apply to the sale. However, provincial sales tax will generally apply to the sale of tangible assets other than manufacturing equipment, but the rules vary depending on the province.

Needless to say, any purchase and sale of a business must be done with detailed professional advice.

If your business goes public without you selling the shares, you can make a special election to "crystallize" part or all of your accrued capital gain, and get the $500,000 exemption as if you had sold the shares (see 6.4).

13.8 References

The following publications can be obtained (in person or by telephone request) from your nearest Revenue Canada District Taxation Office. Forms and guides may also be available from Revenue Canada's Internet site at *www.rc.gc.ca*.

Interpretation Bulletin IT-66R6, "Capital dividends"

Interpretation Bulletin IT-67R3, "Taxable dividends from corporations resident in Canada"

Interpretation Bulletin IT-109R2, "Unpaid amounts"

Interpretation Bulletin IT-119R3, "Debts of shareholders, certain persons connected with shareholders, etc."

Interpretation Bulletin IT-432R2, "Benefits conferred on shareholders"

Farming

- Establish that your farming business has a "reasonable expectation of profit" (14.1)
- Classify farming as your chief source of income (14.1)
- Claim deductions available for the self-employed (14.2)
- Consider using the "cash method" of accounting to defer taxes (14.2.1)
- Make the most of the $500,000 capital gains exemption for qualified farm property (14.5.1)
- Take advantage of intergenerational transfer rules (14.5.2)
- Claim alternative principal residence exemption where appropriate (14.5.3)

The income tax system has a number of special rules to deal with farming. We outline some of them in this chapter.

14.1 Farming—a business or not?

No matter what kind of activity you undertake, you are only allowed to write off losses for tax purposes if you are engaged in a business "with a reasonable expectation of profit" (see 10.4.1). This issue comes up repeatedly in the case of part-time farmers.

"Farming", for tax purposes, includes a number of activities ranging from growing crops to raising livestock, fur farming, fruit growing, keeping bees and training horses for racing. The *Income Tax Act* classifies people engaged in farming into three groups. The principal difference among the groups is the extent to which they can deduct expenses relating to their farming activities.

At one extreme are the full-time farmers, for whom farming is **a chief source of income**. Such people are allowed to treat their farming business like any other business, and can therefore claim losses against other income for tax purposes if they suffer losses in any given year (see 14.3.1).

> Establish that your farming business has a "reasonable expectation of profit".

At the other extreme are people who do not have a **"reasonable expectation of profit"** from their farming activity. Such people are sometimes called "hobby farmers", as farming is considered to be their hobby rather than something they are doing in order to make money. Hobby farmers may not deduct any losses from their farming activity. You will need to keep records that establish that your farming business is carried on with a "reasonable expectation of profit" on an objective basis. If your activities never actually turn a profit over many years, a claim that you had a reasonable expectation of profit will be hard to sustain in court.

In the middle are the people who do have a reasonable expectation of profit, but whose "chief source of income is neither farming nor a combination of farming and some other source of income", to quote the *Income Tax Act*. Such people are allowed only **"restricted farm losses"**, limited to certain dollar amounts (see 14.3.2).

Example 1:

Darryl lives on his farm and raises dairy cattle. Almost all his income comes from selling the cows' milk. In 1999, Darryl's cows have a bad year and he loses $30,000.

Darryl will be able to deduct his $30,000 against any other income he has (such as investment income) and carry it forward or back to be used in other years (see 14.3.1). His farming loss is very much like a loss from any other kind of business, such as manufacturing or retailing.

Example 2:

Bob is a jeweller who lives and works in Toronto. He spends his weekends on his ranch, where he keeps a stable of racehorses. In past years, Bob's horses have won a fair amount of prize money. In 1999, Bob has a bad year and spends $30,000 on maintaining his horses without winning any prize money at all.

Bob's loss will likely be considered a "restricted farm loss", and only a portion of it (see 14.3.2) will be deductible against his jewellery business income. Although his horse-racing business (which for income tax purposes is considered farming) does have a reasonable expectation of profit, it is not a chief source of income to him and therefore falls into the "restricted" category.

> **Classify farming as your chief source of income.**

Many court cases have considered the question of whether farming, or farming in combination with some other source, constitutes a taxpayer's "chief source of income". You may wish to consult a tax professional to determine what facts will best establish a claim that will entitle you to a full deduction for farm losses, rather than the more limited deduction for "restricted farm losses".

14.2 Computing farming income

If you are engaged in a farming business—whether or not your losses will be "restricted" as we saw in 14.1—you may take advantage of a number of special rules when calculating income for tax purposes.

> Claim deductions available for the self-employed.

In addition to the specific rules for farmers discussed in this chapter, see 10.2 for ideas as to deductions that can be claimed by the self-employed. If you successfully establish that you are carrying on a farming business with a reasonable expectation of profit, such deductions will be available to you.

14.2.1 The cash method

Businesses are generally required to follow the accrual method of accounting for income. That is, you take your sales for the year into income, even though you may not have been paid for some of those sales until after your business year-end. You claim expenses the same way (see 10.2.2).

> Consider using the "cash method" of accounting to defer taxes.

For a farming business, you may choose to use the **"cash method"** instead. In general, this means you will count payments received, rather than your sales—and only deduct amounts that you have paid, but not still-unpaid expenses that you have incurred. This usually provides a certain amount of deferral of income, and may result in lower tax payable. Once you have chosen the cash method, you are normally required to continue to use that method for the farming business for all subsequent years.

When you are using the cash method, you may, if you wish, include into income any amount up to the fair market value of your inventories on hand at year-end. The amount you include will then be deductible in the following year. You might wish to do this for 1999, for example, if you had very low income in 1999 and can see by the spring of 2000 (when you file your return) that your 2000 income will increase substantially, enough to put you into a higher tax bracket.

14.2.2 Purchases of inventory and prepaid expenses

If you are using the cash method of accounting, it is clearly possible to generate a loss for tax purposes by purchasing large amounts of inventory. Special rules have been introduced to deal with this possibility and to limit the loss you can claim.

Example:

Darryl, from the example in 14.1, purchased dairy cows for $5,000 just before his year-end on December 31, 1999. This purchase has been included as an expense in arriving at his farming loss of $30,000. He did not purchase any other items of inventory at the end of the year. For income tax purposes, he will be required to include $5,000 as a mandatory inventory adjustment to his 1999 income, reducing his farm loss to $25,000. In 2000, this $5,000 mandatory inventory will be treated as a farm expense.

In general, you will be denied a loss that is attributable to purchases of inventory. However, for horses and certain registered bovine animals, you can deduct a portion of the loss. Professional advice should be obtained when dealing with these complex rules.

Claims for prepaid expenses will also be restricted if the expenses relate to a year that is two or more years after the year of payment.

14.2.3 Cost of improving land for farming

Normally, when calculating income from a business, the cost of work done to improve land is considered a capital expense and is not deductible. However, for a farming business, amounts paid for clearing land, levelling land or installing a land drainage system are deductible.

14.2.4 Sales of livestock in a drought region

If you are farming in a region designated for the year as a "drought region", special relief is available if you sold a significant portion of your breeding herd. This rule is designed to allow you to defer paying tax where you are forced to sell off part or all of your herd because of drought. The list of regions designated for the year is determined by Agriculture Canada's Prairie Farm Rehabilitation Administration in Saskatoon each September.

The rule only applies where, by the end of the year, you have sold off (and not replaced) at least 15% of your "breeding herd". When it applies, some or all of your sales of the breeding animals are not counted into your income, but are deferred until a later year when your area is no longer designated as a drought region.

14.2.5 Forced destruction of livestock

If you have livestock that is diseased, you can be forced by the government to destroy the livestock under the *Animal Contagious Diseases Act* or similar legislation. If you receive compensation for the destruction, the compensation is included in your income. However, a special rule allows you to deduct all or part of this compensation and include it in your income in the next year. This allows you to defer paying tax on the compensation by one year.

14.2.6 Net Income Stabilization Account (NISA) and other income or disaster relief programs

The NISA program has created a number of tax issues including certain planning opportunities. Additionally, the various federal and provincial farm income and disaster relief programs should be considered by all farm operators. Consult your tax advisor to ensure that you are taking maximum advantage of these program from an income tax perspective.

14.3 Farming losses

14.3.1 Ordinary farm losses

As we saw in 14.1, if your chief source of income is farming, or your chief source of income is "a combination of farming and some other source of income", you may deduct your farm losses as though they were ordinary business losses.

The carryover available for such losses is somewhat more generous than that for normal business losses (non-capital losses), which we saw in 10.4.1. Like normal losses, farm losses can be carried back and used against income of the past three years. They can also be carried forward, and used against income in any of the next 10 years (rather than seven).

14.3.2 Restricted farm losses

As noted in 14.1, a loss from farming cannot *all* be used if you do not meet the "chief source of income" test. In this case, the loss you claim is limited to the first $2,500, plus one-half of the next $12,500 (that is, up to an additional $6,250).

Example:

Bob the jeweller, who we met in 14.1, loses $30,000 on his racehorses in 1999.

Bob's "restricted farm loss" will be $2,500, plus one-half of the next $12,500. Since his total loss is more than $15,000, he reaches the maximum, and he can only deduct $8,750 against the income from his jewellery business for 1999.

Any amount of loss that cannot be used because of the "restricted farm loss" rules can be carried back for three years and forward for 10 years, but can be used only against farming income. So, in our example, Bob has $21,250 that can be used to offset income from his horse operations during the years 1996 to 1998 and 2000 to 2009.

14.4 Investment tax credits

Investment tax credits (see 10.2.14) are available for investment in agricultural equipment in the Maritimes and the Gaspé region of Québec. The amount of the credit is generally 10%. Unused credits may be carried back three years and forward for 10.

14.5 Transfers of farming assets

A number of special rules, as outlined below, are available to alleviate the tax burden of selling or transferring a farm and the assets of a farming business.

14.5.1 The $500,000 capital gains exemption

> **Make the most of the $500,000 capital gains exemption for qualified farm property.**

As discussed in 6.4.2, a $500,000 exemption from capital gains is available on the disposition of "qualified farm property"—if you are disposing of farm property, investigate whether it qualifies. In general terms, farm land and buildings, shares of farm companies and interests in farming partnerships may qualify for the exemption if they meet certain tests; equipment, inventory and most other assets do not qualify. In some circumstances you may be able to take action, such as delaying the sale, so you can gain time to reorganize your affairs in order to take advantage of the exemption. You also may be able to take steps to increase the cost base of your qualifying farm property to reduce the tax liability that will arise in the future on the property's sale. The tax rules in this area are quite complex so you should seek professional tax advice if you own farm property that qualifies for the exemption.

14.5.2 Transferring farm property to your children or grandchildren

Normally, if you sell or give property to members of your family other than your spouse, you are deemed to have sold the property for its "fair market value", and will thus have to recognize as a capital gain or income the difference between your original cost (or the value on February 22, 1994 if you elected to use your capital gains exemption on the farm property) and the property's current value. (See 6.5.4 and 6.4.4.)

> Take advantage of the intergenerational transfer rules.

If you transfer property used in a farming business to a child, grandchild or great-grandchild (including a spouse of your child, a child of your spouse, etc., where "spouse" includes a common-law spouse as outlined in 2.2.1), you can avoid this rule. If you simply give the property, it will be deemed to be transferred at your cost (adjusted cost base [see 6.2] for capital property, or undepreciated capital cost [see 10.2.7] for depreciable property). If you sell it for something in between your cost and the current market value, that amount will be accepted for tax purposes. Any gain on the property will thus be deferred.

For this "rollover" rule to apply, you or your spouse or one of your children must have used the property "principally" in a farming business in which you, your spouse or children were actively engaged on a regular and continuous basis.

When the rollover applies, the recipient (your child, grandchild, etc.) will be deemed to have acquired the farm property for the amount at which you are deemed to have sold it. This means that the gain will eventually be taxed, if the child sells the property at some later time.

Example:

Florence operates a wheat farm in Saskatchewan. In 1998, Florence decides to retire and gives the farm to her grandson Daniel. The farmland cost her $10,000 in 1975 and is now worth $150,000.

Florence is deemed to receive $10,000 for the land, and so has no capital gain. Daniel is deemed to have acquired the land for $10,000; if he ever sells the land, the $10,000 figure will be used as his cost for capital gains calculation purposes. (Of course, if Daniel transfers the farm one day to his child, a further rollover will be available, assuming the rules have not changed.)

If you are transferring farm property to a child, grandchild, etc., you may wish to realize a partial capital gain, in order to use up your $500,000 capital gains exemption and give your child a higher cost base in the property. In such a case, you will need to sell the property to your child for an amount greater than your cost. (Where land is being transferred, don't forget to consider the possible cost of provincial land transfer tax. GST, HST or QST may apply as well, depending on the circumstances.)

Note that the tax rules do not let you transfer farm inventory to a child on a tax-free basis. Gifting farm inventory results in the same income inclusion as a sale of farm inventory at fair value.

14.5.3 Principal residence exemption

As we saw in 6.5.2, the exemption in respect of the gain on the sale of a principal residence normally applies to the house itself plus one-half hectare of surrounding land. The gain on any land beyond one-half hectare is subject to the normal rules for capital gains.

> **Claim alternative principal residence exemption where appropriate.**

For land used in a farming business, another option is available. Instead of the ordinary principal residence exemption, you may elect to claim a special exemption of $1,000 plus $1,000 for each year since 1972 during which the house was your principal residence. You subtract this amount from your total gain on both house and land.

This election can be useful where you have occupied the property for many years and the value of the house is small relative to the land. Alternatively, consider whether you might claim more than the one-half hectare under the principal residence exemption if you can substantiate that such additional land was necessary for your personal use and enjoyment of the property.

14.5.4 Capital gains reserve on sale of farm to your child

We discussed capital gains reserves briefly in 6.5.1. It was noted there that the capital gain must be recognized at a cumulative rate of one-fifth each year, so that no reserve can last for more than four years after the year of sale.

Where you sell property used in a farming business (including land) to your child, grandchild or great-grandchild, the allowable reserve is 10 years rather than five. As with the rules discussed in 14.5.2, a spouse of your child, grandchild or great-grandchild, and a child, grandchild or great-grandchild of your spouse also qualify. (For this purpose, "spouse" includes a common-law spouse as outlined in 2.2.1.)

14.6 References

The following publications can be obtained (in person or by telephone request) from your nearest Revenue Canada District Taxation Office. Forms and guides may also be available from Revenue Canada's Internet site at *www.rc.gc.ca*.

Interpretation Bulletin IT-156R, "Feedlot operators"

Interpretation Bulletin IT-232R3, "Losses—Their deductibility in the loss year or in other years"

Interpretation Bulletin IT-268R4, "*Inter vivos* transfer of farm property to a child"

Interpretation Bulletin IT-322R, "Farm losses"

Interpretation Bulletin IT-349R3, "Intergenerational transfer of farm property on death"

Interpretation Bulletin IT-373R, "Farm woodlots and tree farms"

Interpretation Bulletin IT-425, "Miscellaneous farm income"

Interpretation Bulletin IT-427R, "Livestock of farmers"

Interpretation Bulletin IT-433R, "Farming or fishing—Use of cash method"

Interpretation Bulletin IT-485, "Cost of clearing or levelling land"

Interpretation Bulletin IT-526, "Farming—Cash method inventory adjustments"

"Farming Income Tax Guide"

Form T2042, "Statement of farming activities"

If you practice a profession

- Defer tax by electing to follow the modified accrual method for computing income (15.1.1)

- Adjust billings and drawings to maximize your 1971 receivables (15.1.2)

- Maximize your deductible interest (15.2.1)

- Pay retiring partners income or capital as appropriate (15.2.2)

- Consider paying club dues at partnership level (15.2.3)

Most of income tax planning for professionals is the same as that for other self-employed people (see Chapter 10). Self-employed professionals are, after all, carrying on business. However, a number of special rules exist which we consider in 15.1. Since many professionals carry on their practice in partnership, we also look at some rules that apply to partnerships in 15.2.

15.1 Specific rules for professionals

15.1.1 The modified accrual method of accounting for income

As we noted in 10.2.2 and 14.2.1, businesses other than farming businesses are generally required to report income on the accrual basis. That is, you take your sales into income even though you may not be paid until after your year-end.

Most businesses must also account for work in progress—work that has been done but not yet billed. However, there is an exception for the professional practice of an accountant, dentist, lawyer, medical doctor, veterinarian or chiropractor. If you are practising one of these professions, you may elect to exclude work in progress from your income.

> **Defer tax by electing to follow the "modified accrual" method.**

This method of accounting is sometimes called the "modified accrual" method. It is not the cash method, since once an amount has been billed, it must be reported as income even if not yet paid. But excluding work in progress is a step away from the full accrual method.

Example:

Dianne is a lawyer who is in sole practice. She spends almost the entire month of December 1999 preparing for a major trial to defend her client Michael. The trial takes place in January. She does not bill Michael until the conclusion of the trial, in January 2000.

If Dianne elects to exclude work in progress from her income for 1999 she will not have to recognize as income any amount in respect of her work in preparing for the trial until her business year ending December 31, 2000.

As you can see, electing to exclude work in progress from your income can create a substantial deferral of tax. If you are practising one of the eligible professions, you will almost certainly want to follow this method. The only reason not to do so might be if you are in your first year or two of practice, with relatively low income, and you wish to recognize income earlier while it can be taxed at relatively low rates.

Once you choose to exclude work in progress, you must normally continue to do so for all future years.

Upon retirement or withdrawal from the business, the remaining work in progress is brought into your income. Such income is considered to be "earned income" for RRSP contribution limit purposes (see 3.1.3).

15.1.2 1971 receivables

If you have been in practice continuously since before 1972, you may still have a "1971 receivables" balance.

Before 1972, professionals were allowed to use the cash method of accounting, much as farmers still are. In your 1971 taxation year, therefore, you would exclude from income your billings which had not yet been paid.

With the change to the accrual (or modified accrual) method, a special allowance was provided as a transitional rule, to preserve the deferral of taxation of these receivables and avoid taxing the professional too heavily in any one year. The allowance takes the form of a deduction for "1971 receivables".

Each year, you can deduct your original 1971 receivables, up to a limit of your receivables at the end of the current year. (For a partnership, however, the limit is the adjusted cost base of your interest in the partnership.) However, whenever the amount you claim goes down in any year, that lower amount will be your maximum for future years. As your receivables fluctuate from year to year, therefore, your 1971 receivables deduction may eventually become very small.

> **Adjust billings and drawings to maximize your 1971 receivables.**

If you have been in sole practice since before 1972, and you still have an untaxed "1971 receivables" balance, you will want to make sure your receivables are high enough at the end of each year that your deduction is not reduced at all. This can be done by issuing billings towards the end of the year.

If you are a member of a partnership and you have a 1971 receivables balance, you need to keep the adjusted cost base of your interest in the partnership at a high enough level to preserve the 1971 receivables. This can be done by delaying drawings towards the end of the year, or even by investing additional capital in the partnership before the year-end.

15.1.3 Professional corporations

Some provinces allow certain professionals to incorporate their professional practices. For example, lawyers in Alberta and physicians in Nova Scotia can be incorporated.

For tax purposes, a professional corporation is generally treated like any other small business corporation—see Chapter 13. If you are considering incorporating your practice, see 10.5 for a discussion of some of the pros and cons.

Professional corporations which are members of partnerships must use a December 31 business year-end (see 10.2.1). Other professional corporations may use an off-calendar year-end.

15.2 Specific rules that apply to partnerships

In 10.3 we discussed the taxation of partnerships in general. In this section we shall look at two rules applicable to partnerships that are of particular relevance to professionals.

15.2.1 Deductibility of interest paid by the partnership

As we saw in 7.2.3, interest paid is normally deductible as long as the funds borrowed are used to earn income from business or property. Where a partnership borrows funds for working capital, the interest is therefore clearly deductible.

> Maximize your deductible interest.

As a member of a partnership, consider whether you can accelerate your drawings or have the partnership repay a portion of your capital contribution. You could then use the funds to pay off non-deductible debt (such as a home mortgage), while the partnership can borrow funds to replace the lost working capital. The interest would then become deductible. Alternatively, you yourself could borrow funds to inject back into the partnership. However, Revenue Canada could challenge such an arrangement under the general anti-avoidance rule (discussed in 5.2.6) if it considers this type of refinancing technique to be a misuse or abuse of the *Income Tax Act*.

If the partnership borrows funds in order to make a distribution of profits and/or capital to the partners, the interest paid on such borrowings is normally deductible, but only up to the amount of the partnership's "net equity" as determined under generally acceptable accounting principles.

15.2.2 Income payments to retired partners

Normally, if you withdraw from a partnership, and you receive a payment to compensate for your interest in the partnership, the payment will be considered capital. That is, any excess over your adjusted cost base in the partnership will be a capital gain, and taxed as discussed in Chapter 6. (Your adjusted cost base is essentially the amount you contributed to the partnership, plus your share of the profits on which you have been taxed, minus your drawings. See 10.3.5.)

Another option is available under the *Income Tax Act*, however. If your partners agree to pay you a share of the income from the partnership, and to treat it explicitly as an income payment, you will be considered as still being a partner for tax purposes. You will therefore be taxed on that income, but your former partners will effectively pay less tax, since their partnership income will in part be allocated to you.

Example:

Joel, an accountant, retires from his firm at the beginning of 1999. There are three other partners, who share equally in profits. The firm's income for 1999 is $300,000. The partners agree to pay Joel $60,000 upon his retirement, and declare the $60,000 to be a share of the income from the partnership (rather than as a repayment of his capital interest).

Joel will be required to report the $60,000 as income. However, each of the partners will effectively get a deduction of $20,000, since after Joel's allocation, there is only $240,000 to be divided three ways. Each partner will thus report $80,000 in income instead of $100,000.

Note that the continuing income payments to a retired partner are not included in "earned income" for purposes of calculating the retired partner's RRSP contribution limit.

> **Pay retiring partners income or capital as appropriate.**

When you (or a partner of yours) decide to withdraw from a partnership, you will need to calculate the best way of paying out the retiring partner's interest.

On the one hand, if you are retiring and have a high cost base in your partnership, it may be best to receive a capital payment. This amount could be entirely exempted from tax, or, if there is a gain, only three-quarters of the gain will be taxed. However, it will effectively be paid in after-tax dollars by the other partners.

On the other hand, if your partners choose the option of an income payment, you will be fully taxed on it (possibly at lower rates than the continuing partners, if your income is going down substantially). However, your partners will effectively receive a deduction for the amount paid to you.

If you have a 10-year reserve in respect of your 1995 "stub period" income due to the 1995 budget's calendar-year reporting rules for unincorporated business income discussed in 10.2.1, you are entitled to claim the appropriate amount of the reserve in the year that you retire. However, you will only be able to continue claiming the reserve in later years if you retain an income interest in the partnership. Otherwise, you will have to bring your remaining reserve amount into income in the year after the year in which you retire.

15.2.3   Club dues

As you may know, most club dues are not allowed as business expenses. Many professional partnership agreements therefore provide that such dues should be paid by the partners personally (since they are not deductible in computing the partnership's income anyway).

> **Consider paying club dues at the partnership level.**

You should consider having the partnership pay such dues even though they are not deductible. The reason is that the individual partners' adjusted cost bases in the partnership are not reduced by such disallowed expenses, even though the assets of the partnership are reduced by making the payments. (As noted above, your adjusted cost base is essentially the amount you contributed to the partnership, plus your share of your after-tax profits, minus your drawings. See 10.3.5.) As a result, having the partnership pay the club dues can reduce the capital gain (or increase the capital loss) on an eventual sale of the partnership interest.

15.3   References

The following publications can be obtained (in person or by telephone request) from your nearest Revenue Canada District Taxation Office. Forms and guides may also be available from Revenue Canada's Internet site at *www.rc.gc.ca*.

Interpretation Bulletin IT-90, "What is a partnership?"

Interpretation Bulletin IT-138R, "Computation and flow-through of partnership income"

Interpretation Bulletin IT-242R, "Retired partners"

Interpretation Bulletin IT-358, "Partnerships—Deferment of fiscal year-end"

Interpretation Bulletin IT-457R, "Election by professionals to exclude work in progress from income"

Information Circular 89-5R, "Partnership information return"

"Business and Professional Income Tax Guide"

"Guide to the Partnership Information Return"

Form T2032, "Statement of professional activities"

Form GST 370, "Employee and partner GST/HST rebate application"

Form T5013, "Partnership information return"

If you live in Québec

- Calculate your Québec taxes under the general and simplified systems to find out your best filing option (16.1.2)
- Be aware of differences between the federal and Québec tax systems (16.2)
- Claim a refundable credit if you adopt a child (16.2.3)
- Claim the credit for housing "direct ascendants" (16.2.7)
- Withdraw your RHOSP funds to buy a home or furniture or for another qualifying purpose before 2000 (16.2.15)
- Boost your Québec business entertainment expense deduction by subscribing to eligible Québec cultural performances (16.2.21)

Québec is different from all other provinces in that it does not piggy-back on the federal system of personal taxation. Québec residents must file a separate tax return. The *Québec Taxation Act* (Loi sur les impôts) is largely modelled on the federal Income Tax Act, but there are a number of differences. We review those in 16.2. In 16.3 we discuss the incentive plans that are unique to Québec. These plans—QSSP, QBIC (or SPEQ), CIP (or RIC) and others—form a veritable alphabet soup of incentives to investment in various kinds of Québec activities.

16.1 Québec income tax rates

Major reforms to Québec's personal tax system took effect in 1998. These changes include paring down the number of tax brackets, eliminating the province's surtaxes, increasing the rate of refundable tax credits, and introducing an optional, simplified method of calculating your Québec tax.

16.1.1 1999 Québec tax rates

As a result of Québec's tax reform, there are now only three tax brackets, instead of five. Québec's 1999 provincial income tax rates are listed in Appendix II.

Québec residents are allowed a Refundable Québec Abatement on their federal tax return, which reduces their federal tax by 16.5% of basic federal tax. As a result, Québec residents earn federal non-refundable tax credits at a rate of about 14.2%, instead of at the 17% rate earned in the other provinces. Québec non-refundable tax credits are earned at a 23% rate, so an amount that is eligible for federal and Québec credits is effectively worth about 37% of the related amount.

16.1.2 Québec's optional simplified tax filing system

When you file your 1999 Québec tax return, if you are a Québec resident on December 31 of that year, you will be able to choose between the province's general tax filing system and a new simplified system.

The main features of the simplified system are as follows:

- A series of Québec deductions and non-refundable tax credits is replaced by a single, lump-sum amount of $2,430 per person (worth $559)—Appendix II shows the treatment of deductions and credits under the simplified system.
- If you and your spouse both opt into the simplified system, you can transfer the lump-sum amount to your spouse, which is often advantageous since most of the deductions and credits being replaced are not currently transferable. (See 2.1.3 for some planning ideas involving the transfer of credits.)
- If you and your spouse both opt to use the simplified system, the two of you can elect to file a joint Québec tax return.

> Calculate your Québec taxes under the general and simplified systems to find out your best filing option.

Obviously, your choice will depend on which system will give you the greater tax savings, so you will need to estimate your taxes payable under both systems. Whether you stand to benefit under the simplified system will depend on whether the lump-sum amount under the new system is greater than the sum of the replaced deductions and non-refundable credits.

Québec's tax return package includes a workchart for figuring out your taxes under both systems. If you choose to file your return using the general system, Revenu Québec government will calculate your taxes payable under both systems and return any additional tax savings that you would have obtained by following the simplified system.

16.1.3 Calculating net income under the simplified system

Even if you decide to file under Québec's general tax system, you have to calculate your net income under the simplified system since many tax credits are now based on the simplified system's net income amount. These include the credits for spouse, dependent children and other dependants, charitable donations, age and pension income, persons living alone, medical expenses, family tax reduction, refundable Québec sales tax credit, child care expenses and the real estate tax refund.

To calculate your net income under the simplified system, add up all your income as you would under the general system (after deducting expenses related to professional, business or rental income). From this amount, subtract your RRSP and RPP deductions, employment expenses and certain other amounts to arrive at your net income under the simplified system.

16.1.4 Income tax reduction for Québec families

Québec offers a non-refundable tax reduction for couples or single-parent families with at least one dependent child. The tax reduction for families is worth up to $1,195 for a single parent and up to $1,500 for cohabiting spouses, less the "designated" child's income over $5,900. If you have more than one child, you should designate the child with the lower net income in order to maximize the tax reduction.

If a single parent's or couple's Québec family net income calculated under the simplified system is over $26,000, the tax reduction is reduced by 6% of family net income over $26,000.

16.2 Differences from federal tax

In this section we highlight the principal differences between Québec and federal tax law that affect personal tax. We present the topics in approximately the same order as the relevant material appears in the rest of the book.

> Be aware of differences between the federal and Québec tax systems.

You should review the differences between the federal and the Québec income tax systems, as highlighted below. Be cautious of the possible Québec tax implications of any step you take for federal tax purposes.

16.2.1 Basic personal and family credits

Like the federal basic and spousal credits discussed in 2.2 and 2.2.1, Québec offers basic personal tax credits, worth up to $1,357 each for you and for your spouse. The $5,900 amount used to calculate the Québec spousal credit is reduced by your spouse's net income (calculated under the simplified system) and then multiplied by the 23% credit rate.

If you have dependent children 18 and under, or over 18 and attending school full-time, a non-refundable Québec tax credit is available of up to $598 for the first child and $552 for each additional child.

You can claim an additional single-parent family credit of $299 for the first dependent child if you did not live with, support or receive support payments from your spouse at any time during the year. If you made support payments to your spouse that are tax-deductible, you may still claim the single-parent family credit. You cannot claim the credit if you can claim the spousal amount (or could otherwise claim it if your spouse's income were lower).

No "equivalent-to-spouse" credit is available in Québec; instead a credit is available for "other dependants" who are related to you by blood, marriage or adoption. The person must ordinarily live with you unless the person is your dependant due to infirmity. For example, an "other dependant" could be a parent, grandparent, aunt or uncle, or a child over 18 who does not attend school full-time. Except for dependent children and grandchildren, infirm dependants must live in Canada to be eligible. The credit is worth up to $552, plus $805 if the person is infirm. The $2,400 or $3,500 amount used to calculate the credit is reduced by the dependant's net income (as calculated under the simplified system) and then multiplied by the 23% credit rate.

Québec also allows a non-refundable tax credit of $242 for a "person living alone". To qualify, you must have lived by yourself for the entire calendar year in a self-contained home with no person other than dependent children whom you claim for tax purposes. If you are separated but you support your spouse, you cannot claim this credit; however, if you pay only alimony which you deduct on your tax return, you and your spouse can both claim the credit. The credit is reduced by 15% of Québec family net income (i.e., combined net income of you and your spouse under the simplified system) over $26,000, so that the credit is fully eliminated if your family net income is $33,000 or more in that year.

The $26,000 family net income test is used to reduce the tax credit for persons living alone and to reduce the Québec age credit, and the Québec pension income credit (see 16.2.5). Your amounts eligible for claiming all three of these credits will be totalled and then reduced by your family net income over $26,000.

16.2.2 Child care expenses

There are a number of differences between the federal rules discussed in 2.3.2 and the Québec rules. Child care expenses give rise to a refundable credit in Québec instead of a deduction. (See 2.1.2 for a discussion of refundable credits and the difference between a deduction and a credit.) The credit is on a sliding scale, worth 75% of the expenses of low-income families, down to 26% for families with Québec family net income (see 16.1.3) over $74,000. Thus, the Québec credit for child care expenses is more valuable to lower-income families, such as where both parents are attending school full-time.

For federal purposes, only the lower-income spouse can claim the deduction for child care expenses. As of 1999, either spouse may claim the child care expenses credit for Québec purposes.

For Québec purposes, eligible child care expenses are limited to 100% of earned income, instead of the federal limit of two-thirds of earned income. Québec disregards any income earned by the child in determining whether child care expenses are eligible. For 1999, Québec child care expense claims are capped at $7,000 per child under seven and $4,000 per child aged seven to 16.

In addition to the other special circumstances where the lower-income spouse is not expected to care for the children (see 2.3.2), the higher-income spouse can claim the child care credit for periods in which he or she is operating a business that generates a loss or low profits. As with the other situations, the amount of child care expenses that the higher-income spouse can claim is limited to $150 per week for each child under 7 or for each child of any age suffering from an impairment, and $90 per week for each child aged 7 to 16.

Example:

Nicole and Daniel have two pre-school children. In 1999 Daniel earns $70,000, and Nicole earns $8,000 working part-time. They pay $5,500 in day care, required to enable them both to work.

For federal purposes, Nicole can claim the least of (a) the amount paid—$5,500; (b) $7,000 per child—$14,000; and (c) two-thirds of her earned income—$5,333. She can thus deduct $5,333 from income.

For Québec purposes, Nicole's credit will be based on the least of (a) the amount paid—$5,500; (b) $7,000 per child—$14,000; and (c) 100% of Nicole's earned income—$8,000. Since Nicole's and Daniel's Quebec family net income (calculated under the simplified system) is more than $74,000, the credit is 26% of $5,500, or $1,430.

The $5 per day contribution that has to be paid by parents of children attending the province's early childhood centres is not eligible for purposes of the Québec child care expense credit.

16.2.3 Adoption expenses

> **Claim a refundable tax credit if you adopt a child.**

Québec offers a refundable credit for adoption expenses to help finance the expenses associated with adopting children from overseas, but is available even for local adoptions. For 1999, the credit is 20% of up to $15,000 in expenses paid by you, or by you and your spouse, to a maximum $3,000 credit per child. Qualifying expenses include court fees, legal fees, travelling and translation expenses (for adoptions from other countries), and fees charged by approved agencies.

Since the credit is refundable, it is available even if you have no tax to pay for the year. You will have to keep records of your expenses and claim only those that qualify. The credit is available under the general and simplified systems.

16.2.4 Tuition fees and interest on student loans

Tuition fees qualify for a 23% non-refundable credit for Québec tax purposes. Unlike the federal tuition fees credit (see 2.4), Québec does not allow the transfer of undeducted tuition fees to the parent. Since 1997, unused tuition fees can be carried forward indefinitely and claimed as a credit in later years.

Québec does not have a credit to parallel the federal education amount. Instead, Québec increases the parents' non-refundable credit for dependent children and other dependants (see 16.2.1) by $380 per semester (for up to two semesters) if the dependant is a full-time student at a post-secondary institution.

A non-refundable tax credit is available of 23% of interest paid in the year on a student loan that you received under a federal or Québec student loan program. You can carry forward any unused portion of the credit to a later year. To claim the credit, you must file under Québec's general system (see 16.1.2) and you must include a voucher from your financial institution showing the amount of interest paid.

16.2.5 Seniors

Québec offers a 23% non-refundable tax credit similar to the federal credit for persons who are 65 and older (19.3.4) and for pension income (see 19.3.5). The Québec age credit is worth up to $506 and the Québec pension credit is worth up to $230. If you are 65 or older and your Québec family net income (see 16.2.1) is $26,000 or more, these credits are reduced by 15% for each dollar over $26,000.

The amounts available for claiming each of these credits and the credit for persons living alone are added together and then reduced by 15% of your Québec family net income over $26,000 (before 1998, the amount was applied to reduce each credit individually).

16.2.6 Home support for elderly persons living alone

Québec proposes to introduce a new refundable tax credit in 2000 for the home support of persons age 70 or older living alone who are losing their autonomy (as certified by a local community service centre). The credit will be equal to 23% of eligible expenses paid to obtain certain home support services. The credit will be capped at $2,760. If the expense also qualifies for the Québec medical expense credit, you cannot claim it for purposes of both credits—you will need to determine which credit will be worth more to you.

16.2.7   Adults housing "direct ascendants"

> Claim the credit for housing "direct ascendants".

Québec provides a refundable tax credit of $550 for adult taxpayers who live with their parents, grandparents or great-grandparents (including in-laws). Since the credit is refundable, it is available even if you have no tax to pay for the year and regardless of whether you file under the general or simplified system.

To claim the credit, your "ascendant" must be 70 or older (or 60 or older and disabled), but there is no requirement that the "ascendant" be financially dependent on you or in a low-income bracket. (In fact, the "ascendant" could be financially supporting you. However, the person making the claim must own or rent the home.)

16.2.8   Legal fees for establishing support payments

Under the federal system, legal fees to enforce payment of taxable amounts of alimony or maintenance (support) owing are deductible, but not fees paid to establish a right to alimony or maintenance (see 2.8.1). Nor are fees deductible where they are paid in connection with a court application to increase or decrease such payments. Québec taxation is different, in that fees paid in connection with a court application to increase or decrease the level of support are deductible. This deduction is only available if you file under the general system.

16.2.9   Charitable donations

Québec provides a 23% credit for charitable donations, in addition to the 17%/29% federal credit discussed in 2.7.1. Since 1998, you can claim annual donations of up to 75% of your Québec net income (as calculated under the simplified system) on your Québec return, or higher in some cases if you donate property that the charity will use for its activities or if you donate ecologically valuable property to the Québec government. In the year of death and the year before, the limit is increased to 100% of Québec net income. However, the province has not followed the federal lead in reducing the income inclusion rate for capital gains arising from gifts of publicly traded securities and other appreciable property (see 20.7). The credit is available under both the general and simplified systems.

For Québec purposes there is a special restriction on the credit for gifts of works of art. The valuation of the gift is limited to the price the charity receives when it sells the art and the credit can only be claimed (by the donor) if the charity sells the art within the next five years of accepting the donation. This rule does not apply to donations to certain museums and galleries, recognized artistic organizations, governments or municipalities.

16.2.10 Medical expenses

Like the federal credit for medical expenses (see 2.7.2), the parallel Québec credit is reduced by 3% of Québec family net income as calculated under the simplified system (see 16.1.3). However, for Québec purposes, the maximum reduction is not capped at $1,614. Further, the net income amount is now based on the combined income of *both* spouses. As a result, many Québec residents are no longer eligible for the credit.

Québec has also introduced a refundable tax credit for medical expenses similar to the federal medical expense supplement for low-income workers discussed in 2.7.2. For Québec purposes, the credit is reduced by 5% of your Québec family net income (under the simplified system) over $17,500 (instead of the $16,069 threshold for claiming the federal supplement).

The list of allowable expenses is generally identical to the federal list. In addition, however, if you (or a dependant) require long-term care that can only be provided in a Québec health establishment located 250 km or more from your residence, your moving expenses will be allowed as medical expenses by Québec. For this purpose, "moving expenses" are those listed in 12.1.2. Québec medical expenses also include the cost of a course taken to learn how to provide care to a disabled spouse or dependant.

Also, as noted in 16.2.17 below, the taxable benefit for employer-paid private health insurance premiums qualifies as a medical expense for Québec purposes.

16.2.11 Credit for disabled persons

Québec offers a non-refundable tax credit for persons with severe and prolonged physical or mental impairment. You can claim this credit whether you file under the general or simplified system (see 16.1.2). The Québec credit is similar to the federal credit discussed at 2.5.1 and you must meet essentially the same criteria to be eligible. (As of 1999, you are entitled to the Québec disability credit if you spend a lengthy amount of time several times a week having therapy that is necessary to maintain your vital functions.)

To claim the Québec credit for the first time, you must file Form TP-752.0.14-V with your Québec tax return for that year. The maximum amount available for the credit is $2,200, which means it may be worth up to $506 to you. If you have a dependant who suffers from an impairment, your dependant's unused disability credit can be transferred to your Québec return.

16.2.12 Political contributions

As noted in 2.7.3, many provinces provide credits for contributions to provincial political parties, riding associations and election candidates. In Québec's case, the credit is 75% of the first $200 of such contributions and 50% of the next $200, as a credit against Québec tax. The maximum credit is $250. It can be claimed under both the general and simplified systems.

16.2.13 Québec Sales Tax credit

Québec offers a sales tax refund similar to the GST credit available to low-income families (see 2.9.3). The refund is $154 for you and $154 for your spouse, plus an extra $103 if you live alone or with only dependants.

The total credit is reduced by 3% of your Québec family net income (see 16.2.1) over $26,000. The credit is refundable and is claimed on your Québec tax return (whether you file under the general or simplified system).

Québec also offers a sales tax rebate that parallels the GST rebate for employees (see 9.10) and partners (see 10.3.7).

16.2.14 Real estate tax refund

You may be entitled to a refund of a portion of the property taxes that apply on your dwelling. If you own the property, taxes eligible for the refund include school, water and municipal taxes. If you rent, the eligible amount is indicated on the Relevé 4 supplied to you by your landlord each year. The credit is claimed on your Québec tax return.

The eligible property tax is reduced by $430 for each spouse. The refund is 40% of this amount, to a maximum of $514, minus 3% of your Québec family net income (see 16.1.3) over $26,000, subject to various adjustments. Since it is refundable, the real estate tax refund is paid to you even if you have no Québec tax to pay for the year.

16.2.15 Registered Home Ownership Savings Plans (RHOSPs)

RHOSPs were a popular savings plan until 1985, when they were abolished under the federal tax system. Before 1985, contributions to an RHOSP could be deducted (subject to certain dollar limits), and the withdrawals were not taxed at all provided the funds were used to purchase a first home. In 1996, Québec announced that the province will be eliminating RHOSPs by the year 2000.

When RHOSPs were abolished federally, the federal rules were changed to allow withdrawals from all existing plans without paying any federal tax, so most Canadians simply withdrew their RHOSP funds. However, since Québec did not follow this federal change at the time, it is possible that you may still have funds in an RHOSP—if so, you have until December 31, 1999 to use the funds or the value of the funds will be taxable at that time.

In order to withdraw funds without paying Québec tax, the funds withdrawn must be spent on the purchase of a home or new household furnishings (residential furniture and major appliances) or for eligible renovation work to a home you own and occupy as long as the work is carried out by a Québec licensed contractor.

> **Withdraw your RHOSP funds to buy a home or furniture or for another qualifying purpose before 2000.**

If you still have an RHOSP, you should consider using up the funds on your next home purchase, on qualifying renovations to your current home, or on a shopping spree for new furniture and appliances before the end of 1999. Otherwise, the remaining balance will be taxable in Québec at that time.

No matter when in the year you withdraw the funds, you have until 60 days after the end of the year to take delivery of the goods or have the renovation work completed and paid for without triggering tax on the RHOSP withdrawal.

If you withdraw funds from an RHOSP account to make an eligible purchase, you should file Form TP-955-V ("Statement of the use of funds from a Registered Home Ownership Savings Plan") with your income tax return for the year of the withdrawal to ensure that the amount withdrawn is not included in your income for Québec tax purposes.

16.2.16 Cumulative net investment loss

As we saw in 6.4.3, investment expenses and tax shelter write-offs create a cumulative net investment loss ("CNIL"), which reduces your ability to claim the $500,000 capital gains exemption.

For Québec tax purposes, the special investment incentives, some of which we will discuss in 16.3, are *not* included in your CNIL calculation. That is, they will not affect your ability to claim the capital gains exemption on your Québec tax return.

These incentives are the deductions you claim under the Québec Stock Savings Plan (see 16.3.1), the Cooperative Investment Plan (see 16.3.3), Québec Business Investment Corporations (see 16.3.2), certain scientific research and development expenses, certified Québec film and television productions, and resource exploration expenses incurred in Québec (see 7.4.2). These collectively form the "strategic economic investment account", or "compte d'investissements stratégiques pour l'économie" ("CISE").

16.2.17 Employer-paid private health insurance

As we saw in 9.1.1, employer contributions to a private health services plan are non-taxable employee benefits for federal purposes. These contributions are, however, taxable for Québec tax purposes. Thus, if your employer pays for your group sickness, drug or dental plan, the value of the benefit will be included in your employment income on your Relevé 1 and must be reported on your Québec tax return, even though it does not appear on your T4 for federal income tax purposes. As a result, employer health plan contributions will normally make your employment income for Québec tax purposes higher than it is for federal purposes. You (or your spouse) can claim the taxable benefit as a medical expense on your Québec tax return (see 16.2.9).

16.2.18 Union and professional dues

Union and professional dues (excluding professional insurance), which are deductible for federal tax purposes (see 9.9.4), are not deductible on your Québec tax return but instead entitle you to a 23% non-refundable tax credit (under the general system only; see 16.1.2). This rule applies to employees and self-employed individuals alike. The cost of professional insurance is deductible under both the general and simplified systems.

16.2.19 Artists' deduction from copyright income

If you are a painter, writer, performer or other artist, a special deduction is available that effectively exempts from Québec tax a portion of your income from your original copyrights. The deduction is limited to $15,000 a year, and is reduced by 1.5 times the amount of the eligible copyright income over $20,000. Thus, it is effectively eliminated for artists who earn over $30,000 in copyright income. To be eligible for this credit, you must be eligible for membership in one of several recognized associations of artists and you must file under the general system (see 16.1.2).

16.2.20 Overseas employment tax deduction

We discussed the federal overseas employment tax credit in 9.8. The Québec rules accomplish essentially the same goals of not taxing certain income earned while working on projects outside Canada, but do so rather differently.

First, the Québec system allows the overseas income as a deduction (under the general system only; see 16.1.2), rather than allowing a tax credit for a percentage of it. For each consecutive 30-day period that the employee works outside Canada on a qualified project, 1/12 of the income earned abroad in the year can be deducted.

Second, foreign living allowances are completely tax exempt, provided they do not exceed one-half of the income earned abroad.

Third, the recognized activities for purposes of the deduction are broader than under the federal system. As well as the projects that qualify for federal purposes, the installation of computer or office automation systems or data communications systems, and the provision of scientific and technical services, entitle you to the deduction for Québec purposes.

16.2.21 Meals and entertainment expenses

> Boost your Québec business entertainment expense deduction by subscribing to eligible Québec cultural performances.

As under the federal rules (see 10.2.9), if you are self-employed and you take a client or business contact out for a meal or to an entertainment event, your deduction for your costs as a business expense is limited to 50% of the amount paid for Québec tax purposes.

Some business entertainment expenses for cultural events held in Québec are still 100% deductible for Québec tax purposes. These include the cost of a subscription to a symphony orchestra, classical or jazz ensemble, and opera, dance, theatre, and vocal performances. To qualify for this special deduction, the subscription must be for at least three performances in eligible artistic disciplines.

16.2.22 Home office expenses

The federal tax rules governing deductions for home office expenses are discussed in 9.9.3 and 10.2.10. For Québec tax purposes, the deduction for self-employed individuals is limited to 50% of eligible home office expenses (but not if they relate to the operation of a tourist home, bed and breakfast or similar establishment). The home office expense claims of employees are not subject to this restriction.

16.2.23 Rental expenses—documentation

If you use a building located in Québec to earn rental or business income and you claim any expenses for renovation, improvement, maintenance or repair of the property, you must include with your Québec income tax return Form TP-1086.R.23.12-V with the contractor's name, address, social insurance number (if an individual) and QST registration number (if available) as well as the amount paid for the work carried out. This measure is designed to combat tax evasion in the contracting and renovation sectors.

16.2.24 Minimum tax

The Québec alternative minimum tax ("AMT") differs from the federal AMT (see 7.6) in three ways:

- The minimum tax rate is 23%, while the federal rate is 17%.
- Certain tax benefits, such as deductions for resource exploration in Québec, investment tax credits for research and development, the 25% deduction for employees' stock option benefits (see 9.4.1) and a portion of the deduction for certain investments in QSSPs, QBICs (see 16.3.2) and CIPs (see 16.3.3) are not considered tax preferences for minimum tax purposes.
- The Québec basic exemption is $25,000, which is significantly lower than the $40,000 federal exemption.

Note that Québec minimum tax will not apply if you file under the simplified system.

16.2.25 Instalments

Québec instalment requirements are parallel to those for federal tax described in 8.3.2, with some minor differences.

The penalty for late or insufficient instalments is an extra 10% in addition to the normal interest rate. This penalty is substantially higher than the federal penalty, so if you can only pay part of your instalments, you are better off to pay your Québec instalments on time.

The determination of who has to pay instalments is the same as under the federal system, as outlined in 8.3.2. Instalments are required where your balance of Québec tax owing at the end of the year exceeds $1,200 for both the current year and either of the previous two years.

For Québec residents, quarterly *federal* tax instalments are payable if you have federal taxes owing of $1,200 in the current year and either of the previous two years. Since Québec tax can be higher or lower than federal tax for any individual (depending on many factors including those outlined throughout 16.2 above), there can be cases where you must remit federal instalments but not Québec instalments, or vice versa.

16.2.26 Health Services Fund contribution

Your income from all sources (other than employment income) is subject to a "contribution" to the Health Services Fund (i.e., another tax). The income taxed is generally the total shown on your income tax return including business income, investment income, pension or retirement income and taxable capital gains, but not employment income, Old Age Security or alimony. Certain specific deductions are permitted to arrive at the base amount for the contribution, and a further $5,000 exemption (rising to $11,000 in 2000) is allowed.

The Health Services Fund contribution is calculated on a graduated scale, which tops out at $1,000 once your income exceeds $125,000. In the top bracket, the contribution is $150 plus 1% of the excess of your income over $40,000 (but not over $125,000). Your contribution is then offset by a non-refundable tax credit of 23%.

If you are required to pay income tax instalments (see 16.2.25), you must also pay quarterly instalments on your Health Services Fund contribution.

16.3 Special Québec incentives

16.3.1 Québec Stock Savings Plans ("QSSP")

A QSSP (also know as a "Régime d'épargne action", or "REA") is a Québec tax incentive available to Québec residents that is designed to encourage investments in certain companies that have assets under $300 million ($250 million for most shares issued before April 1, 1998) and that operate mainly in Québec. Essentially, if you buy a qualifying investment as part of a public issue and you reside in Québec on December 31, you will be entitled to a Québec tax deduction of 50%, 75%, or 100% of the cost of your investment, depending on the type of investment you purchase. Generally, your total deduction cannot exceed 10% of your net income for the year.

If you are an employee of the corporation in which you are investing, you may be able to deduct an additional 25% of your investment. To qualify for the additional deduction, you must buy the shares through a stock ownership plan that offers financing and that is only available to employees who (together with their families) each own less than 5% of the corporation's shares. Your total deduction will still be capped at 10% of your net income.

A further deduction is available where the qualifying corporation is a "regional venture capital corporation" that finances businesses outside the Hull-Montréal-Québec City triangle. Although this deduction is not limited by 10% of your net income, the total deduction cannot exceed 200% of your investment.

If you deduct an amount for your QSSP investment, you cannot sell the investment until the third year after the year of purchase. Otherwise, you will have to include the amount of your previous deduction in your income for Québec tax purposes in the year of sale. You can avoid the income inclusion by purchasing sufficient qualifying shares in the year of sale to make up for the value of your previous deduction.

Because the deduction for your QSSP investment only applies for Québec tax purposes, if your income is over $50,000, the maximum value of the deduction is about 26% of the amount you deduct, depending on the amounts of any other tax credits that you claim.

The QSSP rules have undergone a number of changes over the past few years and have become quite complex. However, if a share issue qualifies as a QSSP investment, your investment broker should be able to help you to determine how the rules apply in respect of your particular QSSP investments.

16.3.2   Québec Business Investment Corporations ("QBIC")

The QSSP, as we have seen, encourages investment by Québec residents in *publicly-traded* corporations. The QBIC, on the other hand, is a vehicle for investing capital in *private* corporations, typically ones that are newly formed and not yet ready to go public.

A QBIC is more commonly referred to as an "SPEQ" (Société de placements dans l'entreprise québécoise). It is a private investment corporation whose purpose is to invest in new shares of "eligible corporations". It must be registered with the Société de développement industriel.

When you invest in a QBIC, you receive a basic deduction for 150% (125% before April 1, 1998) of the QBIC's eligible investments, in proportion to your interest in the QBIC. However, your deduction may not exceed 30% of your net income.

Example:

Jean and four of his friends get together and invest $20,000 each in a QBIC. The QBIC invests $60,000 (60% of its funds) in eligible corporations in May 1999.

Jean's deduction for 1999 will be limited to $18,000, which is 150% of 60% of his investment. If Jean's net income is less than $60,000, his deduction will be reduced to 30% of his net income.

A QBIC deduction that cannot be used because of the net income limitation can be carried forward and used in any of the next five years, subject to the same limitation.

Additional deductions

For QBIC investments before April 1998, the basic deduction was 125% of the investment, although two additional deductions were available for incentive purposes provided the total deduction did not exceed 200% of the investment. First, where the investor was an employee of an eligible corporation, an additional 25% deduction was available for investments of the QBIC in that corporation or a subsidiary of it. Second, an additional 25% deduction was available for investments in a "regional QBIC", or a QBIC which invested exclusively in "regional corporations". ("Regional" refers to the remoter areas of Québec, and covers most of the province outside the Hull-Montréal-Sherbrooke-Québec City triangle.) The additional deductions were available to you as an investor in the QBIC, but the 30%-of-net-income limitation continued to apply.

16.3.3 Cooperative Investment Plans ("CIP")

Cooperative Investment Plans, or Régimes d'investissement coopératif ("RIC"), are parallel to QBICs. They provide incentives to investment by members and workers in units issued by co-operatives governed by the *Cooperatives Act*—typically producing, processing, agricultural or workers' co-operatives. Various conditions and requirements must be met for the units to qualify.

16.3.4 Resource exploration expenses

Québec also offers special tax incentives for investments in flow-through shares of a mining or oil and gas company—see 7.4.2.

16.4 References

Revenu Québec has offices in Hull, Jonquière, Montréal, Québec, Rimouski, Rouyn-Noranda, Sainte-Foy, Sept-Iles, Sherbrooke, Sorel, Trois-Rivières and Toronto.

Revenu Québec produces a number of publications to assist taxpayers, the most notable of which is the *Guide and General Information* book that accompanies the provincial income tax return. Québec tax forms and guides are also available in French and English from the government of Québec's Internet site at *www.revenu.gouv.qc.ca*.

If you are a U.S. citizen in Canada

- If you're married, file a joint return where appropriate (17.7.1)
- Claim the foreign earned income exclusion if beneficial (17.2.1)
- Aim for maximum foreign tax credit (17.2.2)
- Keep records of expenses deductible on your U.S. return (17.3.1)
- Beware of differences between Canadian and U.S. rules governing retirement income (17.3.4)
- Elect to defer U.S. taxation of income accruing in your RRSP and other Canadian retirement plans (17.3.4)
- Look into the potential advantages of contributing to a Roth IRA (17.3.4)
- Watch out for ownership of Canadian corporations earning passive income (17.3.6)
- Be cautious of using the Cdn$500,000 capital gains exemption (17.4.3)
- Elect out of "instalment sale" rules where appropriate (17.4.4)
- Watch out for U.S. minimum tax (17.5)
- Review income splitting arrangements to prevent double taxation (17.6.2)
- Plan to minimize U.S. estate and gift taxes (17.8.1)
- Consider using the annual $10,000 U.S. gift tax exclusion to transfer wealth to children (17.8.2)
- Beware of U.S. gift and foreign trust reporting rules (17.8.3)

In this chapter we address the difficult and complicated tax problems of the United States citizen who lives in Canada. We can only scratch the surface, due to the interaction of two highly complex tax systems which are both subject to continual change. You should seek professional advice if you are a U.S. citizen living in Canada.

17.1 Two systems of taxation

The income tax systems of the United States and Canada are similar in some general ways, but very different in their details. A U.S. citizen resident in Canada must deal with both systems.

The United States is one of the few countries in the world that taxes its citizens on their worldwide income, whether or not they are physically in the United States. Canada taxes only Canadian residents on their world income; non-residents (including Canadian citizens) are taxed by Canada only on certain income from Canadian sources.

The result is that U.S. citizens living in Canada must file returns under both systems, and often must pay tax to both governments. Safeguards exist to prevent double taxation: clearly, you could not afford to pay a large percentage of your income to each country. But the safeguards, which are outlined in 17.2 below, are not perfect. Much of this chapter deals with the double taxation problems that arise due to differences between the two systems' ways of calculating income and tax.

In general, you will find that U.S. taxation is lower than Canadian. U.S. federal tax currently reaches a maximum rate of 39.6%. Canadian federal tax reaches 31.32% (including surtaxes), but as a resident of Canada you also have a provincial tax liability, which raises the top rate to 50% or more, depending on your province of residence. As a U.S. citizen not resident or domiciled in any state, you have no liability for any U.S. state tax except, perhaps, to the extent you have income arising in a state.

The 1999 U.S. income tax rates for single persons with no dependants and for married couples filing joint returns (see 17.7.1) are:

Single (see 17.7.1) Taxable income	Federal tax
$0 – $25,750	15%
$27,751 – 62,450	$3,863 plus 28% of excess over $25,750
$62,451 – 135,250	$14,139 plus 31% of excess over $62,450
$135,251 – 283,150	$35,157 plus 36% of excess over $130,250
$283,151 and up	$90,201 plus 39.6% of excess over $283,150

Married filing joint income tax returns (see 17.7.1) Taxable income	Federal tax
$0 – $43,050	15%
$43,051 – 104,050	$6,458 plus 28% of excess over $43,050
$104,051 – 158,550	$23,538 plus 31% of excess over $104,050
$158,551 – 283,150	$40,433 plus 36% of excess over $158,550
$283,151 and up	$85,289 plus 39.6% of excess over $283,150

(The rates for other types of taxpayers are different; see 17.7.1 for a discussion of the types of filers.)

The highest effective marginal rate is thus 39.6% for most taxpayers. Due to certain adjustments such as a phaseout of personal exemptions and a limitation on itemized deductions for high-income taxpayers, the effective marginal rate can be higher still in some cases.

The 39.6% marginal rate applies to taxable income over US$283,150 regardless of filing status. However, married individuals filing separately (see 17.7.1) become subject to the highest rate at taxable income in excess of US$141,575.

17.2 Basic mechanisms for avoiding double taxation

There are three mechanisms in place to help you avoid paying tax twice on the same income.

17.2.1 Foreign earned income exclusion (U.S. tax law)

The simplest way to avoid double taxation is the U.S. "foreign earned income exclusion." On your U.S. tax return, you may exclude from your income up to US$74,000 of "earned income" (employment or services income) earned from services provided outside the United States. (The exclusion is scheduled to increase by $2,000 per year for the next few years until it reaches US$80,000 for 2002 and later years.)

If you do not have any income other than your employment or professional services income, and your annual income is under US$74,000, this exclusion will be all you need to escape U.S. tax entirely. You must still file a U.S. return (see 17.7.2 below) and claim the exclusion.

Example:

Mark is a U.S. citizen who lives in Waterloo. He works as an accountant and earns Cdn$100,000 in 1999. (Assume the Canadian dollar is worth an average of US70¢ through 1999.) He has no other income.

On his U.S. tax return, Mark will report his income of approximately US$70,000. He will then elect to use the foreign earned income exclusion, and will deduct the same $70,000, to show a total income of $0. As a result he will pay no tax to the United States. His Canadian tax return will not be affected by his U.S. citizenship.

Note that if you file as "married filing jointly" (see 17.7.1 below), you and your spouse can each claim up to US$74,000 for purposes of the exclusion against your respective earned incomes. This can be done even if your spouse is not a U.S. citizen.

> **Claim the foreign earned income exclusion if beneficial.**

The regulations make it possible to elect the foreign earned income exclusion on late-filed returns in a number of cases. If you are eligible for the foreign earned income exclusion, you should normally claim it. However, there are some unusual circumstances (mostly involving carryovers of foreign tax credits—see 17.2.2) where claiming a foreign tax credit can be more beneficial than claiming the exclusion. If you claim the exclusion and then, in a later year, elect not to claim it, you cannot normally claim it again for five years. Because of this restriction, and on the off-chance that the foreign tax credit might be more valuable in some future year, many tax return preparers will calculate tax both ways and not claim the exclusion if no tax is payable in either case.

17.2.2   Foreign tax credit (both U.S. and Canadian law)

The foreign tax credit is a unilateral mechanism provided by many countries to prevent double taxation. Both the U.S. and Canada provide foreign tax credits. While the details differ, the concept is basically the same for both.

Consider the U.S. foreign tax credit as an example. If you are subject to U.S. taxation (because you are a citizen), but you have paid tax to Canada on Canadian-source income, you can, in general, claim a foreign tax credit to offset your U.S. tax on that income. Your credit cannot be greater than the Canadian tax you paid.

Example:

Dale is a U.S. citizen who lives and works in Winnipeg. He earns Cdn$1,400 (equivalent to US$1,000) in interest on his Winnipeg bank account in 1999. He also receives a salary in Canada and income from investments in the United States.

Dale will be required to include the US$1,000 in his income for U.S. tax purposes. (Because it is investment income and not earned income, it is not eligible for the foreign earned income exclusion.) Assume that he is in the 31% bracket (i.e., his taxable income is less than US$130,250 and he is single), so his additional U.S. tax is US$310. If he is in a 50% tax bracket in Canada, so that he has paid the equivalent of US$500 to Canada (and Manitoba) on the income, he can receive a foreign tax credit for the full US$310 on his U.S. return. On the other hand, if his Canadian tax rate were lower and he paid only US$270 to Canada (and Manitoba), he could only claim US$270 as his foreign tax credit.

The above example is highly simplified, but it demonstrates the basic effect of the credit. When you total up the tax to both countries (including provincial and state tax) and the foreign tax credits of each, you should end up paying a total that is equal to the higher of the two countries' rates of tax.

The Canadian foreign tax credit follows essentially the same principles. Since Canada taxes Canadian residents on their worldwide income, Dale in our example will have to report his U.S.-source investment income on his Canadian tax return. He will then be eligible for a foreign tax credit for U.S. taxes paid on his U.S.-source investment income to offset the Canadian tax that applies, but only up to the amount of U.S. tax he would have paid if he was not a U.S. citizen. Canada only allows foreign tax credits for the amount of U.S. tax payable by non-U.S. citizens and therefore Canadian-resident U.S. citizens earning U.S.-source dividends and interest may pay more tax on such income than Canadian residents who are not U.S. citizens. The U.S. will then allow an additional credit under the treaty, which many taxpayers neglect to claim. (Note that each country's foreign tax credit applies only to foreign taxes on income from sources outside that country.)

The details of the foreign tax credit rules are very complicated. For U.S. foreign tax credit purposes, your non-U.S. income is grouped into several different "baskets", or pools, and a separate foreign tax credit is available for each. Expenses, deductions and Canadian taxes must be allocated to each basket using prescribed allocation rules. Canadian tax you have paid on your employment income, for example, generally cannot be used to create a foreign tax credit for tax on investment income or capital gains.

For U.S. foreign tax credit purposes, excess (non-creditable) foreign tax can be carried back two years and forward five years. For Canadian foreign tax credit purposes, excess foreign tax can be deducted from income in the current year. If the excess foreign tax relates to business income, the excess generally can be carried back three years and forward seven years.

Aim for maximum foreign tax credit.

Over the course of the year, you may be able to structure your income from various sources—U.S. and Canadian, employment and investment income, etc.—in such a way as to maximize your "pools" of foreign tax paid on foreign-source income for purposes of the foreign tax credits of both the U.S. and Canada.

While normally you cannot receive credit for all Canadian tax paid because Canadian taxes are higher than U.S. taxes, you may be able to take particular advantage of the credit if you are resident in Canada for a relatively short time before another foreign posting. That is because you may apply your excess Canadian taxes when determining the foreign tax credit on income earned in other foreign countries.

If you receive income for personal services performed in both the U.S. and Canada, it is a good idea to keep a diary to record U.S. and Canadian work days.

If you have various sources of income and need to claim a foreign tax credit under one or both systems, you should consult a professional advisor.

17.2.3   Canada-U.S. tax treaty

The third safeguard against double taxation is the Canada-U.S. tax treaty (also known as a tax convention). Both Canada and the U.S. have such treaties with many countries. The purpose of a tax treaty is twofold: to prevent double taxation, and to reduce tax evasion by allowing exchange of taxpayer information between the two governments.

The Canada-U.S. treaty, for the most part, does not apply to United States citizens resident in Canada except in specific circumstances.

For example, the treaty allows a U.S. citizen resident in Canada to defer U.S. taxation of funds accruing in an RRSP or other pension plan. Were it not for this provision, U.S. tax could apply to the accruing funds, which are specifically exempt from Canadian tax under the RRSP rules (see 3.1.5 and 17.3.4).

Another treaty provision clarifies how to calculate the foreign tax credit (see 17.2.2) where you are claiming credits on both returns, and each one depends on the tax paid to the other country (which in turn depends on the credit available, leading to circularity). The rule is that you compute your U.S. tax first, without taking your U.S. foreign tax credit into account. Then you calculate your Canadian tax, and base the Canadian foreign tax credit on that U.S. tax figure. Finally, you go back to your U.S. return, and claim your U.S. foreign tax credit based on the Canadian tax actually paid. If you have U.S.-source interest, dividend or royalty income, this treaty provision may even result in a U.S. foreign tax credit for a portion of the Canadian and provincial taxes paid on your U.S.-source income.

Yet another provision in the treaty deals with child support paid by a U.S. resident to a resident of Canada. For U.S. tax purposes, such support (as distinct from alimony or maintenance that goes to support the spouse) is not included in income. As a result, the treaty provides that child support that is otherwise taxable (i.e., received under a pre-May 1997 agreement or court order—see 2.6) will not be included in income for Canadian tax purposes either. This applies whether or not you are a U.S. citizen.

If you are using the treaty to reduce your U.S. tax liability, you are generally required to disclose the specific details on your U.S. tax return. If you do not, the treaty benefits can be denied.

As a result of recent treaty changes, if you are a Canadian resident and you receive U.S. social security benefits, you are no longer subject to U.S. withholding tax on these amounts. However, 85% of the amount received is subject to tax in Canada.

17.3 Differences in calculating income

In theory, the foreign tax credit mechanism prevents you from paying tax twice. However, there are many differences between U.S. and Canadian calculations of income for tax purposes. These differences can lead to unexpected tax liabilities.

17.3.1 Deductions available in the U.S. but not in Canada

While you can normally deduct home mortgage interest and property taxes on your U.S. tax return, it is not deductible in Canada, except to the extent you can claim an office in your home (see 7.2.3 and 10.2.10).

State taxes, which may be imposed to the extent you reside in or have income arising in a U.S. state, are generally deductible for U.S. income tax purposes, while provincial income taxes are not deductible in Canada.

> Keep records of expenses deductible on your U.S. return.

Certain employment-related expenses not available in Canada can also be deducted on your U.S. return. If you are claiming deductions on your U.S. return that are not allowable in Canada, make sure to keep additional records sufficient to establish your claim.

17.3.2 Deductions available in Canada but not in the U.S.

As we saw in 7.2.3, interest paid may be deducted for Canadian tax purposes where the funds were borrowed for the purposes of earning income from investments. There is no strict requirement that you actually earn more income from your investments than you spend in interest.

For U.S. tax purposes, your investment expense deduction is limited to your investment income. You cannot write off interest expense against other income such as employment or business income. This principle extends, under a separate set of complex rules, beyond interest expenses to all deductions relating to "passive" activities, including limited partnership write-offs and most rental losses.

Certain other expenses and deductions permitted for Canadian purposes such as tuition fees will not be allowed on your U.S. return.

17.3.3 Limitations on U.S. deductions for high-income taxpayers

Two limitations apply to high-income taxpayers.

First, personal exemptions (US$2,750 for you, your spouse and each dependant) are phased out once adjusted gross income ("AGI") exceeds a threshold. (Adjusted gross income is gross income minus certain deductions such as foreign earned income exclusion, alimony, and IRA

[Individual Retirement Account] or Keogh plan contributions.) For married persons filing jointly, the threshold is US$189,950; for single taxpayers it is US$126,600; for married filing separately, it is US$94,745. For each $2,500 ($1,250 for married individuals filing separately) or part thereof by which AGI exceeds the threshold, *each* exemption is reduced by 2% (not to exceed 100%).

Second, itemized deductions are reduced once AGI exceeds a threshold, which is US$126,600 for single taxpayers and married filing jointly, and US$63,300 for married filing separately. For each dollar over the threshold, itemized deductions that could otherwise be claimed are reduced by 3% (other than medical expenses, investment interest, casualty or theft losses and gambling losses). However, even for very high-income taxpayers, a base amount of 20% of itemized deductions can always be claimed (i.e., the reduction cannot go beyond 80% of the deductions).

Example:

Byron is married and earns US$219,950. His wife Linda has no income and the couple is able to file jointly. Byron will claim two personal exemptions worth US$5,500. He has itemized deductions of US$20,000 consisting of home mortgage interest and property taxes.

Byron's income is US$30,000 (12 × US$2,500) over the US$189,950 threshold. Each of Byron's US$2,750 personal exemptions is thus reduced by 12 times 2%, or 24%. His total claim for exemptions is therefore US$4,180 (that is, US$5,500 − (5,500 × 24%)).

Byron's itemized deductions are reduced by 3% of US$93,350 (which is the excess of his adjusted gross income over the US$126,600 threshold), or US$2,800. So Byron may deduct only US$17,200 of his US$20,000 in itemized deductions in determining his taxable income. (Note that the reduction can never exceed 80% of the itemized deductions, so no matter how high Byron's income was, he would always be able to deduct US$4,000 of his US$20,000 of itemized deductions.)

17.3.4 Retirement and profit-sharing plans

RRSPs, RPPs and DPSPs (see Chapter 3) can cause problems for U.S. citizens, because they are not given any special status in the U.S. Internal Revenue Code.

> **Beware of differences in rules governing retirement income.**

Employer contributions to a registered pension plan or a deferred profit-sharing plan are exempt from immediate Canadian tax (see 9.1.1). As we saw in 3.4.1, you are taxed on the funds only when you receive them (usually on retirement).

For U.S. tax purposes, there is no such exemption. The amount contributed by your employer is treated as an employment benefit and is taxed, once the contributions have vested in you (that is, you are entitled to them even if you leave your employment). Furthermore, these amounts are explicitly excluded from the definition of "foreign earned income" under U.S. tax law, so you cannot make use of the foreign earned income exclusion (see 17.2.1). You may have to pay U.S. tax on these contributions, depending on the circumstances and the amount of your unused foreign tax credit carryover. When you later withdraw the funds, they should not be taxable in the U.S.

Your own contributions to an RRSP or RPP, which are deductible on your Canadian return, are not deductible for U.S. tax purposes.

> **Elect to defer U.S. taxation of income accruing in your RRSP or other Canadian retirement plans.**

Income accruing in your RRSP, RRIF and other Canadian retirement plans (see Chapter 3) would normally be taxable in the U.S. As noted in 17.2.3, the Canada-U.S. tax treaty allows you to elect each year to defer the taxation of the accruing income until you actually receive the funds from the plan. This allows you to report the income in the same year for Canadian and U.S. purposes.

If you contribute to a regular IRA (U.S. Individual Retirement Account) while resident in Canada, your contributions are deductible for U.S. tax purposes but not for Canadian tax purposes. Income accruing in an IRA is not taxed by Canada. When you withdraw funds from an IRA, Canada will tax the same amount that you would have had to include in your income under U.S. laws if you were a resident of the U.S. at the time of withdrawal. While you may be able to transfer lump sum payments received from an IRA into an RRSP free of Canadian tax, the amount transferred would be subject to U.S. tax. Foreign tax credits may alleviate double taxation.

> **Look into the potential advantages of contributing to a Roth IRA.**

A new type of IRA became available in 1998. Known as the "Roth IRA", this type of plan is essentially the same as a regular IRA but contributions are not deductible for U.S. tax purposes and the income can be received tax-free in most cases. Also, the ability to contribute to a Roth IRA is phased out at a higher level of income than it is for regular

IRAs and there are no minimum distribution requirements at age 70 1/2 (in fact, you can continue making contributions until death). Your ability to make Roth IRA contributions is phased out if your U.S. adjusted gross income is more than $95,000 (if you are single), $150,000 (if you are married filing jointly) or nil (if you are married filing separately).

The benefit of contributing to a Roth IRA generally will be greater than the benefit of contributing to a deductible IRA. Unless you expect your income to be in a lower marginal tax bracket during retirement, the ability to make tax-free withdrawals from a Roth IRA, combined with the tax-free growth within the plan, will probably be worth more to you than a current tax deduction. Regular IRAs can be rolled over to Roth IRAs; although the amount transferred is taxable, the potential benefit of future tax-free growth can make this alternative worthwhile in many situations, especially if you have other funds available to pay the current tax on the transfer.

Contributions to a U.S. deferred income plan by a U.S. employer may be taxable in Canada as an employment benefit or "retirement compensation arrangement" (see 9.5.4).

17.3.5 Dividends

As we saw in 7.1.2, Canada taxes dividends from Canadian corporations using the "gross-up and credit" system, which results in less tax being levied than on other kinds of income. For U.S. purposes, dividends are taxed at the same rate as other income. The actual amount that you receive, rather than the grossed-up amount, is included in income for U.S. purposes.

Since Canadian tax rates (when provincial tax is counted) are normally higher than U.S. federal rates, the effect of the dividend tax credit roughly equalizes the tax rates of the two countries on dividends. The maximum U.S. rate is 39.6%; the maximum Canadian rate on dividends received is about 36%, depending on your province of residence.

17.3.6 Canadian corporations earning passive income

Watch out for ownership of Canadian corporations earning passive income.

Owning an interest in a Canadian corporation that earns passive income can result in unexpected U.S. tax liability. Under U.S. law, if you invest in a non-U.S. corporation that earns a substantial part of its income from investments (a "passive foreign investment corporation"), and then sell the stock or receive an "excess" distribution, there may be a theoretical deferral of U.S. tax (which would have applied if you had earned the investment income directly). In such a case, an interest charge on this "deferred tax" may be imposed under U.S. tax law.

There is no minimum U.S. ownership required in a Canadian corporation to be subject to these rules. There are ways to avoid the interest charge, however; one way is to elect to include your *pro rata* share of the corporation's earnings in your income on a current basis each year (which may result in a mismatching of income for Canadian and U.S. purposes).

17.3.7 Charitable donations

As discussed in 2.7.1, charitable donations of up to 75% of your net income entitle you to a credit for federal Canadian and Quebec tax purposes.

For Canadian tax purposes, charitable donations must normally be made to a Canadian charity to qualify (subject to certain specific exceptions). The Canada-U.S. tax treaty, however, provides that donations to U.S. charities will qualify, up to a limit of 75% of U.S.-source net income. You will need to obtain receipts from the U.S. charities and file them with your Canadian return.

Similarly, charitable donations are normally deductible in the U.S., subject to a limit of 50% of income for most charities. However, donations to Canadian charities may only be deducted for U.S. tax purposes to the extent of 50% of your *Canadian-source* "adjusted gross income". If you are excluding much or all of your Canadian-source income due to the foreign earned income exclusion (see 17.2.1), this limitation can cause problems.

17.4 Differences in taxation of capital gains

17.4.1 Basic calculation

It is in the field of capital gains that one finds the most glaring differences between the Canadian and U.S. tax systems. Not only are many details different, but the basic scheme of taxation of capital gains is itself fundamentally different, which creates a large number of problems for U.S. citizens resident in Canada.

For Canadian tax purposes, only three-quarters of capital gains are taxed (see 6.2).

For U.S. tax purposes, short-term capital gains from property held for one year or less are normally taxed like other income, at your marginal rate of 15%, 28%, 31%, 36% or 39.6% (see table in 17.1 above). However, the rate for long-term capital gains (generally from property held more than 12 months) is limited to 20% or 10%, depending on your tax bracket. A special lower rate of 18% (or 8%) will apply to transactions in 2001 and later years when the property is held for more than five years.

17.4.2 Use of capital losses

For Canadian purposes, allowable capital losses (three-quarters of your capital losses) can only be used to offset taxable capital gains, though they can be carried back three years and forward indefinitely against such gains (see 6.3.1). An exception exists for allowable business investment losses (on shares or debt of small business corporations), which can be used against any income (6.3.2).

For U.S. purposes, capital losses can be used against capital gains. In addition, US$3,000 of capital losses can be written off against other income (US$1,500 for a married person filing separately). Unused capital losses can be carried forward, to be applied against capital gains or against US$3,000 per year of other income in any future year.

17.4.3 The Canadian capital gains exemption

> Be cautious of using the Cdn$500,000 capital gains exemption.

A Cdn$500,000 capital gains exemption is available in Canada for certain small business shares and farm property (see 6.4.1 and 6.4.2). No such exemption exists for U.S. tax purposes.

The Canadian foreign tax credit is calculated so as not to apply to any portion of a gain on foreign property for which the capital gains exemption was claimed. In other words, if you sell U.S. property and pay U.S. tax on the sale, you cannot claim a Canadian foreign tax credit for the portion of the U.S. tax that relates to the gain on which you or your spouse previously claimed the capital gains exemption for Canadian purposes.

If you sell small business corporation shares or farm property, the Cdn$500,000 capital gains exemption won't protect you from U.S. tax on the gain, even if you are not subject to Canadian tax. Generally, you should steer clear of the planning ideas discussed in 13.1 to "crystallize" your gains and use up your exemption.

The U.S. does have a limited form of capital gains exemption. U.S. citizens who invest in the shares of certain active small U.S. corporations after August 10, 1993, and hold the shares for at least five years, may be entitled to exclude up to 50% of any gains from income when the shares are sold. The recognized gain will not be taxed at the lower capital gains rate.

17.4.4 Reserves vs. instalment sales

Problems can arise when you sell capital property but do not receive full payment in the year of sale. As we saw in 6.5.1, a reserve is allowed for

Canadian tax purposes, if you claim it. The reserve is based on the proportion of gain that has not yet been received, but at least one-fifth of the gain must be recognized cumulatively each year, so the reserve cannot be claimed for more than four years after the year of sale.

> **Elect out of "instalment sale" rules where appropriate.**

For U.S. tax purposes, instalment sale rules cover the same situation. However, the rules apply unless you elect to have them not apply. The basic concept is the same—a "gross profit ratio" will apply to include a portion of each payment into your income—but the five-year rule does not exist. This can lead to mismatching of Canadian and U.S. income, and thus foreign tax credits, in a given year. If you are not claiming a reserve for Canadian tax purposes on the sale of a particular capital property, consider electing out of the "instalment sale" rules on your U.S. return.

If you are claiming a reserve that can last only five years, but deferring a large portion of your proceeds beyond five years, the instalment sale rules will again lead to a mismatch of Canadian and U.S. income.

If the gain is taxed in the U.S. some years after it is taxed in Canada due to the instalment sale rules, Revenue Canada may allow you to reopen an earlier year's return (back to 1985) in order to claim a foreign tax credit.

There are further differences between Canadian reserves and U.S. instalment sale rules. In particular, the instalment sale method may not be available if the instalment obligation is pledged as security for a debt.

17.4.5 Foreign exchange gains or losses

When you sell Canadian property, your gain for U.S. tax purposes must be calculated using the U.S. dollar equivalent of your cost, as of the date you purchased the property. This can lead to a foreign exchange gain or loss that is independent of your (Canadian-dollar) gain or loss on the property.

Example:

You purchase 100 shares of XYZ Corporation on the Toronto Stock Exchange when the Canadian dollar is at US70¢. You pay $20 per share including commission, or Cdn$2,000 (US$1,400). You sell the shares several years later, when the Canadian dollar is at US78¢, for $19 each (after commission), or Cdn$1,900 (US$1,482).

For Canadian tax purposes, you have a $100 capital loss, three-quarters of which can be deducted against taxable capital gains. For U.S. tax purposes, however, you have an $82 capital gain, which is taxed. Since you do not pay any Canadian tax on the gain, no foreign tax credit is available to offset your tax (maximum 20% or 10%, depending on your tax bracket) on US$82.

A taxable foreign exchange gain can also arise on the sale of your principal residence. The problem is that the foreign exchange gain realized on the discharge of a mortgage denominated in Canadian dollars is not a gain to which the U.S. principal residence exemption rules (see 17.4.7) apply.

Similarly, when you sell U.S. property, your gain for Canadian purposes must be calculated in Canadian dollars. The first Cdn$200 of your gain or loss on foreign currency in each year is ignored.

17.4.6 Pre-1972 holdings

As noted in 6.5.4, Canada taxes only capital gains accrued since 1972. The U.S. does not have any such rule. If you are a U.S. citizen and have owned property since before 1972, your gain for U.S. tax purposes could be substantially higher than your gain for Canadian tax purposes.

17.4.7 Principal residence

As we saw in 6.5.2, a gain on a "principal residence" is normally completely exempt from tax in Canada. The U.S. has simplified its rules related to sales of a principal residence occurring after May 6, 1997, but they are very different from the Canadian rules and more restrictive.

Under the new U.S. rules, you may claim an exclusion of US$250,000 of gain on a principal residence. The exclusion is increased to US$500,000 for spouses filing jointly.

Certain requirements must be met to claim the exclusion; for example, you and your spouse must have actually occupied the home for at least two of the past five years, and neither you nor your spouse must have claimed this exclusion in the past two years.

If you and your spouse file jointly but do not share a principal residence, the US$250,000 exclusion is available on the sale of one of the principal residences. Similarly, you can claim the US$250,000 exclusion if you marry someone who has used the exclusion in the past two years.

Be careful if you and your spouse buy more than one home during the two-year period. You will have to pay tax on any gain arising on the "middle" home.

A further difference between Canadian and U.S. exemptions for a principal residence lies in the definition of the term. As we saw in 6.5.2, a vacation property such as a cottage will generally qualify for Canadian tax purposes, although you can only designate one principal residence for each year. For U.S. purposes, a home will only qualify if it is the place where you "regularly reside".

17.4.8 Other capital gains differences

Canada and the U.S. have very different rules with respect to the transfer of capital property to corporations, corporation reorganizations, mergers, windups, recapitalization, debt forgiveness, etc. If you are involved in such transactions, professional advice is essential, especially since there have been many changes to both systems.

17.5 Minimum tax

Canada's minimum tax was discussed in 7.6. The U.S. alternative minimum tax ("AMT") has the same general structure, but there are a number of important differences.

> Watch out for U.S. minimum tax.

First, the U.S. AMT exemption is US$45,000 for married taxpayers filing jointly (or a surviving spouse) and US$33,750 for a single taxpayer. (The Canadian exemption is Cdn$40,000 for federal tax purposes and Cdn$25,000 for Québec tax purposes.) As well, the U.S. exemption is phased out for those with adjusted minimum taxable income over US$150,000 if married filing jointly (US$112,500 if filing as a single taxpayer).

Second, the U.S. AMT rate is calculated under a two-tier graduated rate schedule. A 26% rate applies to the first US$175,000 of alternative minimum taxable income over the AMT exemption amount, and a 28% rate applies to alternative minimum taxable income over US$175,000. The 28% rate comes into effect at an alternative minimum taxable income over US$87,500 for married individuals filing separate returns. For long-term capital gains, the maximum AMT rate is reduced to 20%. (The Canadian rate, including provincial tax, is about 27%.)

Third, the list of "AMT adjustments"—items added back to income for AMT purposes—is, of course, different between the two countries. For U.S. tax purposes, the list includes the standard deduction, itemized property and state taxes paid, oil and gas drilling costs, mining exploration and development costs, a portion of accelerated depreciation, and various other specific deductions.

Fourth, the U.S. foreign tax credit can only be used to offset 90% of your AMT payable. This means that if your income (not counting income eligible for the foreign earned income exclusion) is higher than the AMT exemption level, you will almost always end up paying at least some tax to the United States.

Example:

Sam is an unmarried U.S. citizen living and working in Canada. In 1999, his employment income is Cdn$65,000, and he makes Cdn$100,000 (US$70,000) in interest income.

Sam will pay Canadian tax on his employment income and on his interest income. For U.S. regular tax purposes, the employment income will be eligible for the foreign earned income exclusion, and the U.S. tax on the interest income will be fully offset by a foreign tax credit for the Canadian tax he pays on the interest.

For U.S. AMT purposes, however, Sam's income will be US$70,000, minus his $33,750 AMT exemption. The AMT liability will therefore be 26% of $38,250, or $9,425. Only 90% of this amount can be offset by foreign tax credits, so Sam will have to pay $942 in U.S. tax. This will be in addition to his Canadian tax liability. No Canadian foreign tax credit will be available, since the interest is Canadian-source income even though it is being taxed by the U.S.

As you can see, if your income is high enough, you may have to pay a certain amount of U.S. alternative minimum tax even though your income is fully taxed by Canada. One way to reduce this liability is to earn additional U.S.-source income. Canada will give you a foreign tax credit for regular U.S. tax paid on the U.S.-source income, but not for U.S. AMT payable on Canadian-source income.

17.6 Income earned by children

17.6.1 Effects on dependant deduction

If you claim a deduction for a dependent child (US$2,750) on your U.S. return, that child may not claim the regular personal exemption on his or her own tax return. The effect is that any income the child earns is taxed.

In Canada, there is no federal credit for dependent children. As a result, income earned by your children will not affect the tax you pay unless you pay Québec provincial tax (see 16.2.1).

17.6.2 Attribution rules

We discussed the Canadian attribution rules with respect to minor children in 5.2.3. The basic rule is that if you give or lend funds to your child, the income from those funds (but not the capital gains) will be taxed in your hands rather than the child's, until the child turns 18.

The U.S. tax system accomplishes the same general anti-income-splitting objective in a very different way. The income of the child is taxed in the child's hands, but may in part be taxed at the parent's marginal tax rate.

The first US$700 of unearned income (roughly equivalent in meaning to Canadian "income from property") of a child under 14 is not taxed. The next US$700 is taxed as the child's income. Beyond US$1,400, if the child has no *earned* income (compensation for services rendered), any further unearned income will be taxed at the rate of the parent with the greater taxable income. So, beyond the $1,400 level, little is usually gained from a tax point of view by having a child under 14 earn investment income.

If certain requirements are met, the parent whose taxable income is used for calculating the child's tax rate may elect to include the child's income directly. This will eliminate the need to file a tax return for the child, and also lead to a better matching of incomes between the Canadian and U.S. tax systems.

> **Review income splitting arrangements to prevent double taxation.**

Income splitting arrangements that are set up for Canadian income tax purposes can result in double taxation if you are not careful. For example, suppose you and your 13-year-old son are both U.S. citizens and your son has no income, and you lend funds to him with the intention of building up "secondary" income over time which will not be attributed back to you (see 5.3.5). The income on the funds you have loaned will be taxed in your hands under Canadian law, but in your son's hands (albeit at your marginal rate while the child is under 14) under U.S. law. Because different taxpayers are paying the tax, no foreign tax credit will be available and you may end up being taxed twice on the same income.

In this example, as long as your son is under 14, you can elect to include his unearned income on your return for U.S. tax purposes. That should solve the double taxation problem, since the income will be taxed in your hands under both systems.

Bear in mind that attribution problems may arise in certain cases if you and your spouse do not file a joint U.S. return (see 17.7.1). For example, if you give your spouse $100,000 to invest and the investment earns $10,000 in Canadian-source dividend income, you will pay Canadian tax on the income and your spouse will pay the U.S. tax. If you and your spouse file a joint U.S. return, all Canadian taxes will be combined for foreign tax credit purposes. But if you and your spouse do not file jointly, no foreign tax credit will be available because different taxpayers are taxable on the income.

17.7   U.S. filing requirements

17.7.1   Joint return or not?

For federal Canadian tax purposes, every taxpayer is distinct and must file separately. Combining the income of two spouses is only considered for certain specific purposes, such as eligibility for the Child Tax Benefit (see 2.3.1) and the GST credit (see 2.9.3). For Québec purposes, spouses have the option of filing joint returns in certain circumstances (see 16.1.2).

> **If you're married, file a joint return where appropriate.**

For U.S. tax purposes, you have the option of filing a joint return with your spouse. If one spouse has little or no income, this will usually result in less tax than if you file as "married filing separately". For U.S. purposes, spouses must be legally married; in Canada, spouses include common-law spouses (see 2.2.1).

For U.S. purposes, a joint return is mandatory (if you are married) if you wish to claim certain deductions and credits. The child care credit is one example. Another is the US$25,000 loss allowance for an owner who actively participates in rental real estate.

If you do not have a spouse, your filing status will be one of "single", "head of household" or "surviving spouse", all of which have different implications for your U.S. tax return.

If your spouse is a U.S. citizen, the decision as to whether to file jointly can be made annually. If your spouse is not a U.S. citizen, the decision to file jointly can only be made once.

If your spouse is not a U.S. citizen and has no U.S.-source income, and thus is not subject to U.S. tax, consider filing a "married filing separate" return. As a "non-resident alien", your spouse's Canadian income will not be relevant for U.S. tax purposes. On the other hand, if your spouse has little income from any source but you are paying tax to the U.S., filing a joint return can be beneficial, as it will give you larger exclusions and wider tax brackets at the lower rates.

Note also that if you file jointly with a non-resident alien spouse, you must always file jointly unless the election to file jointly is revoked; but once revoked, the decision can never be made again (unless you have a new spouse).

17.7.2 Time requirements for filing

The requirements for filing Canadian tax returns were discussed in 8.1.

U.S. tax returns must normally be postmarked by April 15 each year.

If you are a U.S. citizen whose "tax home" (place of employment) and "abode" (place of residence) are *both* outside the U.S., your filing deadline is automatically extended to June 15 each year. You must attach a statement to your return identifying that you are eligible for this extension. You mail your U.S. tax return to the IRS in Philadelphia.

If you are unable to meet your U.S. filing deadline, you may file for an extension of the deadline to August 15. The extension will be granted automatically.

Even though you are permitted to file your return in June or August, interest on any balance of taxes owing will run from April 15. If more than 10% of your tax for the year is owing, a late payment penalty may also apply.

17.7.3 Estimated taxes

We discussed the Canadian tax instalment requirements in 8.3.2. The U.S. has parallel requirements, which are called payments of "estimated taxes".

Estimated tax payments are due quarterly, on April 15, June 15, September 15 and the following January 15. As with the Canadian system, you can generally choose either last year's tax or this year's tax as the basis for your quarterly estimated tax payments.

If you are basing your payments on the current year's tax, you need only pay 90% of the year's tax liability (regular tax or AMT) in estimated tax payments—22.5% each quarter. If you are using last year's tax, you must normally pay 25% of that amount each quarter. In order to use last year's tax, you must have filed a return in the previous year and the year must have been a 12-month period.

In either case, any balance still owing will be due with your tax return. No estimated tax payments are required if your total tax for the year is less than US$1,000.

If you do not make your estimated tax payments on time, non-deductible late payment penalties will apply.

17.7.4 Disclosure requirements

As well as filing a tax return, you must disclose a substantial amount of financial information under U.S. law.

First, you must disclose holdings in any non-U.S. corporations which you control directly or indirectly, or in which you have increased your interest and which are controlled by other U.S. citizens or corporations. You are required to provide this information by filing a separate Form 5471 for each foreign corporation that you control. The IRS uses this information, among other things, to help determine your liability for tax on any undistributed income of closely-held non-U.S. corporations that earn passive income.

In some cases, a Canadian corporation's reporting year must be the calendar year for U.S. reporting purposes.

Second, you are required to file annually a "Report of Foreign Bank and Financial Accounts" form with the U.S. Department of the Treasury. This form is mailed separately from your tax return and is due by June 30. It is required if the total value of your foreign bank accounts, brokerage accounts, RRSPs, etc. exceeds US$10,000 at any time in the year.

As discussed in 17.8.3, reporting rules are also in place for gifts and bequests over $100,000 received in one year. Any transfers to and from foreign trusts (including loans) must also be reported by filing an "Annual Return to Report Transactions with Foreign Trusts and Receipt of Certain Foreign Gifts". The return is due at the same time as your U.S. personal tax return.

Severe penalties apply under U.S. law for not complying with these disclosure requirements.

17.7.5   U.S. passport renewals

If you apply for a U.S. passport, or a renewal of your passport, while living outside the U.S., you will be required to provide your Social Security Number and file an IRS information return. If you have not been regularly filing U.S. tax returns, you may receive a request to file from the Internal Revenue Service. Ignoring such requests can leave you liable to criminal penalties. In the future, the IRS hopes that legislation will be passed permitting the U.S. government to withhold renewal of your passport for non-filing of tax returns.

17.8   U.S. estate and gift taxes

17.8.1   Estate tax

The U.S. imposes estate tax on death of U.S. citizens, where the net value of the estate (when combined with certain previous taxable gifts) is over US$650,000 (this threshold is scheduled to increase gradually to US$1 million by 2006). The tax applies at graduated rates, ranging from 18% for the value of an estate under US$10,000 to 55% of the value of an estate over US$3 million. See 18.4 for a more detailed discussion.

> Plan to minimize U.S. estate tax.

A deduction is allowed for any amounts left to your spouse on death, if your spouse is a U.S. citizen. As a result, leaving all of your estate to your spouse will result in no estate tax applying on your death. This will cause one US$650,000 exemption amount to be wasted, since only one US$650,000 exemption on your combined estate would be available on your spouse's death.

Generally, a marital deduction is only permitted for property passing to the spouse outright with no restrictions on its use. But you may intend for the assets to be used by your spouse and pass to your children or other individuals on your spouse's death, even if, for example, your spouse remarries. Such property may be treated as "qualified terminal interest property", which is eligible for the marital deduction, if an election is made on the estate tax return and certain other requirements are met.

Life insurance proceeds are subject to U.S. estate tax if the insured had a beneficial interest in the policy, such as a right to change beneficiaries, borrow against the policy or cancel the policy. In many cases, life insurance proceeds comprise the bulk of the taxable estate. Certain techniques are available to minimize the estate tax burden on life insurance proceeds, including the use of life insurance trusts and gifting plans. To use these strategies, advice from an estate planning professional is essential.

If your spouse is not a U.S. citizen, the deduction is not available.

As noted in 6.5.3 and 20.1.2, Canada effectively taxes accrued capital gains on death by deeming capital property to have been disposed of at fair market value immediately before death.

Since the U.S. tax on death is an estate tax and the Canadian tax is an income tax, neither one would normally permit a foreign tax credit in respect of the other. This can result in double taxation. Subject to various restrictions, the Canada-U.S. treaty allows Canadian residents a credit against Canadian income tax payable on U.S.-source income on death for U.S. estate tax, and allows U.S. citizens or residents a credit against U.S. estate tax for Canadian income tax imposed on Canadian property on death. These treaty provisions alleviate (but will not eliminate) the risk of double taxation. See 18.4.

The treatment of Canadian RRSP funds held by a U.S. citizen at death is currently unclear. The RRSP funds would be included in the deceased's income for Canadian tax purposes and would be subject to U.S. estate tax. The treaty provisions technically only cover amounts resulting from a deemed disposition that results in tax, making it unclear whether a credit will be available to alleviate double taxation of the RRSP funds.

Note that although U.S. estate tax will only apply to the extent the net value of the estate exceeds US$650,000 in 1999, an estate tax return must be filed whenever the gross value of the estate exceeds that figure. Furthermore, to the extent you have made taxable gifts (see 17.8.2) during your lifetime, the $650,000 threshold is reduced.

Some items in an individual's estate are subject to both U.S. income and estate taxes. These items include accrued compensation or commissions for personal services received after death, investment income, instalment sales, employment survivor benefits and retirement plans such as IRAs. Planning strategies may be available to reduce the resulting double taxation. For example, you could gift income-producing assets to individuals or trusts during your lifetime or bequeath specific assets to charities. Professional advice on implementing these strategies is recommended.

17.8.2   Gift tax

Canada does not have a gift tax, although the giver of a gift (except to a spouse) is deemed to have sold the property at its current fair market value, possibly leading to income tax on a resulting taxable capital gain (see 6.5.4).

> **Watch out for U.S. gift tax.**

The U.S. does have a gift tax, which applies only to those who make very substantial gifts. The *giver* is liable for the tax. Where the giver and recipient are spouses who are both U.S. citizens, no gift tax applies at all. Otherwise, if only the giver is a U.S. citizen, gift tax may apply.

The gift tax generally does not apply to gifts to charities, U.S. political parties, and directly to institutions to pay for another person's tuition or medical expenses.

Up to US$10,000 may be given tax-free each year to any one donee, and up to $101,000 to a spouse who is not a U.S. citizen. In addition, every U.S. citizen has a cumulative lifetime exemption of $650,000 (for 1999) against gift and estate taxes; the credit is scheduled to increase gradually to $1 million by 2006. Over the course of your lifetime, this can effectively exempt about $650,000 (in 1999) of gifts over the $10,000 and $101,000 annual levels. Any exemption amount used during your lifetime is not available on death.

Beyond the $10,000 and $101,000 levels, gift tax applies at the same graduated rates as estate tax, ranging from 18% on taxable gifts under $10,000 to 55% on the portion of taxable gifts over $3 million.

> **Consider using the annual $10,000 U.S. gift tax exclusion to transfer wealth to children.**

A common estate planning technique is to make use of the $10,000 annual gift tax exclusion to transfer wealth to children. However, for the gift to be eligible for the exclusion, the recipient must have the right to use the gift without restriction. In these cases, steps should be taken to ensure that an adult retains control over the assets while the child remains a minor such as opening a *"Uniform Gift to Minors Act"* account in the U.S. or establishing a formal trust.

The Canadian tax (if any) that applies on a gift is an income tax, while the U.S. tax is not. As a result, no foreign tax credit applies in either system for taxes of the other system. Caution must therefore be exercised if you are making large gifts. One further problem with gifts is that, for U.S. purposes, your cost base of property (plus a portion of the gift tax paid) will be carried through to the recipient of a gift, whereas on death, any property left to your beneficiaries is treated as acquired by them at its fair market value.

You must also watch out for the Canadian attribution rules, as outlined in Chapter 5.

The Canada-U.S. tax treaty does not provide any relief for U.S. gift tax, although you can elect to have a deemed disposition for U.S. purposes in order to match income recognition in the U.S. and Canada. Making this election would allow you to increase the property's cost base to its fair market value at the time the gift is made.

As discussed below in 17.8.3, U.S. recipients of gifts from foreign individuals must also report gifts over $100,000 in a calendar year.

17.8.3 U.S. reporting rules for gifts and foreign trusts

If you are a U.S. citizen and you transfer money or property to a foreign trust, or you receive a distribution from one, you must report the transfer to the IRS. The penalty for not complying with these new reporting rules is 35% of the gross value of the money or property transferred, and additional penalties for continued failure can run up to 100% of the transferred amount.

> Beware of U.S. reporting rules for gifts and foreign trusts.

U.S. citizens must also report each gift or bequest received in a year if the total of all gifts and bequests received from foreign persons in that year is more than US$100,000. Penalties for non-compliance are the same as those for transfers to and from foreign trusts.

17.9 References

The following publications can be obtained (in person or by telephone request) from your nearest Revenue Canada District Taxation Office. Forms and guides may also be available from Revenue Canada's Internet site at *www.rc.gc.ca*.

Interpretation Bulletin IT-221R2, "Determination of an individual's residence status"

Interpretation Bulletin IT-270R2, "Foreign tax credit"

Interpretation Bulletin IT-395R, "Foreign tax credit—capital gains and capital losses on foreign property"

Interpretation Bulletin IT-506, "Foreign income taxes as a deduction from income"

Interpretation Bulletin IT-520, "Unused foreign tax credits—carryforward and carryback"

Form T2209, "Calculation of federal foreign tax credits"

Form T2036, "Calculation of provincial foreign tax credit"

Brochure, "Emigrants and Income Tax"

Brochure, "Newcomers to Canada"

The following may be obtained from any office of the Internal Revenue Service, and are generally available at U.S. embassy and consular offices, or from the IRS' Internet site at *www.irs.ustreas.gov.* Help is also available from the IRS office in Ottawa at 1 (800) 829-1040.

Publication 17, "Your Federal Income Tax"

Publication 54, "Tax Guide For U.S. Citizens and Resident Aliens Abroad"

Publication 521, "Moving Expenses"

Publication 523, "Selling Your Home"

Publication 514, "Foreign Tax Credit For Individuals"

Form 1040, "U.S. Individual Income Tax Return"

Form 1116, "Computation of Foreign Tax Credit"

Form 2119, "Sale Of Your Home"

Form 2350, "Application For Extension Of Time to File U.S. Income Tax Return"

Form 2555, "Foreign Earned Income"

Form 3520, "Annual Return to Report Transactions with Foreign Trusts and Receipt of Certain Foreign Gifts"

Form 3520A, "Annual Information Return of Foreign Trust With a U.S. Owner"

Form 3903, "Moving Expenses"

Form 3903F, "Foreign Moving Expenses"

Form 4868, "Application for Automatic Extension of Time to File U.S. Individual Income Tax Return"

Form 5471, "Information Return With Respect To A Foreign Corporation"

Form 6251, "Alternative Minimum Tax—Individuals"

Form 8833, "Treaty-Based Return Position Disclosure under Section 6114 or 7701(b)"

Form TD F 90-22.1, "Report of Foreign Bank and Financial Accounts"

18

U.S. residency and ownership of U.S. property by Canadians

- Avoid becoming a U.S. resident while visiting (18.1)
- If you own rental real estate in the U.S., elect the net rental income method (18.2.1)
- Sell real estate to a buyer who will occupy it as a residence (18.3.1)
- Apply for a U.S. "withholding certificate" on the sale of real estate (18.3.1)
- Consider using your Canadian principal residence exemption on the sale of your U.S. residence (18.3.2)
- Be cautious when acquiring shares in U.S. corporations (18.4.1)
- Keep the value of your worldwide estate below $1.2 million (18.4.6)
- Split your worldwide assets with your spouse (18.4.7)
- Leave property to your spouse or a qualified domestic trust (18.4.7)
- Mortgage property (non-recourse) to reduce the value of your U.S. real estate (18.4.7)
- Acquire property jointly with your spouse or another person (18.4.7)
- Consider a split interest purchase with your child (18.4.7)
- Hold your U.S. property through a Canadian corporation (18.4.7)
- Hold your U.S. assets through a Canadian partnership that elects to be treated as a corporation in the U.S. (18.4.7)
- Sell U.S. property before death (18.4.7)
- Consider taking out life insurance to cover U.S. estate taxes (18.4.7)

In this chapter we discuss the United States taxes that apply to Canadian residents who are not U.S. citizens and who acquire U.S. investments such as stocks and real estate. (Taxation of U.S. citizens resident in Canada was covered in Chapter 17.) Such investments are taxed in four ways: on the income they generate; on their sale; on gift; and on death of the owner. We also discuss the "snowbird" rules that can make you resident in the U.S. for tax purposes.

In general, the interaction between the U.S. and Canadian tax systems can be highly complex. Transactions in U.S. real estate should not be undertaken without qualified professional tax advice.

18.1   Snowbirds—U.S. residency rules

Avoid becoming a U.S. resident while visiting.

If you spend a substantial portion of the year in the U.S., you may become a U.S. resident for tax purposes. If this happens you may be required to file U.S. tax returns and pay U.S. tax on your income from *all* sources, including Canada (except to the extent that you can claim foreign tax credits—see 18.3.2). If you accidentally become a U.S. resident for tax purposes, the tax cost can be substantial.

If you hold a green card, you have the status of a U.S. permanent resident and will be considered resident in the U.S. for tax purposes wherever you live.

If your "physical presence" in the U.S. totals 183 days or more in the year, you will be deemed a U.S. resident. For this purpose, you must total up the number of days you spend in the U.S. in the current year, 1/3 of the days from the preceding year and 1/6 of the days from the second preceding year.

Example:

Simone spends the winter each year in Miami and the fall, spring and summer in Montréal. For 1997, 1998 and 1999, she is physically in the U.S. for 150, 90 and 140 days respectively.

For 1999, Simone's "physical presence" calculation is 140 + (1/3 × 90) + (1/6 × 150), or 195. Since this figure exceeds 183, she is considered resident in the U.S. for 1999 (subject to the "closer connection" rule described below).

If you are deemed a U.S. resident under the "physical presence" test but the number of days you spend in the U.S. in the *current* year is less than 183, you can be treated as non-resident for purposes of U.S. tax if you can establish that you have a "closer connection" to Canada than to the U.S. This information is reported on Form 8840 (see 18.5), which is due by June 15 of the following year.

If your current year's days in the U.S. are 183 or more, or if you hold a green card, you can gain a measure of protection from the Canada-U.S. tax treaty if you can establish that under the treaty you are resident in Canada rather than the U.S. (This protection is not as broad as being treated as non-resident under the "closer connection" rule above, however.) For this purpose you would need to show that you have a permanent home in Canada and not in the U.S.; or, if you have a permanent home in both countries or neither, that your personal and economic relations are closer to Canada. You will have to file information with the IRS within certain time limits to be entitled to this treaty "tiebreaker" protection. If you have a green card, filing on this basis may jeopardize your U.S. immigration status.

18.2 Income from U.S. properties

Certain U.S.-source income is subject to U.S. tax even if you are not resident in the U.S.

18.2.1 Rent from real estate

A withholding tax of 30% normally applies to the gross amount of any rent paid to a resident of Canada on real estate located in the United States. (Unlike withholding taxes on interest and dividends, this tax is not reduced by the Canada-U.S. tax treaty.)

Example:

You live in Canada and own a condominium in Texas. You rent out the condominium for the entire year, receiving US$10,000 in rent. Your mortgage interest, maintenance costs, property taxes and depreciation total US$8,000.

Over the course of the year, 30% of the rent paid to you, or US$3,000, should be withheld by your tenant and remitted to the IRS.

At the end of the year, you may elect to file a U.S. tax return and to pay U.S. tax on your net rental income. In the example above, your net rental income would be only US$2,000 rather than US$10,000. You can then receive a refund for the withholding tax, to the extent it exceeds the tax payable on your U.S. return. However, note that state tax (and possibly a small amount of city tax) may be payable on the rental income.

> **Elect the net rental method.**

If your expenses are significant (mortgage interest, maintenance, insurance, property management, property taxes, etc.), you will almost always want to elect the "net rental income" method. The amount subject to tax at your marginal rate will be substantially lower than the amount subject to 30% withholding.

Once you've elected to file on a net basis, the election is permanent and you will be taxed on the net basis in future years. If you make the election, it applies to all of your rental real estate. Make sure you take into account the fact that the election can only be revoked in limited circumstances.

If you make the election, you can provide Form 4224 (see 18.5) to your tenant or agent, and 30% of the rent will not need to be withheld.

Depreciation must be claimed for U.S. income tax purposes. Unlike Canada's capital cost allowance system (see 10.2.7), depreciation is not a discretionary deduction in the U.S. Any allowable amount that you don't claim will reduce the property's cost base and increase the gain on its disposition.

If you wish to file on a net basis, the IRS sets a deadline by which you must file. For the 1999 year, your return must normally be filed by October 15, 2001, or you will not be able to claim any deductions and tax will be assessed on the gross income. This rule applies not only to real estate rent, but to any U.S.-source income against which you may wish to claim deductions, such as partnership income.

18.2.2 Dividends and interest from U.S. corporations

Like rental payments, payments of dividends and interest by U.S. corporations to residents of Canada are subject to U.S. withholding tax. The Canada-U.S. tax treaty limits the tax to 15% for dividends and 10% for interest in most cases. Certain interest may qualify for a "portfolio debt" exemption from U.S. tax.

You do not file a U.S. income tax return in respect of dividend and interest income on which the correct tax is withheld.

18.3 Sale of U.S. properties

18.3.1 Withholding tax ("FIRPTA") on sale of real estate

If you sell real estate located in the U.S., a withholding tax of 10% of the sale price is normally payable under "FIRPTA" (the *Foreign Investment in Real Property Tax Act* of 1980). The tax withheld can be offset against the U.S. income tax payable on any gain you realize on the sale, and refunded if it exceeds your U.S. tax liability when you file your U.S. tax return to report the disposition.

> **Sell real estate to a buyer who will occupy it as a residence.**

If you are selling U.S. real estate for less than US$300,000, selling it to a buyer who intends to occupy it as a residence can be advantageous. Withholding under FIRPTA will not apply if the property is sold for less than US$300,000 and the purchaser intends to use it as a residence. For this exception to apply, the purchaser must have definite plans to reside at the property for at least half of the time that the property is in use during each of the two years following the sale. The purchaser does not have to be a U.S. citizen.

Bear in mind that the gain on the sale will still be taxable in the U.S. A U.S. tax return must be filed for every disposition of U.S. real property.

> ### Apply for a U.S. "withholding certificate" on the sale of real estate.

Another way of reducing the FIRPTA withholding is to apply to the IRS before the sale for a "withholding certificate" on the basis that your expected U.S. tax liability will be less than 10% of the sale price. The certificate will indicate what amount of tax should be withheld by the purchaser rather than the full 10%. You must file the application before the sale's closing date.

Be sure to apply for a "withholding certificate" if you are making an instalment sale—otherwise, the 10% withholding will be required on the entire sale price up front.

Some states such as California and Hawaii have state withholding tax provisions that parallel FIRPTA.

18.3.2 Income tax on the sale of U.S. real estate

For income tax purposes, you must file a U.S. tax return to report the gain on the sale of U.S. real estate. You can then claim a credit for the FIRPTA tax withheld. The maximum U.S. tax rate on capital gains for assets held for more the 12 months is 20%. Regular graduated U.S. rates apply for assets held for less than one year. The effective highest Canadian rate is about 37% because Canada only taxes 75% of the gain (see 6.2). However, 100% of the gain is taxed for U.S. purposes.

If you have owned the property and have been resident in Canada since before September 27, 1980 and used it only for personal use, you can likely take advantage of the Canada-U.S. tax treaty (see 17.2.3) to reduce the amount of your gain that is taxable in the U.S. In this case, only your gain accruing since January 1, 1985 will be taxed.

Example:

Riley bought a cottage in the U.S. for personal use in 1977 for US$10,000. On January 1, 1985 it was worth US$30,000. In 1999, Riley sold the cottage for US$60,000.

The U.S. will tax only US$30,000 of Riley's gain, which is the increase in value of the property since the beginning of 1985. State income tax may be based on a gain of either US$30,000 or US$50,000, depending on whether the state adheres to the Canada-U.S. tax treaty.

If you cannot establish a January 1, 1985 valuation, the gain accrued to that date is determined by assuming that the entire gain accrued equally over each month in the holding period.

The above rules also apply to certain rental properties. The Canadian tax will still be based on your entire gain.

To claim the benefit under the treaty, you will need to make the claim on your U.S. return and include a statement containing certain specific information about the transaction.

> **Consider using your Canadian principal residence exemption on the sale of your U.S. residence.**

U.S. tax on the sale of U.S. property will generate a foreign tax credit that can be used to reduce the Canadian tax on the sale. (See 17.2.2 for an explanation of the operation of foreign tax credits.) If the property qualifies, you can shelter the amount of the gain taxed in Canada by claiming the Canadian principal residence exemption (see 6.5.2). However, using the exemption will reduce the foreign tax credit available to you for Canadian tax purposes.

18.3.3 Sales of U.S. stocks and bonds

As long as you are not a resident or citizen of the U.S., U.S. tax will normally not apply to sales of shares in U.S. corporations, whether public or private and no matter where they are traded.

However, if the majority of the corporation's assets are U.S. real estate, the corporation may be considered a "U.S. real property holding corporation" (unless it is a publicly traded company and you own less than 5% of the shares). In such a case, any gain on the sale of the shares of the corporation will be taxed by the U.S. in a manner similar to sales of real property.

18.4 U.S. estate taxes on death and the Canada-U.S. tax treaty

U.S. estate taxes can impose a very serious burden on the death of Canadians who own U.S. stocks and real estate. We shall discuss federal estate taxes only; many states also have estate taxes, and these must be considered as well.

The rules discussed here only apply in situations where both the deceased and the surviving spouse are Canadian citizens and residents. If either spouse is a U.S. citizen or resident, the planning alternatives outlined in this section may not be appropriate.

18.4.1 Determination of property subject to estate tax

U.S. estate tax applies to the deceased's "property situated within the United States". This includes:

- real property located in the U.S.

- certain tangible personal property located in the U.S.
- shares of U.S. corporations, regardless of the location of the share certificates and regardless of where the shares are traded
- debts of U.S. persons, including the U.S. government (such as U.S. Government Savings Bonds)
- interests in partnerships carrying on business in the U.S. (although this is not free from doubt)
- U.S. pension plan and annuity amounts (including IRAs).

U.S. estate tax could apply to any of your personal assets that are located in the U.S. at the time of your death. U.S. case law has established that the assets must be located in the U.S. with a degree of permanence, so the tax probably will not apply to jewellery or other items you might take with you on vacation. However, furniture and artwork in your condominium, for example, may be subject to U.S. estate tax.

> **Be cautious when acquiring shares in U.S. corporations.**

Assets normally excluded from the definition of property situated within the U.S. include: shares of a non-U.S. corporation, regardless of where the corporation's assets are situated; U.S. bank deposits; certain U.S. corporate bonds that are publicly traded outside the U.S.; and certain debt obligations that qualify for the "portfolio debt" exemption from U.S. tax.

The "taxable estate" for estate tax purposes is the gross value of all of the deceased's property situated in the U.S., minus certain allowable deductions. The most significant deductions are:

- amounts left to the deceased's spouse if the spouse is a U.S. citizen (and will therefore be subject to U.S. estate tax on death)
- amounts transferred to a "qualified domestic trust" (a trust which meets certain requirements, as set out in 18.4.7)
- a deduction for a non-recourse mortgage (see 18.4.7) encumbering U.S. property
- a deduction for an allocable share of the deceased's liabilities at time of death in respect of which the estate becomes liable— including Canadian income taxes payable.

To calculate and claim the allocable share of liabilities, the estate tax return must disclose the deceased's worldwide assets and liabilities.

18.4.2   U.S. federal estate tax rates

Once the "taxable estate" has been determined, U.S. federal estate tax applies at graduated rates ranging from 18% on the first US$10,000 to

55% on any amount over $3 million. An applicable credit amount will then reduce this tax, as we shall see below.

Some examples of the U.S. federal estate tax payable at the graduated rates (all figures in U.S. dollars) are shown below:

Taxable estate	Tax (before credit)
$10,000	$1,800
$50,000	$10,600
$100,000	$23,800
$200,000	$54,800
$500,000	$155,800
$1,000,000	$345,800

18.4.3 Enhanced applicable credit amount

Under U.S. domestic law, non-residents of the U.S. who are not U.S. citizens can apply an applicable credit amount of US$13,000 against the estate tax. This credit amount effectively exempts US$60,000 of the estate from taxation. The estate will also be liable for state death taxes, but will receive a credit against federal estate tax for such state taxes. Most states limit their death taxes to the amount of this credit, so the total combined amount of tax is not increased by the application of state tax unless the treaty is applied for federal purposes.

The Canada-U.S. tax treaty increases the U.S. applicable credit amount for residents and citizens of Canada from the US$13,000 allowed under U.S. law to US$211,300 in 1999. This amount is scheduled to increase gradually to US$345,800 for 2006 and later years. This credit must be prorated by the value of the Canadian deceased's U.S. estate over the value of the deceased individual's worldwide estate (as determined under U.S. rules).

The proration of the credit means that Canadians will not be subject to U.S. estate tax unless the value of their worldwide gross estate exceeds US$650,000 (rising to US$1 million in 2006 and after). It also means that wealthy Canadians who hold a relatively small proportion of their total estate in the United States will still be subject to substantial U.S. estate tax. These Canadians may, therefore, choose to avail themselves of the planning techniques discussed in 17.4.7.

Example:

Tony, a Canadian citizen and resident, acquired undeveloped land in Washington state for US$180,000 in 1999. At the time of his death later that year, Tony's worldwide assets had a fair market value of US$650,000 and the value of the land in Washington was still US$180,000. Due to the treaty's enhanced applicable credit amount of up to US$211,300, Tony's U.S. estate tax on the value of the Washington property would be zero.

But what if the value of Tony's worldwide assets at death was US$1.2 million (instead of US$650,000)? Since the enhanced applicable credit must be prorated by the value of Tony's U.S. estate, his U.S. estate tax credit would be US$31,695 (US$180,000 ÷ US$1,200,000 × US$211,300), and Tony's U.S. estate tax liability would be US$16,705 (US$48,400 – US$31,695).

All information necessary for the computation and verification of the credit must be provided to the U.S. authorities or the credit will be denied.

A deceased Canadian's worldwide estate for purposes of the pro rata calculation includes some surprising items that may erode the amount of the credit. The value of life insurance policies may be included if the deceased had "incidents of ownership" (e.g., the right to change beneficiaries at the time of death). This may be the case even though the deceased was not a named beneficiary under the policy. The worldwide estate includes the value of the deceased's principal residence.

Even if no U.S. federal estate tax is payable as a result of the treaty credit, state estate tax may be payable as the treaty generally does not apply for state tax purposes.

If you own U.S. real estate, the enhanced applicable credit amount may not wipe out all of your estate tax. In such a case, any personal assets could be subject to estate tax. You may wish to limit the value of the personal assets such as artwork which you keep in the U.S.

18.4.4   Marital credit

A "marital credit" will be available if an estate tax marital deduction would have been available had the surviving spouse been a U.S. citizen. However, this credit will be capped at the lesser of the applicable credit amount allowed to the deceased's estate and the U.S. estate tax payable after other credits. This effectively allows a minimum $26,000 credit (i.e., 2 × $13,000) where U.S. property is transferred to a spouse on death.

The executor of the estate must elect to take advantage of this provision and must irrevocably waive the benefit of any estate tax marital deduction which may have otherwise been allowable. In effect, the executor must either claim the treaty marital credit or create a qualified domestic trust (but not both) (see 18.4.7). The deadline for the election and waiver is usually nine months after the date of death.

18.4.5   Canadian credit for U.S. estate taxes

On death, Canada will normally tax the accrued capital gains in the deceased's estate (see 20.1.2). A foreign tax credit is available in Canada to offset foreign income taxes paid on foreign-source income. However,

U.S. estate taxes are not income taxes. As a result, no foreign tax credit is available under Canadian domestic law to offset taxes on death.

Under the treaty, Canada now permits U.S. estate tax to be deducted from a Canadian resident's Canadian tax otherwise payable for the year of death. The credit will, however, be limited to the Canadian tax attributable to the deceased's U.S.-source income for the year of death. It may be beneficial to elect out of the Canadian spousal rollover rules to use the estate tax as a credit and bump the basis of the assets for Canadian tax purposes.

18.4.6 Special rules for smaller estates

If the value at death of the worldwide estate of a Canadian resident individual (other than a U.S. citizen) is less than US$1.2 million (determined under U.S. rules), the treaty narrows the range of U.S. assets on which estate tax may be levied to properties the gain on the sale of which would have been subject to U.S. income tax under the treaty.

As we saw in 18.4.1, U.S. estate tax normally applies to the deceased's "property situated within the U.S.", including U.S. real estate, certain tangible personal property located in the U.S., shares of U.S. corporations (regardless of the location of the share certificates and of where the shares are traded), debts of U.S. persons, and interests in partnerships carrying on business in the U.S.

> **Keep the value of your worldwide estate below US$1.2 million.**

Under the treaty, the U.S. may only tax U.S. real estate (including U.S. real property holding corporations) and personal property constituting business property if your worldwide estate is less than US$1.2 million at the time of death. As a result, you'll want to exercise caution if the value of your worldwide estate is close to US$1.2 million.

Example:

Harry, an unmarried Canadian citizen and resident, died owning U.S. stocks with a fair market value of US$1 million. His other assets were all situated in Canada. If Harry's worldwide estate was worth US$1,199,000 at the time of his death, Harry's U.S. estate tax liability would be zero.

However, if Harry's worldwide estate was worth US $1,201,000 at the time of his death, his applicable credit amount would be US$175,937 (US$1,000,000 ÷ US$1,201,000 × US$211,300), which would reduce his U.S. estate tax liability of US$345,800 on his US$1 million U.S. estate to US$169,863.

In order for Harry's estate to use the entire U.S. estate tax amount as a foreign tax credit for Canadian tax purposes, the deemed gain on the shares at Harry's death would have to be at least US$452,968—the amount of capital gain that would attract US$169,863 of Canadian tax (US$452,968 × 3/4 × 50% rate of tax).

18.4.7 Ways to reduce your exposure to U.S. estate tax

Once you have determined which of your assets are subject to U.S. estate tax, there are a number of strategies you can put in place to reduce your estate's potential U.S. estate tax exposure.

> **Leave property to your spouse or a qualified domestic trust.**

Where property is left to a surviving spouse who is a U.S. citizen, or to a qualified domestic trust ("QDOT"), the estate tax can be deferred until the death of the surviving spouse.

To qualify as a QDOT, the trust instrument must provide that at least one trustee be a U.S. citizen or U.S. corporation, and that no distribution of capital may be made from the trust without the U.S. trustee being able to withhold U.S. estate tax. Any capital paid out of a QDOT will then become subject to estate tax. More stringent rules apply to QDOTs with assets exceeding US$2 million in value. A properly structured QDOT may qualify as a "spousal trust" for Canadian tax purposes (see 20.4.2).

> **Mortgage property (non-recourse) to reduce the value of your U.S. real estate.**

A "non-recourse" mortgage is one that entitles the lender to have recourse only against the property mortgaged. That is, if you default on payment, the mortgagee can seize the mortgaged property, but cannot bring suit against you for the balance if the property is not worth enough to pay off the debt. A non-recourse mortgage outstanding on your U.S. real estate will reduce your equity in the property, and thus reduce the value of your taxable estate.

Consider taking out a substantial non-recourse mortgage on your U.S. property, even where it is already fully paid off.

Example:

You are not married and you own a condominium in Florida, now worth US$200,000 and clear of all mortgages. Your worldwide assets are substantial. If you die, the U.S. estate tax will be US$41,800.

Assume you borrow US$100,000 against the property at 11%, on a non-recourse basis, and invest the funds in Canada at 10%. Subject to currency fluctuations, your annual cost will be approximately US$1,000. If you die after taking out this mortgage, your taxable estate will be only US$100,000, and the estate tax will be US$10,800—a US$31,000 saving.

The mortgage generally should be obtained from a lender resident in Canada (however, Canadian financial institutions generally are reluctant to lend on a non-recourse basis, so you will have to seek out other sources). Canadian withholding tax (usually 10%) will apply to the interest payments you make to a non-resident lender if you are deducting the interest paid for Canadian tax purposes. In Canada, your interest expense will normally be denied to the extent it exceeds the investment income you earn from investing the loan proceeds. This has the effect of reducing the hoped-for estate tax savings.

Over time, the property's value may increase and the mortgage amount will decrease. Because of this, the exposure to U.S. estate tax will increase as time goes by.

Acquire property jointly with your spouse or another person.

Another way you can reduce your estate tax exposure is by acquiring U.S. assets jointly with your spouse (or another person). For this to work, you and your spouse will each have to supply your own funds; you cannot simply give half of the interest in the property to your spouse, or give your spouse the funds to invest. Where assets are jointly held and it can be proven that each joint tenant paid for their interest with their own money, on the death of the first joint tenant, each tenant is deemed to own their share of the property. If it cannot be proven that each spouse paid for their own interest, the first joint tenant to die is deemed to own 100% of the property for purposes of determining the value of the taxable estate.

If you have each invested your own funds and you and your spouse jointly own a condominium worth US$200,000, for example, only US$100,000 of that value will form part of your estate on your death.

Split your worldwide assets with your spouse.

If your spouse has no assets or assets of minor value, consider having your spouse acquire full ownership of one or more of your U.S. assets, such as a vacation property, worth up to the US$650,000 exemption amount. Seek professional tax advice before doing so, however, since the transfer could trigger the attribution rules or gift tax if your spouse does not use their own funds and/or liability for U.S. property purchase tax.

> ## Consider a split interest purchase with your child.

In some situations, it may be beneficial for U.S. estate tax purposes for you to split your interest in an asset with your child. In this strategy, you would acquire a life interest in the property and your child would acquire a remainder interest with his or her own funds. The rules in this area are extremely complex—if you want to pursue this strategy, professional advice is a must.

> ## Hold your U.S. property through a Canadian corporation.

An obvious solution to U.S. estate tax is to hold any U.S. stocks and real estate in a Canadian corporation rather than personally. When you die, your corporation does not, and no U.S. estate tax applies to holdings in shares of a Canadian corporation. You have effectively converted the "location" of your assets from the U.S. to Canada. While this solution is often useful, it is fraught with pitfalls, and qualified professional advice should be obtained. Some possible problems that should be addressed include:

- Beyond the initial setup costs, there are ongoing costs to maintaining a corporation, including legal and accounting fees, and capital taxes in some Canadian provinces.
- The acquisition of the U.S. assets by the corporation must be legally complete, and all corporate formalities must be observed. If it is determined that the corporation was only acting as an agent or mere title holder for you, estate tax can still apply to the property on your death.
- Any income earned by the corporation on its U.S. assets (such as interest, dividends, rent) will be subject to tax both when originally earned and when paid out to you in the form of dividends. The combined effect of the taxes may be higher than the tax you would pay if you held the assets directly.
- If the property is U.S. real estate that you already own personally, any accrued gain will normally be taxed by the U.S. when you transfer the property to the corporation. (As noted in 18.3.2, the tax can be reduced where you have owned the

property since before September 27, 1980.) This suggests that the corporation route may only be useful for future acquisitions of U.S. real estate, and not for transfers of existing holdings.

- If the U.S. real estate is a personal use property, the accrued gains will generally be taxable in Canada at the time of its transfer to the corporation.
- If you or members of your family will be using the property for personal purposes (e.g., a vacation property which you occupy for a few weeks each year), you may be taxed in Canada as having received a shareholder benefit from the corporation.
- If the property is sold after death and the funds distributed, the total income tax cost may be higher than the potential estate tax cost in certain cases.

Hold your U.S. assets through a Canadian partnership that elects to be treated as a corporation in the U.S.

Instead of using a Canadian corporation, you could consider establishing a Canadian partnership with your adult child to hold your U.S. assets and having the partnership elect to be treated as a corporation for U.S. tax purposes. On your death (or your spouse's death), your partnership interest and the underlying assets can be transferred directly to your child. Since the U.S. will treat the partnership as a corporation, the assets held by it should bypass your estate entirely for U.S. estate tax purposes. And since Canada will treat the entity as a partnership, you can avoid the negative Canadian tax implications discussed above of holding U.S. property through a Canadian corporation. Again, this strategy is quite complex and should not be pursued without professional tax advice.

Sell U.S. property before death.

If you sell your U.S. assets (say, to a family member) before your death, and receive in exchange assets that are not "located in the U.S." (e.g., cash or a promissory note situated in Canada), you will have no U.S. assets left to form a taxable estate.

This step may be useful when death is anticipated within a short time period. For example, property could be sold to a child to whom you intend to leave the property anyway, in exchange for a bona fide promissory note. The note might then be left to your spouse or to another family member. If the note were left to the child, the sale may be treated as a gift and subject to U.S. gift tax.

On such a sale, U.S. and Canadian income tax will apply to any gain (the Canadian tax applying to three-quarters of the capital gain—see 6.2). A foreign tax credit will normally be available in Canada to offset part or all of the U.S. tax paid. The U.S. instalment sale rules (see 17.4.4) may apply where you take back a promissory note rather than cash.

Be aware of the possible application of the Canadian attribution rules (see Chapter 5) where you have transferred property to your spouse or to a family member who is under 18. Also, make sure you do not take back debt (such as a promissory note) from someone resident in the United States, since certain debts of U.S. residents are generally considered to be property located in the U.S. Before undertaking any transaction, be sure to compare the tax consequences that will arise on death to the tax consequences that will arise on a transfer before death.

> **Consider taking out life insurance to cover U.S. estate taxes.**

If you anticipate that substantial estate tax will apply on your death, consider taking out life insurance as a way of funding the payment of the tax without requiring the sale of your U.S. assets. Life insurance proceeds will not form part of your estate on death, even if provided by a U.S. insurer (although they will be included in your worldwide assets for purposes of determining the applicable credit amount discussed in 18.4.3). Bear in mind that premiums paid on a life insurance policy are not deductible for either Canadian or U.S. income tax purposes. Also, if the policy is with a U.S. insurer, have your professional advisor review the Canadian income tax implications of holding the policy.

18.5 References

Revenue Canada publishes a booklet titled "Canadian Residents Going Down South", available (in person or by phone) from any District Taxation Office or via the Internet at *www.rc.gc.ca*. Written jointly with the IRS, it includes information on U.S. tax laws.

The following publications may be obtained by telephoning or writing to any office of the Internal Revenue Service (IRS). They may also be available at United States embassy and consular offices, or from the IRS' Internet site at *www.irs.ustreas.gov*.

Form 706NA, "United States Estate (and Generation Skipping Transfer) Tax Return: Estate of nonresident not a citizen of the United States"

Form 1040NR, "U.S. Nonresident Alien Income Tax Return"

Form 4224, "Exemption from Withholding of Tax on Income Effectively Connected with the Conduct of a Trade or Business in the United States"

Form 8288-B, "Application for Withholding Certificate for Dispositions by Foreign Persons of U.S. Real Property Interests"

Form 8840, "Closer Connection Statement"

Publication 515, "Withholding of Tax on Nonresident Aliens and Foreign Corporations"

Publication 519, "U.S. Tax Guide for Aliens"

19

Planning for your retirement

- Start planning and saving for retirement at least 15 years before you plan to retire (19.1)

- Consider topping up your RRSP and using the tax refund to pay down your mortgage (19.1)

- Prepare detailed cash flow forecasts to project changes in your expenses and sources of income as you get older (19.2.1)

- Revise your investment strategy as you near retirement (19.2.2)

- Split income by assigning CPP/QPP benefits to the lower-income spouse (19.3.1)

- Delay or defer income until 2000 where possible to minimize the OAS clawback (19.3.2)

- Aim for at least $1,000 of pension income for both spouses (19.3.5)

- Top up your RRSP before the end of the year in which you turn 69 (19.4.1)

- Convert your RRSP to a RRIF or annuity at the end of the year in which you turn 69 (19.4.6)

This chapter discusses a number of financial planning issues to consider as you enter your retirement. Since the decisions you make when you reach retirement will greatly affect your quality of life throughout your retirement and the financial resources you can make available to your heirs, we strongly recommend that you seek professional financial and tax planning advice. Since retirement planning and the estate planning issues discussed in Chapter 20 are closely related, you should consider developing your retirement and estate planning strategies at the same time.

19.1   Saving for your retirement

Most people can live comfortably in retirement on 70 to 80% of their pre-retirement income (adjusted for inflation). To meet this target requires dedicated long-term planning. Generally, the principal sources of retirement income for Canadians are employer pension plans, government pension plans, and registered retirement savings plans ("RRSPs") and other retirement savings.

If you are a member of a company pension plan (see 3.4), you should consider this as one potential source of retirement income, not as your total retirement fund. Nor should you plan to rely too heavily on Old Age Security ("OAS") or the Canada and Québec Pension Plans ("CPP/QPP") since these programs will not provide much more than subsistence level income.

> **Start planning and saving for retirement at least 15 years before you plan to retire.**

Beyond these types of income, you'll have to develop resources on your own through other savings and investment strategies. If you don't start at least 15 years before you reach retirement age, you'll probably find yourself working longer than you had intended and/or unable to afford the retirement lifestyle you expect.

By your mid- to late-forties, you should find it easier to put larger amounts of funds toward your retirement nest egg: you will be entering your peak income-earning years, your children will be nearing independence, and most of your major lifestyle acquisitions (except maybe your home) will probably be bought and paid for. But don't wait until then—due to the exponential growth of your retirement investments through compounding, the earlier you can start saving for retirement, the better off you will be.

Your RRSP is one of the best available retirement savings vehicles since it allows you to set aside money and to defer the taxes you would otherwise pay on it. You should try to contribute as much as possible, and do so early in the year so your contribution can earn tax-sheltered income for the entire year. The tax rules governing RRSPs and a number of strategies for maximizing your RRSP's growth are covered in Chapter 3, along with registered pension plans ("RPPs") and other deferred income plans.

> **Consider topping up your RRSP and using the tax refund to pay down your mortgage.**

Building equity in your home and building up funds in your RRSP should be two key components of your retirement savings plan. A commonly-asked question is whether you would be further ahead in the long run to maximize your RRSP contributions or to put the same funds toward paying down your mortgage (see 1.2.2). The answer will depend on a variety of factors, including your mortgage's interest rate and remaining amortization period, your RRSP balances and the number of income-earning years you have left until you plan to retire, and the availability of other pension plans. To hedge your bets, consider taking advantage of both strategies by making maximum annual RRSP contributions and using the resulting tax refund to make a lump-sum mortgage payment.

19.2 Getting ready to retire

19.2.1 Assessing your financial situation

As you get close to retirement, you will need to update your net worth statement (see 1.1.3) to get a clear picture of the retirement income resources that will be available to you. You will also need to prepare new cash flow forecasts to reflect the upcoming changes in your financial situation and to determine your monthly disposable income. As in preparing a budget (see 1.1.4), your cash flow forecasts should list the amounts you expect to receive and pay out monthly.

> Prepare detailed cash flow forecasts to project changes in your expenses and sources of income as you get older.

You should prepare several cash flow statements to take into account changes in your expenses and sources of income as you get older. For example, preparing a statement at retirement will show cash flow changes resulting from your loss of employment income and your receipt of pension income; it should also reflect reduced employment-related expenses for items such as commuting and clothes and perhaps increased expenses for items such as travel and medical bills. Cash flow statements at ages 60 and 65 will reflect the impact of your CPP/QPP and Old Age Security benefits (see 19.3) on your finances. A further cash flow statement at age 69 or when you mature your RRSP should forecast RRIF or annuity income you will receive.

These detailed forecasts will indicate if your resources will be adequate or if you will need to sell any assets to help meet your cash flow needs (see 19.2.3). These projections will also give you the information you need to make decisions such as when you should apply to receive CPP/QPP benefits (see 19.3.1) and whether you should opt for an integrated pension (see 19.3.6).

You should review your retirement projections every one or two years to take into account any changes in your personal circumstances or goals, tax law amendments, economic events and changes to any other assumptions on which your plan is based.

19.2.2 Revising your investment strategy

In 1.1.5, we discussed the importance of determining your objectives and risk tolerance in developing your investment strategy. As you enter retirement, your investment objectives will change from building your asset base to preserving or drawing on your capital gradually so it will provide a steady and dependable source of income throughout your own and your spouse's lifetimes.

> ## Revise your investment strategy as you near retirement.

The closer you get to retirement, the less able you will be to replace substantial investment losses and the less risk you should tolerate. Consider changing your investment mix in the years leading up to your retirement so that a greater proportion of your wealth is invested in more secure, fixed income assets such as government or other high quality bonds, preferred shares and guaranteed investment certificates ("GICs"). Since your retirement could last 30 years or more, you will probably need to have some proportion of your portfolio invested in growth equities such as shares or other equities.

19.2.3 Planning for the sale of assets

On reaching retirement, you may need to reorganize your finances to meet your cash flow needs. This could involve selling some of your assets, withdrawing funds from your RRSP or selling your home. Before doing so, watch out for unintended consequences.

Many tax incentives and social programs are based on your net income for tax purposes (essentially your total income less certain deductions— see 2.1.1). The capital gains arising from asset sales or the income inclusion resulting from your RRSP withdrawals could significantly increase your net income and your tax bill for the year. If your net income is too high, some tax and social benefits will be reduced or eliminated. These include the federal age credit (see 19.3.4) and the Québec age and pension income credits (see 16.2.5). You could also wind up having to pay back some of your Old Age Security benefits for the current year and receiving reduced OAS cheques in July through June of the next year (see 19.3.2). A liability for minimum tax could also arise (see 7.6).

Before you sell your investments or dip into your RRSP funds, consider the following strategies for avoiding a significant income inclusion:

- Consider using resources that do not affect your income for tax purposes first. For example, withdraw from your savings account (without using your emergency fund; see 1.3.1) or certain fixed income investments before withdrawing from your RRSP.
- Spread your sales of assets such as shares and RRSP withdrawals over several years to avoid creating a large income inclusion in any one year.
- Instead of receiving your sales proceeds in one payment, consider making it part of the terms of sale that the proceeds are to be paid to you in equal instalments over five years. This will

enable you to spread the income inclusion over the five years by claiming a capital gains reserve (see 6.5.1). Of course, you'll want to consider the risk of default of payment.

- Remember that selling your home or cottage will not affect your income for tax purposes if the property is eligible for the principal residence exemption (see 6.5.2).

- Instead of selling your home, consider a reverse mortgage whereby the lender pays you a fixed amount of money each month toward a mortgage that the lender holds on your property. When your home is ultimately sold, the lender will get back the total amount of its payments plus interest and you or your estate will be entitled to the remainder of the sale proceeds. Since a reverse mortgage is not a beneficial strategy for everyone, be sure to consult a financial advisor before entering into such an arrangement.

19.2.4 Insurance coverage under your pension plan retirement benefits

As a retiree, your life insurance needs are somewhat different from those discussed in 1.3.2. While you will still want to be sure that funds will be available to cover your estate's tax liability arising on your death and to provide for your spouse and other dependants, you will likely have fewer debts to service and no need for coverage for loss of employment or self-employment income.

In reviewing your insurance needs, be sure to investigate the death benefit and the survivor's benefits available on your death. Many companies provide life insurance to their pensioners, although the amount may decrease over time. Some companies also pay a death benefit (see 9.7) which may help out your spouse financially.

You should also review your spouse's medical insurance coverage under your pension plan in the event of your death. Many survivors lose their entitlement to medical insurance coverage on their spouse's death and you should make alternate arrangements in advance to ensure your spouse will have coverage after your death.

Since life insurance fills many important roles in estate planning, your review of your coverage on retirement should take place in the wider context of the issues discussed in 20.6. For example, you may wish to consider purchasing life insurance to fund a capital gains tax or other tax liability that may arise on your death.

19.2.5 Survivor's benefits

Upon retiring, if you are a member of a company pension plan, it will normally provide you with several choices regarding the payment of your pension after your death. These options may include a life-only benefit, a specified guarantee period, a joint and last survivor benefit at amounts ranging from 50% to 100%, a 50% spousal benefit, or a combination of these options.

If you choose a specified guaranteed payment period of, say, five, 10 or 20 years, your company guarantees it will pay your pension for that period of time. If you die before the period is over, your pension cheque will be paid to your estate until the period expires.

If you choose a 100% joint and last survivor guarantee, the company will pay you a pension until you die and will continue to pay a pension to your spouse until your spouse dies.

Under a 50% spousal guarantee, your spouse will receive half of your pension upon your death. Most provinces require that the spouse receive 50% of your pension amount upon your death, unless the spouse specifically renounces this entitlement in writing when you choose your pension guarantee.

When you are assessing the various options, bear in mind that the longer the guarantee period, the lower the pension payment. For example, the monthly pension payment for a five-year guarantee period will be much higher than payments under a joint and last survivor guarantee.

19.3 Government assistance for retirees

19.3.1 Canada Pension Plan/Québec Pension Plan benefits

Between the ages of 60 and 70, you can apply to begin receiving your monthly pension benefits under the Canada Pension Plan or Québec Pension Plan. To receive benefits before age 65, your annual employment or self-employment earnings must be less than the maximum annual pension payable at age 65 for the current year.

The amount of your CPP/QPP cheques will depend on how many years you have contributed to the plan, the amount of your contribution and the age at which you decide to start receiving your pension. CPP/QPP benefits are adjusted annually for inflation; the maximum monthly retirement benefit at age 65 was about $750 at the time of writing. These benefits are taxable as income.

Although you can apply to receive pension amounts as early as age 60, you will have to pay a penalty in the form of reduced benefits for receiving these amounts early. The penalty is 0.5% of your benefits otherwise payable at age 65 for every month (or 6% a year) before your 65th birthday that you collect CCP/QPP benefits and will apply to reduce your benefits for life. If you decide to apply for the benefits after age 65, your benefits will increase by 0.5% for every month after age 65 (but up to age 70) that you do not collect CPP/QPP benefits and will continue to increase your benefits for life.

Example:

Vanessa accepts an early retirement package from her company and decides that she wants to start receiving her CPP/QPP benefits at age 62. Since she will begin receiving her pension benefits 36 months before her 65th birthday, she estimates her monthly CPP/QPP pension benefits at $750 less $135 ($750 × 36 × 0.5%), for a total monthly pre-tax pension amount of $615.

To estimate your benefits, you may request a Statement of Participation from Human Resources Development Canada or the Régie des rentes du Québec.

Many factors will influence your decision about when to apply for your benefits. If you expect your expenses to be higher during the early part of your retirement, perhaps because you wish to travel, you may appreciate receiving benefits before age 65. On the other hand, if you do not need the funds to pay your living or other expenses, you may be better off delaying your application since the benefits will be included in your taxable income. Your life expectancy should also be considered—if you are likely to live beyond age 81, think about applying for your CPP/QPP benefits at age 65, so that your payments will not be reduced, and using your benefits to make investments.

The CPP/QPP also pay a death benefit equal to six months of regular CPP/QPP benefits to a maximum of $2,500; this amount is taxable to the estate or the survivor in the year received. The surviving spouse may also apply for a survivor's benefit under the CPP/QPP, which will be a percentage of the deceased's benefits based on the survivor's age and other factors. If the surviving spouse is 65 or older, for example, the survivor's benefit will generally be 60% of the deceased's CPP/QPP benefits.

You will need to apply for your CPP/QPP benefits at least six months before you wish to begin receiving them. CPP applications are filed with Income Security Programs, Human Resources Development Canada; QPP applications are filed with the Régie des rentes du Québec.

Split income by assigning CPP/QPP benefits to the lower-income spouse.

As a strategy for saving taxes through income splitting, you may direct that up to 50% of your CPP benefits be paid to your spouse, provided both of you are over age 60. If either of you does this, a portion of the other spouse's CPP is assigned automatically back to the first spouse.

If both spouses are eligible for maximum CPP benefits, assignment will not change anything, since each will assign half of the maximum to the other. But if one has high CPP benefits and the other has low benefits or none, the assignment can effectively transfer up to half of the CPP income to the lower-income spouse. The amount that can be split is based on the length of time you and your spouse have lived together as a proportion of your total contributory period, to a maximum of 50%.

The attribution rules discussed in Chapter 4 specifically do not apply to an assignment of CPP benefits. If you and your spouse are both over 60, and you have higher CPP benefits and are in a higher tax bracket, you should consider such an assignment. This assignment might not be advantageous, however, if it affects your spousal tax credit claim (see 2.2.1).

CPP benefits can be assigned by completing a form available from Human Resources Development Canada; QPP benefits can be assigned by completing a form available from Régie des rentes du Québec.

If you are resident in the U.S. and you receive CPP/QPP benefits, see 19.3.3.

19.3.2 Old Age Security benefits and the OAS clawback

OAS benefits are a taxable pension available at age 65. Unlike CPP/QPP payments which are based on prior contributions, your entitlement to the OAS benefit is based on your age and how long you have lived in Canada. To receive the maximum pension, you must have lived in Canada for 40 years or more after turning 18. Partial pension may be available if you lived in Canada for 10 or more years after turning 18. A social security agreement between Canada and another country may allow you to add your period of residence in the other country to your period of Canadian residence for purposes of determining your OAS entitlement.

OAS benefits are paid monthly and benefit rates are indexed quarterly for inflation. At the time of writing, the maximum OAS payment is just over $400 per month. For high-income taxpayers, these payments are completely taxed back through a special tax, known informally as the "clawback". The tax reduces benefits for taxpayers whose net income (after most deductions such as RRSP contributions) is over $53,215. If your net income exceeds about $85,000, the clawback will apply to 100% of your OAS benefits. Spouses' incomes are not pooled for purposes of the clawback; each taxpayer's income is considered separately.

The tax on OAS benefits is deducted from your monthly benefits cheque. The amount withheld is based on your income in the prior two years. For example, for the first six months of 1999, your tax withheld was based on your 1997 income while your tax withheld for the last half of 1999 is based on your 1998 income. If too much tax is withheld, the excess will be applied to reduce your taxes owing or refunded to you after you file your return for the year. If the tax withheld falls short of your liability, you will have to repay the difference.

> **Delay or defer income until 2000 where possible to minimize the OAS clawback.**

To minimize the clawback's potential effect, try to delay or defer recognition of income until the following year where possible. For example, if you are thinking about selling investments that have appreciated in value in 1999, consider waiting until 2000 to cash them in—preservation of your OAS benefits may well outweigh the returns you'll forgo by waiting a few months for the proceeds from your appreciated investments (provided their value does not decline in the meantime).

To start receiving your OAS benefits as quickly as possible after turning 65, you should file your application with Income Security Programs, Human Resources Development Canada at least six months before your 65th birthday. If you make your application after turning 65, it may be approved retroactively for up to one year.

If you are resident in the U.S. and you receive OAS benefits, see 19.3.3.

19.3.3 Cross-border payments of CPP/QPP, OAS and U.S. social security benefits

Amendments to the Canada/U.S. tax treaty retroactive to 1996 have changed the tax treatment of certain cross-border income security payments. Due to these changes, U.S. residents who receive CPP/QPP or OAS benefits are no longer liable for Canadian withholding tax on these amounts. These benefits received by U.S. residents are now taxable only in the U.S.

Similarly, if you are a resident of Canada and you receive U.S. social security benefits, you are no longer liable for U.S. withholding tax on these amounts. The U.S. no longer requires U.S. tax to be withheld on social security benefits paid to Canadian residents; 85% of the benefits will be subject to Canadian tax.

19.3.4 Age credit

If you are 65 or older by the end of the year, you get an additional federal credit of up to $592. This credit is linked to your income and is phased out by 2.55¢ for each dollar that your net income (see 2.1.1) exceeds $25,921. Thus, the credit completely disappears once your net income reaches $49,134. (Your spouse's net income does not affect this calculation.) The Québec age credit is discussed at 16.2.5.

19.3.5   Pension income credit

You are entitled to a federal tax credit of 17% of your pension income, up to $1,000 of pension income for the year. A similar credit is available in Québec—see 16.2.5.

Pension income does not include Canada Pension Plan, Old Age Security or Guaranteed Income Supplement payments. It basically means private pension income received through a life annuity. If you are 65 and over or are receiving payments as a result of your spouse's death, it also includes annuities out of an RRSP or a deferred profit-sharing plan, a payment out of a RRIF (see 19.4.4), or the income portion of a regular annuity.

> **Aim for at least $1,000 of pension income for both spouses.**

To make the most of this credit, you should aim to have at least $1,000 of qualifying "pension income" annually, plus another $1,000 for your spouse if possible.

19.3.6   Integrating government assistance with your pension benefits

Many pension plans (particularly public sector employee pension plans) offer the choice of an integrated or normal pension. An integrated pension takes into account the amount of government assistance payments you will receive over the course of your retirement, providing higher payments in the first retiring years and lower payments when you decide to start receiving CPP/QPP payments (see 19.3.1) and when you become entitled to receive OAS payments at age 65 (see 19.3.2).

If you choose the integrated pension, you will normally have the same monthly income before and after age 65 (unless you decide to apply for CPP/QPP before then). Maintaining a consistent level of income before and after you start receiving your OAS and CPP/QPP benefits can help keep your income in a lower tax bracket and avoid having your government payments taxed back or reduced.

19.4   Maturing your RRSP

In Chapter 3 we discussed the tax rules and some planning ideas regarding RRSPs. This section discusses your options for maturing your RRSP. There are basically four routes for getting your money out of an RRSP—you must make use of one of the options described below by the end of the year in which you turn 69. Note that life income funds discussed in 19.4.5 are only available in respect of locked-in RRSPs.

19.4.1 RRSP contributions at age 69 and after

If you turn 69 and must wind up your RRSP in 1999, remember that you only have until December 31, 1999 (and not February 29, 2000) to make your RRSP contribution for 1999. If your spouse hasn't yet reached age 70, you can continue making deductible contributions to a spousal RRSP as long as you have earned income in the previous year or unused RRSP contribution room carried forward from prior years.

> **Top up your RRSP before the end of the year in which you turn 69.**

If you have earned income (generally salary and wages—see 3.1.3) in 1999, this will create new RRSP contribution room for 2000. But if you turned 69 in 1999, you must contribute your 2000 amount before you wind up your RRSP at the end of this year. If you have contributed your maximum amount for 1999 and your $2,000 penalty-free overcontribution, your additional contribution will attract a penalty tax of 1% per month. But the penalty will only apply for the period between the date of the overcontribution and January 1, 2000—after that, your 2000 deduction room will be available. The tax savings from your 2000 RRSP deduction will probably far outweigh the penalty, especially if you make your overcontribution in December 1999.

19.4.2 RRSP maturity option #1—Withdraw the funds

The first, and easiest, way to cash out your RRSP is simply to withdraw the funds in a lump sum. The amount withdrawn from the RRSP is included in your income for the year in which you do so. It is taxed as ordinary income, just as if it were salary, even if some of the value of the RRSP represents capital gains (which outside an RRSP are normally only partially taxed and, in some cases, could be entirely exempt). A percentage to cover income tax will be withheld at source by the financial institution and remitted to Revenue Canada (and Revenu Québec if appropriate) on your behalf (see 3.2). You will then report the income and the amount of tax withheld on your annual income tax return and either receive a refund or, if not enough tax was withheld, pay the difference.

19.4.3 RRSP maturity option #2—Purchase an annuity

The second method is to purchase an annuity. None of the RRSP proceeds will be taxed immediately, but the annuity payments will be taxed as you receive them. (As discussed in 19.3.5, currently up to $1,000 per year of the income may be effectively exempted through the pension income tax credit.)

There are three general kinds of annuities: "term-certain", payable to you or your estate for a fixed number of years; "single life", payable to you as long as you are alive; and "joint and last survivor life", payable as long as either you or your spouse is alive. Numerous additional options are available, such as a guaranteed term as part of a life annuity, indexing for inflation, reduction of payment on the death of your spouse, reduction of payment when Old Age Security payments begin, and so on. Unless you purchase a life annuity with a guaranteed period or a survivor option, your annuity dies with you and no residual balance will be left to your heirs.

You should discuss the available options, and their effect on the monthly annuity payment you receive, with your life insurance agent or trust company. Prevailing interest rates must also be considered to determine whether annuities alone, or a combination of annuities and RRIFs might provide greater flexibility and returns.

19.4.4 RRSP maturity option #3—Convert RRSP to RRIF

The third option for maturing your RRSP is to convert it into a Registered Retirement Income Fund, or RRIF (pronounced "riff"). A RRIF is somewhat like an RRSP, in that you can have it invested in various kinds of securities. However, you must withdraw at least a "minimum amount" from the RRIF each year and report what you withdraw for tax purposes. (Again, currently up to $1,000 per year of such income may be effectively exempted through the pension income tax credit, as explained in 19.3.5.)

For RRIFs set up before 1993, the amount that must be withdrawn from the RRIF each year up to age 78 is 1/N of the value of the RRIF at the beginning of the year, where N is the number of years left until you (or your spouse) turn 90. After age 78, and for all ages for RRIFs set up in 1993 or later, the amount that must be withdrawn is a fraction (i.e., 1/90 – your age in the year) that increases gradually each year, levelling out at 20% once you turn 94.

19.4.5 RRSP maturity option #4—Convert locked-in RRSP to life income fund

A life income fund ("LIF") provides an alternative to a life annuity when certain individuals, who were formerly members of a registered pension plan, terminate employment or plan membership. The LIF is also an option for individuals who have transferred pension funds to a locked-in RRSP (see 3.3.2).

A LIF is a RRIF for tax purposes (see 19.4.4) with additional restrictions. Like any other RRIF, a minimum amount must be withdrawn each year. As well, under a LIF there is a maximum amount that can be withdrawn each year until age 80. (Thus, the funds remain "locked in", just like a pension or locked-in RRSP.) The remaining balance of funds in the LIF must be used to purchase a life annuity by December 31 of the year in which the individual turns 80.

A LIF can offer an attractive income alternative to a life annuity option. LIFs are now available in all provinces except Prince Edward Island and they can be purchased with funds governed by either federal or provincial pension regulations. You should consult your financial advisor to determine whether this option is available to you.

19.4.6 What's the best option?

By the end of the year in which you turn 69, you will have to decide what to do with your RRSP. While your personal cash flow needs should be your primary concern, your decision should take into account your overall investment and estate planning goals. A straight withdrawal will rarely be the best option, since you will be taxed on the total income in the current year—and none of it will be eligible for the pension tax credit (see 19.3.5).

> **Convert your RRSP to RRIF or annuity at the end of the year in which you turn 69.**

Instead, if you wish to retain some control over the investment of your RRSP funds, you should purchase a RRIF (see 19.4.4). If you prefer simply to have a steady monthly income that you don't have to worry about, you could contact your life insurance agent and purchase an annuity (see 19.4.3).

A RRIF will give you more flexibility than an annuity in establishing the amount withdrawn each month, although you must still withdraw a monthly minimum. LIFs also offer flexibility within a range of minimum and maximum monthly withdrawals.

If you are setting up an annuity, consider the effect of the tax brackets on your income. Your main goal, of course, is to ensure that you have enough income each month to meet your needs. If you can satisfy those needs with a longer-term annuity that keeps your income below the high-tax brackets, you may be financially better off.

19.5 Cross-border retirement planning

If you have lived and worked in Canada and the U.S. (or in another country) and you are considering which country you want to live in after you retire, your retirement planning will be quite complex. In addition to two sets of income tax rules, you will have to consider differences in your health care coverage, government-assisted investment vehicles and how your assets will be taxed at death. The taxation of your investment and pension income in Canada and the U.S. should be a key factor in your decision about where to retire.

If you have lived and worked in both countries, you may have built up retirement assets on both sides of the border. These assets can include RRSPs (see Chapter 3), U.S. Individual Retirement Accounts (IRAs) (see 17.3.4), Canadian company pensions (see 3.4), U.S. company pension plans (also known as 401(k) plans) and a variety of other types of plans. You may have paid into both the Canada/Québec Pension Plan and "FICA", the U.S. social security plan.

Retirement planning in cross-border situations involves the same retirement planning steps discussed in 19.1: you need to assess your net worth, outline your goals and objectives, review your cash flow requirements now and in retirement, and determine your sources of retirement income. You will also need to consider the usual areas of risk management (including disability and life insurance), taxation, investment strategies and estate planning. Due to differences between the laws of the two countries, planning opportunities may be available to minimize your overall tax liability and maximize your retirement assets and cash flow. But without proper advice, double taxation can result, especially on death.

As we saw in 19.2, retirement planning typically involves the preparation of financial projections to incorporate outside sources of retirement income such as government and company pensions and to determine which assets should be accessed and in what order to maximize your retirement income. Before these projections can be prepared, you will need to review the rules for withdrawal of funds from the various Canadian and U.S. tax-sheltered plans. The tax treatment of withdrawals from these funds will vary depending on their status under the tax laws of Canada and the U.S. The same income may be taxable in both countries and, in certain cases, a foreign tax credit will be available to minimize or even eliminate double taxation (see 17.2.2).

When you are deciding whether to retire in the U.S. or in Canada and developing your retirement plan, you will need to address the following questions. The answers will depend on your particular situation; professional advice is strongly recommended.

- What is your tax status in each country and how are you taxed as a result? Is this the best result from a tax perspective? Do you have any choices?
- How will your RRSP be taxed as a non-resident of Canada? Can you still contribute to your RRSP if you do not live in Canada? If you do not return to Canada, should you withdraw your RRSP in a lump-sum?
- Will your expenses be higher in Canada or in the U.S.?

- How will you pay for your health care coverage? How does your provincial medicare coverage compare to your U.S. coverage, if any?
- How will your U.S. tax-deferred plans be treated for Canadian tax purposes if you are resident here?
- Can you transfer the funds in your U.S. plans to an RRSP? Is this beneficial?
- How do the CPP and the U.S. social security pensions interact in your situation? Can you collect two separate pensions and when should you start collecting them?
- Is it more advantageous to hold U.S. or Canadian-denominated investments? Should you adopt a different investment strategy depending on the country of retirement?

In creating your estate plan for the distribution of your assets on death, you will need to review the laws of both Canada and the U.S. in detail. From a tax perspective, residing in the U.S. at death or simply holding U.S. property can be costly. For a detailed discussion of U.S. estate taxes on death, see 18.4.

19.6 References

Old Age Security and Canada Pension Plan application kits are available (in person or by telephone request) from Human Resources Development Canada. Information on the following topics is available from the Human Resources Development Canada Internet site at *www.hrdc-drhc.gc.ca.*

Guide, "Retirement Pension"

Guide, "Disability Benefits"

Guide, "Survivor Benefits"

Guide, "Credit Splitting"

Guide, "International Benefits"

Guide, "Your Guaranteed Income Supplement"

Guide, "Your Old Age Security Pension"

Guide, "Your Spouse's Allowance"

You can obtain the following publications (in person or by telephone request) from your nearest Revenue Canada Taxation Services Office. Forms and guides may also be available from Revenue Canada's Internet site at *www.rc.gc.ca.*

Information Circular 72-22R9, "Registered Retirement Savings Plans"

Information Circular 78-18R5, "Registered Retirement Income Funds"

Interpretation Bulletin IT-517R, "Pension tax credit"

Information Bulletin IT-500R, "Registered Retirement Savings Plans—Death of an annuitant"

Guide, "RRSPs and Other Registered Plans for Retirement"

Guide, P119, "When You Retire"

20

- Take steps to minimize probate fees (20.1.3)
- Make a will or review your existing will (20.2)
- Consider the advantages of establishing one or more family trusts (20.4.3)
- Take action before the 21st anniversary of a trust's creation to minimize the impact of a deemed disposition of all of a trust's capital property (20.4.3)
- Look into the potential benefits of an "estate freeze" (20.5)
- Make sure you have sufficient life insurance (20.6)
- Consider planned charitable gifts and bequests (20.7)
- Think about donating publicly traded securities instead of cash (20.7.4)
- Plan for the succession of your business (20.8)
- Watch out for the effects of foreign estate taxes (20.9)
- Consider a pre-paid plan to finance your funeral and cemetery arrangements (20.10)

In this chapter we provide an overview of the rules that apply on death and some estate planning strategies you can use to minimize the taxes arising on death and to leave as much as possible to your beneficiaries. Estate planning can be extremely complicated, and depends very much on your personal situation and goals. It should be undertaken in conjunction with the development of your retirement plan, as discussed in Chapter 19. Professional advice is highly recommended. If you or your spouse are not Canadian, much of our commentary in this chapter will not apply to your situation; if you or your spouse is a U.S. citizen, see Chapter 17.

20.1 Taxes on death

20.1.1 Tax payable by the estate

When a person dies, the executor or administrator of the estate (called the "estate trustee") must file a "terminal return" for the deceased to report income up to the date of death. Although the regular T1 and Québec TP1 return forms are used, there are a number of special rules for these returns. For example:

- charitable donations, which can normally be claimed for the year of donation or carried forward to future years (see 2.7.1 and 20.7.1), can be carried back and claimed in the year prior to death (subject to the limits discussed in 20.7.1)

- medical expenses paid, which can normally be claimed for a 12-month period ending in the year (see 2.7.2), can be pooled for any 24-month period that includes the day of death
- the full amount of the deceased's RRSP (see 3.1) is brought into income for the year of death, unless the beneficiary of the RRSP is the deceased's spouse or certain dependants (see 3.3.3); if the RRSP funds are not transferred to the spouse's own RRSP, the spouse must report the funds as income for tax purposes
- any balance borrowed by the deceased from an RRSP under the Home Buyers' Plan (see 3.3.6) and not yet repaid must be included in income unless an election is made to have the liability assumed by the surviving spouse
- minimum tax (see 7.6) does not apply to the year of death
- capital property is generally deemed disposed of at its fair market value, resulting in either a capital gain or a capital loss (see 20.1.2)
- capital losses, which are normally only allowed to offset capital gains (as discussed in 6.2), may be deducted from other income (except to the extent you have previously claimed the capital gains exemption)
- certain kinds of income earned but not received by the deceased before death can be reported on a separate return (against which the deceased's personal credits can be claimed a second time).

The terminal return for the deceased is due by the usual deadline (see 8.2.1) or six months after death, whichever is later. For example, if the date of death is March 10, 1999, the deceased's 1999 return is due by April 30, 2000.

A similar extension is allowed for filing of the return for the year before the year of death if the individual dies before the return's normal due date. Continuing our example above, the deceased's 1998 tax return would be due by September 10, 1999 instead of the usual April 30, 1999 deadline. Any balance of tax owing is due on April 30 of the year after the year of death or six months after death, whichever is later.

Any income earned after death will be subject to tax as part of the estate. The estate is treated as a separate person which must file a return as a trust each year until all of the assets are distributed. (Sometimes this distribution can take several years, but normally an estate can be wound up within one year.) Any income paid to beneficiaries of the estate may be taxed in their hands directly, instead of in the estate.

Note that life insurance proceeds received as a result of an individual's death are not subject to income tax. Life insurance is discussed in more detail in 20.6 below.

20.1.2 Deemed disposition of capital property

Canada has no federal estate tax or inheritance tax, nor do any of the provinces. To the extent you simply have cash in the bank and you leave it to your family, there will be no tax to pay at all (other than probate fees, discussed in 20.1.3 below).

Many people, however, have capital assets such as stocks, real estate and jewellery. As a general rule, capital assets are deemed for tax purposes to have been sold at their fair market value immediately before death. This results in the realization of any accrued capital gains or losses at that time. This rule was discussed in 6.5.3 as well. If you own depreciable property, recaptured depreciation or a terminal loss may also be triggered.

Example:

Agnes dies in 1999. Her only capital assets are her house, which has a cost base of $50,000 and is now worth $600,000; a diamond ring, which has a cost base of $5,000 and is now worth $10,000; and a stock portfolio, which has a cost base of $10,000 and is now worth $17,000.

The house will be deemed sold at fair market value just before Agnes' death, but there will be no capital gain because it is Agnes' principal residence. The ring and the stocks will also be deemed sold at their current values, for a total gain of $12,000. Three-quarters of the capital gain, or $9,000, will be taxed as a taxable capital gain on Agnes' terminal return.

As you can see, the normal capital gains rules apply, together with the availability of exemptions, such as the $500,000 capital gains exemption (see 6.4).

The main exception to the "deemed disposition" rule is the case where you leave assets to your spouse (including a common-law spouse) or to a spousal trust (a trust that meets certain requirements, as outlined in 20.4.2 below). In such a case, you are deemed to have sold your assets immediately before your death at their cost, so no capital gain results, as long as your spouse or a spousal trust obtains ownership and unfettered rights to the property. Your spouse (or the trust) then inherits that cost for tax purposes along with the assets. When your spouse (or the trust) sells the assets, or on your spouse's death, the full capital gain or loss from your original purchase price will be taxed.

There is, however, a special rule under which your estate trustee may elect to realize a capital gain or loss on a property-by-property basis when assets are left to your spouse on your death. This election may be beneficial if your estate trustee elects to trigger a capital gain in order to use loss carryforwards or a capital gains exemption. Alternatively, triggering a capital loss may recover tax in the year prior to death, since capital losses in the year of death may be carried back to the immediately preceding year and used against any income, except to the extent that the deceased previously claimed the capital gains exemption (see 6.4).

20.1.3 Probate fees

Probate fees are charged by the courts in each province (except Québec) to grant letters probate which confirm that the deceased's will is valid and the executor has the authority to administer the estate. Although they are theoretically administrative fees charged to cover the courts' costs for probating wills, probate fees functioned as an unofficial tax until 1998, when the Supreme Court ruled that they were legally a tax.

Whether it's called a tax or a fee, the probate charge generally applies to the total value of an estate's assets at the time of death, without any deduction for debts other than those encumbering real property. In some cases, the assets can be distributed and the estate wound up without probate but probate is generally required before third parties such as financial institutions (e.g., banks, investment dealers) will release property to the executor or estate trustee. If there is no will, probate is still required because the court has to confirm that an executor has been appointed to distribute the deceased's property as required by law.

Probate fees are highest in Ontario and British Columbia, where they are 1.5% and 1.4%, respectively, of the value of the estate in excess of $50,000. In other provinces the top rates are typically 0.5% to 0.7% of the value of the estate. Alberta has progressive flat rates to a maximum of $6,000; the probate fees for large estates in other provinces can be substantial as there is no maximum.

The fee generally applies to the total value of the assets of the estate at the time of death, without any deduction for debts other than those encumbering real property. Property held by two people as "joint tenants" with right of survivorship (rather than as "tenants in common") is not subject to probate, since on the death of one joint tenant the property does not form part of the estate but simply becomes wholly owned by the other.

Example:

Jonah, who lives in Ontario, dies in 1999. His estate consists of a house worth $500,000, with a $200,000 mortgage on it, $100,000 in personal effects, and the shares of his business, worth $1 million. He also owes $80,000 on a personal line of credit to the bank at the time of his death.

The value of Jonah's estate for probate purposes is $1,400,000. The house is counted as $300,000 (i.e., minus the mortgage), and his other assets are $1,100,000. The $80,000 debt is not deducted. The fee for probating Jonah's will is $20,500.

Take steps to minimize probate fees.

Some of the following techniques can reduce the cost of probating your estate. Note, however, that any planning to reduce probate fees must take numerous other issues (such as family law, income tax effects, land transfer tax, GST and other sales taxes) into account—professional advice is strongly recommended.

- If you are leaving property to your spouse (or another person), consider holding the property as joint tenants with your spouse (or that other person with a right of survivorship). On your death, the property will pass automatically to the other joint tenant and will not form part of your estate. Note that there may be immediate adverse tax consequences if you transfer the property to a joint tenant who is someone other than your spouse (for example, your child). Also, there are some situations where a joint tenancy will be severed on death by provincial legislation.

- Try to keep certain assets out of the estate. This is quite practical in the case of life insurance and RRSPs issued by life insurance companies, where beneficiaries (other than the estate) can be designated in the RRSP plan documents or in the life insurance policy. Also consider transferring property during your lifetime, either directly to your intended beneficiaries or to a trust. Again, take care that this does not result in the premature recognition of accrued capital gains.

- Change the location of property to a jurisdiction where probate fees are low or fixed (for example, Alberta) through the use of a holding company incorporated in the lower-fee jurisdiction. You would then prepare a separate will dealing with the shares of that company.

- If you own real estate with no mortgage, and you also owe money (perhaps on a personal line of credit or on a debt secured by other assets), consider having the debt converted to a mortgage or charge on the real estate. It may then reduce the value of the real estate for probate purposes.

- If you have certain assets that can be passed to beneficiaries without probate, such as shares in a private company, you may be able to reduce probate fees by making a secondary will that only includes these assets. Your executor would then apply for probate on the primary will but not the secondary one. (In 1998, the Ontario court ruled that this strategy was permitted under Ontario law but the case is currently under appeal. If you live in Ontario you may still want to go ahead with creating multiple wills — even if the decision is overturned, your estate won't end up paying more in probate fees on two wills than it would pay on one.)

20.1.4 Death benefits

Death benefits may be paid by the deceased's employer to the surviving spouse, other family members or to the estate. Up to $10,000 of such benefits may be received tax-free (see 9.7).

20.2 The will

20.2.1 Purpose of a will

The will is a key element of estate planning. It allows you to provide for an orderly distribution of your assets in accordance with your desires and in a way that minimizes the tax burden on your estate and on your beneficiaries. Depending on your circumstances, having more than one will may be advantageous—for example, multiple wills can help reduce probate fees (see 20.1.3) and facilitate the administration of your estate if you have assets in different countries.

> **Make a will, or review your existing will.**

Your will's primary function, of course, is to specify where and when your assets are to be distributed. You may want to leave specific properties (e.g., jewellery, furniture or shares in your business) to specific beneficiaries. You may want to leave a stated sum of money to certain people or to named charities (make sure you get the correct legal name of the charity). You will also want to specify a "residual" beneficiary, who will get everything left in the estate after your specific bequests are satisfied.

For example, you may wish to simply leave everything to your spouse. Alternatively, you may want to make use of a "spousal trust" which, as we'll see in 20.4.2, can offer certain tax advantages and a measure of protection from potential creditors without any loss in flexibility for your surviving spouse. As discussed in 20.1.2, there will be no tax on the accrued capital gains on your property when the property is transferred to your spouse or the spousal trust, provided your spouse or spousal trust obtains ownership and unfettered rights to the property.

If you do not make a will, the provincial law will determine how your assets are distributed. The result can vary significantly, depending on where you reside at the time of death. In Ontario, for example, the law provides that the surviving spouse gets the first $200,000 of the estate and divides any additional amounts with the deceased's children in accordance with a formula. However, in Alberta, the surviving spouse is only entitled to the first $40,000, with the balance of the estate divided among the surviving spouse and the deceased's children under a formula (these provisions are currently under review).

Note also that, in some provinces, family law can effectively override the instructions in your will. In Ontario, for example, your spouse can elect to ignore the will and take the amount of money due to him or her under the "net family property" rules (see 20.3). If this is done, your estate may lose the benefit of the capital gains rollover described above.

If you have specific desires as to who should have custody of or guardianship over your children after your death and while they are under 18, you can put these desires into your will for consideration by the courts. However, in some provinces, this designation is not binding.

While in some provinces an entirely handwritten will may be valid, it is strongly advisable to have your will prepared or reviewed with the assistance of a lawyer, or a notary in Québec, and a tax adviser to ensure it meets your wishes and takes tax and family law considerations into account.

Periodic reviews of your will are necessary to ensure that your estate plan is consistent with changes in the tax law, which occur regularly, as well as any changes in provincial family law and succession law.

Changes in your own personal circumstances such as the birth of a child or a change in marital status could also necessitate a change to your will. For example, in many jurisdictions, a will becomes void if you marry after making the will, unless it was made in contemplation of the marriage. On the other hand, a will may not become void after a divorce.

If you do not make a will or if your will is invalid, the process of obtaining court approval for distribution of your assets may be cumbersome and expensive. Your representative or heirs must apply to the court to appoint an administrator (also called an "estate trustee") to administer and distribute the estate in accordance with a formula set out in legislation.

As discussed in 1.3.4, consider also executing powers of attorney in the event you become unable to act by reason of disability or mental incompetence—one for decisions related to your finances and one for decisions related to your personal care. If, for example, you become mentally disabled, the continuing powers of attorney would enable the named "attorney" to act in your stead. You may wish to give the powers of attorney to the same person you name as your executor, such as your spouse.

20.2.2   Your executor and estate trustee

In your will, you should designate one or more persons as your executor and estate trustee. The person should be someone you can trust to take charge of your affairs and distribute your assets in accordance with your desires as set out in your will. The executor and estate trustee will normally apply to the court for "letters probate" (see 20.1.3), which will give court approval for the executor to take over your property, manage it and distribute it to your beneficiaries.

The responsibilities of your executor and estate trustee include determining the assets and liabilities of the estate, filing all income tax returns for you and the estate (including any foreign succession duty or tax returns) and paying the debts (including all taxes) outstanding at the date of your death.

Ideally, you should choose an executor and estate trustee who is familiar with your personal situation. Often the executor will be your principal beneficiary (such as your spouse). Sometimes this may not be appropriate, however, because of a possible conflict of interest with other beneficiaries.

You should consider naming an alternate executor and estate trustee should your executor die before you do. Otherwise your estate may be handled by the executor of your executor's estate. Naming an alternate executor and estate trustee is also important in case the named executor is either unable to or chooses not to act. This can avoid costly court proceedings.

If you are an executor and estate trustee yourself, you should seek advice with respect to how to minimize the tax burden on the estate which has been left under your care. If you do not, you could be sued by the beneficiaries. The courts have found executors liable for failing to take active steps to structure the estate's affairs to minimize income tax.

20.2.3   Will planning to minimize your estate's tax liability

There are many tax-oriented clauses that can be included in a will to help minimize the tax liability. The will should include a provision granting executors and trustees broad authority to make or join in any election, designation or allocation under tax legislation. This will ensure that your executor can use benefits such as the principal residence designation and capital gains exemption. The following clauses should also be considered:

- forgiveness of certain loans made to family members
- a discretionary power permitting trustees to determine which assets are to form the trust property of a spousal trust
- a reminder to your executors that if you have not made your maximum RRSP contribution at the time of your death, one

should be made by your estate to your spouse's RRSP before the required deadline.

In your will, you can name the beneficiary of your RRSP, deferred profit-sharing plan, death benefits and life insurance proceeds. Alternatively, these plans and policies may allow for naming a beneficiary directly within the plan documents. While designating beneficiaries directly in the plan documents may reduce probate costs, there may also be implications for spousal rights under family law.

Note that your estate may have to pay tax on the full value of your RRSP on your death if you designate as the beneficiary of your RRSP someone other than your spouse or (as of 1999 and under a special election after 1995) your financially dependent children (see 3.3.3).

If you are planning to make a charitable gift through your will, instead of donating cash, consider donating publicly traded securities, mutual funds or segregated funds of a life insurance company in order to minimize taxes payable at death (see 20.7.3).

20.3 Family law

Provincial family law can have a significant impact on your estate planning. Every province has legislation to protect the interests of spouses on marriage breakdown. This legislation may apply on death as well. We shall use Ontario family law for purposes of this discussion. The laws of each province are different, however, and professional advice should be obtained.

On marriage breakdown, Ontario's *Family Law Act* provides for an equal division of "net family property", which includes almost all property acquired during the marriage and the increase in the value of property owned at the time of the marriage. Business assets, shares in a privately-held or public corporation and investments are typically all included in "net family property". Each spouse's assets are totalled and an equalizing payment is required, so that each spouse ends up with half of the value of the net family property.

The above provisions apply on death as well. The surviving spouse may elect to take an equalizing payment for one-half of the difference in net family property rather than whatever has been left to him or her under the deceased's will. Clearly, such rules can interfere with one's estate planning, and should be considered when making a will.

Spouses can agree to have these provisions of the *Family Law Act* not apply by signing a "domestic contract". Separate independent legal advice for each spouse is required before signing such a contract.

20.4 Trusts

20.4.1 What is a trust?

A trust is an arrangement whereby one or more persons (the trustees) hold legal title to property (the trust property) for the benefit of other persons (the beneficiaries). The person who creates the trust and puts ("settles") property into it is called the settlor.

Example:

Brian is leaving the country to work in Africa for several years. He gives Paul $80,000 to hold in trust for Brian's two teenagers, Dianne and Darryl. Brian draws up a trust agreement that allows Paul to use the trust funds to pay for Brian's children's education, to invest the funds not yet used, and to pay half of the capital of the trust to each child when he or she turns 23.

In this example, Brian is the settlor, Paul is the trustee and Dianne and Darryl are the beneficiaries. Paul will have legal ownership of the $80,000, but he is required to use it only for Dianne and Darryl's benefit and not for his personal use. If the trust document permits, he can pay himself a fee for his services as trustee.

There is no legal requirement that the settlor and the trustee be different people. (In the example above, Brian could simply declare and document that he is holding funds in trust for his children, and a trust would be created.) Similarly, the settlor and the beneficiary can be the same person. (This is what happens when you put funds into a self-directed RRSP, for example. You are the settlor and beneficiary, and a trust company is the trustee of your assets—see 3.1.6.) However, the choice of settlor, trustee and beneficiaries will affect the taxation of the trust and its beneficiaries. For example, there are a number of attribution rules that apply to trusts, including those outlined in Chapter 5. Careful planning is required.

Note that the mechanics and terminology of trusts are somewhat different in Québec, which is governed by the province's *Civil Code* rather than by the common law which governs the rest of Canada.

20.4.2 What kinds of trusts are there?

A trust can be set up during the settlor's lifetime (as in the example above). Such a trust is called an *inter vivos* (Latin for "among the living") trust.

A trust can also be created by the settlor's will, in which case it is called a testamentary trust.

A trust for the settlor's spouse that meets certain conditions is a spousal trust. The principal conditions are, first, that all of the income of the trust must be paid to the spouse during the spouse's lifetime, and second, that none of the capital can be distributed to anyone other than the spouse during the spouse's lifetime. (After the spouse's death, however, the capital can be distributed to someone else, such as the settlor's children.)

Such a trust can be either testamentary or *inter vivos*. A transfer of property from the settlor to a spousal trust does not trigger tax on any accrued capital gain; instead the property passes at the settlor's cost, and any capital gain is taxed only when the trust eventually disposes of the property or the spouse dies (see 6.5.3 and 20.1.2).

Note that if your will creates a trust, that trust will be separate from your estate. The estate is taxed as a trust for as long as it takes to wind up your affairs and distribute your assets. A trust set up in your will, on the other hand, can be designed to continue for many years beyond your death.

20.4.3 How is a trust taxed?

A trust is a separate person for income tax purposes. The trustee(s) must file a T3 trust tax return (and a TP-646 Québec trust return in some cases) and pay tax on the trust's income. A trust is generally taxed as an individual, but is not eligible for the personal credits (see Chapter 2). A testamentary trust pays tax at the same marginal rates as individuals (see 5.1), but an *inter vivos* trust pays tax at a flat rate—the top rate of combined federal and provincial tax for individuals (about 50%).

The trust's income includes its income from carrying on business (see Chapter 10), from taxable capital gains (see Chapter 6) and from investments (interest, dividends, rent, etc.—see Chapter 7). Amounts that are payable or paid to beneficiaries are deducted from the trust income, and the beneficiaries report such income on their tax returns.

Certain kinds of income, such as capital gains and dividends, preserve their character when flowed through to a beneficiary. Thus, such income can be treated as capital gains (see Chapter 6) or as dividends (see 7.1.2) on the beneficiary's tax return.

A special election called the "preferred beneficiary election" is available where a beneficiary is disabled (as defined for tax purposes in 2.5.1). This election allows the trust and a certain kind of beneficiary to agree that the trust's income will be taxed in the beneficiary's hands so that, in a later year, the income can be paid out by the trust to the beneficiary free of tax.

Other special tax rules allow income and capital gains to be taxed in the trust even if these amounts have been paid out to the beneficiary during the year. This can be beneficial if the trust has unused losses from previous years which can offset this income. For certain testamentary trusts, this election may also save taxes if the beneficiary would otherwise be subject to tax at a higher rate than the trust.

> Consider the advantages of establishing one or more family trusts.

In your will, you can provide a separate testamentary trust for each beneficiary. This will allow each trust to benefit from lower graduated rates of tax for the income retained in such a trust.

Every 21 years a trust is deemed to dispose of all of its property, so that accrued capital gains are taxed. In the past, a trust could make an election with Revenue Canada to defer this deemed disposition as long as the trust continued to have a living beneficiary who was related to its settlor.

> Take action before the 21st anniversary of a trust's creation to minimize the impact of a deemed disposition of all of a trust's capital property.

In 1995, the government announced that trusts would no longer be able to elect to defer the deemed disposition. A trust which made such an election in the past will automatically have had a deemed disposition of all capital property on January 1, 1999.

If you are considering a family trust, advice from a qualified tax professional will be essential.

20.4.4   The benefits of setting up a family trust

A trust offers tremendous flexibility in structuring your affairs and controlling the future use of your property. The powers of the trustees can be strictly limited and defined; or they can be given full discretion as to when and whether to pay income or distribute capital to the beneficiaries, how to manage the trust property and when to wind up the trust.

Setting up the trust while you are alive can also provide several advantages:

- by making yourself a trustee, you can keep control of the trust assets (such as shares of your business)
- by getting the assets out of your estate, you can reduce probate fees (see 20.1.3)
- because the assets will not be in your estate, they will not form part of the public record that anyone can examine in the court office
- income splitting may be possible, depending on the application of the attribution rules (see Chapter 4).

A trust can also be useful as part of an estate freeze plan (see 20.5). In many cases, you may not know at the time you set up the freeze how you will want the growth allocated among your children. You may also not yet want to give them direct ownership in the business. In such an event you should consider setting up a family trust and having the trust subscribe for the "growth" common shares (or, preferably, have them gifted to the trust). If you are the trustee and have discretion as to how to allocate the income and capital of the trust, you can decide several years later (or even in your will) which of your children should inherit the business. This may also provide some protection for your children against family law legislation (see 20.3). If you have already established such a plan, ensure that its benefits will not be neutralized by the new income-splitting tax on certain income received by minors (see 5.2.4).

20.5 Estate freezing

20.5.1 What is an estate freeze?

"Estate freezing" is the term used to describe steps taken to fix the value of your estate (or some particular asset) at its present value, so that future growth will accrue to your children (or to a trust for your children) and not be taxed on your death. Several provisions of the *Income Tax Act* are designed to facilitate this type of planning.

Estate freezing is most often used when you own a business that you expect will increase in value in future years. Your children may be involved in running the business. Even if they are not, you may want them to own it after your death.

20.5.2 How do you freeze an estate?

There are many different approaches to an estate freeze, some of them very complex. The following example is one of the simplest types:

Example:

You own all of the common shares of X Corp. (your business). Your original share investment in X Corp. was $100, and it is now worth $1 million. You expect it to increase in value significantly over the next several years. You have two children, both in their early 20s, who work in the business.

First, you exchange your common shares of X Corp. for 1,000 new preferred shares (a step that can be taken without triggering any income tax). The preferred shares are voting shares. They are also retractable at any time, at your option, for $1,000 per share. In other words, you can demand that the corporation pay you $1 million for your shares at any time.

Each of your children then subscribes for 50 new common shares in X Corp., paying $1 per share. Since X Corp. is worth $1 million, and your preferred shares are retractable for $1 million, the common shares have negligible value at the moment.

Over the next few years, the value of X Corp. rises to $1.5 million. Now your preferred shares are still worth only $1 million, but the common shares are worth $500,000. You have thus transferred the post-freeze "growth" in the corporation to your children at no tax cost to you.

Note also that since your preferred shares are voting shares, you have kept control of the corporation. You have 1,000 votes and your children together have only 100.

The mechanics of an estate freeze are complex, and there are numerous income tax rules that have to be considered. The basic concept, however, is generally as outlined above. Often you will set up a holding company and a family trust (see 20.4.4) as part of the freeze, rather than having your children subscribe directly for shares in the operating company.

> **Look into the potential benefits of an estate freeze.**

An estate freeze can significantly reduce the tax payable on your death, if the value of your business is "frozen" sufficiently early. The value of the business will be fixed at the time of the freeze, so the tax on the subsequent capital appreciation will be deferred until your children sell the business (or until their deaths). You can also multiply the availability of the capital gains exemption for certain small business shares (see 6.4.1), if it is still available when your children eventually dispose of the shares. At the same time, you do not need to give up control of the business.

You can also continue to receive income from the corporation, either by declaring dividends on the preferred shares, or by drawing a salary if you continue to work in the business.

If you use a trust to acquire the common shares, you can retain flexibility with respect to allocating the shares of the business among your children later.

At the time you set up the freeze, you can trigger part or all of the accrued capital gain on your shares to date. This may allow you to use your $500,000 capital gains exemption (see 6.4.1), for example. Be aware of the various restrictions on claiming the exemption (see 6.4.3).

Depending on how the freeze is structured, you can achieve income splitting (see Chapter 5) by directing income into the hands of your children for tax purposes. Note that certain attribution rules do not apply if your corporation qualifies as a "small business corporation" (see 6.3.2) or your children have reached the age of 18 (see 5.2.6). However, existing arrangements may be affected by the new income-splitting tax on certain income received by minor children (see 5.2.4).

Whether an estate freeze is useful to you will depend very much on your business, your financial position, your future plans and your goals. Qualified professional advice should be obtained before this type of planning is undertaken.

20.6 Life insurance

Life insurance plays many roles in estate planning. For example, it can

- provide replacement income for your dependants
- provide a fund for emergency expenses or children's education in future years
- pay for final expenses such as funeral costs
- assist in funding the succession for a business in a closely-held corporation
- fund capital gains tax liability that arises on death (see 20.1.2)
- allow you to accumulate funds on a tax-sheltered basis to supplement retirement income.

Insurance proceeds received on the death of the life insured are not taxable. Similarly, the premiums you pay for your life insurance are generally not tax deductible.

If your corporation is the beneficiary of a policy on your life, the corporation may be able to distribute the life insurance proceeds to its shareholders without any tax applying.

Make sure you have sufficient life insurance.

Your need for insurance will change as factors such as your income, investment portfolio and dependants change. Therefore, a regular review of your coverage is important.

There are many different life insurance products available. These products can generally be divided into two types: term insurance and permanent insurance.

Term (or "pure") insurance policies usually have lower premiums at younger ages. You are paying the cost of insuring against the risk of your death in the current year, and nothing more. As long as you continue to pay the premiums, your coverage will continue; many policies guarantee renewal without additional medical evidence as long as you remain in the plan. However, the cost of premiums will increase dramatically in later years. Most term policies terminate at age 70 to 75, which is lower than the current average life expectancy.

A permanent insurance policy (often called "whole life" or "universal life") combines pure insurance coverage with an investment fund. As a result, the cost of premiums when you are young is often much higher than term insurance. However, many permanent insurance policies offer fixed premiums for guaranteed maximum terms (say, 10 or 20 years). At the end of the term, the policy is often fully paid up. The policy can be designed so that the investment fund or cash surrender value accumulates tax-free. Such a fund can be borrowed against or "cashed out" in later years. However, doing so will have a tax cost.

Permanent insurance products are usually desirable for the following purposes:

- capital gains tax funding
- estate equalization (to allow for an even distribution of your estate, such as where you wish to leave business assets to beneficiaries active in a family business and non-business assets to those family members not active in the business)
- business succession planning
- tax-sheltered, long-term investment strategies.

When buying insurance, consider who should be the beneficiary. If your estate is the beneficiary, the insurance proceeds will form part of your estate on your death, and will be subject to any claims that creditors have on your estate. The proceeds will also be subject to probate fees (see 20.1.3 above). You may therefore want to have the insurance proceeds payable directly to your spouse or another beneficiary, in order to bypass the estate. The investment fund or cash surrender value of a policy can also be protected from creditors during your lifetime where certain beneficiaries are named.

20.7 Charitable gifts and bequests

In this section we look at some ways you can structure charitable gifts, both during your life and through your will, to further your estate planning goals and make the most of the available tax credits. The options are much broader than simply leaving a sum of money to a charity in your will.

> Consider planned charitable gifts and bequests.

There are many ways in which gifts may be made to charitable organizations—including gifts of property (such as securities, artwork, real estate), life insurance and annuities—with significant tax benefits. These benefits depend on the type of gift, the timing of the donation and the nature of the charitable organization.

A gift made today can provide a current tax saving and, in addition, a charitable gift annuity (see 20.7.7) or a gift of a remainder interest in a trust or property (see 20.7.9) will also allow you the continued use of, or income from, the property itself.

Proper will planning can help ensure that your bequest will be made as you intend and provide significant tax savings for your estate.

Careful planning together with an informed advisor can ensure your philanthropic goals are met and the tax benefits are available when you need them most.

20.7.1 The tax credit for charitable donations

As discussed in 2.7.1, the federal government has enriched the federal tax credit for charitable donations for the past few years (the Québec credit is discussed at 16.2.9). To the extent your total donations exceed $200 per year, you receive a credit worth about 50% of the donation in most cases. The limit of donations you can claim each year is 75% of your "net income" plus 25% of the taxable capital gains arising from donations of capital property (see 20.7.3). Any donations you do not claim can be carried forward for up to five years.

Charitable gifts can be made through your will. A bequest in your will is treated as if the gift was made in your final year and is claimed for credit on your final tax return. The charitable donations limit in the year of death and the immediately preceding year is 100% of the deceased's "net income" (20% of net income for Québec purposes).

It is possible that large bequests in your will (or large donations during your lifetime) may become unusable for tax purposes, if they far exceed the allowable threshold. You may therefore want to consider other options, so as to maximize both the tax credits and the funds available to your beneficiaries—both family members and charities.

20.7.2 Gifts to the Crown

Before 1997, gifts to the federal or a provincial government ("Crown gifts") were not subject to the charitable donations limits. You could claim up to 100% of your net income for Crown gifts, including gifts to Crown agency foundations set up for the benefit of universities, colleges, hospitals and museums. The advantage of the pre-1997 higher income limit allowed on Crown gifts often made it more attractive for donors to make large gifts to the Crown rather than to other charities. To level the playing field for all charities, the federal limit for claiming Crown donations has been reduced to 75% of net income, the same limit that now applies to gifts made to other charities.

20.7.3 Gifts in kind

Both during your lifetime and on your death, you can donate property to a charity as an alternative to money. A gift of property is called a gift in kind. Examples include artwork, shares and real estate, as well as some more esoteric gifts we discuss below, such as life insurance or a residual interest in real property. (You cannot "give" services, however—only property.)

A gift in kind is normally valued at its fair market value. For purposes of determining the tax credit for your donation, it will be the same as a gift of cash. Thus, the tax credit will generally be worth about 50% of the value of the property. However, at the time of the donation you are deemed to have disposed of the property at its fair market value— meaning that you must recognize any capital gain or income that would apply had you sold the property for that price.

For purposes of the tax credit, the 75% net income limit is effectively increased to 100% of net income for:

- donations of capital property resulting in taxable capital gains (as of 1996)
- donations of depreciable property that trigger recapture of capital cost allowance (see 10.2.7)
- gifts of ecologically sensitive lands to municipalities and certain charities
- gifts of "certified cultural property" (and capital gains on such property may not be taxable—see 20.7.5).

However, if you have large capital gains in a year from other dispositions, gifts that trigger significant gains could result in a liability for alternative minimum tax ("AMT"—see 7.6). Before you make such a donation, be sure to run the numbers to ensure that AMT will not result.

Individuals and corporations who donate securities listed on prescribed stock exchanges, mutual funds and segregated funds of life insurance companies to charities (other than private foundations) may only include in their taxable income 37.5% of the capital gain (instead of the usual 75%) that arises on the securities' disposition. If your corporation makes the donations, its capital dividend account (see 13.2.4) will be increased by the non-taxable portion (or 62.5%) of the capital gain (instead of 25%); this amount can then be paid to the corporation's shareholders tax-free. This tax treatment applies to such donations made between February 18, 1997 and the end of 2001 (after which the government will review this measure's effectiveness in encouraging donations). (If you live in Québec, see 16.2.9.)

Example:

David lives in Prince George and owns shares in a mining company traded on the Vancouver Stock Exchange that have a cost base to him of $10,000. In 1999, the shares are worth $70,000, and on April 15, 1999 David donates them to a hospital foundation. David's employment income in 1999 is $75,000.

David is deemed to have disposed of the shares for $70,000, and so must recognize a $60,000 capital gain, 37.5% of which is brought into his income as a $22,500 taxable capital gain (see 6.2). His total income for tax purposes is thus $75,000 + $22,500, or $97,500.

David gets a receipt from the hospital foundation for $70,000. David's charitable donation limit for 1999 is $78,750—25% of the amount of the taxable capital gain of $22,500 (or $5,625) plus 75% of his net income of $97,500 ($73,125). As a result, David will be allowed to claim the entire $70,000 as a charitable donation on his 1999 tax return. This will entitle him to a credit worth about $35,000.

If you make a gift of capital property, you can file an election with your tax return to use a lower amount than the fair market value, for purposes of determining both your proceeds of disposition of the property and the value of your donation. You can elect any amount between the adjusted cost base (see 6.2) and the actual fair market value.

Whether the election is useful depends on a number of factors, including your tax bracket, your other sources of income and deductions, and your prospects for income in future years against which to use up the charitable donation carryforward.

The election described above can also be used by artists for gifts of work they have created (which is inventory rather than capital property).

20.7.4 Cash vs. shares—which should you donate?

> **Think about donating publicly traded securities instead of cash.**

Say you want to make a $2,000 donation to a favourite cause and you have publicly traded securities that originally cost you $1,000 and that are now worth $2,000. Should you sell the securities and donate the proceeds or should you simply donate the securities? Assuming your income is taxed at the top marginal rate of about 50% and you have already donated $200 in the year, the tax effects of both choices are as follows:

- If you sell the shares and donate the before-tax proceeds, a $1,000 capital gain will arise on the securities' sale ($2,000 proceeds − $1,000 original cost). You would then have to pay $375 in tax on the taxable portion of your gain (75% of $1,000 × 50% tax rate). Your $2,000 donation will give you a tax credit of $1,000 (50% × $2,000). In the end, the donation will result in net tax savings of $625 ($1,000 tax credit − $375 capital gains tax).
- If you donate the shares directly, the charity will still get the full $2,000 value of the shares. The taxable portion of the $1,000 capital gain will only be 37.5%, so your tax payable will only be $187.50 (37.5% of $1,000 × 50%). You will also get a tax credit of $1,000 for the donation (50% of $2,000). The net tax savings resulting from your donation will be $812.50 ($1,000 tax credit − $187.50 capital gains tax).

As you can see, under the new rules in effect for the period between February 18, 1997 and the end of 2001, you will come out ahead if you donate the securities directly. In the above example, you give up property of the same value but your after-tax cost is $187.50 less than had you sold the securities and donated the proceeds.

20.7.5 Gifts of cultural property

Gifts of "cultural property" to certain public authorities or institutions (such as museums) also produce tax benefits. This property must be certified by the government as a national treasure with cultural significance to Canada. The donation will be equal to the property's fair market value for purposes of the credit but no taxable capital gain will result. Any capital loss that may arise may be deductible in some circumstances.

20.7.6 Gifts of life insurance

If you have a "permanent" life insurance policy (see 20.6), such as whole life or universal life, you can donate it to a charity by transferring the ownership of the policy to the charity and having the charity become the beneficiary of the policy. For tax purposes, the value of your donation will be the policy's cash surrender value, plus any accumulated dividends and interest that are also assigned, minus any policy loan outstanding. However, to the extent that value exceeds the tax cost of the policy to you, you must recognize the excess as income, as if you had cashed in the policy.

Once you have donated the policy to the charity, if you continue to pay the premiums on the policy, each such payment will be considered to be an additional charitable donation entitling you to a tax credit.

Note that if you simply make the charity a beneficiary of a life insurance policy that you continue to own, there will be no tax benefits available to you or your estate.

20.7.7 Purchasing an annuity from a charity

You can purchase an annuity from a charity, whereby you give the charity a sum of money up front and receive a fixed annual payment for the rest of your life.

While the "cost" of this type of annuity is usually more than the market price to purchase an annuity from a life insurance company offering the same annual income, the annuity purchased from a charity may actually provide you with more annual disposable income and allow you to make a sizable gift to the charity at the same time. If the total payments that you expect to receive from the charity during your lifetime are less than the original sum you gave to the charity, the annual payments to you will be tax-free. You will also be entitled to a tax credit on the difference according to the usual rules as outlined above.

Revenue Canada has published a table outlining the number of annual payments that donors can expect to receive based on their age at the time the annuity is purchased.

If the total payments that you expect to receive are more than the original sum given to the charity, the excess amount will be taxable on an annualized basis.

20.7.8 Charitable insured annuity

Another strategy is to set up a "charitable insured annuity". You buy an annuity from a life insurance company, and use part of the monthly payments to pay the premiums on a life insurance policy with a charity as the owner and beneficiary. Thus, you receive an income stream over your lifetime (from the annuity), and tax credits for the insurance premiums you pay. On your death, the charity receives the insurance proceeds.

20.7.9 Charitable remainder trusts

If you have property that you would like to donate to a charity, but you need the income from the property during your lifetime, consider donating a "residual" interest in the property—that is, the capital that will remain on your death. One way to do this is to set up a "charitable remainder trust". This is a trust (see 20.4) whose conditions are that the income be paid to you during your lifetime, while the *capital* will go to the charity on your death. In some cases, you can transfer the residual interest in property (e.g., real estate) directly, without setting up a trust.

The value of a gift of the residual interest in a property is its discounted present value. This value will depend on factors such as the current fair market value of the property, current interest rates, and your life expectancy. The gift entitles you to the normal tax credit for charitable donations. If you arrange to receive less income from the trust (or property) than you might otherwise be entitled to, the value of your donation may be higher.

Such a gift has several attractions. First, the charity gets a vested right to the property immediately, and need not worry about whether you will leave the property to it in your will (or whether your will might be contested). Second, you get an immediate tax credit based on the amount of your donation (the residual value). Third, you continue to receive the income from (or use of) the property for the rest of your life.

You will be deemed to have disposed of the remainder interest in the property transferred to the trust for its fair market value. This may lead to a capital gain and an income inclusion for tax purposes, with an enhanced tax credit as illustrated in the example in 20.7.3 above. In addition, the trust will have to file an annual tax return (see 20.4.3), though it will normally not pay any tax since all of its income will be paid out to you.

20.8 Business succession

> **Plan for the succession of your business.**

If you own and manage a business, it could well be your family's largest asset. After your death, the business may be crucial for meeting your family's financial needs. Taking steps to ensure your business' ongoing profitability and management can be just as important as considering the planning opportunities available to minimize taxes on your death.

One of the first issues you must resolve is what will happen to the business when you die. You could plan for the business to be kept in the family, sold to a buyer outside the family, or liquidated. The option you choose will depend on things such as the nature of the business, the likelihood of its continued success after your death, and the abilities of your family members and/or key employees to run the business' operations.

If the family is not capable or does not want to run the business, it may be in everyone's best interests to sell or liquidate the business on or before your retirement. If some family members are quite active in managing the business while others are not, dividing ownership equally among your family might seem fair but it could disrupt the business and create tension in the family. Often in these cases, you could use other family assets or life insurance to ensure fairness for all family members.

If you decide to keep the business in the family, you should seek professional advice to help you decide whether to transfer ownership during your lifetime or on death, who will receive the business' shares and in what proportion, whether the shares will be gifted or sold, and the most tax-effective way to structure the transfer.

If you do not own 100% of your company's shares, the transfer of its legal control may be smoothed by a carefully drafted shareholders' agreement (see 13.4).

Life insurance owned by you or your company can facilitate the sale of your shares of the company and help to fund any tax liability arising on death. Recent income tax changes may allow you to maintain certain tax advantages associated with life insurance-funded arrangements if your company was the beneficiary of a life insurance policy held for this purpose held on or before April 25, 1995, or if there was an agreement in place at that time relating to the disposition of your shares.

20.9 Planning for the succession of wealth

In some cases where a family business has been sold, the family's largest asset after the sale is the net sale proceeds. In other cases, wise investment decisions have resulted in the accumulation of significant wealth. Since the bulk of such estates will ultimately accrue to your children, you should assess the age at which they should have access to this wealth and whether controls or restrictions should be placed on the use of these resources for certain periods of time.

Inter vivos and testamentary family trusts (see 20.4.4) can facilitate the transfer of wealth to children over pre-determined ages. Such trusts are also useful in situations where the child is dependent by reason of mental or physical infirmity. They can also be of assistance when dealing with children who lack an appreciation for the value of money and with the safeguarding of assets from family law legislation.

If you will be passing on a sizable estate to your children, you should consult with your legal and tax advisers to develop a plan to transfer the wealth into their hands.

20.10 Foreign estate taxes

> Watch out for the effects of foreign estate taxes.

If you own assets in other countries, investigate the possibility of estate, inheritance or succession taxes of those countries (or their states or provinces) applying on your death.

Note that estate taxes and succession duties imposed by other jurisdictions are not normally eligible for a foreign tax credit in Canada, even though you may have a Canadian income tax liability as a result of the deemed disposition described in 20.1.2. Double taxation can result. You may need to plan for this ahead of time.

If you are a U.S. citizen, see our discussion of U.S. estate tax in 17.8.1.

If you are not a U.S. citizen but own assets legally located in the U.S., including real estate, debts owed to you by U.S. citizens or shares in U.S. corporations, see the planning techniques discussed in 18.4.7.

20.11 Pre-paid funeral and cemetery arrangements

Planning and paying for your funeral and cemetery arrangements in advance can go a long way toward easing the stress on your survivors at a difficult time. Many funeral and cemetery service providers offer plans through which you can deposit funds as pre-payment for their services.

> Consider a pre-paid plan to finance your funeral and cemetery arrangements.

To help Canadians finance these arrangements, the tax rules provide a special tax exemption for the interest earned on eligible pre-paid amounts. Like the deferred income plans discussed in Chapter 3, the sooner you contribute to a pre-paid funeral or cemetery arrangement, the longer your funds will benefit from the effect of tax-free compounding of interest.

You can contribute up to $35,000 to an arrangement that covers both funeral and cemetery services. If the funeral and cemetery services will be provided by separate businesses, you can contribute up to $15,000 to an arrangement that covers only funeral services and up to $20,000 to an arrangement that covers only cemetery services. The funds in your account can be used to cover your own funeral and cemetery arrangements or those of anyone you choose; the limits only restrict the amount that any one person can contribute to such plans over his or her lifetime.

Although the amounts of your lump-sum or periodic contributions are not tax-deductible, any interest income earned on the deposited amounts will not be subject to tax while they are in the plan. If you withdraw the funds and use them for other purposes, any amounts in excess of your total contributions will be taxable in the year of withdrawal.

Any amounts left over after the funeral and cemetery expenses have been paid for will be refunded to the contributor or the contributor's estate. The tax payable on the refund is calculated with a formula that ensures that only the fund's investment income is subject to tax.

20.12 References

There is little published information on estate planning that is easily understood by the layperson. As well, every individual's case is different. Consult a qualified tax professional for advice.

Revenue Canada publishes the following, which are available (in person or by telephone request) from your nearest District Taxation Office. Forms and guides may also be available from Revenue Canada's Internet site at *www.rc.gc.ca.*

> Interpretation Bulletin IT-111R2, "Annuities purchased from charitable organizations" and Special Release IT-111R2SR
>
> Interpretation Bulletin IT-210R2, "Income of deceased persons— periodic payments"

Interpretation Bulletin IT-212R3, "Income of deceased persons—rights or things" and Special Release IT-212R3SR

Interpretation Bulletin IT-226R, "Gift to a charity of a residential interest in real property or an equitable interest in a trust"

Interpretation Bulletin IT-234, "Income of deceased persons—farm crops"

Interpretation Bulletin IT-244R3, "Gifts by individuals of life insurance policies as charitable donations"

Interpretation Bulletin IT-278R2, "Death of a partner or retired partner"

Interpretation Bulletin IT-288R2, "Gift of capital properties to a charity and others"

Interpretation Bulletin IT-297R2, "Gifts in kind to charity and others"

Interpretation Bulletin IT-305R4, "Testamentary spousal trusts"

Interpretation Bulletin IT-313R2, "Eligible capital property—rules where a taxpayer has ceased carrying on business or has died"

Interpretation Bulletin IT-349R3, "Intergenerational transfers of farm property on death"

Interpretation Bulletin IT-407R4, "Disposition of cultural property to designated Canadian institutions"

Interpretation Bulletin IT-508R, "Death benefits"

Brochure, "When You Retire"

"Preparing Returns for Deceased Persons"

"T3 Trust Income Tax and Information Return"

Appendices

Appendix I
1999 Personal Tax Credits – Federal

	Maximum Dollar Amount	Value of Credit[1]
Basic personal[2]	$6,794	$1,155
Supplementary personal[3]	250	43
Spousal[4]	5,718	972
Equivalent-to-spouse[4, 5]	5,718	972
Infirm dependants age 18 and over[6]	2,353	400
Age 65 and over[7, 8]	3,482	592
Disability[8, 9]	4,233	720
Caregiver[10]	2,353	400
Pension income[8, 11]	1,000	170
Canada Pension Plan		
Employed	1,187	202
Self-employed	2,373	403
Employment Insurance	995	169
Education[12]		
Per month – full-time	200	34
Per month – part-time	60	10
Tuition fees[12]		17%
Interest paid on student loans[13]		17%
Medical expenses[14, 15]		17%
Charitable donations[16]		
On the first $200		17%
On the remainder		29%

1   The federal credit values are calculated at a rate of 17%. Most of these credits are factored in to the calculation of basic federal tax and therefore they also reduce the federal surtax, provincial tax and provincial surtaxes (other than Québec). As a result, these credits are generally worth about 50% to 75% more than indicated.

2   The 1999 federal budget increased the basic federal credit by $675 for all taxpayers as of July 1, 1999. Due to the mid-year implementation date, the credit rises by $338 to $6,794 for 1999. In 2000, the full increase to $7,131 will apply.

3   As of July 1, 1999, the supplementary credit is combined with the basic personal credit. For individuals with income below about $19,500, up to one-half of the supplement will be available in 1999. This credit is reduced by 2% of net income over $7,294. An additional $250 amount is available if the individual is claiming the

spousal or equivalent-to-spouse credit, but only if the spouse's or dependant's net income is less than $7,294.

4   The spousal and equivalent-to-spouse credits also increase by $675 as of July 1, 1999. The dollar amount of the credit is thus increased by $338 for 1999, with the full increase to $6,055 applying in 2000. The spousal amount of $5,718 is reduced by the excess of the spouse's or other individual's net income over $572 ($606 in 2000) and is thus reduced to zero where net income exceeds $6,290.

5   The equivalent-to-spouse credit is calculated in the same way as the spousal credit. Eligible dependants are dependants under 18 related to the taxpayer, or the taxpayer's parents or grandparents, or any other person who is related to the taxpayer and infirm.

6   The dependant amount is reduced by the excess of the dependant's income over $4,441 and is thus reduced to zero where net income exceeds $6,794.

7   The age amount is reduced by 15% of the excess of the taxpayer's net income over $25,921 and is thus reduced to zero where net income exceeds $49,134.

8   These credits are transferable to the taxpayer's spouse. The amounts available for transfer are reduced by the excess of the spouse's net income over $6,794.

9   The disability credit is transferable to a supporting person. The transferable amount of $4,233 is reduced by the excess of the dependant's taxable income over $6,794 and is thus reduced to zero where taxable income exceeds $11,027.

10   The caregiver credit is reduced by the excess of the dependant's net income over $11,500 and is thus reduced to zero where net income exceeds $13,853.

11   Calculated as a percentage of eligible pension income, to a maximum of $1,000 of pension income.

12   The tuition fee credit is calculated as a percentage of eligible tuition fees paid in the calendar year. The tuition and education credits are transferable to a spouse, parent or grandparent. The maximum amount transferable for both credits is $5,000 less the excess of the student's net income over $6,794. Any amounts not transferred may be carried forward by the student.

13   This credit is calculated as a percentage of interest paid in the year on student loans under federal and provincial programs. The credit is not transferable but it can be carried forward for up to five years.

14   The medical expense credit is calculated as a percentage of qualifying medical expenses in excess of the lesser of 3% of net income or $1,614.

15   A refundable medical expense credit is also available equal to the lesser of $500 and 25% of qualifying medical expenses. This credit is reduced by 5% of the excess of family net income over $16,745.

16   The maximum amount of donations that you can claim in a year is limited to 75% of net income. In the year of death and the preceding year, the limit is 100% of net income.

1999 Personal Tax Credits — Québec

	Maximum Dollar Amount	Value of Credit[1]
Basic	$5,900	$1,357
Spousal[2]	5,900	1,357
Person living alone or with dependant[3]	1,050	242
Single parent[4]	1,300	299
Dependent children:[4]		
First	2,600	598
Second and subsequent	2,400	552
Other related dependants age 19 or older[5]	2,400	552
Dependent post-secondary student (per semester)[4, 6]	1,650	380
Infirm dependant age 19 or older[5]	5,900	1,357
Person 65 or over[3, 9]	2,200	506
Disability[7, 9]	2,200	506
Pension income (maximum)[3, 8, 9]	1,000	230
Québec Pension Plan		
Employed	1,187	273
Self-employed	2,373	546
Employment Insurance	995	229
Tuition fees[10]		23%
Interest paid on student loans[11]		23%
Medical expenses[12]		23%
Charitable donations[13]		23%

---

1 The Québec credit values are calculated at a rate of 23%. For purposes of determining many Québec credits, net income must be calculated under both the regular filing system and the simplified filing system, even if the simplified system is not used (see 16.1.2 and 16.1.3). "Net family income" is the total income of both spouses, as calculated under the simplified system, minus $26,000. "Family income" is the total income of both spouses as calculated under the simplified system.

2 The spousal amount is reduced by the amount of the spouse's net income. There is no equivalent-to-spouse credit in Québec.

3 The amounts for a person living alone, age 65 and over, and pension income are added together and reduced by 15% of net family income (see note 1).

4 The amounts for a single parent, dependent children and dependent post-secondary students are added together and reduced by the amount of the dependant's net income.

5   The amounts for other related dependants and infirm dependants are reduced by the amount of the dependant's net income.

6   The credit is limited to two semesters per year, and can only be claimed by a supporting person.

7   The disability credit is transferable to a supporting person. The amount available for transfer is reduced by any income tax payable by the dependant.

8   The pension credit is based on the lesser of eligible pension income and $1,000.

9   These credits are transferable to a spouse. The credits available for transfer are reduced by any income tax payable by the spouse.

10   This credit is calculated as a percentage of tuition, professional examination and mandatory ancillary fees paid for the calendar year. The credit is not transferable but the student may carry it forward to future years indefinitely.

11   Interest paid on student loans but unclaimed in a particular year may be carried forward indefinitely.

12   The medical expense credit is calculated based on qualified medical expenses in excess of 3% of family income (see note 1). A refundable medical expense credit is also available equal to 25% of qualifying medical expenses, net of the 3% deduction; it is reduced at a rate of 5% of the excess of family income over $17,500.

13   The maximum amount of donations that you can claim in a year is generally limited to 75% of your Québec net income (as calculated under the simplified system). In the year of death and the preceding year, the limit is 100%.

Appendix II
1999 Federal Income Tax Rates

If Taxable Income is:

Over—	But not over—	The tax is:	Of the amount over—
$ 0	$ 29,590	$ 0 + 17%	$ 0
29,590	59,180	5,030 + 26%	29,590
59,180	—	12,724 + 29%	59,180

Federal Surtax

The 1999 federal budget eliminated the 3% surtax that was previously levied on federal tax as of July 1, 1999. The 1998 budget had eliminated the surtax for taxpayers with income up to about $50,000 and reduced it for those with income between about $50,000 and $65,000. Because of the mid-year implementation, taxpayers earning over $50,000 will pay one-half of the surtax otherwise payable in 1999, to a maximum of 1.5% of federal tax.

Where basic federal tax, after deducting any applicable credits and before adding the general surtax, exceeds $12,500, an additional surtax of 5% of the basic federal tax in excess of $12,500 is applicable.

1999 Québec Provincial Income Tax Rates*

If Taxable Income is:

Over—	But not over—	The tax is:	Of the amount over—
$ 0	$ 25,000	$ 0 + 20%	$ 0
25,000	50,000	5,000 + 23%	25,000
50,000	—	10,750 + 26%	50,000

---

* Québec residents and persons carrying on business in Québec receive a reduction of federal taxes equal to 16.5% of basic federal tax. There is also a mandatory contribution to the "Fonds de lutte contre la pauvreté par la réinsertion au travail" equal to 0.3% of Québec tax payable.

Québec's Simplified Filing System

Since 1998, Québec residents have been able to choose between a general filing system and a new simplified system. The simplified system replaces many deductions and credits with a single lump-sum amount of $2,430 for 1999 (worth about $559). The only deductions allowed under the simplified system are deductions related to RRSPs and RPPs, repayments of certain social assistance, OAS, CPP/QPP and EI payments, employment expenses, expenses of disabled persons and capital cost allowance amounts for certain film investments. The only non-refundable credits allowed under the simplified system are the basic personal, single parent and married amounts, amounts for dependants and persons living alone, age and pension amounts, disability (for yourself or a dependant), charitable donations, tax reduction for families, political contributions and labour-sponsored fund contributions. For more details, see 16.1.2 and 16.1.3.

1999 Provincial Income Tax Rates

Percentage of Federal Tax

British Columbia	49.5%[1]
Alberta	44.0%[2]
Saskatchewan	48.0%[3]
Manitoba	48.5%[4]
Ontario	39.5%[5]
Newfoundland	69.0%[6]
New Brunswick	60.0%[7]
Nova Scotia	57.5%[8]
Prince Edward Island	58.5%[9]
Northwest Territories/Nunavut	45.0%
Yukon	50.0%[10]
Non-resident	45.0%

1   A surtax of 30% applies to B.C. tax in excess of $5,300. An additional surtax of 19% applies to B.C. tax in excess of $8,660.

2   Alberta levies a surtax of 8% of basic Alberta tax in excess of $3,500 and a flat tax of 0.5% of Alberta taxable income.

3   There is a flat tax of 2% of net income and a surtax of 15% on Saskatchewan tax (including flat tax) in excess of $4,000. A 10% "deficit surtax" applies to basic Saskatchewan tax plus the flat tax.

4   Manitoba levies a surtax equal to 2% of net income over $30,000 and a flat tax of 2% of net income.

5   A surtax (i.e., the Fair Share Health Care Levy) of 20% applies to basic Ontario tax in excess of $3,750 and at a rate of 36% of basic Ontario tax in excess of $4,681.

6   A surtax of 10% applies to Newfoundland tax in excess of $7,900.

7   A surtax of 8% applies to New Brunswick tax in excess of $13,500.

8   A surtax of 10% applies to Nova Scotia tax in excess of $10,000.

9   A surtax of 10% applies to Prince Edward Island tax in excess of $5,200.

10   A surtax of 5% applies to Yukon tax in excess of $6,000.

Index